THE ROYAL TANK REGIMENT

A Pictorial History 1916 – 2001

The First tank attack. Flers, 15 September 1916. A Mark I (Male) of C Company, HBMGC, moves into action. TM

Challenger, Chieftain and Centurion make an impressive lineup, spanning the postwar years. (Crown Copyright)

THE ROYAL TANK REGIMENT
A Pictorial History 1916 – 2001

George Forty

First published in the UK in 1988 by Spellmount Ltd, Kent.

First published in the USA in 1988 by Hippocrene Books Inc, New York.

New revised and expanded edition published in Great Britain in 2001

British Library Cataloguing-in-Publication Data
A CIP record for this title is available from the British Library

ISBN 1 84114 124 0

HALSGROVE
PUBLISHING, MEDIA AND DISTRIBUTION

Halsgrove House
Lower Moor Way
Tiverton, Devon EX16 6SS
Tel: 01884 243242
Fax: 01884 243325
email: sales@halsgrove.com
website: http://www.halsgrove.com

Printed and bound in Great Britain by
Bookcraft Limited, Midsomer Norton

*Whilst every care has been taken to ensure the accuracy of the
information contained in this book, the author disclaims responsibility
for any mistakes which may have inadvertently been included.*

CONTENTS

FOREWORD

The Royal Tank Regiment is deeply indebted to Lieutenant Colonel George Forty for having compiled this condensed, pictorial History of the Regiment. From the origin of the tank itself, manned by men of the Heavy Section of the Machine Gun Corps, drawn from many different regiments and corps, in the First World War, through the life of the Royal Tank Corps to that of the Royal Tank Regiment, within the Royal Armoured Corps, a consistent thread runs. It is a combination of high professionalism and warm comradeship. Both are needed to ensure that the tank performs its task effectively on the battlefield, and the latter is strengthened by the close relationship of the tank crew.

The contemporary accounts and photographs produce a vivid picture of life for the man in the tank. I commend this volume most warmly to those who have served, serve now or think of serving in the future in the regiment of which I am proud to have been a member for over half a century.

Opposite page: Sporting its 'Chinese Eyes', this 1 RTR Challenger 1 was photographed on the Soltau Training Area. TM

House of Lords

The Regiment is further indebted to George Forty for bringing this historic volume up to date, recording in aptly chosen words and pictures the activities of the Regiment, sadly now reduced to the 1st and 2nd only, since it was originally published in 1988.

Michael Carver
FM

June 2001

Portrait of Field Marshal Lord Carver, GCB, CBE, DSO, MC. TM

INTRODUCTION

When I was first asked to write a new history of the Royal Tank Regiment I was very aware of the fact that there were many books on the subject, some of almost classic stature. I have in mind such distinguished works as the two volumes by Sir Basil Liddell Hart which, together with the companion third volume by Major Kenneth Macksey, trace the history of the Regiment from the year of its formation up to 1975. Then there is Macksey's earlier book *To the Green Fields Beyond*, one of a number of shorter histories published between the wars and since 1945, and Kenneth Chadwick's slim but invaluable volume in the 'Famous Regiments' series. These and many other excellent studies fill the shelves of military libraries and together they present a most formidable challenge to any author approaching the subject afresh. And since it was inevitable that much of the same ground would be covered, it seemed to me that I would be well advised to adopt a different method from that of my predecessors, in order to arouse the reader's interest and to hold his attention. Therefore I decided to adopt the same technique as I had used in the 'At War' series of histories, such as *Desert Rats at War*, where I brought together

first-hand accounts and 'action' photographs in a pictorial evocation, telling the story through the eyes of those who had actually been there at the time.

That was the situation in which I found myself nearly two decades ago and nothing has changed since, apart from the fact that the intervening years have seen even more books published! Now, however, I am fortunate enough to have been given the chance to bring my history up to date, or at least up to the end of the Millennium.

Fortunately also, I have been able to maintain a strong connection with the Regiment during the intervening years, having been Editor of *Tank* ever since I left the Tank Museum in 1993, with the added advantage of being able to draw upon its pages for material. Although the text remains complete in the

bound volumes of the magazine I have been disappointed to discover that some of the original photographs published in the magazine have vanished, although the Tank Museum has managed to retain quite a few thank goodness, so that the story can still be properly told. So much has happened - and continues to happen - in these supposed tranquil days of peace, that there is much to cover and I am bound to have left out some of the detail. However, I hope that I have managed to convey the main highlights of the story of our first eighty-five years.

And what a story it is! There can be no other regiment in any army anywhere in the world, that has seen and made so much history in such a short time. There are so many heroic acts and remarkable events to recall. The very first action at Flers in September 1916, then Cambrai where, with

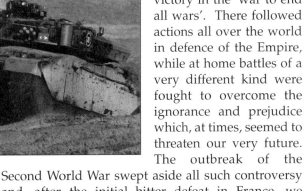

Regimental flag unfurled, Elles led the Corps to its first great victory, then on to Amiens and final victory in the 'war to end all wars'. There followed actions all over the world in defence of the Empire, while at home battles of a very different kind were fought to overcome the ignorance and prejudice which, at times, seemed to threaten our very future. The outbreak of the

Second World War swept aside all such controversy and, after the initial bitter defeat in France, we survived to take our revenge in the Western Desert, Italy, North-West Europe and all the other theatres of war. Nor must we forget the five and a half decades of uneasy peace that have followed the end of the Second World War

Indeed, the vast majority of our soldiering has been in the 'piping days of peace' with more than enough to do, be it in 'shooting wars' like Korea and the Balkans, or showing the flag in distant outposts of Empire such as Aden, the Persian Gulf, Malaysia and Borneo, or dealing with the troubles nearer home in Northern Ireland. I am sure that any RTC or RTR soldier would agree that there has always been more than enough to do, the patterns of duty have been many and varied, but through them all have run the same threads of comradeship, loyalty, devotion to duty, technical skill and, above all, professionalism, which are the hallmark of all those who wear the black beret. There are other constants as well, despite the many and rapid changes that have taken place over the years. The very special loyalty that exists between members of the same tank crew has not changed, and the crew of a Great War Mark IV with its thin armour and naval six-pounders would still find much in common with today's crew in their state-of-the-art Challenger with its computer-assisted fire control system. A Crossley crew on the North-West Frontier between the wars would have seen little difference between their task and that of a Saladin crew in Aden during the 1960s. Many other parallels can be found as the story unfolds.

Regimental Headquarters RTR, was in the process of moving to Bovington from London when I first wrote this book. Now it is in the process of moving for a third time within the camp, its new 'home' having been designated as Bovington Farm, probably the oldest building in Bovington as it was here before the army arrived at the turn of the nineteenth century. Undoubtedly, Bovington is the place in which our story really began, so it is fitting that RHQ should have returned to its roots.

Like every other regiment in the British Army, the Royal Tank Regiment has, over the years, expanded and contracted according to the defence needs as defined by political circumstance. We are luckier than many of our companions-in-arms because, whilst many of our units have been disbanded or amalgamated, we have always kept our identity and corporate image. Be there 25 regiments as in the First World War, or only two as there are today, we keep our name, our traditions and our badge. The RTR remains to carry on the traditions of the past, and it is to all its members, past, present and future, that this book is proudly dedicated.

George Forty
Bryantspuddle
Dorset
June 2001

The Regimental Standards on parade in Whitehall Court, London, at the Unveiling of the RTR Memorial Statue by HM The Queen, 13 June 2000. (Crown Copyright)

ACKNOWLEDGEMENTS

Last time I included an 'en masse' acknowledgement for all those who had helped me with the preparation of this history and I must do so again, because if I try to name everyone individually then I am bound to leave out someone important. This time I have deliberately tried to use a slightly different selection of photographs from the last edition, so as to ensure that this one is different from its predecessor. However, there are some photographs which, because of their subject matter, must be included again. I must thank my friend and highly respected Tank Museum Historian, David Fletcher, and my son Adam, whose help with the photographic research has been invaluable. In this connection I must also thank the Regimental Colonel, Col John Longman, the COs of 1 and 2 RTR, the Tank Museum and Crown Copyright, all of whom have provided the majority of the photographs. The text remains generally unaltered, apart from a number of significant additions for which I am indebted to another good friend, Brigadier Bryan Watkins, who has generously given freely of his time to carry out a first class: 'Staff College Red Ink Edit' on the early and wartime chapters. Finally, I must thank Field Marshal Lord Carver for once again writing the Foreword.

My thanks go to everyone who has given me help and encouragement with what has again been a labour of love. I hope all will be pleased with the result.

RTRA Standard Bearers lower their Standards as the Last Post is played. (Crown Copyright)

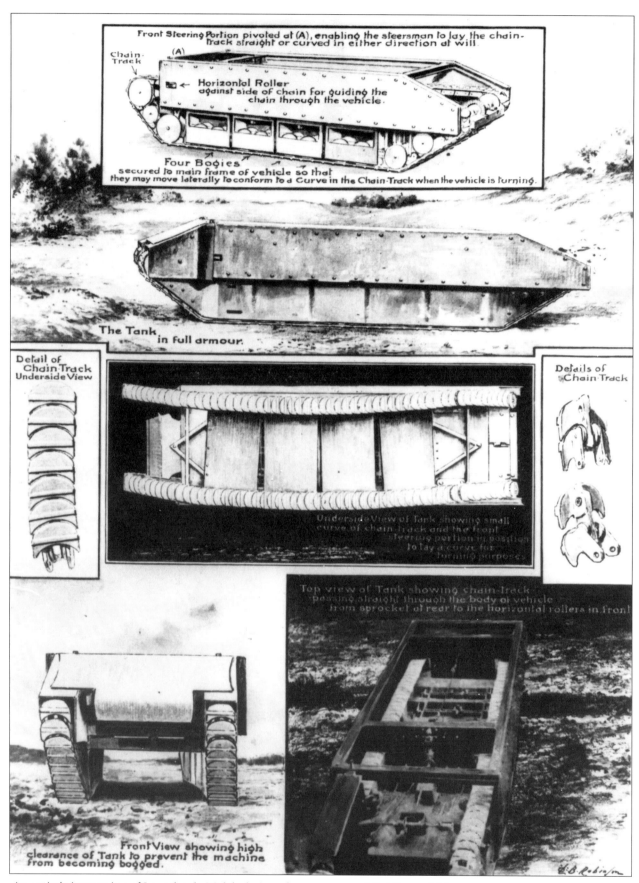

An artist's impression of Lancelot de Mole's designs for an armoured fighting vehicle which he submitted to the War Office as early as 1912 and which they completely ignored.

Chapter 1

THE FIRST TANKS AND THEIR CREWS

THE DEVIL IS COMING!

A German correspondent, reporting the appearance of the first tanks in action on the Somme in September 1916 wrote:

> When the German outposts crept out of their dugouts in the mist of the morning of 15 September and stretched their necks to look for the English, their blood was chilled to their veins. Two mysterious monsters were crawling towards them over the craters. Stunned as if an earthquake had burst around them, they all rubbed their eyes, which were fascinated by the fabulous creatures… One stared and stared as if one had lost the power of one's limbs. The monsters approached slowly, hobbling, rolling and rocking, but they approached. Nothing impeded them; a supernatural force seemed to impel them on. Someone in the trenches said: 'The devil is coming' and the word passed along the line like wildfire.

The brief intensive period of preparation which had taken place before the initial manifestation of these *Devil's Coaches*, as the reporter colourfully called them, had itself been preceded by an unbelievably short preparatory phase, during which the revolutionary new weapons had been secretly designed, built, tested and then put into production. At the same time an entirely new unit had to be raised and trained, to provide the crews to man these strange machines.

THE FIRST TANKS

Before describing that first tank engagement, it is necessary to devote some space to the evolution of the new weapon and to the training of its crew. The basic idea of the tank goes back to ancient times and there have been many attempts throughout history to produce a weapon system able to carry protected firepower about on the battlefield. The war chariot is usually considered to be the original ancestor of the tank, although the armoured elephant could perhaps lay equal claim. It was not until the twentieth century that it became possible to combine the necessary prerequisites of firepower and protection with the mobility needed to propel a suitably armoured vehicle, containing both crew and weapons, across all types of terrain. The invention of the internal combustion engine and new, improved methods of fabricating armour plate, broke the deadlock. However, what was also needed was a reason to get fertile imaginations working on the design of such a vehicle. This impetus came early in the First World War and was brought about by the stalemate which existed after the First Battle of Ypres in 1914. The battle not only effectively halted further German advances, but also prevented the Allies from advancing. The reason was that the defences of both sides had become too strong. The machine gun, the artillery shell, the miles of barbed-wire barricades and the formidable lines of opposing trenches, stretching from Nieuport on the Belgian coast to Switzerland, had effectively brought the fighting to a grinding halt. Until some way could be found of protecting the attacking soldiers from the machine-gun bullets and the shell splinters, and a method devised for getting the attackers safely through the wire and over the obstacles, any attack was bound to fail, and would merely result in horrendous casualties. Before the war, plans for various mechanical devices had been put forward to the War Office and either pigeon-holed or summarily discounted. Foremost among these designs were those of an Australian engineer, Mr Lancelot de Mole, which were submitted in 1912 and bore a striking similarity to the first real tank. Makeshift wheeled armoured

'The Devil is coming!' Artist's impression of the first British tanks advancing against the Germans. TM

The Big Wheel *project, was designed to carry an armoured vehicle forward on huge 40ft diameter wheels, but was never built. Here William Tritton, Managing Director of William Foster's (in bowler hat), inspects the smaller* Big Wheel *machine. This never got any further than a wooden mock-up.* TM

cars had already been used in small numbers by the Royal Naval Air Service (RNAS) to protect landing sites or as a means of rescuing downed pilots, while the Belgians employed a few armoured cars in a light cavalry raiding role. These vehicles, despite their limitations, convinced the Commander RNAS, Capt. Murray Sueter, of the value of armour and prompted him to suggest to Winston Churchill, then First Lord of the Admiralty, the development of a tracked armoured vehicle, using Diplock Pedrail crawler tracks. Another RNAS officer, Flight Commander Hetherington, suggested a similar vehicle but with three enormous 40ft diameter wheels instead of tracks. The *Pedrail* and *Big Wheel* land battleships were naval proposals; the army also had its own ideas, but they got a much cooler reception. Foremost among these was the proposal made by a Royal Engineer officer, Lt-Col Ernest Swinton, for a tracked armoured vehicle using American Holt farm-tractor caterpillar tracks as the means of getting across broken ground. Swinton was then serving as Assistant Secretary of the Committee of Imperial Defence and had been sent to France as war correspondent in September 1914. In his book *Eyewitness*, Swinton writes:

Throughout this time I had been racking my brains to discover an antidote; and within the last two weeks my vague idea of an armoured vehicle had definitely crystallised in the form of a power-driven, bullet-proof, armed engine, capable of destroying machine guns, of crossing country and trenches, of breaking through entanglements, and of climbing earthworks.

While Swinton and his contemporaries had the ideas, it was Winston Churchill who saw merit in their proposals and diverted the necessary funds to pay for development. A Landships Committee was formed under the chairmanship of Tennyson d'Eyncourt, then Director of Naval Construction, containing such brilliant men as William Tritton, Managing Director of William Foster's of Lincoln - the firm which eventually built the first tanks - and Lts Walter Gordon Wilson and Albert Stern of the RNAS. The basis of their work on the Swinton proposals was enshrined in the memorandum he submitted to the General Staff in France, entitled 'The Necessity for Machine-Gun Destroyers', which gave the following description of the proposed new weapons:

These machines would be petrol tractors on the caterpillar principle, of a type which can travel at 4 miles an hour on the flat, can cross a ditch up to 4ft width without climbing, can climb in and out of a broader cavity and can scramble over a breastwork. It is possible to build such tractors. They should be armoured with hardened steel plate, proof against the German steel-cored, armour-piercing and reversed bullets and armed with - say - two Maxims and a Maxim 2pdr gun.

LITTLE WILLIE

Swinton continues in his autobiography:

Meanwhile the Landships Committee had made substantial progress in the construction of an experimental machine - later to be known as Little Willie - which had been put in hand on information furnished by the War Office shortly before my specification had been communicated. Halfway through September this machine was sufficiently advanced for demonstration, and on Sunday, the 19th, in company with Mr d'Eyncourt and other members of his Committee, I went by invitation to see it perform. The trial took place at Lincoln, not far from the works of the constructors - Messrs W. Foster and Sons.

Swinton was not a little surprised to discover a large crowd of spectators lining the fence at the side of the test ground and protested about this serious breach of security. However, it was too late to do anything about it and as he goes on to explain:

Luckily, from the point of view of secrecy, the machine failed to comply with the test to which it was put; and in order to discount the revelation of what we were aiming at, it was arranged that a report should be put about that the whole idea was impracticable and should be dropped. *Little Willie*, in addition to suffering from certain technical shortcomings, chiefly connected with the tracks, was unable to fulfil my conditions, for which, in truth, it had not been designed…

Swinton was then taken to a nearby building where, behind tightly closed doors, he saw a nearly completed, full-sized wooden mock-up of a much larger tracked machine, expressly designed to meet his conditions:

Although an engineer it took me some minutes to size the thing up at close range. Its most striking features were its curious rhomboidal, or lozenge, shape, its upturned nose, and the fact that its caterpillar tracks were led right round the hull, instead of being entirely below it… Unwieldy as this contrivance appeared in the confined space in which it was housed, it promised to solve the most difficult problems involved - the power to climb and the ability to span broad trenches; and I felt that I saw in front of me - though only in wood - the actual embodiment of my ideas and the fulfilment of my specification… Dinner on the train on the return journey to London was a joyous occasion.

BIG WILLIE[1]

The mock-up which Swinton had seen was of course the vehicle that was later to be known as *Big Willie*, HMLS *Centipede* or, more affectionately, *Mother*, even though 'she' was strictly a male tank, being armed with two, long-barrelled, 6pdr naval guns, while female tanks were to carry only machine guns. *Mother* was completed in January 1916 and moved by rail to a secret trials area where the makers could show off her prowess. The chosen location was the Marquess of Salisbury's park at Hatfield, where Swinton and Flight Commander T.G. Hetherington, RNAS, another member of the Landships Committee, had been laying out a 'steeplechase course' which would enable the tank to prove it could achieve all the conditions laid down in the 'official test' and 'active service test'.[2] The trial took place on 2 February 1916 and was watched by representatives of the Cabinet, the Army Council, the Admiralty and GHQ France. Swinton also attended and later recalled:

Wednesday, 2 February, was the great day of the official trial. So far as was humanly possible everything had been done to ensure that there

should be no breakdown. On this point I was particularly nervous, for so much hung in the balance … it is the first impression which counts … The demonstration was attended by Lord Kitchener, Mr Balfour, Mr Lloyd George, Mr McKenna, members of the Admiralty Staff, General Robertson, several senior officers from the War Office, those connected with the creation of Mother, and last but not least, representatives of GHQ.

Maj-Gen Sir Ernest Swinton - 'Father of the Tank Corps' - seen here wearing the distinctive tank arm badge which he designed. TM

13

Mr William Tritton (later Sir William) with his Tritton Trench Crosser, *an early attempt at a cross-sountry vehicle which carried its own bridge. His tenacity and enterprise would finally bear fruit as his firm, William Foster & Sons of Lincoln, would build the first tanks.* TM

The trial was a great success and most observers were enthusiastic and showed it. Lord Kitchener, however, was entirely sceptical and called *Mother* a 'pretty toy'.[3] Swinton was very disappointed, as Kitchener had been the man he most wished to convince. However, as he recalls:

> It was the opinion of the representatives of GHQ which counted. As potential buyers they had come to inspect the sample before placing an order…. Though not exuberant, the buyers were very satisfied with the possibility now offered them, of competing with the hitherto impregnable German defence.

They agreed that they would recommend to the Commander-in-Chief that he ask for some machines. His Majesty the King, who had always been kept informed of the progress of the development, now said that he would also like to see *Mother*, so a private trial was held on 8 February. The King followed every manoeuvre with great attention, expressed his satisfaction and even congratulated the driver personally. Swinton wrote shortly afterwards:

> We were waiting for the word 'Go'. All was in train. On Friday, 11 February, things began to move. After eight days the War Office received a request for forty machines. Considering the

During September 1915, behind this conference room door at the White Hart Hotel, Lincoln, the idea for the first practical fighting tank were hammered out in great secrecy by William Tritton and Major Wilson. TM

nature of the weapon and the way in which it was to be employed, this number was, to my mind, quite inadequate and I suggested that it should be increased to at least 100. This was the number finally decided upon.'

WHAT'S IN A NAME?

There have been many theories advanced as to why the name *Tank* was given to the new weapon system. In fact it was Swinton and Lt-Col Dally Jones who coined the name when they were acting as assistant secretaries of the Landships Committees. Swinton wrote later:

> The structure of the machine in its early stages being boxlike, some term conveying the idea of a box or container seemed appropriate. We

The very first prototype tank in the world was the No 1 Lincoln Machine. Initially it was fitted with Bullock tracks which proved unsatisfactory. A modified version, known as Little Willie, *was soon fitted with new tracks with armoured frames. It is seen here at Wembley Park towards the end of the war, minus its tailwheels.* TM

rejected in turn - container - receptacle - reservoir - cistern. The monosyllable Tank appealed to us as being likely to catch on and be remembered. That night in the draft report of the conference the word 'Tank' was employed in its new sense for the first time.

During the First World War, however, the crews were far more likely to talk about the tanks as *Willies,* or to refer to them by their special nicknames, or the letter-number allocated to each tank for identification purposes.

THE FIRST CREWS

A few days after the initial order had been placed for the first 100 tanks, Swinton happened to meet General Bird, Director of Staff Duties, in one of the corridors of the War Office. To his astonishment he was told that the Army Council had selected him to raise and command the Tank Detachment, as the new unit manning the tanks was to be called. He set about his task with a will, and as he recalled later '...found the ensuing eight months to be the most strenuous, stimulating, and trying period I have ever experienced.'

Siberia Farm near Bisley Camp, was chosen as the birthplace of the Tank Detachment, on 16 February 1916, mainly because it was very close to the depot and training school of the Motor Machine-Gun Service, which had been formed in late 1914 to increase the machine-gun strength of infantry divisions, by adding specially trained batteries of motorcycle and sidecar combinations carrying medium machine guns. Because trench warfare had rendered their sidecar guns virtually useless, quantities of excellent soldiers were thus immediately available for transfer to the Armoured Car Section of the Motor Machine-Gun Service, the new name of the Tank Detachment, which was adopted in March 1916 as a safer disguise.[4] Thus a ready-made and already partly-trained nucleus of a number of officers, about 700 Other Ranks and the CO of the Motor Machine-Gun Service, Lt-Col R. W. Bradley, DSO, South Wales Borderers, were transferred *en bloc* at the beginning of March. One of these 700 was L-Cpl A. E. Lee who recalled those days in an article published in the *Tank* magazine:

> We were moved from the huts of Bisley Camp to tents at Siberia Farm, about a mile away. Our training was extended to include the .303in Hotchkiss Light Automatic Rifle (formerly a cavalry weapon) and the 6pdr Hotchkiss Naval Quick-Firing Gun. Gunnery training was difficult. Practical training, with live ammunition, was easy as far as the .303 Vickers and Hotchkiss were concerned as we had the use of the Bisley Ranges, but the 6pdr gun could not be used there.

Mother - also known as Big Willie *or* HMS Centipede *- at the Burton Park trials in 1916. Designed in August 1915, it moved under its own power on 13 January 1916, a remarkable achievement of swift design and production. Production versions were known as the Heavy Tank Mark I.* TM

The Machine-Gun Corps capbadge was worn by soldiers of the Heavy Section from 16 February 1916, but officers continued to wear the badges and accoutrements of their parent units. TM

Due to the shortage of machine guns in the BEF early in the Great War, a Motor Machine Gun Service was created to provide a battery of motorcycle-mounted machine guns for each division. These are Vickers-Clyno combinations. In due course many of the men would transfer to the Tank Corps as the batteries were disbanded. TM

Some of the very first tankmen are seen here in this group photograph of 'B' Company, Heavy Section Machine Gun Corps, taken in July 1916. TM

We were taken to Larkhill on Salisbury Plain for firing practice, but that was soon given up as impractical. Then the problem was solved - by the Royal Navy. (From the beginning the Navy had a finger in our pie!)

Winston Churchill, who had been First Lord of the Admiralty, had taken a great interest in the idea and had put up a large proportion of the money needed for the development. We were to use naval guns, and it was considered that the movement of a tank in action might be comparable to that of a small ship in a heavy sea. What then could be more natural than we should be trained in gunnery by the Navy?

Large numbers of us were sent to Whale Island (HMS *Excellent*) for training. Whale Island was a small island just off the coast at Portsmouth. The training was first-class. The old Petty Officer Instructors went to great lengths and nothing was too much trouble to ensure that we became efficient gunners. At the conclusion of the course we were taken down the English Channel and fired our classification tests from one of the Monitors which had previously been used to bombard enemy positions on the Belgian coast. And so we returned to Siberia Farm camp as fully qualified gunlayers, entitled to wear that badge on our sleeves.

The first 100 drivers and the workshops were provided by 711 Company, Army Service Corps, who mostly came from the Caterpillar Companies in France and the Siege Batteries of the Royal Garrison Artillery, while Mr Geoffrey Smith, editor of the *Motor Cycle* magazine, was very helpful in recruiting men for the Motor Engineering trades. More

volunteers, especially officers, were still required, so Swinton and Bradley toured the country visiting officer cadet units and similar, looking for likely men. Others responded to publicity and one such volunteer was Lt Victor Huffam, who was later to command one of the first tanks into action. He recalled being shown an order which read:

WAR OFFICE
Strictly Secret and Confidential

Volunteers are required for an exceedingly dangerous and hazardous duty of a secret nature. Officers who have been awarded decorations for bravery, and are experienced in the handling of men, and with an engineering background, should have their names submitted to this office, and suitable officers will be required to attend Wellington Barracks at a date to be specified later.

Huffam's name was submitted and in company with 300 other lieutenants, volunteers from units all over the British Isles, he went to Wellington Barracks to meet Swinton:

who warned us that we had volunteered for a very dangerous mission and said if any man had any doubts he was to step back one pace. Not one moved. He told us that only 28 were required and that the others would probably be wanted later. I was one of the 28 and returned to Felixstowe under orders to hold myself in readiness.

In May 1916, I duly reported to Bisley and was issued with a badge of crossed machine guns and found myself a Lieutenant in the Heavy Section Machine-Gun Corps (HSMGC). This provided no clue whatsoever as to our real Unit! The veil was soon lifted a little when we saw, stuck on a sandy ridge, a sponson with machine guns. A sponson was a steel protrusion with room for two Vickers guns, which was bolted on each side of a female tank. All officers and some 300 men underwent a machine-gun course, but no one was shown a tank.

ORGANISATION

During April and May 1916, after various tentative organisations had been tried, it was decided to form six companies (lettered A to F), each of 25 tanks, a total of 150 machines. 75 would be machine-gun destroyers or MALE tanks, armed with two 6pdr guns, firing cannon shell and also case-shot; the remaining 75 would be man-killing FEMALE tanks, armed only with machine guns. Each company was to be divided into four sections, each with six tanks and one spare tank. Each section had three male and three female tanks and was divided into three subsections. Every group of two companies was provided with an administrative branch of one officer and four ORs, plus a workshop branch of three officers and fifty ORs. A company establishment was 28 officers and 255 ORs, while the total strength of the Heavy Section was 184 officers and 1610 ORs. The original six company commanders wer e:

A – Major C.M. Tippetts (South Wales Borderers)
B – Major T.R. McLellan (The Cameronians)
C – Major A. Holford-Walker, MC (Argyll and Sutherland Highlanders)
D – Major F. Summers, DSC (Armoured Car Division, RNAS)
E – Major N.H. Nutt (Armoured Car Division, RNAS)
F – Major W.F.R. Kyngdom (Royal Artillery)

MOVE TO THETFORD

The Heavy Section did not stay in Bisley for long, moving during June 1916, to Lord Iveagh's estate at Elveden, near Thetford, as Victor Huffam recalls:

Shortly after this we were ordered to move to a new camp at Thetford in Norfolk, and on arrival marched from Thetford Station, the seven miles to Canada Farm, Elveden. We marched in through a typical white farm gate and were surprised to see soldiers from the Hampshire Regiment, cavalry and Indian Units stationed on the perimeter surrounding the farmhouse and buildings. We also learned that there was a railway siding in the camp. We were soon introduced to Little Mother, our first tank, a real tank to train on, and a reminder of what 'hazardous duty' could mean.

Early tanks being built at Foster's factory in Lincoln. TM

At once the veil was completely lifted. We were told that more tanks were coming and that we were to make ourselves proficient in tank handling, so as to be able to train others who were to follow. We were also told that there was an armed guard on the three perimeters surrounding the camp and that not only could we not get out but nobody could get in, and that our future safety and maybe our very existence depended on one thing: Absolute Secrecy.

'D' Company now at Canada Farm, had 28 officers and 300 men and with 'A', 'B', and 'C' Companies over 100 officers and 1000 men were in this guarded reserve. No one outside knew our secret. Our privileged visitors were: His Majesty King George V, Lloyd George, the Prime Minister, Winston Churchill and Earl Haig, who had attended a tank demonstration and knew our secret. The demonstration had impressed Haig so much that it altered his plans to break the stalemate on the Somme. 'A', 'B', 'C' and 'D' Companies were then equipped with tanks and we all did some training with individual tanks and crews.

Training at Elveden mainly concentrated upon crew duties, such as driving, negotiating battlefield obstacles and vehicle maintenance. There was neither the time nor the experienced instructors available to work out or to teach any elaborate tactical manoeuvres. L-Cpl Lee recalls:

We learnt by a system of trial and error and somehow, by sharing our knowledge, we got results and soon every man in the crew became a competent driver, working on the principle that every man must be able to do the job of everyone else in an emergency.

TANK TIPS

Swinton had earlier written a memorandum he entitled: 'Notes on the Employment of Tanks', in which he spelt out his basic rules for the tactical employment of the new machines. Despite the fact that he sent copies over to GHQ in France, they were studiously ignored. His rules for tank warfare were encapsulated in 'Tank Tips' - what he described as being his 'Child's guide to knowledge'. They were written in down-to-earth, easily understandable language and are as relevant today as they were all those years ago.

ON TO FRANCE

On 13 August 1916 the first detachment of tanks left England for France, as L-Cpl Lee recalls:

Training was finally completed except for actual practice in battle, and in August we were given

TANK TIPS

Remember your orders

Shoot quick

Shoot low. A miss which throws dust in the enemy's eyes is better than one which whistles in his ear.

Shoot cunning

Shoot the enemy while they are rubbing their eyes. Economise ammunition and don't kill a man three times.

Remember that trenches are curly and dugouts deep - look round the corners

Watch the progress of the fight and your neighbouring Tanks

Watch your infantry whom you are helping

Remember the position of your own line

Shell out the enemy's machine guns and other small guns and kill them first with your 6pdrs

You will not see them for they will be cunningly hidden

You must ferret out where they are, judging by the following signs: Sound, Dust, Smoke

A shadow in a parapet

A hole in a wall, haystack, rubbish heap, woodstack, pile of bricks

They will be usually placed to fire slantways across the front and to shoot along the wire

One 6pdr shell that hits the loophole of a MG emplacement will do it in

Use the 6pdr with care; shoot to hit and not to make a noise

Never have any gun, even when unloaded, pointing at your own infantry, or a 6pdr gun pointed at another tank

It is the unloaded gun that kills the fool's friends

Never mind the heat

Never mind the noise

Never mind the dust

Think of your pals in the infantry

Thank God you are bullet proof and can help the infantry, who are not

Have your mask always handy

The cranes at Southampton were initially unable to load tanks, so they had to be sent to Avonmouth for loading to start their cross-Channel journey. TM

ten days' leave. This was the first leave we had had since our formation, apart from one weekend pass, and we had worked hard at training for 6½ days every week… so we considered our leave well deserved. On returning to camp, equipment and kit was packed and we entrained for Southampton… and from thence by ship to Le Havre.

The tanks were to be collected on arrival in France; they were travelling via Avonmouth as there wasn't a crane at Southampton at that time powerful enough to load them. The tanks were named by their crews and some were very ingenious. One was, I remember, named *Autogophaster*, another was *Otasel*. A male and female were the *One-Eyed Riley* and *Riley's Daughter* respectively. One member of the crew must have been an artist, for delightful portraits of these two characters were painted on and covered the whole front of each tank. The tanks in my section were all named after revues which were popular in London at the time: *Oh, I Say; Look Who's Here; Watch Your Step; We're All In It; So Search Me;* and my own tank was *Keep Smiling*. We joined up with our tanks at Yvrench, a small

village near Abbeville, and then came the job of bolting on the sponsons which carried the guns each side of the tank. These had to be removed for any journey by rail as the tank would otherwise be too wide to pass through bridges and tunnels. The sponsons each weighed three tons and were carried on small trolleys intended to be towed by the tanks. On arrival at the railhead they had to be manhandled into position on each side of the tank, the sponsons lifted off the trolley, and manhandled into position until the bolt holes in tank and sponson coincided exactly, then the bolts were inserted and tightened. It sounds easy, and so it was, in theory; but have you ever tried to lift three tons of metal into a position where not one but every pair of bolt holes must exactly coincide? And if the fit was not exactly perfect, even to one sixteenth of an inch, the bolts would not fit. Sometimes, just as the bolt was being inserted, something would slip and the whole operation had to be re-started. At other times the first bolt hole went in, but perhaps because the sponson had warped slightly none of the others would… then it was a case of using drifts, levers and brute force… but it was done eventually. Each crew was responsible for fitting its own sponsons and the first crew to finish went round the others making caustic remarks and offering unhelpful suggestions. The last crew to finish had the worst time, with the remaining part of the section chipping them. Fortunately this job was rendered unnecessary the following year, when the Mark I was replaced with the Mark IV. The sponsons then were smaller and were located inside the tank, so they merely had to be slid outwards into position and then bolted up.

PREPARATIONS FOR BATTLE

The great Somme offensive had opened on 1 July and on the very first day the British alone had suffered nearly 60 000 casualties, including over one-third killed. It was the heaviest loss the British Army had ever known and what made matters even worse was that the sacrifice was all in vain. The enemy defences were immensely strong and nothing the Allies could do had any effect on them. General Sir Douglas Haig, C-in-C British Expeditionary Force, conscious of mounting criticism at home, was desperately seeking a solution to this stalemate and seized on the tanks as the panacea for all his problems, despite the fact that they were still very few in number and completely untried in battle, Swinton wrote:

On 19 August, I paid a hurried visit for one day to Advanced GHQ at Beaquesne. Sir Douglas saw me and pointed out on the map the sector where he proposed to throw in the tanks. He did not enter into any discussion of his reasons for using them at that time.

Four Mark I tanks of C Company HBMGC being prepared for the first battle at Flers. There are three female and one male, which is named Clan Leslie. TM

Swinton's further visits to France were not much better. He was met everywhere with a strange mixture of amused tolerance and contemptuous scepticism by some senior officers, while others on the Staff had an almost blind faith in what the tanks would be able to achieve. He remarked that the thing which struck him most forcibly was that the tanks were being looked on as some 'new kind of toy' and he objected most strongly to the endless displays which the Heavy Section were made to give on their arrival in France, but was powerless to stop them. One tank commander summed up the situation succinctly:

It all reminded me of Hampstead Heath. When we got there we found the Infantry Brigades had been notified that the tanks were to perform from 9.00 to 10.00 and 2.00 to 3.00 and every officer within a large radius and an enormous number of the Staff came to inspect us. We were an object of interest to everyone. This did not help one's work.

So, during that most critical period of preparation, instead of being left alone to get ready, the men barely had time to eat and sleep, let alone service their machines.

MOVING UP

'C' Company had been the first to arrive, coming over in two groups during the second half of August. On arrival in France they moved to an improvised training centre at Yvrench, near Abbeville. 'D' Company also arrived by instalments, entraining on 25 and 30 August, reaching Yvrench so late that they had to move immediately on to the concentration area at the Loop, a rail centre near Bray-sur-Somme, close behind the front. This move started on 7 September, but was not completed until 13 September, just two days before the attack. They had the barest time to prepare, while 'A' Company, which did not arrive at Yvrench until 14 September was too late for the battle, as was 'B' Company which followed even later. Lt-Col John Brough and one

Before the first battle. C19 Clan Leslie *is seen here with a crowd of admirers. The wood and chicken-wire framework on the top was as a defence against hand grenades. Note the tank has the long-barrelled six pounder guns in its sponsons.* TM

staff captain formed the HQ of the Heavy Section, and he fell out with GHQ almost immediately because he was understandably 'difficult' over lack of training time and the use of all the available tanks at this early stage. Swinton had to replace him with the only other Lt-Col in the Section - Bradley, who arrived less than two weeks before they went into action. There was also, of course, a great deal of administration to do, establishing workshops and supply depots, working out how the tanks would be supplied and repaired in the field, in addition to all the battle preparations, so these enforced staff changes did not help.

Haig had decided to spread all the available tanks (49 total) in twos and threes across the entire front, with the XIVth and XVth Corps on the right and centre-right being allocated 17 tanks each; IIIrd Corps in the centre eight; while the remaining seven were kept with the Reserve Army. The tanks' main tasks would be to deal with enemy strongpoints and to provide fire support for the infantry.

The tanks were finally loaded up for battle at the Loop, as Victor Huffam recalls:

> ...petrol, oil, half a cow, pigeons, signalling flags and 33 000 rounds of .303 ammunition which was already loaded into belts for use with the four Vickers guns, in addition to one .303 Hotchkiss gun.

That afternoon, while the loading was in progress yet another visitor arrived, got into D9, bumping his head in the process and 'letting fly some real oaths'. Huffam was slightly taken aback to discover that his visitor was none other than the Prince of Wales, who then sat on the engine platform and talked as they loaded up the stores. The crew were delighted, as HRH only visited D9, so they felt that put them 'one up on everyone else'. That night (13 September) the tanks moved forward from the Loop to their respective assembly areas: 'C' to the Briquetterie near Trones Wood, and 'D' to the Green Dump behind Delville Wood. They moved forward on their tracks, guided by tapes laid along the routes they were to follow. Lt Arnold recalled his move forward thus:

> Towards nightfall on the 13th we set off on the last stage of our journey, with guides detailed by the infantry. We arrived before daylight at Green Dump. Here we hived up for the day; we were on a slight rise in the ground and took no partic- ular precautions as regards camouflage. At daybreak the tank commanders were taken in small parties to look at the ground over which they would be operating, then they walked back to Green Dump, filled their two 60gal petrol tanks, got a little sleep and waited for 9pm. Then we started off, with the noise of our 105 Daimler

engines lost in the battle effects of the continuous bombardment. We all moved off together and were to cross our front line in pairs of tanks at various points. We were scheduled to advance just before the infantry, zero hour being 6am.

Green Dump was only some three miles behind the front trenches, yet it took the tanks a full nine hours to reach their starting positions, despite the fact, as Arnold recalled, that they seemed to be travelling most of the time. However, they had to use bottom gear all the way and at times one of the crew had to dismount and look for routes round the very bad patches. With occasional enforced stops and much laborious climbing in and out of shellholes, they could only maintain about 700yds an hour. At one stage Arnold was so convinced that they would never make it in time, he even contemplated sending off a pigeon message, but decided against it. In fact they were much nearer to the front line than he had imagined and so managed to reach their starting position just after the infantry left their trenches.

INTO BATTLE

The morning of 15 September 1916 was fine, but there was a thin ground mist, the kind one associates with the onset of autumn. Zero Hour had been set at 0620hrs, (not 0600 as Arnold recalled). However, the tanks had to be on the move well before them, as these orders issued to 'D' Group explain:

COMPANY ORDERS FOR 'D' GROUP OF TANKS FOR 15th SEPT 1916[5]
HASTIE M (D17) COURT F (D14) HUFFAM V (D9)

You will leave your starting line at Zero minus 35 (Zero 6.20am)

Distance - 480yds out is taken at 600 as you are in column, ie: at 10yds per min - 60mins.

You must arrive at plus 25 as you are W of Flers Road 60 minus 25 equals 35. Throughout the advance you will follow the route laid down on Map and adhere to time given to you. The following points in your advance are to be noted. The first Vickers car of the Group that arrives at Tea Trench will stop there - where he will deal with the German machine guns and advance posts until the arrival of the Infantry, when he will advance in line with them overtaking the Group at the Switch Trench. All Tanks of Group on arrival at Switch Trench wait until arrival of Infantry when the Group will advance 150yds and thence conform to time table.

The objectives, routes, and responsibility for dealing with strong-points encountered by Group of Tank D will be as follows: Tea Support

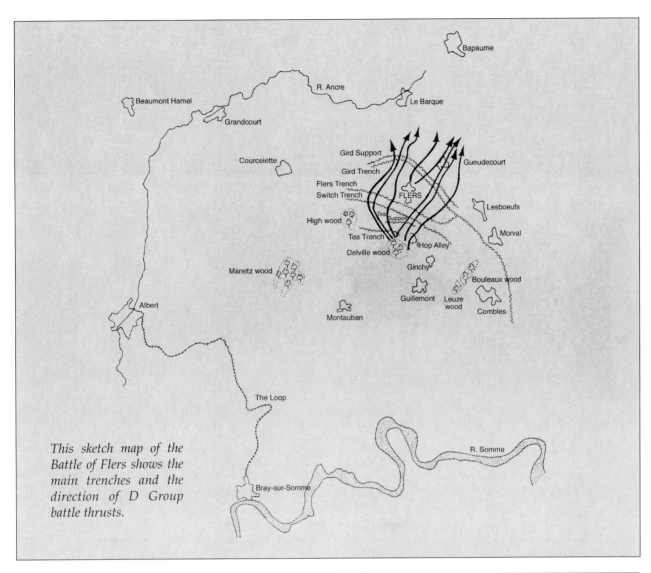

This sketch map of the Battle of Flers shows the main trenches and the direction of D Group battle thrusts.

Trench (where one Tank MG will be dropped until arrival of Infantry). Switch Trench - Flers Trench sunken road at TIA35 thence to follow sunken ditch at NW corner of Flers Village N31A8.2 Hog Head strong-point. During the advance to the second objective from Switch to Flers Trench along routes chosen.

You will make every effort to deal with sunken roads and machine-gun emplacements as far as Flers Trench. Should any strong-point succeed in holding up the Infantry, the Tanks will immediately deal with it.

It had been planned to precede the main attack with a small operation to clear the enemy out of a pocket on the British Front, between Ginchy and Delville Wood, where the Germans were occupying a trench known as Hop Alley. Three tanks had been allocated for this task. Unfortunately one immediately broke down and one was ditched, so the remaining tank (D1), commanded by Capt. H.W. Mortimore advanced on its own at about 0515hrs, followed fifteen minutes later by two companies of 6th KOYLI - the first infantry to go into action with tanks.

The first reports of the battle at Flers, with pictures of tanks did not appear in the Daily Mirror *until 22 November 1916, over a month after the event.* TM

Artist's impression of Hastie's Dinnaken *(D17 of No 3 Section, 'D' Company) on 15 September 1916, 'walking up the High Street of Flers with the British Army cheering behind.'* TM

Mortimore and the KOYLIs cleared out the pocket successfully but the tank was disabled by a shell which hit the steering gear. Thus D1 was the very first tank to go into action and the location of this first action is now the site of the Tank Corps Memorial.

Due to the way in which Haig had decided to use the tanks - in 'penny packets' spread across the entire front, and because there were so few actually battleworthy, most of the actions which took place on that first day were fragmentary and, in the main, single tank actions.

Thus the two eyewitness accounts of Huffam and Arnold which follow give just their own isolated view of the battle. They are stirringly written and give a fascinating insight into the tankman's problems in that first action. First, Victor Huffam:

With the dawn 26 tanks rolled into action. In crossing a disused support trench, Lt Court (D14) when halfway across started to dig in, the parapet collapsed and D9 and D14 were immobilised. We climbed to the roof of our tanks and watched the other tanks go in, immediately behind a creeping barrage. It was a wonderful experience to see this barrage of terrific intensity and the rising ground in front seemed to disappear. Jerry, dumbfounded at our firepower, then saw for the first time our tanks rolling towards him. They fled from their trenches and retired to Flers, but even there they could not stop our tanks and the uplifted Infantry drove them out and the battle for Flers which had previously cost

tens of thousands of lives was over.

Huffam and Court were dug out that afternoon by a Chinese labour force, then went on to Flers that night, so as to be ready for the attack on the second objective (Gueudecourt) the following day:

D14 and D9 started up. As D9 entered Flers piles of dead British and Germans were in our path. Attempts to clear a passage had to be abandoned, shelling was too intense and eventually we left Flers. D14 was leading on our right and appeared to be smothered in shells. Our own prismatic mirrors and periscopes were already useless and my driver, Archer, had been blinded by splinters so I called my Corporal, H. Sanders, to take his place. We were now getting too much attention from Jerry. We opened our armoured flap to see where we were and found we were almost astride the enemy trench and that our two starboard guns were doing terrible execution of the bewildered Germans.

On moving off we were watching D14. It appeared to stop suddenly and immediately exploded. I then went to the port-side gunners to see why their guns were silent - they never fired again as both gunners were dead. Several bullets and small shells had penetrated our armour plate and we were in a bad shape. We were then hit by a larger shell and there was an explosion followed by a fire. I came round to find myself lying on top of my Corporal whose shins were sticking out in the air. I had already been issued with morphia tablets so I quietened him with these and bandaged him with first-aid dressings from the others of my crew. It was not a very nice situation as we were in enemy lines and I had my Corporal in agony and all the others damaged and shell-shocked. Later that morning the infantry attacked and captured Flea trench which lay between us and our own men, so I sent two men back to them for help. Whether they ever got back I do not know but eventually the Infantry went back which left us in No Man's Land. Sanders was now in a very bad way and perhaps I had given too much morphine to quieten his cries. I knew that somehow I had to get him back and so as to help him and myself, I fastened my belt to his and as I crawled back from hole to hole he came with me.

Huffam eventually got back to safety and some months later was reunited with Cpl Sanders when he visited him in hospital in Kent.

Arnold's battle was just as hectic, as he relates:

...It was now half light; we were getting along better and were amongst the infantry, who were in turn advancing and sheltering in shell holes as our creeping barrage gradually lifted. The German shelling was severe and one felt comparatively safe inside the tank. The German front-line trenches had been shelled practically out of existence and I think the infantry met little opposition there. And *Dracula* reached the support line first. A row of German heads appeared above the parapet and looked - doubtless in some amazement - at what was approaching out of the mirk of the bombardment. At point blank range, I drew a bead with my Hotchkiss and pressed the trigger. It did not fire! Instead the mechanism gave forth a dull and impotent click. Instantly I performed the immediate action indicated for the particular stoppage - it was only to pull back the loading lever. Again I fired, and again the same result. But those inquisitive Germans gained only a momentary respite for the tank was on top of the trench - and there we paused whilst the Vickers machine guns raked the enemy to port and starboard. Then on we went again, myself furiously attempting to make the Hotchkiss fire. I cursed myself. Fool! I thought, you must have got excited, done the wrong thing and jammed the gun. But how? The mechanism and the drill were so simple - and so familiar - I would have backed myself to fire and remedy the few possible stoppages almost in my sleep. I dismounted the gun and discovered the trouble. A shell splinter had struck the exposed portion of the gun and

dented the metal guard over the piston which works the mechanism. This still permitted the gun to be loaded and almost to fire, but the firing pin could not quite reach the cartridge in the breech. I mounted the spare gun - and tried it to make sure that it was firing. Meanwhile it was growing lighter and we were advancing in the direction of Flers. The bombardment had slackened right off. Opposition was slight and the New Zealanders who were here attacking were advancing and taking prisoner any remaining Germans. We soon covered the mile or so to Flers - on my right I saw the tank proceeding up the road into Flers, 'with the British Army cheering behind' (vide reports). The New Zealanders immediately set about consolidating the position and took possession of a sunken road which leads out of the village to the north-east. I sent off a pigeon with a message notifying the situation to Corps HQ. It was now about 8am; things were quiet, except for spasmodic shelling, and it was a lovely morning. Not liking the look of the German observation balloons, I withdrew *Dracula* behind the shelter of a belt of trees. There we made tea and had breakfast; filled up with petrol from the reserve which we carried in a box on the stern wheels. We went over with fire

A shaken German soldier crawls out of his bunker which has been crushed by a Mark I tank (note the tail-wheels which were supposed to help with steering). TM

Kein Eintritt! TM

Drawing by Sam Goddard Crowder of the first tank attack is accompanied by details of 'D' Company, Heavy Section Machine-Gun Corps crews, who took part in the action. 25 tanks, 25 officers and 200 crew trained in secret in Canada Farm, Thetford. TM

extinguishers to see if we could help another tank which was on fire, but it was raging furiously, with the ammunition going off inside like squibs, and there for some time we stood by. I moved our position occasionally as, from the incidence of the shelling, I felt sure we were visible to one of the German 'sausage' balloons. I was talking to a New Zealand Company Commander when we saw a large party of Germans advancing into a sunken road. They were some two miles away to the left - in the direction of the Butte de Warlencourt - and one longed for a swift tank to scurry over and take a look into that sunken road! But it was off my beat and it would have been no use lumbering over there at two miles an hour anyway. A bit later on the infantry commander sent me a message: 'Counter attack brewing, can you do anything about it?' We emerged from our lair, crossed the sunken road and went out to the front. We were rewarded with the sight of long lines of Germans advancing in open formation, and opened fire with our port-side Vickers guns at 900yds range. It was impossible to tell just

what effect our fire took, but it certainly checked the advance. *Dracula* cruised about for a while in front of the village and then came under what seemed to me to be direct fire from a field gun. A difficult matter to judge but someone was making useful practice against us. One shell in particular seemed to miss us by inches. I had, in the meantime, collected a bullet through my knee, whilst outside. It was late afternoon now and as our infantry had been reinforced, I judged it was time to get back. We had taken aboard a badly wounded New Zealander and putting the village with its trees between us and the imme-diate front we made tracks for the slight ridge that intervenes between Flers and Delville Wood. We must have been visible to an observation balloon for we were faithfully hunted back by shells. One fell just in front of us - the next 20yds behind us. Where would the next one land? Ah! just off to the side. Then after a while we were apparently ignored and as it grew dark we lumbered over the rise and out of sight. We handed over our wounded New Zealander to a doctor who appeared and proceeded on our toilsome way back through Delville Wood to our Headquarters at Green Dump. It was pretty late when we got there and although we had medical comforts' aboard - and had not forgotten the fact - I was pleased to meet a tumbler full of medicine which my CO handed to me. About fifty-fifty whisky I think. At any rate it induced a nice muzzy feeling which took the jolts out of a some-what bumpy ride in an ambulance car.

As Arnold has explained, he saw a tank moving up the road into Flers, which became the subject of the now famous newspaper heading: 'A tank is walking up the High Street of Flers with the British Army cheering behind.'[6] There has always been some controversy as to which tank this could have been, because a number of tanks were in and around the village at some stage of the battle. It seems most likely, however, that it was Hastie in D17 (*Dinnaken*) which drove right through the village.

A GLIMPSE INTO THE FUTURE

Perhaps the most prophetic action took place a few days later, during the Fourth Army's offensive which was launched on 25 September. 21st Division of XV Corps had been given Gueudecourt as its objective. However, the two leading brigades were soon held up by uncut wire and machine-gun nests, in front of the formidable Gird Trench. It was decided that the one and only available tank would be brought up to help the infantry the following morning. It was a Female tank, commanded by 2/Lt C.E. Storey. Just before dawn the tank moved up the road from Flers and then motored along the edge of Gird Trench from west to east, flattening the wire and firing its machine guns to great effect. The two companies of infantry following up found no difficulty in capturing 370 demoralised enemy, especially after a British aero-plane had also flown along the line of the trench, raking it with machine-gun fire. In addition to those

captured, nearly half-a-mile of trench was occupied and many casualties were inflicted on the enemy in this first infantry/tank/air co-operation, while the British suffered a mere five casualties. Storey, who had fought his tank until all but two of the crew were wounded and his petrol tanks were empty, received a well-deserved DSO. The XV Corps battle report read: 'What would have proved to be a very difficult operation, involving probably very heavy losses, was taken with the greatest of ease, entirely owing to the assistance rendered by the tank.'

THE AFTERMATH

Despite the undoubted success of some individual tanks, it could not be said that the new weapons had either proved themselves or been a tremendous influence on the battle. Indeed, while the Press were ecstatic, going overboard and calling them names like 'Motor Monsters', 'Touring Forts' and 'Jaberwocks with eyes of Flame', many senior officers viewed their performance with scorn and remem-bered their faults, without making any allowance for the inexperience of the crews, or the fact that they had been rushed into action. Haig's reaction was fortunately more favourable and when Swinton and Stern went to see him at his Advanced HQ on 17 September, he thanked them warmly for what they had done, and said that, although the tanks had not achieved all that had been hoped for, they had saved many lives and fully justified themselves. According to Stern's report on their meeting, he had added: 'Wherever the tanks advanced we took our objectives and where they did not advance we did not take our objectives.' He also said that he now wanted as many tanks built as possible, that they should have better armour and be heavier. His request was translated into a firm order for 1000 bigger and better tanks, plus a further 100 Mark Is to keep the factories going until the new design was settled. It also meant the major expansion of the Heavy Branch together with a move from Elveden to a new location in the UK.

---

[1] See Annex A for detailed specification of *Big Willie*.

[2] The official test comprised climbing a parapet 4ft 6ins high and crossing a 5ft wide trench; for the active service test it had to crawl into a prepared dug-out shelter, climb out and over a British-style trench, cross two 12ft wide x 6ft shell craters, ford a stream with marshy edges, then up a slope, through a German wire entanglement, over the trench beyond, turn round and go back to the stream, down the marshy bed and finally surmount a double breastwork of 5ft 6ins. All this *Mother* did with ease and then achieved a final feat by crossing a 9ft wide trench which Kitchener had specially demanded.

[3] One school of thought credits Kitchener with more foresight, and his remarks are explained as a desire to preserve secrecy by not discussing the new weapon's capabilities. If this was the case, then

he did a remarkably good job, as no one intimately concerned with the new project was aware of his subterfuge!

[4] In May 1916, this name was again changed to Heavy Section Machine-Gun Corps, and on 16 November 1916 to Heavy Branch Machine-Gun Corps, a title that remained in use until it finally became known as the Tank Corps on 28 July 1917.

[5] Extract from original held in Tank Museum Library (Acc 4966-04.203)

[6] This stirring piece of journalistic writing was based upon a much more matter-of-fact message sent back by an air observer. It read: 'Tank seen in main street Flers going on with large number of troops following it.'

Annex to Chapter 1

DESCRIPTION OF BIG WILLIE
(As given in the 'Tank Trial' programme)

This machine has been designed under the direction of Mr E.H.T. d'Eyncourt, by Mr W. Tritton (of Messrs Foster of Lincoln) and Lt W.G. Wilson, RNAS, and has been constructed by Messrs Foster of Lincoln. The conditions laid down as to the obstacle to be surmounted were that the machine should be able to climb a parapet 4ft 6ins high and cross a gap 5ft wide.

Over-all dimensions	ft	ins
Length	31	3
Width with sponsons	13	8
Width without sponsons	8	3
Height	8	0

Protection

The conning tower is protected generally by 10mm thickness of nickel-steel plate, with 12mm thickness in front of the drivers. The sides and back ends have 8mm thickness of high tensile steel, and the belly is covered with the same.

Weight	tons	cwts
Hull	21	0
Sponsons and guns	3	10
Ammunition, 300 rounds for guns & 20 000 rounds for rifles	2	0
Crew (8 men)	0	10
Tail (for balance)	1	8
Total weight, armament, crew, petrol & ammo	28	8

Horse power of engines	105 hp
Number of gears	4 forward
	2 reverse
Approximate speed on each gear	¾ mile
	1¼ miles
	2¼ miles
	& 4mph

Armament
Two 6pdr guns & three automatic rifles (one Hotchkiss and two Madsen)

Rate of Fire
6pdr: 15-20 rounds per min: Madsen 300 rounds per min: Hotchkiss 250 rounds per min.

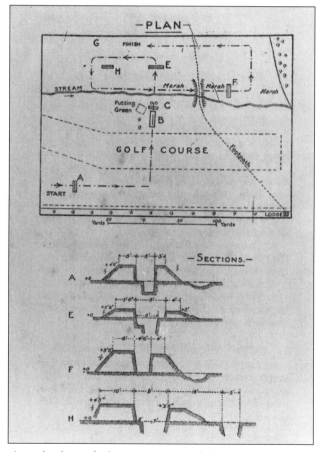

Actual plan of the tests successfully carried out by Mother at Hatfield Park on 2 February 1916, to everyone's satisfaction apart from Lord Kitchener. TM

Chapter 2
GROWING PAINS

EXPANSION

Despite Haig's satisfaction with their performance, which had led directly to the order for a further 1000 tanks, all was not well. There were still many senior officers, such as Generals Rawlinson and Robertson, who had little faith in the new machines, the latter having already described them as a 'somewhat desperate innovation'. The outcome of this dissension was the sudden and unexplained cancellation of the tank order. Immediately, Stern - who was by then Director of Tank Supply - saw the War Minister, Lloyd George, who intervened personally and cancelled the cancellation!

The proposed increase in the tank numbers meant that there had to be a major increase to the strength of the Heavy Section. In October 1916, after various proposals had been discussed, it was agreed that a total of nine battalions would be formed - the four tank companies already in France being expanded into twelve companies, divided between four battalions; while a further five battalions would be formed, based on the two remaining companies still in England. Although moves were afoot to form the battalions into a new Corps, this did not happen immediately. The internal organisation of battalions also underwent a number of changes. The first plan was to have three companies per battalion, each with four fighting sections of five tanks apiece and an HQ section of four tanks, making a total of 72 tanks in each new battalion. However, early in 1917, it was decided that four tanks per fighting section were easier to handle, while one of the sections was made a 'spare', thus significantly reducing the operational tank strength. Each battalion also had its own workshop.

There were, in addition, changes at the top. Brough had already been replaced by Bradley; now Bradley was replaced on the grounds that the commander of the Heavy Section in the field should be someone who had active service experience on the Western Front. Swinton chose another Sapper, Lt-Col Hugh Elles, who had originally been selected by Haig in late 1915 to enquire on his behalf into the subject of tanks, so he was most acceptable to GHQ, while Swinton considered him to be:

a first class officer...*persona gratissima* at GHQ

who knew everyone and all the 'ropes'... in spite of the fact that he knew as little about tanks as his two predecessors did about the niceties of the tactics current in France... I could think of no one more suitable.

On 29 September 1916 Elles was appointed, with the rank of Colonel, to command the Heavy Section in France. His small headquarters, then in a single hut in the village of Beauquesne, comprised just four other officers: Brigade Major (Capt. G. le Q. Martel), DAA & QMG (Capt T.J. Uzielli), Staff Captain (Capt J.H. Tapper) and Intelligence Officer (Capt F.E. Hotblack). One of Elles' first actions was to move the headquarters to Bermicourt, a small village near St Pol, where it would remain for the rest of the war. The staff would of course grow considerably as the Corps increased in size, but it was on the shoulders of those initial four already mentioned, plus Fuller (who would later play a major role in Tank Corps development), and a few others, that, as the original short history of the Corps put it:

...fell the onerous task of creating order from chaos and forming a disciplined corps with high morale, out of very hetero-geneous material... who had the very difficult task of not only creating, organising and administering this new body, but of inventing a suitable and comprehensive system of training in the new arts of tank gunnery, tank driving and maintenance. The whole of tank tactics for the future, co-operation, communication, supply and many other problems incidental to the use of the new arm in battle had to be worked out most carefully, with very meagre data to work from.

In view of their importance in the evolution of the Corps, it is relevant to name them:

GSO 2	Major J.F C. Fuller (later Maj-Gen)
GSO 3 Operations	Capt G. le Q. Martel (later Lt-Gen)
GSO 3 Intelligence	Capt F. E. Hotblack (later Maj-Gen)
DAA & QMG	Capt T.J. Uzielli (later Col)

Elles plus some of his staff officers at Bermicourt in 1917. Left to Right: Fuller, Uzielli, Elles, Atkin-Berry, Dundas and Butler. TM

Typical tank crew – this was the crew of HMLS Dragon Fly III, minus one man but with their mascot! TM

Left: Maj Gen Sir Hugh Elles, KCMG, CB, DSO, was appointed to command the Heavy Section in France on 29 September 1916, at which time he was a Colonel in the Royal Engineers. This painting of him was by Sir William Orpen, ARA. TM

Crews at work on their tanks and sorting out kit at a 'Tankodrome' on the Western Front, probably Rollencourt. TM

Staff Capt A.   Capt H.C. Atkin-Berry
Staff Capt Q.   Capt R.W. Dundas
Chief Engineer   Lt-Col F. Searle (later Col)
Assistants: Major G.A. Green
                   Major J.G. Brockbank

Stephen Foot, in his book *Three Lives*, described Fuller as being 'the brains behind it all', going on to say that:

> For their success Tanks require tactics no less than petrol: Fuller devised them. Before an attack can be launched there must be a plan: Fuller made it. After an attack lessons must be learnt both from success and failure: Fuller absorbed them. And sad to relate, in the case of the Tanks a constant war had to be waged against apathy, incredulity and short-sightedness of GHQ, Fuller fought that war and won.

Fuller himself, in the introduction to his own book *Tanks in the Great War*, painted vivid character sketches of his chief associates which Liddell Hart reproduced in the Corps history:

> It was a great brotherhood, the Tank Corps, and if there were 'duds' in it there were certainly not old ones, for the Commander of the Corps, Major-General H.J. Elles, CB, DSO, was under forty, and most of his staff and subordinate commanders were younger than himself. Youth is apt, rightly, to be enthusiastic, and General Elles must frequently have had a trying time in regulating this enthusiasm, canalising it forward against the enemy and backward diplomatically towards our friends.
>
> We of the Tank Corps Headquarters Staff knew what we wanted. Realising the power of the machine which the brains of England had created, we never hesitated over a 'No' when we knew that hundreds if not thousands, of lives depended on a 'Yes'…
>
> There was Col F. Searle, CBE, DSO, Chief Engineer of the Corps, a true civilian with well-cut khaki jacket and lion-tamer's boots. He could not understand the military ritual and we soldiers seemed never to be able to explain it to him. Throughout the war, in spite of his immense mechanical labours, I verily believe he had only one wish, and this was to erect a guillotine outside a certain holy place. There was Major G.A. Green, MC, Col Searle's deputy, the father of terrible propositions, the visitor of battlefields, the searcher after shell-holes, the breather of profane words. The Corps owed a lot to Green; a firm believer in seeing things before criticising them, he was a very great asset.
>
> The 'King of Grocers', this was Col T.J. Uzielli, DSO, MC, DA and QMG of the Corps, business-like and an administrator from boot to crown. Suave yet fearless, tactful yet truthful, the Corps owed much to his ability. It was never left in want, his decision gave it what it asked for, his provision cut down this asking to a minimum. Ably seconded by Major H.C. Atkin-Berry, DSO, MC, and Major R.W. Dundas, MC, the 'A' and 'Q' branches of the Tank Corps Staff formed the foundation of the Corps efficiency.
>
> On the 'G' side there was myself. Under me came Major G. le Q. Martel, DSO, MC, very much RE and still more tanks, the man who 'sloshed' friend or foe. One day, in March 1918, I was at Fricourt, then none too healthy. Martel walked down the road; 'Where are you going?' I shouted. 'To Montauban,' he answered. 'I hear it is full of Boches,' I replied. 'Well I will go and see,' said Martel and off he moved eastwards. There was Major F.E. Hotblack, DSO, MC, lover of beauty and battles, a mixture of Abelard and Marshal Ney…

Elles not only had operational command of the tanks in France, but also was responsible for their advanced training and tactical employment under the C-in-C. He was soon to have a large Central Depot and Repair Shop to support his battalions, forming a large and complex organisation as the following description explains:

> …and in the meantime developments even more striking had been taking place in France. From four rather forlorn little companies, living as it were from hand to mouth, the Corps sprang at a bound into a huge and complicated organisation, with its own territory, works and depots, and every apparatus for carrying on its lethal industry. A large area, lying between the river Ternoise and the direct Hesdin-St Pol road, was allotted to it. To Bermicourt, a village almost in the centre of this country, Colonel Elles removed his headquarters from Beauquesne early in October 1916. Twenty-four acres near the river were taken for central workshops and stores. In a few weeks, as well as the ubiquitous hangars, immense steel and iron sheds had arisen, and continued to grow in numbers and size until they covered six acres. Stalls for tanks, like the old elephant stables of Carthage, lined one side of the testing-ground. There were huts for a staff which grew to 1200 officers and men, cinema-theatres, a rest-camp and hospital, a compound holding 500 Chinese labourers and, for a time, a reinforcement depot. From Erin Station, eleven lines of rail, with 10 500ft of sidings, led into the main enclosure. A few hundred yards away was a driving and mechanical school, with its own training-ground. Long before the end of 1917 the original twenty-four acres of stores and work-

Refuelling at the Rollencourt 'Tankodrome'. Each tank held 70 gallons, plus extra cans were carried for topping up, so refuelling was a long and arduous task. TM

Mark I tanks plus the mobile workshop wagon at the Rollencourt 'Tankodrome' 20 June 1917. TM

shops were getting overcrowded. In addition to the vast accumulation of equipment, ranging from engines and armour-plate down to split-pins and motor-bicycle parts, there were always there two or three hundred tanks in every stage of dismemberment or reconstruction. Every machine sent out from England (perhaps 3000 in all) came from Le Havre to Erin to be tested, equipped and issued to units; and every machine salved on the battlefield was returned there for repair. More ground, therefore, was taken over in the area itself; a great driving-

school was formed on the old front line at Wailly, near Arras; the whole reinforcement depot moved out to Le Treport; and a school of gunnery, capable before long of taking three battalions at a time, came into being among the sand-dunes and gimcrack villas of Merlimont on the coast near Etaples. In the Bermicourt area there was not a village now which did not house some detail of the Corps - MT, Workshops, Salvage, Supply and Signal Companies, etc - or was not reserved for billeting battalions as they arrived from England or returned from the line to refit. It should be needless to add that the headquarters in Bermicourt Chateau kept pace with this expansion. In the beginning the staff was palpably inadequate; before the end it was comparable in size to that of an army.'

Taking it all in all, I doubt if there can be anything, even in the exceptional records of this war, to equal for extent and variety, the growth of the technical, instructional and supply branches of the Tank Corps during the last two years. It was the natural habit of the combatant units to complain loudly of all three; but to visit Erin at any time, to see there the scores of tanks, the acres of vast workshops and store-sheds, the miles of sidings, and the tons upon tons of gear and equipment, and to reflect that every pound of this material had come from England since the winter of 1916, was enough to make one pause and wonder; and looking back now at the whole industry raised in so short a time from nothing at all, it appears with all its obvious shortcomings a highly remarkable achievement of forethought and energy.[1]

SWINTON REPLACED

Meanwhile, at home in England major changes were also on the way. As the tank strength in France built up, England became just the administrative headquarters, responsible to the War Office for providing the men and material needed in France to fight the war, and for giving the new recruits their preliminary training. In essence its role was to ensure that those on operations were continuously supplied with men, tanks and spare parts. The emphasis had thus shifted to France and for some unaccountable reason the War Office decided that while Elles should have full command in France, Swinton should be replaced at home by Brigadier General F. Gore-Anley, in order to return to his old duties with the War Cabinet Secretariat. Swinton was understandably bewildered by this decision, as he explained in his autobiography:

I thought it best to go direct to the Chief of the Imperial General Staff, to whom I reported what I had heard, asked if it were correct and if so, the reason. General Robertson's reply was to the effect that France wanted a big expansion of the Heavy Section and that I was not considered the man to carry it out... As I walked down the passage of the War Office, bereft of my child, consolation came with the thought that the child was waxing strong.

As Liddell Hart put it:

Thus ended the connection between the new force and the man who had fathered it, until in 1934 he was chosen to be Colonel-Commandant

This early tank officer (Maj Inglis) is carrying an ashplant stick which he would use for testing the depth of mud over which his tanks would have to operate. Note also his mascot, Jock, who followed him everywhere. TM

of the Royal Tank Corps. By that time the significance of his early services had come to be better appreciated; above all, in the Corps itself.[2]

MOVE TO BOVINGTON

'E' and 'F' Companies, together with all their tanks and equipment were still in Thetford when Gore-Anley took over. However, in November 1916 it was finally decided to move everything to a new location which Swinton had chosen some months earlier. Bovington Camp, near Wool in Dorset, was the chosen location, principally because the surrounding countryside was ideal for the training of tank battalions: '...the rolling downs, the woods and the small streets being very similar to, and equally as deserted as the battlefields of France.'[3]

The Tank Training Centre, as it was then called, was squeezed into the existing accommodation. One of the early arrivals, W.F. Lear, recalled those early days at Bovington in an article published in the *Tank Magazine*:

It was a bitterly cold day in November 1916, when, with about 40 others, I arrived at Bovington Camp. We were all ASC men and had been transferred into the new branch of the Army then styled the Tank Corps. We had left comfortable billets at Osterley Park in London for the wilds of Dorset, and I must say we were by no

Left: *Pigeons were used in the early days for message carrying from tanks in the field to base. On one occasion a tank got stuck on a buried tree root, leaving the tracks rotating but to no purpose. The commander decided to send a pigeon to tell HQ of his plight, however, the bird had been fed too generously on whisky-laced seedcake and refused to leave, instead perching itself on the immobile track and refusing to budge. So they started the engine, the track revolved, but the pigeon still refused to leave, marching against the direction of the moving track so as to stay in the same place! Eventually the commander gave up and put the bird back in its pigeon basket.* TM

Below: *'All aboard the Skylark!' I trust this was a static posed photograph or they would have had a very rough ride! The tank is a Mark IV female.* TM

means impressed. Bovington in those far-off days was a dreary spot indeed, and the wintry weather (snow was falling when we reached Wool) did not help to cheer us. I recollect when coming along in the train and nearing our destination we passed through a station named West Moors. Someone asked what station it was and one of the crowd who had been looking out of the window immediately replied 'West Horrors!' On arriving at Wool, we dumped our kit bags at the station and marched the half mile or so to the camp. Here we

were divided up and sent to various battalions then in the course of formation. About a dozen of us had to report to 'H' Battalion where, of course, we had to go through the usual procedure of having our particulars taken. This over, we drew some blankets and eventually were directed to a hut in 'F' Lines which was particularly uninviting as there was no fire and only one small electric light bulb. I think we all felt pretty miserable, but we cheered up somewhat a few minutes later when a Corporal appeared and told us to go to the

Infantrymen looking over a tank which has one of its sponson doors open. TM

cookhouse where we could get some hot soup. I don't think I ever enjoyed army soup more than I did then. It certainly warmed us up and helped to dispel some of the gloom that was hanging over us.

Next day we sorted ourselves out, and after breakfast had a wander round the camp. Nobody appeared to take any notice of us and apparently we were the first arrivals or, at least, if there were any others about they didn't bother us. Bovington in those days of course, was a far different place from what it is now. There were no brick buildings and the Tank Park only possessed about three hangars with about the same number of tanks. We were naturally greatly intrigued by the antics of one of these, which we were fortunate enough to see working, as it lumbered and rolled along, spitting and spluttering and stopping every minute or so. It was the first tank we had seen, and I'm afraid we were inclined to greet it more with merriment, judging from the facetious remarks passed, than as a serious fighting proposition. We little realised then what a force tanks would eventually become.

We soon discovered the YMCA and C of E huts and spent most of our time in these for the first week or two. They were the safest places in which to dodge fatigues! However, our 'scrounge' didn't last. Men were arriving every day and 'H' Battalion began to take shape; 22, 23 and 24 Companies were formed as well as the various Sections to each…

There followed an intensive course of instruction on tanks, the 6pdr gun, Lewis and Hotchkiss guns, map reading, morse, judging distance, lectures on explosives, Mills bombs and German bombs, as well as having to do guard duties, PT, squad drill, route marches and night operations. As there was no wireless in those days each tank had to carry pigeons which were used as a means of communication, so everyone had to learn how to handle those birds. The man who used to give instructions on this course was, to my mind, the saddest fellow I have ever listened to. He seemed surrounded by an atmosphere of the deepest gloom… As time went on more and more tanks began to arrive, and the crews which had been formed were soon at work on these learning their various duties. These early buses had one great drawback. It necessitated having a gearsman inside the tank on the left and right to work the gears, as otherwise the driver could not turn the tank while driving. To swing the tank to either left or right one or other of the tracks had to be stopped, and this was where the gearsmen came into action…

Another thing I recollect is in connection with the 6pdr gun. Originally this was twice as long as the ones eventually used in tanks. I believe it was shortened for convenience. I don't know whether it made any difference to its accuracy, but we were assured that it did not. Speaking of the 6pdr reminds me that we used to be sent in batches either to Whale Island or Chatham to fire our courses. I was fortunate enough to go to Chatham, and I must say, I enjoyed the experience. After Bovington, Chatham Naval Barracks were paradise. We spent a week there and used to go out in a vessel up the Medway to the open sea, where we did our practice at targets being towed some distance away. This was a great thrill as we used the same kind of ammunition that we would use in action. Later however, the visits to the Navy ceased as firing practice was started at Lulworth, which was of greater advantage as the firing was done from the tanks, and that of course was the real thing.

OPERATIONS CONTINUE

Meanwhile in France, the battles on the Somme had dragged on interminably, with the tanks playing as full a part as they were able. The actions they fought normally involved only single tanks or very small groups, yet on many occasions it was the tank which proved to be the battle winner. On 1 October, for example, two tanks assisted the battalions of 141 Brigade just west of Flers, where they were held up short of the German trenches. The tanks drove along the trench line with guns blazing, so frightening the defenders that they surrendered en masse and 141 Brigade was able to capture the trenches and push forward to Eaucourt L'Abbaye. Unfortunately, the tanks became ditched and had to be abandoned when the enemy counter-attacked. As the weather worsened, the going became more and more impossible. On the 5th Army front to the north, it was decided to launch an attack around Beaumont-Hamel and so all available tanks were allocated to V Corps who were providing the attacking force. A total of 52 tanks had been withdrawn behind the lines for refit after the September offensive. One company, with 20 tanks, was moved back in mid-October and held in readiness for suitable weather conditions. Then a further 20 joined them, but they could do nothing in the sea of mud. Eventually, on 13 November, the ground had dried out sufficiently for the attack to be mounted. The assault began half-an-hour before dawn in a thick mist, which helped to blind the enemy, so the attackers were able to break through. The tanks assisted, being used as normal, in small groups. Typical was an action on 14 November when two tanks moved forward into no-man's land, got bogged, but were still able to use their 6pdr guns. An entire enemy garrison - some 400 in all - was so anxious to surrender they did not realise until too late that the tanks were stuck!

Finding good going was so essential that great care had to be taken to reconnoitre and mark suitable

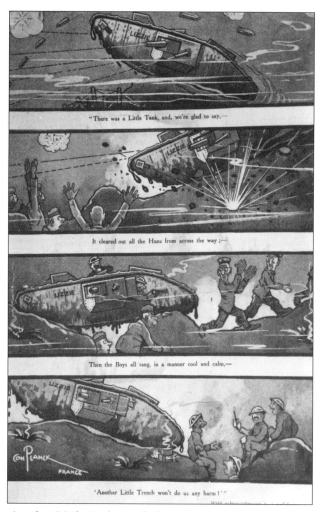

Another Little Tank, won't do us any harm! TM

routes. Whenever possible, tank commanders were taken to suitable OPs and shown the ground over which they would be operating prior to an attack. The Heavy Section's IO - Capt. 'Boots' Hotblack, was awarded a well-deserved DSO for walking ahead of a tank, guiding it close to an enemy stronghold under heavy fire when its route marking tapes were obscured by a sudden snowfall. Later he guided it safely back to the British lines. It was on such occasions that the Regimental custom of officers carrying a long ashplant walking stick, instead of the normal swagger cane, came into being, the ashplant being used to test the depth of mud in front of the tank.

TANK BRIGADES FORMED

On 19 November the Somme offensive ended and the tanks were loaded onto trains and taken back to the Bermicourt area where, during December, the four companies were expanded into four battalions, still retaining their original company letters - 'A', 'B', 'C', 'D'. In January 1917, 1 Tank Brigade was formed, fittingly composed of 'C' and 'D' Battalions who had fought the first tank action. Lt-Col Baker-Carr was given command. He had started the war as a gentleman chauffeur. Fuller described him as being the 'Murat of the Corps, ever ready for a battle or a game'. He had earlier created a Machine-Gun School for the British Army in France and was a man of exceptional vision and drive. In mid-February 1917, 2 Brigade was formed, comprising 'A' and 'B' Battalions. Its chosen commander was a cavalryman, Lt-Col Courage, who had lost half his jaw at Ypres. He had a natural gift for leadership and an eye for detail (Fuller again): '...no trouble was too great and no fatigue sufficient to suggest a pause.' Finally, in the last week of April, 3 Tank Brigade was formed after the arrival of a sixth tank battalion from the UK. Lt-Col Hardess-Lloyd, another cavalryman, was chosen: '...*a beau sabreur* who always kept a good table and a fine stable,' is how Fuller described him. It is perhaps fitting here to record also what Fuller said about Elles: '...he endowed the Corps with that high morale, that fine *esprit de corps* and jaunty *esprit de cocarde* which impelled it from one success to another.' There was the inevitable delay in promoting the new brigade commanders to their appropriate rank (Brigadier-General), while Elles was not made up to Major-General until 1918.

TRAINING CONTINUES

During January and February 1917 the Heavy Branch, as it had been called since 16 November 1916, got down to some serious training. All officers took part in a large indoor exercise during which Fuller put across his thoughts on the tactical and administrative background for the coming operations. It was a great shame that Swinton's 'Notes on the Employment of Tanks' were unknown to Elles' HQ as they would have saved much effort, but they had been ignored by GHQ and never issued.

Towards the end of the exercise Fuller was able to put down his conclusions in a pamphlet (Training Note No 16) - the first real manual of tank tactics. In it Fuller described the tank as a 'mobile fortress' which could escort the infantry right into the heart of the enemy defences, and from behind which they could launch attacks to capture the enemy trenches. Surprise, he contended, was the keynote of any successful attack, with the very minimum of pre-artillery bombardment - sadly this was never taken note of by GHQ, who still felt that at least 17 days of continuous bombardment was essential before an attack!

NEW TANKS

The end of 1916 had seen the production of the stopgap tanks, produced before the main 1000-tank order began. These were equally divided between Mark II and Mark III, also between male and female tanks. There were a few differences with the Mark I as the result of battlefield experience, the most obvious being the omission of the tail-wheels. These had proved a hindrance in action as they fell into shell holes or got stuck in trenches, and fortunately their removal did not affect the tank's steering, which had been their raison d'etre. They were also taken off those Mark Is still in operational use. The Mark IIs and IIIs were intended only for training so their hull plates were unarmoured. Shortages in France were later to lead to their use in action, with the inevitable results. In their unarmoured state they were very vulnerable to the recently developed German armour piercing bullet, but fortunately a better tank was on the way. Designed in October 1916, the Mark IV went into production in March/April 1917. A total of 1220 would eventually be built, more than any other model. The Mark IV incorporated many improvements, including an armoured 60gal petrol tank, mounted outside the tank in between the rear horns, much safer than the earlier internal fuel tanks which had been mounted on either side of the driver! The sponsons were hinged so that they could be swung inboard during rail journeys, rather than having to be taken off and carried separately. Their size was also reduced so that the bottoms were not so close to the ground. Both male and female had Lewis guns instead of Vickers and Hotchkiss. Thicker steel was used in the construction, making them proof against the German anti-tank rifle bullet - which would come as a nasty shock to the enemy after the ease with which it could penetrate the Mark Is and IIs. The long (40 calibres) 6pdr gun barrels were replaced by shorter ones of 23 calibres, which were less likely to be damaged by trees and buildings, or get clogged with mud. Another innovation was the unditching beam - a large bolt of metal-bound timber, carried on top of the tank which, when fixed with chains to the tracks, would be taken underneath the tank as the tracks revolved, giving more purchase in the mud and thus enabling the tank to unbog itself. The glass vision prisms were replaced with armoured shutters with peepholes, much to the relief of the crews who had suffered facial injuries from flying shards of glass when the prisms were shattered by enemy fire. Despite these improvements, fighting inside an early tank remained a desperate business. It still needed four men, working as a team, to drive the vehicle and operate the gears. Although relatively immune to rifle-fire and shell splinters, strikes on the outside gave rise to 'spawl' inside (fragments of hot metal chipping off the inside of the armour plate) which caused small but painful wounds. Primitive chain-mail facemasks and leather helmets soon proved too hot and uncomfortable to wear, while the fumes from the engine and weapons that hung inside the fighting compartment, often accompanied by a generous helping of poisonous gas, were at times overpowering. All in all, the job of these early tank crews was difficult, dangerous and thoroughly uncomfortable, but like all those who have come after, they never let such problems affect their performance in battle.

SPRING OFFENSIVE

While the tank crews trained, GHQ was busy planning new operations for the coming spring. These would involve all available tanks - so much time had to be spent on forward reconnaissance, carried out by Hotblack and the Battalion and Company Recce Officers. Their carefully laid plans suffered a partial setback when the Germans decided to withdraw in late February in the Somme sector, leaving the British to follow through the battle-devastated area of no-man's land. The German move was cleverly timed and nullified much of the pressure along the British Fourth and Fifth Armies frontage, so it was decided to switch the main weight of the attack onto the Third Army front around Arras. As always, GHQ lost all chance of surprise by insisting on a long preparatory barrage, which not only destroyed the good going, but also alerted the enemy as to exactly where the attack would take place. The number of tanks available was small. It had been hoped that 240 of the new Mark IVs would be ready for action, but they did not actually start to arrive in France until late April, when the battle was already over. At the beginning of March not one single tank was fighting fit anywhere in France, so 26 of the Mark II training tanks were rushed over from Bovington to make up numbers. Eventually, a total of 60 tanks, Mark Is and IIs, were scraped together, all vulnerable to the now plentiful German armour-piercing bullets.

Having learnt nothing from previous engagements, GHQ again decided to spread the tanks across the entire front in 'penny packets', while the long and heavy artillery barrage, combined with snow and heavy rain, made the battlefield into a sea of mud. Haig's plan had included a special cavalry pursuit force, but this failed to materialise in the appalling conditions. Many tanks were bogged before they had even reached their assault positions and from then on it was the same old story; excellent work by individual tanks, but never enough available on good going to make a significant impact on the outcome of the battle. Opinions on their value were also mixed. The Australian Division laid the entire blame for their failure on the poor showing of the handful of tanks which had been allotted to them, and this bitterness was to cloud their thinking for the rest of the war. Other commanders were enthusiastic, the: commander of one corps (Lt-Gen Aylmer Haldane), writing to Baker-Carr that:

The great success of the Corps is only attributable to the help you have given us. This has been my first experience of the co-operation of Tanks and I certainly never again want to be without them, when so well commanded and led.

Much was achieved, but sadly those in authority did not learn from the lessons that were staring them in the face. Liddell Hart sums up this period succinctly:

The tank arm, employed merely as a subsidiary defence breaker, had an unhappy part. Tanks sank in the swamp-like battlefield, and the new corps which manned them was nearly sunk in the sequel... by the wave of thoughtless disappointment in high quarters which followed their inevitable failures in such ill-fitting conditions.[4]

And there was worse to follow.

Good shot of another wartime tank crew with the officer in the middle of the rear row, the other seven are: the driver, two gearsmen, two gunners and two loaders on a male tank, the latter four men being replaced by four machine gunners on a female tank. TM

---

[1] *The Tank in Action* by Capt D G Browne, MC (Blackwood 1920)
[2] *The Tanks* Volume 1
[3] War Diary of the Heavy Section
[4] *The Tanks* Volume 1

Chapter 3

CAMBRAI

PROBLEMS IN FLANDERS

The offensive in Flanders, which Haig called 'the main operation for 1917', sadly was to prove once again that GHQ had learnt nothing from the previous battles about the correct way to employ tanks, despite the fact that the new Mark IV had by now (late May) started to arrive. 2 Brigade ('A' & 'B' Battalions) received 76 Mark IVs before moving north to Flanders to take part in the Second Army's attacks on the Messines Ridge, a preparatory phase before the main summer offensive. Although the battalions had been allotted two spare tanks on top of their normal complement of 36, plus six Mark Is converted into supply tanks - to carry the petrol and ammunition needed to maintain the offensive - the new tanks were used only in minor roles, well spread out and, as usual, on poor going, so their potential for offensive action was wasted. The Mark IVs stood up well in action, their armour plate being proof against the new German 'K' armour-piercing bullets. A.A. Lee, who fought in the Battle of Messines, recalled how he was operating in a pair of tanks - his own called *Revenge* and its sister tank *Iron Ration*. A few days previously it had been decided that all the tanks in 'A' Battalion should have names beginning with the letter 'A' [1], so they had offered to change theirs to *Avenger*.

> …for some unknown reason this was considered unacceptable, and as the crew of *Iron Ration* could not decide upon a suitable name, we were given the official names *Apple* and *Apricot*. In our opinion these were most unsuitable names for fighting tanks, so we painted out our original names with a mixture of water and lime, which washed off as soon as we started for the line!

This pair of tanks did well at Messines, penetrating further behind enemy lines than any other tanks in the brigade.

J.C. Allnatt, who served as a sergeant tank driver before receiving a battlefield commission shortly after Cambrai, fought close by Messines in the Ypres salient. His pithy comments reflect the feelings of those who had to do the fighting:

> It was unfortunate that the decision to send the tanks rested with officers in high places. If these officers had been to see the salient, and if they had

Tank crewmen inspecting a German Mauser 13mm anti-tank rifle (tankgewehr), the world's first operational specialised anti-tank weapon. It could penetrate 22mm of steel armour at 100m. This one was captured near Demuin. TM

The Mark IX Supply carrier. Initially battleworn tanks were converted into supply carriers by the removal of their guns, etc. A purpose-built supply tank did not emerge until late in the war. It could carry 10 tons of stores or 30 riflemen, so was in effect, the very first armoured personnel carrier. TM

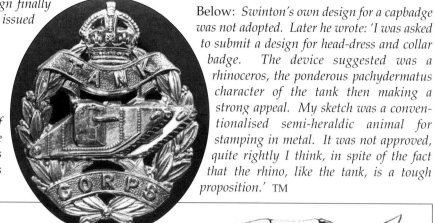

Right: This was the capbadge design finally chosen, to be worn by all ranks and issued on 28 July 1917. TM

Below: This is the original sketch of Swinton's tank armbadge which he designed and insisted that it was worn by all ranks of the Tank Corps as a unifying symbol. TM

Below: Swinton's own design for a capbadge was not adopted. Later he wrote: 'I was asked to submit a design for head-dress and collar badge. The device suggested was a rhinoceros, the ponderous pachydermatus character of the tank then making a strong appeal. My sketch was a conventionalised semi-heraldic animal for stamping in metal. It was not approved, quite rightly I think, in spite of the fact that the rhino, like the tank, is a tough proposition.' TM

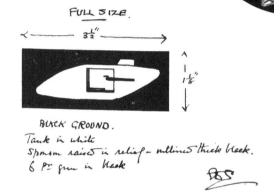

had the brains of a child, they surely would never have committed the tank crews to practically certain death. Every member of the Tank Corps, even those of the lowest rank, knew that they should not be there... Even the commanders of the British Army, from the comfort and security of GHQ should have known that an attack should never have been made where the terrain is bad... There were plenty of places where tanks could have been, and were afterwards used, with great success.

As before, however, Haig seemed quite satisfied with the work of the Corps in Flanders, mentioning in his official despatches:

> Although throughout the major part of the Ypres battle and especially in its later stages, the condition of the ground made the use of tanks difficult or impossible, yet whenever the circumstances were in any way favourable and even when they were not, very gallant and valuable work had been accomplished by tank commanders and crews on a great number of occasions.

Liddell Hart on the other hand, summed up this period more realistically when he wrote:

> On more suitable ground they might have been used to far better advantage in that summer of opportunity.[2]

HM THE KING INSPECTS HIS TANKS

King George V had already taken an active interest in the new arm when it was first formed, so it was no surprise that he made a point of visiting the tanks when he went over to France in July 1917. A spectacular demonstration of a 'tank action' was laid on for him, and Lt-Col Alan Scrutton, then a subaltern in 'B' Battalion, later recalled how the final part of the demonstration went slightly awry, when the leading tank, while negotiating a very large lump of concrete - the top of an ammunition bunker:

> ...came up with a great deal of noise, appeared on the flat top, balanced for a second on the crown of the descent and as it dropped, inch by inch, it suddenly lost all grip and shot to the bottom, burying its nose several feet in the mud of the field below, just in front of His Majesty. We all stood holding our breath, wondering if anyone inside was still alive when, to our amazement, after a short pause, the tank went slowly on its way and came to an even keel alongside the King. Out hopped Haseler (the commander) and two other men looking very shaken, but Haseler, with a grin all over his face, made light of it and was congratulated by the King who, of course, had no idea that the remainder of the crew were still inside the tank unconscious!

This visit was followed by one from the King and Queen of the Belgians, which included a race between a male and a female tank, again vividly recalled by Alan Scrutton:

> The female tank had been specially cleaned inside, had a strip of carpet down and a chair for the Queen to sit in, and this tank was to win the race - the male tank merely being a stooge - When the King saw the Queen hopping into the female tank helped by General Gough, he turned to me and indicated that he wished to get into the male tank. I was completely at a loss because I knew that it was filthy and he would have a very uncomfortable journey, but he insisted and got in… All went according to plan, the Queen's tank won the race and she emerged, helped out by General Gough. The King did not seem so pleased at his very rough journey in a filthy tank in which everything he touched had been red hot!

THE TANK CORPS

On 28 July 1917, the new arm became a Corps in its own right, the design and issue of the metal cap badge following on from the earlier issue of the tank armbadge[3] which had been designed by Swinton. Fate played its part in the choice of the Corps colours, Elles and Hardess-Lloyd finding only a very limited selection of materials when they visited a local draper's shop. They chose brown, red and green, a combination which Fuller later proposed could be interpreted 'from the mud, through the blood, to the green fields beyond'.[4] The Corps motto 'Fear Naught' was chosen in preference to the earlier 'Dread Naught' which Swinton had suggested, presumably because of the latter's use by the Navy to describe one class of warships.

A MIDDLE EAST INTERLUDE

The successes on the Somme in 1916 had led to a decision to send tanks out to Egypt for use against Turkey, Germany's ally in the Middle East. Originally Mark IVs were to have been sent but, in the event, eight old Mark Is were despatched with a detachment of 22 officers and 226 other ranks to man them. They arrived in Egypt in January 1917 and travelled to Khan Yunis near El Arish. They got there in time for the second battle of Gaza, which began on 17 April, and gave excellent support. In a typical example of their prowess one tank called *Tiger* led a divisional advance to capture Sampson Ridge and the El Arish redoubt. It reached its objective without difficulty, but had to withdraw because the infantry were unable to follow up. In the six-hour action it fired over 27 000 rounds out of its machine guns and every member of the crew was wounded. Despite their age,

HMLS War-Baby *was one of the Gaza Detachment.* TM

Tanks in Palestine at Deir-el-Belah. TM

The first Tank Corps Victoria Cross was awarded posthumously to Capt Clement Robertson, 'for conspicuous gallantry and devotion to duty', during the third battle of Ypres on 4 October 1917. TM

Heavy Mark IVs entrained ready to moved up for the Cambrai operation.
All are carrying fascines for trench crossing. Photo taken on 18 November 1917. TM

The tank trains arrive at the Plateau, now the scene of great activity. TM

the Mark Is averaged over 40 miles' motoring - twice the mileage previously considered to be the entire life of the original tank tracks! Three more tanks, all Mark IVs, were sent out later, and all fit tanks took part in the final battle to capture Gaza in early November 1917. This was the last time they were used in the Middle East, as the machines were by then worn out and were also considered unsuitable for the hilly country of Judah, where the advance was continuing. It would be left to tank men of another era to show how effective tanks could be in desert conditions.

FIRST TANK CORPS VC

On 4 October 1917, during an action fought by four tanks of 'A' Battalion, in the area of Polygon Wood, the Tank Corps gained its first Victoria Cross, when Capt Clement Robertson was awarded the medal posthumously, for conspicuous gallantry and devotion to duty. His citation reads:

From 30 September to 4 October this officer worked without a break under heavy fire preparing a route for his tanks to go into action against Reutel. He finished late on the night of 3 October, and at once led his tanks up to the point for the attack. He brought them safely up by 3am on 4 October, and at 6am led them into action. The ground was very bad and heavily broken up by shell fire and the road demolished for about 500yds. Capt Robertson, knowing the risk of the tanks missing their way, continued to lead them on foot. In addition to the heavy shell fire intense machine-gun and rifle fire was directed at the tanks. Although knowing that his action would inevitably cost him his life, Capt Robertson deliberately continued to lead his tanks when well ahead of our own infantry, guiding them carefully and patiently towards their objective. Just as they reached the road he was killed by a bullet through the head, but his objective had been

Left: *An historic photo at the railhead shows the Mark IV Female* Hilda *being unloaded. This was the tank in which Elles rode into action, flying the new Corps flag.* TM

Below: *Unloading Heavy Mark IVs at Plateau.* TM

reached, and the tanks in consequence were enabled to fight a very successful action. By his very gallant devotion, Capt Robertson deliberately sacrificed his life to make certain the success of his tanks.

PREPARATION FOR CAMBRAI

By now it was becoming clear to everyone that unless the Tank Corps was given a chance to show its true potential there was a very real danger that the newly formed Corps would cease to exist. This danger was appreciated at tank-crew level just as much as by Elles and his staff. J.C. Allnatt, for example, later commented caustically, that he thought that the Tank Corps had been deliberately sent to the Ypres salient so it could be discredited in the eyes of the Army commanders and the Government: ...'so that those who disbelieved in the tanks could have their way and disband the Corps. Certainly the proposed expansion of the Corps was held up, due to the unfortunate tendency of the staff at higher headquarters to blame the tanks for the failure in Flanders. It was General Capper[5] who gave Elles the shattering news that: ...on account of the heavy casualties, the Tank Corps expansion had been postponed.' This was an extremely serious situation and, it has to be said, to Haig's credit that he also saw the danger and

agreed to give the tanks a chance to prove themselves by planning and executing a tank battle on a suitable area of ground of their own choosing. Nevertheless, nothing was plain sailing and Elles and Fuller had to battle extremely hard, modifying their plans, until they could find an ally to agree with them. Fortunately they found one in General Sir Julian Byng, then Commander of Third Army, in whose area lay the proposed chosen ground for the 'tank raid', as the operation had by then become. The tank idea appealed to him, but he wanted to make it a far larger affair involving many more resources, so it was promptly vetoed by GHQ! Unfortunately even Haig still considered the tank '...only as a minor factor... an adjunct to infantry and guns.' Byng, however, was not prepared to let the idea drop and eventually won the day, but the plan was by now so altered from its original conception as to be fraught with considerable danger. As Liddell Hart explained: '...there were marked alterations, and in these lay the germ of disaster. The raid had been transformed into a large-scale offensive, with far-reaching aims.'[6]

AREA OF OPERATION

The area which had been selected for the operation (now known by the codeword *Operation GY*) was a stretch of open rolling countryside hardly damaged

Special order No 6 issued to all commanders on the eve of battle. TM

bombardment. Every tank would carry a special obstacle crossing device known as a fascine. This consisted of about 75 large bundles of brushwood, strongly compressed and bound by chains, to form one large bundle some 10ft in length and 4½ft in diameter, and weighing over a ton. This was to be carried on the nose of every tank and then lowered into the trench to be crossed.

Sections had been reorganised from four to three tanks, so that every company now had a fourth (reserve) section. Each section was to advance in arrow-head formation. The leading tanks - known as the advanced guard tank - would go through the wire up to the enemy line and then turn left on the friendly side of the first trench, opening fire with its starboard guns. The lefthand of the following pair (known as infantry tanks), which were initially some 200yds behind, then moved up to the first trench, dropped its fascine, crossed it and then also turned left along the back of the enemy trench. The third tank crossed by the same fascine, advanced to the support-line trench, crossed it using its own fascine and then also turned left. Next, the advanced guard tank returned and crossed via the fascine, met up with the left-hand infantry tank and then both crossed the support trench via the second fascine. All three tanks would now be beyond the enemy support line and still with one fascine in hand. This 'attack drill' had been evolved by Fuller and was to work very well during the battle, except in the 51st Highland Division area whose commander (widely known in the army as 'Uncle' Harper) had rejected the scheme as being 'fantastic and unmilitary' and

by shell fire, just south of Cambrai, between the Canal du Nord and the Canal St Quentin. The soil was hard and chalky, so the going for tanks would be good. The objective contained a number of villages and was strongly defended by fortifications of the famous, hitherto impregnable, Hindenburg Line. Instead of the limited raid as originally planned, the aim was now to advance between the two canals and to capture and hold the objectives, so that a large-scale offensive could then be launched. The fundamental weakness of the general plan was that nothing was kept in reserve for this offensive phase except for five cavalry divisions, and experience had already shown that it was suicidal to contemplate launching such an attacking force while even one enemy machine gun remained in action.

However, at this stage, the 'bigger picture' did not concern the crews, because at the tank level there was a great deal to do, including the learning of new basic tactics for dealing with the strong German defences. It was decided that surprise would be of the essence, so there would be no preliminary

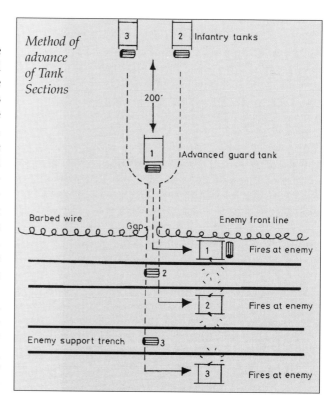

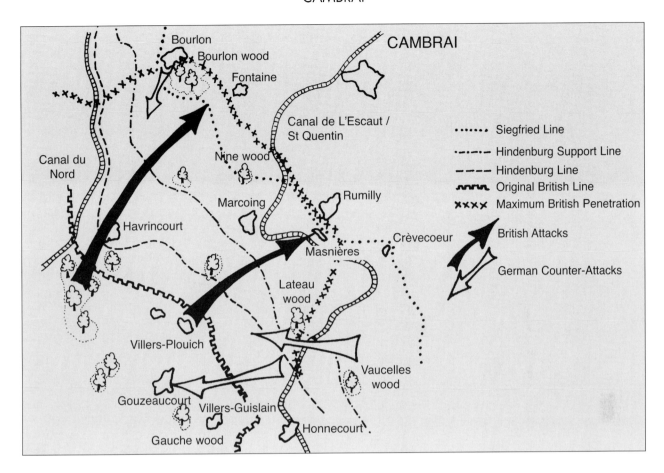

instituted his own system. The failure at Flesquieres was ascribed in the British Official History as being directly caused by this departure from the prescribed attack drills.

BREAKDOWN OF TANK CORPS FORCES

Against the advice of the Tank Corps staff it was decided to attack with tanks all along the entire frontage, rather than concentrating them at selected places or retaining any in reserve, a foolhardy plan which was supported by all the infantry divisional commanders who naturally wanted the fullest tank support. Their requests were agreed to, despite Fuller describing it as '...fighting without a reserve is similar to playing cards without capital - it is sheer gambling. To trust to the cast of the dice is not generalship. ...To leave the present plan as it is and the distribution as it is, is to court failure.'[7] The entire Tank Corps (three brigades now each of three battalions) was to be used for the operation, broken down as follows:

III Corps Sector: attacking with three divisions forward and one in support, with 2nd and 3rd Tank Brigades allocated, from left to right:
12th Division -   'C' and 'F' Bns
20th Division -   'A' (minus one company) and 'I' Bns
6th Division -   'B' and 'H' Bns
29th Division -   one company of 'A' Bn

IV Corps Sector: attacking with only two divisions initially, but with the important objective of taking Bourlon Ridge in the second phase.

1 Tank Brigade allocated with:
51st Division -   'D' and 'E' (minus one company) Bns
62nd Division -   'G' Bn plus one company of 'E' Bn

Each battalion had a full complement of 36 fighting tanks, plus six in immediate reserve. In addition, each brigade had eighteen supply tanks and three signal tanks equipped with wireless, while there were 32 tanks fitted with grapnels to pull away any wire on the cavalry attack routes, and a further two loaded with bridging material to follow the cavalry. Finally, one tank was used to carry telephone cable for Army HQ, making up the total of 476.

PREPARATIONS FOR THE BATTLE

The War History of 'F' Battalion gives a good account of the period prior to the battle, beginning in September when they drew up new tanks at Erin to replace casualties of the Ypres battles and brought them back to the Battalion camp at Blairville:

Life down at the camp proceeded normally, the sections training reinforcements in squad drill, Lewis guns and other classes. The workshop personnel, assisted by the crews, started a

Dawn 20 November 1917. The Sunken Road at La Vacquerie, from a painting by W.L. Wyllie. TM

systematic overhaul of all the tracks. The tanks were jacked up on sleepers, the tracks broken, and the mud of Flanders scraped out from the rollers and switches. Those tanks not on the stocks went out daily under their section officers, training drivers and crews… On 15 October the battalion was ordered to move to Auchy-les-Hesdin and to hand over the camp to 'I' Battalion.

In their new location 'F' Battalion had to regroup into the new three-tank section organisation, train with both grappling irons and steel cables to drag away barbed wire, and with the new fascine, finally leaving Auchy between 13 and 17 November to entrain at Erin for the final move up to the front:

Next day found the whole battalion assembled at Le Plateau, each company in its own train. The day was spent in getting ammunition and stores aboard the trains and getting the fascines, which had been put on the trucks at Central Workshops, into position for conveying on top of the cab. As soon as it was dark the trains left for the various detraining points. 'F' Battalion detrained at Heudicourt, and the spare tanks of the battalion at Sorrell. The first stage of the approach march was from Heudicourt to Gouzeaucourt, while the spare tanks went to Dessart Wood, where the crews continued to work on them.

The three companies of fighting tanks, arrived at Gouzeaucourt about an hour before dawn, and straightway commenced to camouflage them-selves under the ruins which were all the Huns had left of this village. The strictest precautions were taken against discovery. No one was allowed to prowl about during the daytime, and the camouflage of the tanks was kept intact until dusk, when the work of fixing spuds and getting the fascines into battle position began. At night no fires or lights were allowed. Of course by this time everyone realised we were in for the most intensified form of training. During the next two days reconnaissance was made to the front line and the final preparations for action completed.

On the afternoon of 19 November, Lt-Col F. Summers, DSO, DSC, visited the three companies and gave a short outline of the scheme and plan of operations. Maps were given out, and the CO wished everyone the best of luck. Just before this the Special Order of the Day, by Brigadier-General H.J. Elles, DSO, calling upon the Tank Corps for its best efforts, was issued.

As soon as darkness permitted, the ROs taped the last stages of the approach march and marked each tank's position at the jumping-off point.

ELLES SPECIAL ORDER

On the morning before the attack, Elles drafted and issued his Special Order No 6, probably the most famous order ever given in the history of the Corps. In it he explained how at long last the Tank Corps would get the opportunity to operate on good going, in the van of the battle. He ended the order:

Offensive on the Cambrai Front, near Ribecourt. Using a temporarily disabled tank as an observation and signalling post. 'WC' stands for Wire Cutter. TM

'I propose leading the attack of the centre division', something unheard of in modern war, but as Fuller said in his memoirs:

> To lead his command was to give life and soul to all our preparations - it was spiritually the making of the Tank Corps, and in value it transcended all our work.

Press correspondents were later to shorten the order into one sentence: 'England expects every tank to do its damnedest.' Undoubtedly it and Elles' presence on the battlefield had a tremendous effect upon the whole Tank Corps and set the seal on their success.

THE ATTACK COMMENCES

By 0500 on 20 November 1917, the tanks were drawn up in one long line, stretching for six miles in front of the British trenches. At 0610hrs, ten minutes before zero hour, they began to move so that they would be in the correct positions to lead the infantry forward. At zero hour the artillery barrage from 1000 guns began and the tanks were again on the move with Elles in *Hilda* flying the Tank Corps colours, as Major Gerald Huntbach of 'H' Battalion recalled:

> I visited my tanks while they were warming up before zero, and as time got close we - Parsons, McCormick and myself - stood by Lt Leach's *Hilda*. A lithe figure strode past the infantry and the rear rank tanks, pipe aglow, and an ash stick with mysterious cloth wrapping tucked under his arm: unheralded, unexpected then and there, and unattended, Brigadier-General Elles had arrived. 'Five minutes to go,' he said. 'This is the

centre of our line and I'm going over in this tank.' He tapped *Hilda's* off-side sponson, I swung the door open and informed Leach of his distinguished passenger... The General glanced at his wrist. Shaking out his stick, he disclosed the brown, red and green flag soon to be historical, and then he squeezed through the doorway.

Huntbach goes on to describe the advance and later how, after crossing the first enemy trenchline, he met General Elles walking briskly towards the Beauchamp:

> ...still pulling at his pipe, and with his fondest theories vindicated, exultant. He gave us a cheery wave with the now shot-riddled victorious banner. Behind him, at a respectful interval, came several crowds of German prisoners.

Elles was walking because *Hilda* had been ditched in a trench close to Ribecourt, but was later towed out.

J.C. Allnatt was driving one of the tanks in Section 3, XIX Company of 'G' Battalion, called *Gravedigger*, supporting 62nd Division. His graphic description of those early moments begins thus:

> Then the order came to move off. My Crew Commander took his place on my left inside the tank and it was his job to operate the two hand-brakes, one on each track. At the last minute a runner came up bringing us two pigeons in a crate, and then the Section Commander and his runner also got in, making us ten in all, leaving very little space in which to move. We synchronised watches - I had one on either wrist because I knew how important the exact time is on such occasions - and went down the edge of the wood. Now and again a Section would break off, No 1 breaking off to my left and No 4 to my right. No 2 Section were not there, they were engaged on a job of wire pulling, which meant that they had to go behind the fighting tanks and drop chains and anchors amongst the barbed wire and pull it out of the way for the infantry to go through. There was a bit of shelling when we reached our forward jumping-off point and it was not long before we heard that three tanks of No 1 Section had been hit... There were several machine guns operating that night in order to drown any noise that the tanks might make in their approach. It is normally supposed that a tank makes a terrific noise. This was not so, unless it is under speed pressure, so there was very little noise to drown as the tanks were just creeping slowly along with their engines ticking over. The machine guns brought a certain amount of retaliation from the enemy in the way of field-gun shells, which came alarmingly close.

We could tell from our watches that dawn was approaching and about ten minutes before zero hour I said to both my Crew Commander and Section Commander that I would try to get a bit further ahead so as to catch the enemy completely by surprise. This I did. I got into bottom gear and allowed the engine to tick over and went forward at a very slow pace in complete silence. I could tell from my map and my oblique aeroplane photograph exactly where I was. I was 150yds from the German front line. There seemed to be very little activity on this part of the front. From time to time there was a burst of machine-gun fire and rifle fire and an occasional, in fact rather more than occasional, shell. One of these exploded just under the nose of our tank, the Gravedigger. It filled the Crew Officer's eyes with dust as it did mine and a splinter from the shell lodged in the back of my hand. I pulled it out and allowed the blood to dry, so as to stop further bleeding. I then decided that as zero hour was so close I would try to get a bit nearer. I got into bottom gear and allowed the tank to ease itself forward a few more yards... I had hardly arrived at this point when there was a tremendous crash of gunfire, shells went screaming overhead and there was no doubt that the battle had begun.

I immediately got into second gear, revved up the engine and shot forward as fast as possible. I am sure I was on the German front line within ten seconds of zero hour.

The Gunners did exactly as they were told, and when we were astride the front line they let the enemy have it for all they were worth. I did not hesitate, however, and having given them about 25 seconds to get off as much ammunition as they could, went on. We raced as hard as we could to the second support line and could see the flashes of our shells bursting upon the third line. I knew that the safest place was just behind one's own barrage and this I endeavoured to do. This did not please either the Tank Commander or the Section Commander, as they said that we would get cut off. I promptly explained the reason for it and told them that they had better leave it to me. The going was excellent the soil being dry and firm and ideal for tank work. The dawn had almost broken and already the Germans had got to their guns and were giving us something in return. Our own barrage was superb, it was very accurate as to position and the timing was quite precise. If at any time I had any doubt as to where we were I only had to look at my watch and at the position of the barrage and I could find out exactly where my own position was. I kept off the roads because they were almost certainly mined and the going there could not have been any better than it was across the fields. There was a certain amount of machine gunning from the enemy and I could hear the tattooing on the outside steel plates.

I eventually arrived at the place where I had to make a half-left turn and cross a sunken road in order to get to my correct position near the village of Havrincourt, but before I could get there I had to cross a very, very wide and strong barbed-wire defence. I suppose it could not have been less than 50yds across. It is true there were a few gaps but a tank must always avoid a gap in barbed wire defences because they are almost certainly mined. I ploughed my way through, with some satisfaction, knowing that where I had rolled the wire down the infantry could make a crossing. I got through seemingly safely and moved to where I thought I would cross the sunken road. I then noticed that the tank was not behaving as it should, the steering was rather sluggish and the engine seemed to be losing power. I could not make this out because I was quite sure that the tank was in perfect order. The answer soon came, strangely enough. There were two German soldiers lying wounded in my path. I had no intention of course, of running them over but I could see that they were terrified. I could see no reason for it until it suddenly dawned upon me that they were not afraid of the tank but of what I was drawing behind. I looked out of my rearward peep-hole and saw that I was dragging a mass of barbed wire the size of an ordinary house and it was that which was causing the sluggish engine. The wire was also winding itself round the tracks, but I thought that the power of the tank would break it to pieces and I should shake myself free, so I avoided the wounded Germans and made for the sunken road.

On the other side of the sunken road I could see a steep bank, steep enough for any tank even though free of wire. I had a go, in fact I had several

Even tanks found it difficult to break through thick barbed-wire entanglements, the wire and pickets getting entangled with the tracks. TM

goes to get over, and I just could not manage it. We only had 105hp engines and it was simply too weak for the job. So I backed down into the sunken road and told the two second drivers, who were acting as secondary gearsmen, to get out and cut the wire away from the tracks so that I could pull myself free. It is a pity that the tanks which were following me did not pull out and go ahead, leaving me to effect the necessary adjustments. Unfortunately they also stopped and as a result the infantry, who had now caught us up, suffered some needless casualties. However, they did their job very well and under most unpleasant conditions and we went on again, climbing up the steep bank and coming out into level and open country before approaching the strong points, which we were supposed to destroy to help our infantry. It was obvious, at the very first glance, that we were late because the ground in front of the strong points was strewn with our own dead. It was also clear that our infantry had succeeded in taking the strong points and that no mercy had been shown to the defenders. We pushed on at a good speed, perhaps up to eight miles an hour, catching up and passing the infantry. They were only in very small numbers and it is true to say that in the whole of the battle I saw no more than 50 altogether.

My machine-gunners were doing good work and obviously enjoying themselves. The port gunners in particular finding targets to suit themselves and several times they got out and ran alongside the tank to locate targets and, jumping in again, would let the enemy have a burst of fire. It was about this time that I spotted some Germans on our left flank and rather ahead of us, running away. I called my Crew Officer's attention to them but he was unable to get the gun to swing far enough to the left, so I asked him to hand it to me, which he did… I must have been the only tank driver who actually operated a machine gun at the same time as driving a tank, and I believe hit them.

Unlike Sgt Allnatt who saw the battle from the confines of his driving seat, the Hon Evan Charteris, who served as the historian of the Tank Corps, watched it standing in the open, on a spur which projected over the front line. He had walked there with two other officers and had a grandstand view of the battlefield. Later he wrote:

The darkness had paled; partridges were calling to one another; one could distinguish differences of level in the ground; trees began to stand out from the darkness; …it was indescribably still. The hour was very near; it was already 6.15. We were aware of men moving forward on either side of us. We surmised that it must be the 29th Division advancing in support. Suddenly the air

itself seemed to reel under a colossal blow; a dull and curiously mellow roar broke forth and continued with a peculiar rhythm; the atmosphere became alive with the scream of shells. We were at the end of the spur by now, and on the opposite slope we could see the shells bursting on the German trenches; while behind that again rose a huge black curtain thrown up by our smoke shells, which, as they landed gave the effect of the embers of a haystack. Splinters of flame were on every side like exploding stars in a night sky. The German trenches were throwing up rockets and SOS signals all the length of their line; these shone out vividly against the black curtain behind. Now the light of dawn began to creep up quickly - a cold grey light, with little power of illumination.

The surprise had been complete, and our artillery overwhelming; the reply of the German guns was negligible. The sight and the certainty that they had been taken unawares and were in confusion produced in one a sense of supreme exultation. On the slope opposite, tanks showed up like small dull-coloured huts endowed with movement; as they advanced one could see the flashes of their 6pdrs along a line which stretched to both right and left.

Another account, which appeared in the *Tank Corps Journal* soon after the war, told of a tank commander's impression of the battle and, in particular, the use of fascines.

Our mission, as the centre tank of a group of three, was to make for a particular piece of trench, drop our fascine, and get over, the other two tanks of the group crossing the same place. We crossed the narrow outpost line, got to our portion of trench, but found no Huns - they had retired, leaving their machine guns behind; but my gunners had a little practice potting at them.

The Hindenburg Trench was a truly formidable obstacle, and we naturally had a few exciting moments. First, poised over the deep and wide excavation; then releasing the fascine - would it drop all right? - we saw it lumber beautifully into the bottom. But could we get over? One can imagine our doubts, as we had witnessed a few ghastly failures at Wailly. Anyhow, down we dropped and up, up, up - no one thought of the balance point - until at last we crashed upon the other side, splitting open my Section Commander's head, and petrol cans, oil cans and ammunition boxes scattered all over the place. However, we had done the first part of the job successfully - and then the real fun began. The Hun was bravely standing on the first step of his reserve trench; fully exposed, and giving us rather a warm time with machine-gun and rifle fire. The first system was very quickly overcome, and the battle developed into a tank race for the second system. The much feared Grand Ravine was taken in third gear.

Our second objective was Flesquieres Chateau. Here stiff resistance was met - so well did the enemy resist, that it was not cleared until the following morning. Our alignment and positions had been lost by this time, which led to individual attacks on various strong points. My particular tank, being a male, plugged the chateau and machine-gun emplacements in the vicinity for about ten minutes; but, as there was no enemy in sight, I decided to get around to the rear of the chateau. Shells were dropping rather too near just now, which hastened our efforts. After crossing a deep sunken road, in which one of our tank commanders was repairing a broken track, we were asked by the infantry to clear a trench that was holding up their advance. The trench in question was on the reverse slope of Flesquieres Ridge, and therefore out of sight. On gaining the crest of the ridge, we seemed to walk 'right into it'. Tanks were all over the place; some with noses up, some afire, but all motionless. At the time we hardly realised what had happened. However, we spotted the offending trench, packed with Huns, fully exposed, and all their fire seemed concentrated on our tank. The trench was protected by a belt of wire about 50yds deep. My gunners, in spite of the enemy fire, were getting well on to their targets, and I could observe the 6pdrs bursting on the parapet. About 20yds in the German wire we received a direct hit, which left a gaping hole in the side of the tank, and which wounded everyone except the driver and myself, but fortunately left the engine still running. As my gunners were out of action, and another shell had landed amongst the sprockets, I ordered my driver to reverse out of the wire. We just reached the fringe when the motor petered out. A hasty examination showed the carburettor pierced by a splinter. Meanwhile, a fire started on the top of the tank amongst some spare ammunition we were carrying. There was nothing left but to evacuate, which we did one by one, carrying the badly wounded back to our infantry. This left the driver and myself free to wend our way back to the battalion rallying point, and observe how things were going. The Hun appeared to have wakened from his slumbers by this time, for his planes were flying very low, and firing on our troops (one of them, in fact, was actually brought down by a gunner of the 5th Tank Battalion) and the advance, in our sector at any rate, was held up. About noon a drizzle set in and, not having enough tanks left for a further attack, it was decided to wait for dawn for a further effort. Being tankless, we were ordered

back to Havrincourt Wood, and although tired, hungry and very depressed at losing our tank, the sight of all the ground that had been gained with so little bloodshed, and the complete success of the surprise attack acted upon us like a tonic. All troops seemed very pleased with the tanks; so pleased, in fact, that I regret to mention many were the drinks we had on the way back. It is really astonishing how much whisky the British Army carries into battle!

On arriving into camp, we learned of the rough handling the 5th Tank Battalion (then 'E' Battalion) had had - 'C' Company in particular. Out of the 14 officers of that company ten became casualties, including five killed - and this prevented our taking part in the following action.

ANOTHER VICTORIA CROSS AWARDED

At first the attack went incredibly well, the enemy being thrown into complete confusion by the ease with which the tanks were able to breach their impregnable Hindenburg Line, spreading death and destruction everywhere. Large numbers of enemy soldiers surrendered or fled the battlefield, dropping their arms and equipment in their haste to get away. By 0800hrs the first objectives were all but secure. Ribecourt held out until 0920hrs and there was hard fighting in the Havrincourt area where the enemy were holding firm in deep dugouts and cellars. The next phase of the advance swept over the Hindenburg Support Line everywhere, except near Flesquieres, where 51st Highland Division were held up for reasons already explained. On the right centre the assault was led by tanks of 'A' and 'I' Battalions. Here Capt Richard William Leslie Wain was awarded the Victoria Cross for most conspicuous gallantry near Marcoing while in command of a section of tanks. The citation reads:

During the attack, the tank in which he was became disabled by a direct hit near a German strong point in the Hindenburg Support Line, at L24 a.3.6, which was holding up the attack. Capt Wain and one man were the only survivors, and they were both seriously wounded. While the infantry were held up there, this officer, in spite of his wounds, rushed from behind the tank in front of the enemy strong point with a Lewis gun and captured the strong point, taking half the garrison prisoners. Although his wounds were very serious, Capt Wain picked up a rifle and continued to fire at the retiring enemy until he received a fatal wound in the head. Although bleeding profusely from wounds, this gallant officer refused attention of stretcher-bearers in order to carry on clearing the enemy out of the strong point.

CAMBRAI

It was due to this gallant act by this officer that the infantry were able to advance.

Not everywhere did the Germans flee in panic. Artillery batteries in the Flesquires area succeeded in knocking out a number of tanks that had outdistanced their supporting infantry. A further delay occurred at Grand Ravine where, as the tanks came over the crest, they were heavily engaged at close range by artillery fire and 16 were knocked out. This gave rise to a rumour - now part of the folk-lore of the Battle of Cambrai - that a lone German gunner - an under officer named Kreuger, serving a single gun, had alone been responsible for all the casualties. While the evidence is hazy, it appears that the casualties were more likely to have been the result of the fire of several guns which the Germans had pulled out of their gun pits and fired direct at the tanks at point-blank range. Kreuger's gun certainly accounted for at least five or six tanks and the gallant NCO fell by his gun, refusing to withdraw.[6]

By 4pm the battle, as far as the Tank Corps was concerned, was tactically complete. With their aid the most rapid advance of the war had been achieved. From a start line some 13 000yds long, a penetration of about 10 000yds in depth had been achieved in under twelve hours. To put this into perspective, a similarly sized penetration had taken three months to achieve and at the horrendous cost of over 250 000 casualties, while the total casualties suffered by III and IV Corps during the first two days at Cambrai were under 6000 (one-tenth of which were Tank Corps men). This success had been attained by a force of only 690 officers and 3500 men - equal in strength to a strong infantry brigade. With their tanks they had also replaced the normally tedious, expensive weeks of preliminary bombard-ment and the artillery wire-cutting operations. The tanks were all but exhausted and, as none had been kept in reserve, it was now only possible to rally the various units, select the fittest tanks and crews, and then to form them into composite companies for further operations.

This should have been the moment when the cavalry poured through the gap which had been created by the tanks, but they were able to gain prac-tically nothing despite showing great gallantry. The chance for mounted action on a large scale had been lost and the following day the battle reverted to the normal dogfight. On 21 November the composite

The second Tank Corps VC was awarded to Capt Richard William Leslie Wain during the Battle of Cambrai, for conspicuous gallantry near Marcoing, 20 November 1917. TM

companies of tanks fought in co-operation with new infantry but, as the Tank Corps historian put it:

Though the infantry was new, it was unfortunately not fresh. Consequently many strong points, though they were finally captured, gave us more trouble than they would normally have done.

During the next few days the situa-tion went from bad to worse until, on 30 November, the Germans launched a major counter-attack to recapture the salient. The tanks had been withdrawn, starting about the 27th and the withdrawal was almost completed when the counter-attack was launched.

An urgent demand for tanks was then made and, despite their non-fighting condition, numbers were soon made available. In some cases tanks were taken off railway trains, patched up on the siding and sent off to the scene of action and several critical situations were saved through their aid. In 2 Tank Brigade, for example, at 8am on 30 November it was reported that not a single machine was in a fit state or fully equipped for action. At 6am the following morning, seventy-three tanks were launched against the enemy with decisive effect.

When the position was eventually stabilised in early December, the tanks were at last able to withdraw to 'lick their sores and prepare for the 1918 campaign'. The Tank Corps losses over the period from 20 November to 1 December were 1068 officers and men killed, wounded or missing, while 112 tanks had been destroyed by shellfire and a further 64 were mechanically defective and beyond local repair. The cost had been grievous but the victory gained was immeasurable. Haig, for instance, wrote in his despatches that the 'great value of the tanks in the offensive has been conclusively proved'. General Byng, the commander of Third Army wrote a letter to Elles which included the following:

To say that the operation without tanks was an impossibility is merely a truism, but to say that

the far-reaching success was due to the co-operation of your Corps with the infantry and artillery is the point of view I wish you to realise.

No one could have been so well supported, so greatly helped and so consistently strengthened in the plan, as I have been by you and your staff. And no army has ever been so splendidly led and so fully assisted as mine by your Corps.

The many calls on you and your men's endurance have been answered with the greatest alacrity - their losses have been heavy and their work prodigious, but they have established a record now which none can dispute.

A last word from one of the tankmen who fought throughout the battle: J.C. Allnatt's tank had broken down well forward and he had returned to the rallying point to collect rations for his company.

When I got within 50yds of the dugouts the Company Commander hopped out of the ground and shouted 'What the hell are you doing up there?' I replied that I had brought rations for the company. He shouted 'Go back, go back. We are all coming back.'

We about turned, selected some high ground with a handy trench, opened up some of the rations and had a good meal. We also had a grandstand view of a German counter-attack which was taking place. We then took what was left of the rations back to camp and reported the situation. And so, after three days' continuous

fighting the Battle of Cambrai, for my tank crew, was over. Later we received much praise for our part in the battle and it was very nice to know that what we had done had been appreciated.

---

[1] The practice of naming tanks in this way has survived to the present day, although it does vary between regiments.

[2] *The Tanks*, Vol 1.

[3] The tank arm badge, made in worsted embroidery, depicted a Mark I tank without its tail wheels, and was issued to all ranks as a unifying symbol, to be worn on the upper part of the right sleeve. This was done because the officers and men who made up the Tank Corps still wore their old regimental badges and insignia. It it still worn by all ranks in the RTR.

[4] Usually misquoted as 'Through mud and blood to the green fields beyond.'

[5] Maj-Gen Sir John Capper, a distinguished Royal Engineer officer, had been appointed as Director General of the Tank Corps in May 1917.

[6] *The Tanks*, Vol 1.

[7] *The Tanks*, Vol 1.

[8] This incident gave rise to a whole series of stories about the 'lone Flesquires gunner' who single-handed had held up the tanks' advance. Critics of the new arm were quick to seize on this story to show how easily artillery could deal with tanks - if one man could knock out sixteen, then well-trained, properly handled artillery could deal with all large-scale tank attacks in any future wars. How wrong they were!

Opposite page:
Top; *An 'H' Battalion tank* Hyacinth *which belonged to No 10 Section of 24 Company (commander Lt Jackson) in a German trench in front of Ribecourt with infantrymen of 1st Leicesters.* TM

Bottom; *A Mark IV going past the Graincourt Battery, which was overrun and captured by 'G' Battalion tanks during the battle. The crew of* Gorgonzola II *captured one of the guns which is now on show at the Tank Museum.* TM

The Medium A Whippet. Amongst the new generation of tanks to reach the Western Front in 1918, was one designed by William Tritton, called the Tritton Chaser or Whippet of which some 200 were built by Foster's. It was half the weight and twice the speed of the heavy tanks. TM

The best of all heavy tanks to see action was the Mark V, which had a more powerful engine and a new Wilson-designed gearbox which gave much better manoeuverability. It also had thicker armour and better machine guns. The photograph shows the Tank Museum's Heavy Mark V which is still in full running order. Here it is being commanded by the author 'on parade' for Her Majesty in 1985. TM

Chapter 4
ON TO FINAL VICTORY

FURTHER EXPANSION

There were no further tank actions fought in 1917 after Cambrai, the British abandoning the offensive and reverting to static defence, but the tank's great success in the battle had the effect of changing opinions both at home and in France in a remarkable way. Stern who, with Churchill's aid, had been made Commissioner for Mechanical Warfare (Overseas and Allies) was able to convince the Americans to join in the tank building programme so that the target for production in 1918 could be raised to 5000 tanks, while on 27 November, only a week after the battle, the War Office sanctioned the enlarged Tank Corps establishment, which had been the subject of continual prevarication since the previous April. The immediate effect was that on 28 December, 4 Tank Brigade was formed, under command of Brigadier-General E. B. Hankey, DSO, late of 'G' Battalion. A few months later on 3 March 1918, 5 Tank Brigade was formed, being initially commanded by Brigadier-General A. Parker, CMG, who on March 31 exchanged places with Brigadier General Courage then commanding 2 Brigade. The Tank Corps now had five brigades, totalling 13 battalions, and from January 1918 the old battalion lettering was dropped in favour of numbers: 'A' becoming 1st, 'B' 2nd, and so on.

NEW TANKS

In addition, the Tank Corps began to receive new tanks. First to arrive was the Medium A - later called the Whippet, a smaller, lighter and faster machine, which had been specifically designed for the exploitation role with the cavalry once the heavy tanks had broken through the enemy lines. They made their debut at the village of Collincamp on 26 March, when 12 Whippets of the 3rd Battalion surprised 300 Germans in close formation. The enemy fled in disorder, many surrendering to our infantry who were following up. The other new arrival was the Mark V heavy tank. This closely resembled the Mark IV, but had much improved performance because of its more powerful engine; better manoeuvrability, particularly due to a new Wilson-designed gearbox; better armour and mounted Lewis machine guns instead of Hotchkiss.

The new Ricardo 150hp engine gave it a top speed of nearly 5mph, while its epicyclic gears enabled the tank to be driven and steered by one man. Later versions of this type (Mark V Star and Mark V Two Stars) had lengthened bodies[1] while the eventual Mark VIII (known also as the 'International'), which was evolved directly by Stern's newly formed Allied Committee, was much larger, weighing 37 tons, and was powered by a 300hp engine. This was to have been the tank to be built in great numbers by Britain and the USA in France, to 'win the war in 1919'. The war ended before it could take the field. Britain only built a handful and the USA completed about 100 after the war had ended, so none ever saw action. In 1939, a few of the American-built models were refurbished and given to the Canadians to be used for training at the beginning of the Second World War!

'SAVAGE RABBITS' AND LEWIS-GUN SECTIONS

Despite the expansion and increased production there was a desperate shortage of serviceable tanks in France at the beginning of 1918, there being only 320 Mark IV and 50 Whippets fit for action in January 1918. The plan of action devised by General Elles for their employment in the expected German offensive was for the tanks to be used in support of counterattack forces. This meant them waiting, concealed, in ambush positions and then emerging, as he put it, 'like savage rabbits from their holes' to fall upon the German flanks and rear. Unfortunately, due to the speed and scale of the German advance which began at dawn on 21 March, a great deal of useful track mileage was wasted, moving the tanks continually backwards and forwards before they could take part in the battle. Out of a total of the 370 fit to fight, only 180 saw any action and many had to be destroyed or abandoned in the retreat. The lack of tanks led to the formation of a large number of Lewis-gun sections, initially made up from tank crews who had lost their machines. The whole of the 5th Battalion was eventually armed with Lewis guns and later the 9th Battalion also.

These teams did much useful work but they suffered heavy casualties, a cause of great anxiety to Tank Corps HQ, as properly trained replacements were very hard to come by.

FIRST TANK V TANK ACTION

On 24 April 1918 the first tank *v* tank engagement took place. The Germans had designed and built a handful of cumbersome heavy tanks they called the A7V. They also used captured British tanks. In fact an A7V and five captured Mark IVs took part in their offensive on 21 March, but no recorded action appears in the British Official History until 24 April, when the Germans employed tanks around Villers-Bretonneux. Three A7Vs took many prisoners in the village and then pushed on towards Cachy. Here, one A7V encountered a forward section of 1st Battalion, Tank Corps, equipped with one male and two female Mark IVs. Although the section under Capt F.C. Brown had just been badly gassed, they immediately advanced to plug the gap. The two female tanks were the first to meet the enemy, but could make no impression with their machine guns against the enemy armour and were quickly knocked out. Then the male tank (commanded by Lt F. Mitchell, MC) appeared on the scene and engaged the enemy, scoring five direct hits with his 6pdr guns. Trying to escape from this accurate fire, the German tank ran onto a steep bank and overturned. Three more A7Vs arrived but were engaged and routed, one crew abandoning their tank in the process. As Liddell Hart records: 'It was most appropriate that the victor in this first tank versus tank fight was No 1 Tank of No 1 Section, A Company, 1st Battalion, Tank Corps.' On the same morning, quite close to this action, Capt T.R. Price, DSO, MC, with seven Whippets, charged two German infantry battalions while they were massing for an attack. The Germans were mown down and lost some 400 men in a few minutes, while the total British casualties were three killed and two wounded, one tank being knocked out by shell-fire and three others damaged. The Whippets had received the information about the enemy from a reconnaissance aircraft that dropped a message to them while they were leaguered three miles behind the front line. This short action gave a foretaste of the way in which the speed, mobility and firepower of armoured forces could be used to fullest advantage.

ARMOURED CARS IN ACTION

In mid-April 1918, 17th Battalion Tank Corps was converted to armoured cars in England, moved over to France and fought its first engagement on 11 June. Of course, armoured cars had already been in both naval and military service and in action. However, the 17th was the first battalion of the Tank Corps to convert to the armoured car role. They had been training at Bovington on Whippets and were rapidly re-equipped with Austin armoured cars, but with the Maxim heavy MGs replaced by Hotchkiss. Armoured cars went on operating throughout the early summer. However, their most spectacular successes would not come until after the final Allied offensive had begun.

The badge of the 3rd French Division presented to the 9th Battalion, together with the Croix de Guerre, after the offensive in July 1918. The motto means: 'He who rubs me burns himself.' TM

CROIX DE GUERRE AWARDED TO THE 9TH TANK BATTALION

'I owe a special tribute of thanks to the battalion of British tanks whose powerful and devoted assistance has aided and assured our success.' So wrote General Debeney, Commander of the First French Army, in a Special Order of the Day following the Battle of Moreuil on 23 July 1918. He went on to say that the battalion had given:

> 'the finest example of bravery, energy, of comradeship in action and of training for war carried to the highest degree of perfection. Their assistance has enabled the infantry to gain a brilliant victory in which they themselves share largely.'

As a result of this action the 9th were awarded the Croix de Guerre as a corporate decoration and the badge of the French 3rd Division, which the men of that battalion subsequently wore on their left sleeve. General Ludendorff, in one of his orders after the battle wrote: 'It is to the tanks that the enemy owes his success… as soon as the tanks are destroyed the whole attack fails.' It was a lesson that the Germans had learnt far too late.

A BLACK DAY FOR THE ENEMY

It was now the Allies' turn to go into the offensive and by early August the strength of the Fourth Army had been boosted to sixteen divisions (13 infantry and three cavalry). More importantly, the whole of the available strength of the Tank Corps (less 1

Above: *Artist's impression of the first tank-v-tank battle which took place on 24 April 1918, during which Lt Mitchell, MC, routed four A7Vs.* TM

Below: *Two Austin armoured cars setting off on a reconnaissance in August 1918.* TM

Brigade) had been concentrated into one spot. Even larger than the Cambrai concentration, there were over 600 tanks assembled, comprising:

Nine battalions of heavy tanks (324 fighting tanks) which would lead the attack.
Two light battalions (96 Whippets) to exploit with the cavalry.
Miscellaneous - 42 tanks in mechanical reserve, 120 supply tanks (66 with the infantry), and 22 gun-carrier tanks.
Also, the armoured cars of the 17th Battalion.

The tanks were to provide a massed tank assault to lead a surprise attack, timed to commence on 8 August, the main stroke being made south of the Somme by the Australian and Canadian Corps, while III Corps advanced north of the river to give flank protection: The attack was called the Battle of Amiens because its immediate aim was to free Amiens and the Paris Amiens railway from German interference. If the battle proved successful then a second phase would be directed towards the St Quentin-Cambrai line. For the Germans it was the 'Black Day' of the war that sealed their final defeat, the 'Hundred Days' Battle' culminating in the Armistice of 11 November 1918.

As at Cambrai there would be no preliminary artillery bombardment before zero hour. Afterwards: the guns would concentrate mainly on counter-battery. Time for preparation was short, but everything that could be done was done, both

speedily and efficiently - as can be judged by the fact that at zero hour 415 out of a total of 420 fighting tanks went into action.

There was a thick ground mist at 4.45am zero hour, when the early morning silence was shattered by our massed artillery, which opened intense fire along the eleven miles of front. Little did the Germans realise they were going to have so rude an awakening. Their front was drenched in a hurricane of shells, and before they had time to recover their wits, waves of tanks were upon them out of the mist to spread panic and disorder all along the enemy lines.

The forward positions were completely overwhelmed, the tanks not so much destroying the enemy by their fire as simply running down his machine-gun emplacements and crushing the guns and crews beneath them. The attack was an overwhelming surprise, and though the Germans were holding their main position in strength, there was little opposition, for the German machine gunners had learnt how quickly the Mark V tank could turn at the Battles of Hamel and Moreuil and gave very little trouble. The co-operation between the tanks and infantry, especially on the Canadian and Australian fronts, was good and the attack swept on irresistibly. The mist lifted for the second phase of the battle, giving the German artillery their chance, and 100 tanks were temporarily put out of action the first day by artillery fire, chiefly from Chipilly Ridge, and the crews of the remainder were very exhausted. The maximum penetration was, however, seven-and-a-half miles, and 200 guns and 16 000 prisoners had been counted by 6am on 9 August.[2]

BARRHEAD IN ACTION

One of the tanks taking part in the Battle of Amiens was No 9003, named *Barrhead*. It was operating with the 2nd Australian Division, and started just east of Villers Bretonneux. The Tank Commander made this report after the battle:

On the evening of 7 August, we left the Tankodrome at 9.30pm to take up our position on the Jumping-Off Point, ready for the attack next morning. The Approach March is always a most important and trying part of the tank's work. It must be done at night and every precaution has to be taken to prevent the enemy hearing our approach, as much of the success of the tank's action depends on taking the enemy by surprise. The first part of the Approach March was comparatively easy, but afterwards the route became more difficult, therefore guiding tapes were laid down under the supervision of officers detailed for the work.

At a short distance from the Jumping-Off Point, we halted and were informed that the attack was to commence at 4.20am. Watches were synchronised and a final inspection made of the tank to ensure that everything was ready for the attack. Everything worked well, and it is certain from reports of prisoners that the enemy had no knowledge of our presence previous to the attack. We arrived at the Jumping-Off Point just when the barrage commenced and each tank at once got into its own sector in front of the infantry. At zero hour there was a very thick mist which made observation most difficult, and it was only by using the tank compass and following the barrage, that we were able to keep to our proper course. The mist afterwards lifted about 6.45am.

This British Mark IV female heavy tank was 'showing the flag' during a 'Liberty Loan' parade on Fifth Avenue, New York City. The USA built only a few prototype tanks during the Great War, their Tank Corps using British and French tanks instead. TM

A very young Capt Dwight D Eisenhower at Camp Colt, Gettysburg, in June 1918, with Col Clapham, US Army, and two British Tank Corps officers. Ike was responsible for creating the first US Tank corps training centre. TM

Excellent shot of Regimental Sergeant Major McIntyre of the 14th Tank Battalion, who won a DCM during the Battle of Amiens. TM

Very little opposition was met with in the first phase of the attack, we had taken the enemy completely by surprise and they put up a poor fight. Whenever a tank was sighted they ran forward with their hands well up and we passed them and allowed the infantry to deal with them. A few enemy machine guns kept on firing, but they were soon silenced by running over them with the tank. Any of the gun teams who remained were dealt with effectively. We reached our first objective at 7am and, after patrolling in front of the infantry until they had consolidated, we returned to our Rallying Point.

Instructions were then received to proceed with two other tanks to assist the infantry in cleaning up the village of Bayonvillers. We entered the village, followed by the other tanks and infantry and steered a zig-zag course through it, travelling down behind the houses and swinging round, then passing through a house and across the street, passing through a house on the other side and so on. This had the effect of bringing out any of the enemy who were

hiding in houses and they immediately surrendered. There was little resistance met within this village and a good number of prisoners were rounded up and afterwards handed over to the infantry for disposal.

We patrolled the village until the Infantry Commander informed us that the assistance of *Barrhead* was no longer required. We then set off for Harbonnières. On arrival there we found the other tanks of the battalion cleaning up the village, they had also captured an enemy train full of reinforcements. After seeing that the village was cleared of the enemy, all the tanks returned to the Rallying Point. It was a good day's work and the crews were in excellent spirits although somewhat exhausted, having been in their tanks for nearly 16hrs. *Barrhead* was in splendid condition and gave no trouble whatever during this its first action.

That night we again moved and took up a new position ready for further events. We arrived at about 2am and slept in or near our tanks wherever we could make ourselves most comfortable. During the morning (9 August) orders were received to attack with the infantry, the Starting Point being to the south of Harbonnières. The Approach March was over open country and in view of the enemy observation balloons. Whilst waiting for the infantry to come up a number of shells dropped in the vicinity of the tanks, but luckily they did no damage. The attack commenced at 1.30pm. Strong opposition was met from enemy machine guns, anti-tank guns, artillery and bombing aeroplanes.

The machine guns were soon silenced, *Barrhead's* 6pdr guns opened fire on some splendid targets and her machine gun poured forth a leaden hail of bullets on the Germans, who were seen running in all directions. Pushing ahead and getting nearer the objective, the artillery fire became very heavy, shells kept bursting all around *Barrhead* so the driver steered a zig-zag course to avoid them and meanwhile the gunners kept up a heavy fire. At this time one of the crew was wounded and whilst the NCO was examining his wounds the tank was hit by a shell. The concussion from this shell threw the crew all over the tank and filled it with suffocating fumes. I got four of the crew outside and placed them at the rear of the tank as they were all wounded.

On re-entering the tank to ascertain what had happened to the other two members of my crew, I found them both dead. The shell, which must have been a large HE, had hit the tank in front of the right hand sponson and burst inside, wrecking the engine. After dressing the wounded men I sent three of them to the nearest Dressing Station and went in search of a stretcher

THE ROYAL TANK REGIMENT

for the other man whose wounds prevented him from walking. Whilst I was bringing the stretcher, the tank was again hit and burst into flames.

When I returned I found that *Barrhead* was a blazing furnace and the ammunition was going off like a machine gun firing. The seriously wounded member of my crew has since died of his wounds in hospital. The tank's position was near a hospital, midway between Vauvillers and Rosieres, and I expect that it has since been salvaged and brought back to workshops where many of its parts may have been used to repair other tanks.

Thus ended the career of *Barrhead* and the loss of such a reliable tank is very regrettable. It did splendid work on both days of the attack and was instrumental in capturing at least 10 enemy machine guns, and about 200 prisoners. When one considers the number of lives of our own infantry that were saved by this tank owing to its valuable assistance in subduing the enemy's fire and overcoming his resistance, the existence of *Barrhead* was well justified and the initial expense of its construction more than ten times repaid.

In the Field 10.8.1918   Tank Commander

MUSICAL BOX IN ACTION

So far, all the personal accounts of tank actions have been by crews of heavy tanks, so it is fitting to include one written by the commander of a Whippet tank, Lt H.C.B. Arnold of 6th Battalion. He was taken prisoner after his tank *Musical Box* had been knocked out by artillery fire near Harbonnières. However, before this happened he had spent an exciting day behind enemy lines. Later he wrote:

On 8 August 1918 I commanded Whippet tank *Musical Box*, belonging to 'B' Company of the 6th Battalion. We left the lying-up point at zero (4.20am) and proceeded across the country to the south side of the railway at Villers-Bretonneux. We crossed the railway in column of sections, by the bridge on the eastern outskirts of the town. I reached the British Front Line and passed through the Australian Infantry (2nd Australian Division) and some of our heavy tanks (Mark V), in company with the remainder of the Whippets of 'B' Company, proceeded parallel with the railway (Amiens-Ham) across country, due east. After proceeding about 2000yds in this direction I found myself to be the leading machine, owing to the others having become ditched. To my immediate front I could see more Mark V tanks being followed very closely by Australian Infantry.

About this time we came under direct shell fire from a four-gun field battery, of which I could

There had to be order and method in the stores departments, so that everything could be found quickly. The more different the models and types of tanks and other vehicles in service, then the larger the problem became. These two photographs clearly show the range of items held. TM

Another spare part kept at Erin was the 'Tadpole Tail' which effectively lengthened the tank by about 9ft, enabling them to cross wider trenches. TM

see the flashes, between Abancourt and Bayonvillers. Two Mark V tanks, 150yds on my right front, were knocked out. I saw clouds of smoke coming out of these machines, and the crews evacuate them. The infantry following the heavy machines were suffering casualties from this battery. I turned half-left and ran diagonally

A general view of the Tank Corps Central Worksops at Erin, near Bermicourt. The area around Erin encompassed workshops, supply, salvage, signals, etc units and was also the staging place for incoming tank battalions from the UK. TM

across the front of the battery, at a distance of about 600yds. Both my guns were able to fire on the battery, in spite of which they got off about eight rounds at me without damage, but sufficiently close to be audible inside the cab, and I could see the flash of each gun as it fired.

By this time I had passed behind a belt of trees running along a roadside. I ran along this belt until level with the battery, when I turned full-right and engaged the battery in rear. On observing our appearance from the belt of trees, the gunners, some thirty in number, abandoned their guns and tried to get away. Gunner Ribbans and I accounted for the whole lot. I cruised forward, making a detour to the left, and shot a number of the enemy, who appeared to be demoralised, and were moving about the country in all directions. This detour brought me back to the railway siding NNW of Guillaucourt. I could now see other Whippets coming up, and a few Mark Vs also.

The Australian infantry, who followed magnificently, had now passed through the battery position, which we had accounted for, and were lying in a sunken road about 400yds past the battery and slightly to the left of it. I got out of my machine and went to an Australian full lieutenant and asked if he wanted any help. Whilst talking to him, he received a bullet which struck the metal shoulder title, a piece of the bullet casing entering his shoulder. While he was being dressed, Major Rycroft on horseback, Lt Waterhouse in a tank, and Capt Strachan of 'B'

Company, 6th Battalion, arrived and received confirmation from the Australian officer of our having knocked out the field battery. I told Major Rycroft what we had done, and then moved off again at once, as it appeared unwise for four machines (Lt Watkins had also arrived) to remain stationary at one spot. I proceeded parallel with the railway embankment in an easterly direction, passing through two cavalry patrols of about twelve men each. The first patrol was receiving casualties from a party of the enemy in a field of corn. I dealt with this, killing three or four, the remainder escaping out of sight into the corn.

Proceeding further east, I saw the second patrol pursuing six enemy. The leading horse was so tired that he was not gaining appreciably on the rearmost Hun. Some of the leading fugitives turned about and fired at the cavalryman, when his sword was stretched out and practically touching the back of the last Hun. Horse and: rider were brought down on the left of the road. The remainder of the cavalrymen deployed to the right coming in close under the railway embankment, where they dismounted and came under fire from the enemy, who had now taken up a position on the railway bridge and were firing over the parapet, inflicting one or two casualties. I ran the machine up until we had a clear view of the bridge, and killed four of the enemy with one long burst, the other running across the bridge and so down the opposite slope out of sight. On our left I could see, about three-quarters of a mile away, a train on fire being towed by an engine.

This Whippet was named Musical Box *and knocked out was captured behind enemy lines, where it was used as a shelter for wounded. It was later recaptured.* TM

I proceeded further east, still parallel to the railway, and approached carefully a small valley, marked on my map as containing Boche hutments. As I entered the valley (between Bayonvillers and Harbonnières) at right angles, many enemy were visible packing kits and others retiring. On our opening fire on the nearest, many others appeared from huts, making for the end of the valley, their object being to get over the embankment and so out of sight. We accounted for many of these. I cruised round; Ribbans went into one of the huts and returned and we counted about sixty dead and wounded. There were evidences of shell-fire amongst the huts, but we certainly accounted for most of the casualties counted there.

I turned left from the railway and cruised across country, as lines of enemy infantry could be seen retiring. We fired at these many times at ranges of 200-600yds. These targets were fleeting, owing to the enemy getting down into the corn when fired on. In spite of this, many casualties must have been inflicted as we cruised up and down for at least an hour. I did not see any more of our troops or machines after leaving the cavalry patrols already referred to. During the cruising, being the only machine to get through, we invariably received intense rifle and machine-gun fire. I would here beg to suggest that no petrol be carried on the outside of the machine, as under orders we were carrying nine tins of petrol on the roof, for refilling purposes, when well into the enemy lines (should opportunity occur). The perforated tins allowed the petrol to run all over the cab. These fumes, combined with the intense bullet splash and the great heat after being in action (by this time) nine to ten hours, made it necessary at this point to breathe through the mouthpiece of the box respirator, without actually wearing the mask.

At 1400hrs, or thereabouts, I again proceeded east, parallel to the railway and about 100yds

Heavy Mark Vs, carrying fascines, and belonging to the 8th Battalion, are seen here near Amiens in August 1918. Note the enemy prisoners in the foreground. TM

A 'pack' of Whippets being loaded up with stores. The Whippet was more difficult to drive than the heavy tanks as it had a separate engine for each track. TM

north of it. I could see a large aerodrome and also an observation balloon at a height of about 200ft. I could also see great quantities of motor and horse transport moving in all directions. Over the top of another bridge on my left I could see the cover of a lorry coming in my direction. I moved up out of sight and waited until he topped the bridge, when I shot the driver. The lorry ran into the right-hand ditch. The railway had now come out of the cutting in which it had rested all the while, and I could see both sides of it. I could see a long line of men retiring on both sides of the railway, and fired at these at ranges of 400-500 yds, inflicting heavy casualties. I passed through these and also accounted for one horse and the driver of a two-horse canvas-covered wagon on the far side of the railway.

We now crossed a small road going over the main railway, and came in view of large horse and wagon lines, which ran across the railway and close to it. Gunner Ribbans (right-hand gun) here had a view of the south side of the railway, and fired continuously into motor and horse transport moving on three roads (one north and south, one almost parallel to the railway, and one diagonally between these two). I fired many bursts at 600-800yds at transport blocking roads on my left, causing great confusion. Rifle and machine-gun fire was not heavy at this time, owing to our sudden appearance, as the roads were all banked up in order to cross the railway. There were about twelve men in the middle aisle of these lines. I fired a long burst at these. Some went down and others got in amongst the wheels and undergrowth. I turned quarter-left towards a small copse, where there were more horses and men, about 200yds away. On the way across we met the most intense rifle and machine-gun fire

imaginable from all sides. When at all possible we returned the fire until the left-hand revolver port cover was shot away. I withdrew the forward gun, locked the mounting, and held the body of the gun against the hole. Petrol was still running down the side of the back door. Fumes and heat combined were very bad.

We were still moving forward, and I was shouting to Driver Carney to turn about as it was impossible to continue the action, when two heavy concussions closely followed one another, and the cab burst into flames. Carney and Ribbans got to the door and collapsed. I was almost overcome, but managed to get the door open and fell out on the ground, and was able to drag out the other two men. Burning petrol was running on the ground where we were lying. The fresh air revived us, and we all got up and made a short rush to get away from the burning petrol. We were all on fire. In this rush Carney was shot in the stomach and killed. We rolled over and over to try and extinguish the flames. I saw numbers of the enemy approaching from all round. The first arrival came for me with a rifle and bayonet. I got hold of this, and the point of the bayonet entered my right forearm. The second man struck at my head with the butt end of his rifle, hit my shoulder and neck, and knocked me down. When I came to, there were dozens all round me, and anyone who could reach me did so, and I was well kicked; they were furious. Ribbans and I were taken away and stood by ourselves about 20yds clear of the crowd. An argument ensued, and we were eventually marched to a dug-out where paper

Flying the Tank Corps flag, despite the fact that they are well behind enemy lines. The task of the armoured cars was deep range penetration, recce and flank protection. TM

Sautrecourt manoeuvres, 10 August 1918. HM The King always took a keen interest in his tanks. Here, accompanied by Elles, he watches tanks manoeuvring. TM

HM The Queen also took a great interest in the new arm. Here she is visiting the Central Workshops at Erin, 7 July 1917. TM

bandages were put on our hands. Our faces were left as they were. We were then marched down the road to the main railway. There we joined a party of about eight enemy, and marched past a field-kitchen where I made signs for food. We had had nothing since 8.30pm on the night previous to the action and it was 3.30pm when we were set on fire.

We went on to a village where, on my intelligence map, a Divisional HQ had been marked. An elderly stout officer interrogated me, asking if I was an officer. I said 'Yes.' He then asked me various other questions, to which I replied, 'I do not know.' He said, 'Do you mean you do not know or you will not tell me?' I said, 'You can take it which way you wish.' He then struck me in the face and went away. We went on to Chaulnes to a canvas hospital, on the right side of the railway, where I was injected with anti-tetanus. Later, I was again interrogated with the same result as above, except that instead of being struck, I received five days' solitary confinement in a room with no window, and only a small piece of bread and a bowl of soup each day. On the fifth day I was again interrogated, and said the same as before. I said that he had no right to give me solitary confinement and that unless I were released I should, at the first opportunity, report him to the highest possible authority. The next day I was sent away and eventually reached the camp at Freiburg where I found my brother, Capt A.E. Arnold, MC, Tank Corps. The conduct of Gunner Ribbans and Driver Carney was beyond all praise throughout. Driver Carney drove from Villers-Bretonneux onwards.

C.B. ARNOLD, Lt   6th Tank Battalion[3]

THE ARMOURED CARS EXPLOIT

Even further behind the enemy lines than *Musical Box* were the armoured cars of the 17th Battalion, which had raced down the St Quentin road after the tanks had towed them across the enemy trenches. There is a vivid account of their doings in *The Tanks* as provided by the Australian Corps Commander, Sir John Monash:

It was nearly midnight when Carter, with a Staff Officer, got back to Corps HQ to render their report. They were scarcely recognisable, covered as they were from head to feet with grime and grease. They had had a busy time. The substance of what they had to tell was taken down at the time almost verbatim, and reads as follows:

Got Armoured Cars through to Warfusee-Abancourt. When we reached the other side of No Man's Land we found that the road was good but a number of trees (large and small) had been shot down and lay right across it in places. Obstacles removed by chopping up the smaller trees and hauling off the big ones by means of a tank. Pioneers helped us to clear the road all the way down. We did not come up to our

Women played a key role in the building of tanks at Foster's and elsewhere in the UK, especially towards the end of the war. TM

advancing troops until they were almost near the Red Line. When we got past our leading infantry we came upon quite a number of Huns and dealt with them. Had then to wait a little on account of our barrage, but went through a light barrage. When we got to Blue Line we detached three sections to run down to Framerville. When they got there they found all the Boche horse transport and many lorries drawn up in the main road ready to move off. Head of column tried to bolt in one direction and other vehicles in another. Complete confusion. Our men killed the lot (using 3000 rounds) and left them there; four Staff Officers on horseback shot also. The cars then ran down to the east side of Harbonnières, on the south-east road to Vauvillers, and met there a number of steam wagons; fired into their boilers causing an impassable block. Had a lot of good shooting around Vauvillers. Then came back to main road. Two sections of cars went on to Foucaucourt and came in contact with a Boche gun in a wood north-east of Foucaucourt. This gun blew the wheels off one car and also hit three others. However, three of the cars got away. Two other cars went to Proyart and found a lot of troops billeted there having lunch in the houses. Our cars shot through the windows into the houses, killing quite a lot of the enemy. Another section went towards Chuignolles and found it full of German soldiers. Our cars shot them. Found rest billets and old trenches also with troops in them. Engaged them. Had quite a battle there. Extent of damage not known, but considerable. Cars then came back to main road. We were then well in advance of Blue Line. Everything was now perfectly quiet - no shell-fire of any kind.

I went a quarter of a mile beyond La Flaque. There was a big dump there, and Huns kept continually coming out and surrendering, and we brought quite a lot of them back as prisoners. It was then about 10.30am. A party of Hun prisoners was detailed to tow back my disabled car. I saw no sign of any wired system anywhere. Old overgrown trenches but no organised trench system. I proceeded to some rising ground near Framerville. Did not go into Framerville, but could see that the roofs of the houses were intact. Saw no trace of any organised system of defence of any kind during the day coming towards us, but very large numbers of fugitives hastening in the opposite direction. Engaged as many of them as could be reached from the roads. I saw from the hill, open country with a certain amount of vegetation on it.

Two leading armoured cars under Lt E.J. Rollings had shot up the enemy's advanced Corps headquarters in Framerville, capturing the German defence scheme 'complete in every details' of the 20-mile stretch of the Hindenburg Line between Oise and Bellicourt.

TWO MORE VICTORIA CROSSES

In the battles that followed on from Amiens, Tank Corps officers were to be awarded two more Victoria Crosses, Lt Cecil Howard Sewell of the 3rd Battalion winning his on the afternoon of 29 August 1918, while in command of a section of Whippets. The citation reads:

…this officer displayed the greatest gallantry and initiative in getting out of his own tank and crossing open ground under heavy shell and machine-gun fire to rescue the crew of another Whippet of his section, which had side-slipped into a large shell hole, overturned and taken fire. The door of the tank having become jammed against the side of the shell hole, Lt Sewell, by his own unaided efforts, dug away the entrance to the door and released the crew. In doing so he undoubtedly saved the lives of the officers and

Lt Cecil Howard Sewell was awarded the Victoria Cross posthumously, after his bravery near Fremicourt on 29th April 1918, whilst commanding a section of Whippets. His medals and his tank are on display at the Tank Museum. TM

men inside the tank, as they would not have got out without his assistance.

After having extricated this crew, seeing one of his own crew lying wounded behind his tank, he again dashed across open ground to his assistance. He was hit while doing so, but succeeded in reaching the tank, when a few minutes later he was again fatally hit, in the act of dressing his wounded driver.

During the whole of this period he was in full view and short range of enemy machine-gun and rifle pits and throughout, by his prompt and heroic action, showed an utter disregard for his own personal safety.

Lt Sewell's Whippet *Caesar* is now on show at the Tank Museum in the World War One Hall, with a brass plate affixed commemorating his heroic act.

The fourth Tank Corps Victoria Cross was awarded on 2 September 1918 to Lt-Col Richard Annersley West for conspicuous bravery and brilliant leadership at Courcelles, and again for amazing self-sacrifice near Vaux-Vraucourt. Col West had already been awarded the DSO and bar, and the Military Cross. His citation reads:

On 21 August, during the attack on Courcelles, the infantry having lost their bearings in the dense fog, this officer at once took charge of any men he could find. He reorganised them and led them on horseback through the village on to their objective in face of heavy machine-gun fire. He had two horses shot from under him during the morning. Throughout the whole action he displayed the most utter disregard of danger, and the capture of the village was in great part due to his initiative and gallantry.

On 2 September it was intended that a battalion of light tanks under command of this officer should exploit the initial infantry and heavy tank attack. He therefore rode forward on horseback to our front infantry line in order to keep in touch with the progress of the battle and to be in a position at the front line when the enemy were in process of delivering a local counter-attack. The infantry battalion had suffered heavy officer casualties, and its flanks were exposed. Realising that there was a danger of the battalion giving way, he at once rode out in front of them under extremely heavy machine-gun fire and rifle fire and rallied the men. In spite

The fourth VC to be awarded to the Tank Corps was again posthumous. It went to Lt-Col Richard Annersley West, DSO, MC, for conspicuous bravery and brilliant leadership at Courcelles on 21 August 1918 and for an act of courageous self-sacrifice near Vaulx-Vracourt on 2 September 1918. TM

of the fact that the enemy were close upon him, he took charge of the situation and detailed non-commissioned officers to replace the officer casualties. He then rode up and down in front of them in face of certain death, encouraging the men and calling to them: 'Stick it men, show them fight, and for God's sake put up a good fight.' He fell riddled by machine-gun bullets.

The magnificent bravery of this very gallant officer at the critical moment inspired the infantry to redoubled efforts, and undoubtedly saved the situation. The hostile attack was defeated.

VICTORY BY 'GENERAL TANK'

Amiens was followed by further successful battles at Bapaume, Arras, Epehy, Cambrai-St Quentin, Selle and Mauberge, as the Germans were forced farther and farther back. In all these actions the tanks played a: major role, indeed a German historian, General der Infanterie AWH von Zwehl, writing about the Allied successes on the Western Front in 1918 said he considered that they had been beaten: '…not by the genius of Marshal Foch, but by "General Tank"; in other words, a new weapon of war, in conjunction with the widespread reinforcement of the Americans.'[4]

Certainly Sir Douglas Haig was now unstinting in his praise of the Tank Corps as this extract from his despatches shows:

Since the opening of our offensive on 8 August tanks have been employed in every battle and the importance of the part played by them in breaking the resistance of the German infantry can scarcely be exaggerated. The whole scheme of the attack of 8 August was dependent upon tanks, and ever since that date on numberless occasions the success of our infantry has been powerfully assisted or confirmed by their timely arrival. So great had been the effect produced upon the German infantry by the appearance of British tanks that in more than one instance, when for various reasons real tanks were not available in sufficient numbers, valuable results have been obtained by the use of dummy tanks painted on frames of wood and canvas.

It is no disparagement of the courage of our infantry or of the skill and devotion of our artillery, to say that the achievements of those essential arms would have fallen short of the full measure of success achieved by our armies had it not been for the very gallant and devoted work of the Tank Corps, under the command of Major-General H. J. Elles.[5]

The Commander-in-Chief's despatches only concerned themselves with operations in the field, so it is equally relevant to reproduce here the remarks made about the sterling performance of the Tank Corps Training Centre at Bovington Camp and

its outstations at Lulworth, Wareham and Swanage. To quote again from *The Tank Corps Book of Honour*:

With the exception of the 1st to 4th Battalions, one Salvage Company, and the original formation of the Central Workshops and Central Stores - all of which units were raised in France from trained personnel drafted into the corps - the whole of the remainder of the Tank Corps has been raised, trained, equipped and despatched to France and Egypt, together with some 7000 reinforcements, from the training centre. And this has been done from almost entirely raw personnel in the space of two years. The Tank Corps units so raised and despatched to France - many went into action within a few weeks of arrival - include:

5th to 18th Tank Battalions, ie 14 Battalions.
5 Carrier (or Supply) Companies.
2 Gun-Carrier Companies.
1 Salvage Company.
2 Workshop Companies.
Some 7000 Reinforcements.

Which means a total of twenty-four tank units into the field in two years. Surely a record unsurpassed by any training centre at home; considering also that the training centre itself had to be organised at the same time.

Tank Corps Roll of Honour. TM

In addition to the above, all the American heavy tank units were trained at the training centre from absolutely raw material and sent to France, comprising three battalions and two salvage units. A further eight British tank battalions and one Canadian tank battalion had also been raised and were under training at the time of the Armistice.

In all, some 34 units had been raised for the Tank Corps within two years - an average of about one unit every six weeks.

As an average, about four months was the limit of time allowed for the raising, equipping and training of a tank battalion, with a shorter period for subsidiary units. The most difficult problem which had to be overcome was the formation of efficient schools of instruction for the many tank specialist subjects concurrently with the raising and training of the tank battalions and other units, and the organisation and erection of workshops to keep training tanks in running order.

The schools of instruction included: Tank Driving and Maintenance School, Tank Gunnery School (including 6pdr, machine gun and revolver), Camouflage School, Gas School, Reconnaissance School, Compass School, Signalling and Pigeon School. The Tank Gunnery School on several occasions sent their instructors to assist in the organisation of the same school in France.

The strain on the workshop personnel was very great, as only a few tanks were allotted training purposes owing to all being taken for fighting. The wear and tear was therefore very great.

Yet another institution which should receive our recognition is the 24th Tank Corps (Officers Cadet Battalion). This unit has sent to the Tank Corps large numbers of young officers who have received a very thorough early training in this battalion.

We owe our gratitude, also, to the Naval Gunnery Schools of HMS *Excellent* (Whale Island), and HMS *Pembroke* (Chatham), for training our 6pdr gunners before the training centre was able to complete their instruction.

Finally, a tribute is due to the large number of officer and NCO instructors and training-centre staff who had to be retained at the training centre to carry out their work there for the ultimate benefit of the Tank Corps, and so were unable to take their places in the field.

near Mormal Forest, while the fast-moving armoured cars of 17th Battalion operated in the vanguard of the final advance before the Armistice. By then, the Tank Corps was virtually at the end of its tether. It had been fighting non-stop for 96 days, with nearly 2000 tanks and armoured cars in almost continuous action. Nearly half had been knocked out or damaged beyond local repair and sent to salvage, while over 3000 officers and men had been lost, a grievous price to pay out of a Corps whose total strength was only 10 500. Nevertheless, the impact the Tank Corps had made on the land battle was considerable, and warfare would never be quite the same again. The tank was not yet 'Queen of the Battlefield', but the Tank Corps had shown what armoured forces were capable of achieving when properly led and given half a chance.

As the 17th (Armoured Car) Battalion led the march to the Rhine, crossing the German frontier on 1 December and entering Cologne a few days later to deal with civil disturbances in the city, the Corps' colours flying proudly in the leading armoured car, the future must have appeared very secure and rosy. The coming of peace was to shatter their illusions.

Victory! The official Tank Corps Christmas Card for 1918. The painting by George Whitelaw, was called: 'The Roadmaker'. TM

An indication of what the country felt about the Tank Corps' achievements was shown when, on 17 October, His Majesty King George V became the Corps' first Colonel-in-Chief.

LAST TANK CORPS OPERATIONS

5 November saw the last tank action of the war when 8 Whippets of 6th Battalion supported 3 Guards Brigade

---

[1] An earlier device known as the 'Tadpole Tail' could be fitted to both Mark IV and Mark V and lengthened the tank by 9ft. This enabled the tanks to cross wider enemy trenches.

[2] Extract from the *Short History of the RTC* published in the Tank Corps Journal.

[3] 'Weekly Tank Notes for January 1919' published in the *Tank Corps Journal*

[4] *Short History of the RTC* published between the wars.

[5] *The Tank Corps Book of Honour.*

Chapter 5

CONTRACTION

BACK TO 1914

'Thank God we can now get back to some real soldiering!' That is what an officer of the 'old school' said to Fuller on the day the Armistice was signed. As Liddell Hart comments: '…such remarks represented a widespread yearning to return from the "mud and blood" to the green fields *behind*' - the smooth routine of military life, with its ceremonies and social pleasures, as it had been before the war.' While one can sympathise with this view, it was unfortunately applied indiscriminately across the board to everything, including tactics, organisations, weapons and equipment, as well as to the social and ceremonial activities. So the 'Back to 1914' brigade led an ever growing groundswell of opinion against the tank and all its works. They considered that it had merely been a necessary evil, created to deal with trench warfare, but now that was a thing of the past and the 'war to end all wars' was over, then there was no place in the British Army for those dirty, smelly machines, and the horse could return in all its glory! They were aided and abetted by the politicians who saw tanks as an unnecessary expense in peacetime. 'Tanks is tanks and tanks is dear, there shall be no tanks this year', was the way the

Americans saw the problem, abolishing their infant Tank Corps before it could reach maturity. It was also touch and go within the British Army when, through demobilisation, the contraction of the Corps gathered speed. Fortunately Fuller was now in a position of some influence in the War Office and used his position to head off complete disaster. The speed at which the Army Council changed its mind about the future of the Tank Corps gives a good idea of what he had to contend with almost daily. For example, in October 1919 they decided that the Tank Corps should form a *corps d'elite* then only three days later, changed their minds and decided that officers should merely be seconded from other arms and that it should not be established as a separate corps. The next month they favoured a twin corps system - one corps to provide tanks for infantry support, the other to be available for independent action. Two months later, in January 1920, they decided that tanks should become part of the Royal Engineers, yet the following month had gone back to the secondment proposal.

Victory Parade 1919. A quartet of Medium Cs passing the Cenotaph, during the impressive parade which was watched by thousands of people. In front of the tanks was the Tank Corps marching contingent, led by Elles and Fuller on horseback. TM

London Welcomes the Tanks! Another spectacular view of the Victory Parade as the tank contingent crosses the Thames, led by Elles on a white horse. TM

Foreword to the first issue of the Tank Corps Journal, *published on 9 April 1919.* TM

Also featured in the first issue was the formal exchange of messages between General Elles and King George V when, in October 1918, His Majesty became Colonel-in-Chief of the Tank Corps. TM

In April it was back to the twin corps idea and by July they had returned to putting tanks under Sapper control again! It was not until 1922 that a firm decision was made to allow for a permanent Tank Corps, initially of four battalions. The following year, on 18 October 1923, the Tank Corps was given the Royal seal of approval, the Army Order reading:

Tank Corps

$\dfrac{\text{AO 369}}{1923}$

GEORGE RI

WHEREAS WE have noted with great satisfaction the splendid work that has been performed by our Tank Corps during the Great War; $\dfrac{20}{\text{Tanks}}$ 157

OUR WILL AND PLEASURE is that
this Corps shall enjoy the distinction
of 'Royal' and shall henceforth be
known as Our 'Royal Tank Corps'.
Given at Our Court of St James's
this 18th day of October 1923, in the
14th year of Our Reign.
By His Majesty's Command
DERBY.

TANK CORPS WAR MEMORIAL

Preliminary steps to select a suitable site for a Corps war memorial had been taken by Tank Corps headquarters shortly after the Armistice and a site on Pozieres Ridge was chosen, close to where the very first tank went into action. Work commenced in 1919 and was nearly completed by that autumn, when the

TANK CORPS MEMORIAL
ERECTED ON THE POZIÈRS RIDGE

The design of the memorial consists of an obelisk, mounted on a plinth at each of the four corners of which is a model of a Tank. These four models comprise Mark I (with the tail), Mark IV, Mark V and Medium A (Whippet)– the four types of Tanks mainly used during the war.

On each face of the plinth is a bronze plaque 42in. x 36in. The plaques on the North and West faces of the plinth bear the inscriptions shown in the illustration above. On the plaques on the East and South faces are inscribed respectively the years 1916 and 1917. Below these date are inscribed the battles in which the Corps took part during those years.

Pozières Ridge, not far from where the very first tank went into action, was the site chosen for the proposed Tank Corps Memorial. TM

Tank Corps War Memorial. Work commenced on a Corps war memorial at Pozieres in 1919, but it was not completed in 1922. It was unveiled on 22 July 1922, by Lt-Gen Sir T.L. Morland KCB, KCMG, DSO, ADC, representing HM The King and in the presence of Elles (seen here watching the presentation of a bouquet to Gen Morland) plus Swinton, Fuller and Stern. TM

working party from the Tank Field Battalion had to be withdrawn for demobilisation. Construction then dragged on for three years, so it was not until 1922 that the final touches were at long last put to the memorial. It was unveiled on 22 July 1922, by Lt-Gen. Sir T.L.N. Morland, KCB, KCMG, DSO, ADC, representing HM The King, in the presence of Swinton, Elles, Fuller and Stern, together with representative detachments from all battalions. As the *Tank Corps Journal* later reported: 'The whole ceremony was marked by simplicity and sincerity, and will long remain in the memories of those present.'

THE CORPS CONTRACTS

At the time of the Armistice there were 18 tank battalions in France, all of which had seen action except for the 18th Tank Battalion. There were also seven tank battalions in England, four of which were fully trained and ready for battle. In addition, there was

Left: *Austin armoured cars of the 17th Battalion having just crossed the Hohenzollern bridge into Cologne. Instead of going home as they had hoped, they were posted immediately to Ireland for peace-keeping duties.* TM

Below: *Armoured car crews of the 17th Battalion in Cologne. The display boards show their progress during the wartime campaigns and their hopes for 'Blighty' next!* TM

the training and reinforcement centre at Swanage, consisting of two more battalions and a complete battalion of officers. This entire reserve disappeared soon after the Armistice.

The first battalion to leave France was 17th Armoured Car Battalion, which came home in January 1919 and was immediately sent over to Ireland, being split up there into 12 separate detachments and located in the centre and south-west of the country. Next to leave were the 4th, 9th, 12th, 13th and 16th Battalions, who were formed into two Tank Brigades (2 and 5) and sent to join the Army of Occupation in Germany in March 1919, where they were held in GHQ in case of internal trouble. Four tanks took part in the ceremonial march over the Hohenzollern Bridge into Cologne, being the first British tanks ever to cross the bridge.[1]

The remaining battalions in France were reduced to cadre strength as demobilisation took its toll and were brought back to Bovington and Wareham camps, where they eventually became the basis of the regular battalions formed as follows:

1st Depot Battalion formed at Wareham, 26 July 1919.
5th Battalion formed at Bovington, 3 September 1919.
2nd Battalion formed at Bovington, 4 October 1919.
3rd Battalion formed as a cadre only at Bovington during November 1919.
4th Battalion formed at Wareham, 28 February 1920.

On 7 August, Sir Hugh Elles, now like so many other officers reduced in rank (to Brigadier-General[2]) took over command of the Tank Corps Centre, which then included the Central Schools, the Tank Corps Depot and the Workshops Training Battalion at Bovington, and the Gunnery School at Lulworth.

SERVICE IN THE ARMY OF OCCUPATION

On 5 April 1920, 'B' Company of the 5th Battalion was sent from Bovington to Germany to relieve the temporary units of the Corps which had been there since March 1919. By then the two brigades were down to a much reduced 12th Battalion plus the Rhine Army Tank Company which 'B' Company became. Based in Cologne they had to send one section of Mark Vs to Upper Silesia to help deal with unrest between Germans and Poles in this disputed area. They were used in Brebreck to disperse a hostile crowd and in a contemporary article published in the Tank Corps Journal, 'Boots' Hotblack, who was then the Brigade Major of 1 Brigade, British Upper Silesian Force, explained how the tanks' mere presence provided a major incentive towards good behaviour:

The process of separating the German and Polish forces was now in progress and tanks were sent to see that the withdrawal of opposing troops took place according to orders issued. In some cases the Poles found difficulties in organising their moves, but in each case reports that tanks were on the way to 'assist' them, solved all the Polish difficulties and moves took place according to plan.

The section returned to Cologne in July 1922. Their value can be gauged by the remarks made by C-in-C Rhine Army, who wrote at the time:

The prestige of British troops is still high in the eyes of the Germans, and there is abundant evidence that this is largely due to the enormous effect of tanks on the civil population.

THE 'RUSSIAN STUNT'

An article entitled 'With the Tanks in Bolshevik Russia' written by Sgt C.L. Windle and 'Ranker', tells how volunteers were shipped with their tanks to Southern Russia:

Saturday afternoon, 8 February 1919, at 6pm the volunteers for the 'Russian Stunt' as the boys called it, paraded at Erin. Epaulette colours showed that every battalion was represented. The party consisted of three officers and twenty-six NCOs and men.

The general impression was that we were going to visit a land of snow and ice. This impression seemed very real on the following morning as we shifted the snow from the covers of six Mark V Tanks and six Whippets. We worked on the tanks for three days, thawing the frost from the tracks and getting them ready for moving to the train.

Right: These 12th Battalion tanks were drawn up in front of Cologne Cathedral after forming part of the welcoming parade at the main railway station, for a visit by Gen Petain in 1919. TM

Below: Tanks of the 12th Battalion in Cologne in 1919, where they formed part of the British Army of the Rhine (BAOR). TM

On Wednesday evening, 12 February, we entrained the tanks and journeyed to Calais, arriving there on the Friday morning, the rain pouring down in torrents; during the afternoon the train steamed on to the Channel ferry and we crossed over to Richborough, the mystery port situated between Ramsgate and Margate. A guard was mounted on the train and the remainder of the party encamped at the local REs camp.

A week later we ran the tanks on to a South Eastern wreck train and were taken to Woolwich,

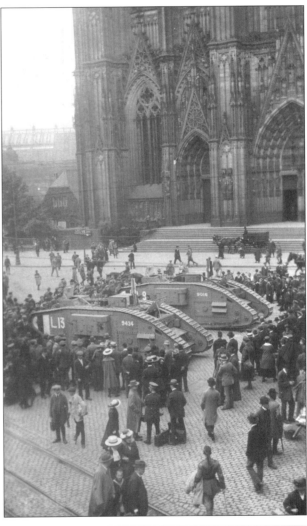

Cavalry and tanks exercising in BAOR in 1919. Very few cavalrymen had then appreciated that their days on the battlefield, mounted on horses, were numbered. TM

This Medium A, named Love Child, was part of the South Russia Tank Detachment, which took part in the 'Russian Stunt' in 1919. Was the euphonium player in the crowd there to welcome them? TM

Their Majesties King George Vth and Queen Mary, visiting Aldershot in 1919. In the background is a Medium C belonging to the 2nd Battalion. TM

where we commenced to embark on the SS *St Michael*... The loading of tanks and cargo was finished on Saturday, 2 March, and the SS *St Michael* sailed from the Royal Albert Docks on the Sunday morning, anchoring off Gravesend for the night; a fine starlit sky gave promise of good weather. We reached the English Channel next day and anchored off Dover. The next morning, Shrove Tuesday, we commenced our journey to Southern Russia.

Once they had got their 'sea legs' the tank crews had an interesting journey via the Bay of Biscay and the Mediterranean to the Dardanelles and thence to Southern Russia, arriving at the port of Novorossysk on 22 March.

Our first sight of the port gave us a very favourable impression; the sunshine was brilliant and the distant snow-capped mountains glistened in the sunlight, the forest-clad mountain slopes reflected a dull green and the town in the foreground completed the pretty picture. We anchored in the harbour and the DNTO came aboard with several Russian officers, whose uniform was considerably the worse for wear. The Russian officer may be recognised by a red line down the centre of his epaulettes, criss-crossed by a white line. These officers seemed very excited over the arrival of the tanks, probably as they were the first they had seen. Scores of people surrounded the ship in their boats but were not permitted to come aboard... The next day the dockers commenced to unload the cargo and when a floating crane arrived the tanks were landed on to the quay (dock work was apparently the only work going on in the town). The unloading took seven days and meanwhile a portable ramp was erected on the quay by the Russians, and a Whippet run over to test its strength. This operation was filmed by a Russian firm. The ramp was found to be strong enough. Crowds of spectators watched the unloading, standing on the quay all the day. Hundreds of Cossack officers and soldiers crowded around the tanks, and did not seem to be convinced they were real unless they were allowed to touch them - many even kissed the armour-plated sides.

On Palm Sunday we drove a Mark V tank around the town; the people of Nova Rossick (sic) lined the route in dense masses; the tank climbed a small cement wall and there was breathless silence as it slowly mounted the wall and stood on its tail; as the tank passed over the wall and crushed it the spectators gave a series of tremendous cheers. During the whole show the Cossacks followed the tank on horseback.

More tanks followed this first batch, until the South

Russian Tank Detachment numbered 57 Mark Vs and 17 Whippets. The combined detachment, under Major E.M. Bruce, then moved to Ekaterinodar in the Kuban peninsula, where they established a large tank school and started trying to train the Russian peasant soldiers as tank crews - a difficult and frustrating task! The British instructors were supposed not to get involved in the fighting. During the climax of armoured operations in South Russia in June 1919 the British did get involved and in one operation, which Liddell Hart describes as 'one of the most remarkable feats in the whole story of the Tank Corps', a British tank crew was primarily responsible for the capture of the important centre of Tsaritsin (renamed Stalingrad and now called Volgograd) and the surrender of 40 000 Bolshevik troops. The tanks (three Mark Vs and three Whippets) were among the reinforcements called up when the attacks on Tsaritsin had twice been repulsed. One of the Mark Vs had a British crew under Capt Walsh. After some breakdowns, Walsh's tank and another Mark V smashed through the enemy wire and crossed their first trench line. Following Cambrai tactics, Walsh then turned and ran parallel with the trench clearing it of enemy, so that the Cossack cavalry could come up and consolidate. After an enforced wait for petrol - it took two days to bring up sufficient for Walsh's tank alone - the advance continued with Bruce taking personal command of the Mark V. He drove straight for Tsaritsin and succeeded in capturing the whole city single-handed , something the Germans did not succeed in achieving during the Second World War with an entire Tank Army!

By February 1920 the initiative was firmly with the Red Army and the tanks had to cover a general withdrawal, being evacuated themselves from Sevastopol in late June 1920.

A second small volunteer detachment under Lt-Col Hope-Carson, DSO, MC, operated in Estonia and North-West Russia with some six Mark V Composites which were given such names as *Brown Bear*, *White Soldier* and *Deliverance*. Hope-Carson had first to train tank crews from Russian volunteers and he also

The 'Long and Short' of the Drums. One of the many photographs taken between the wars by Mitchell, the Bovington photographer. TM

formed a special infantry force called the 'Tank Push Battalion'. The tanks performed wonders, despite their small numbers, and they were always the decisive factor in any of the battles they fought. Eventually, in November 1919, the North-West Russian Tank Detachment was withdrawn and returned to England.

The third detachment - four Mark Vs and two Whippets, under Major J.N. Lewis-Bryan, arrived at

The Tank Park at Bovington Camp, circa 1920. Many of the surviving tanks were brought to Bovington, parked up on the training area and then broken up for scrap. TM

Tanks and tents belonging to the 4th Battalion on the gunnery ranges at Lulworth, with Bindon Hill rising behind them and beyond it - the sea. TM

Left: One of the splendid charabancs which took soldiers to Bournemouth and Poole each weekend. Standing beside the bus is RSM Silverwood – nicknamed 'Tishup' because of the strange noises he made when clearing his throat before shouting words of command! TM

Below: The Tank Corps Band was first formed in 1922, although there had been an unofficial one before that date. Here they lead a parade down to Wool. TM

One of the most famous Tank Corps privates was 7875698 Pte T.E. Shaw, better known as Lawrence of Arabia. He enrolled on 12 March 1923, having been driven to leave the RAF by continual harassment by the Press. He served as a QM storeman at Bovington and rented a cottage at Clouds Hill, quite close to Bovington, where he would entertain his friends. After two years in the RTC, he went back to the RAF and served with them until 1935. When he left the RAF he returned to the Clouds Hill cottage, but some months later, he was seriously hurt in a motor-cycle accident on 13 May 1935 and died six days later at the Bovington Camp Medical Centre. He was buried at Moreton and his effigy is in St Martin's Church, Wareham. TM

Archangel in August 1919, having been asked to cover the withdrawal of British and Allied forces. Once this had been achieved the tanks were handed over to the White Russians and the detachment returned home in October 1919. The tanks were later used very successfully against the Reds, but when Archangel finally fell their crews refused to hand them over, preferring to sink them in the middle of the Dvina River.

PROBLEMS AT HOME

The Tank Corps was mobilised in May 1926, on the occasion of the General Strike. On both occasions armoured car companies were formed all over the country and used throughout the strikes. 'Z' Armoured Car Company, composed of men of the Central Schools, was typical of the Tank Corps units involved:

The company commenced to mobilise after dinner on Wednesday, 5 May, and Nos 2 and 4 Sections left for Hounslow at 8am, and No. 3 Section at 5pm the following Friday, 7 May. Advanced HQ left at 4am on Saturday 8 May and was followed by the remainder of HQ and No 1 Section at 2pm the same day; so that the whole company mobilised and moved within 72 hours of the commencement of mobilisation. Not a bad effort in view of the many things that had to be done and the stores that had to be collected.

On arrival at Hounslow, Nos 2 and 4 Sections were at once moved to Chelsea Barracks, whilst HQ with Nos 1 and 4 Sections were accommodated with the 12th Lancers at Hounslow. On Monday, 10 May, the whole company was concentrated at Albany Barracks, Regent's Park, and accommodated by the Life Guards.

In the meantime, constant demands were made upon it for escort duties, so much so that the question of resting the personnel and maintenance of the cars began to assume serious proportions. Convoys between the docks and Hyde Park - from the Great West Road to the Marble Arch, Shaftesbury Avenue to Staines, etc. provided all ranks with an opportunity of seeing London under odd and interesting circumstances. Cricklewood and Hendon were also scenes of activity, where the LGOC put some 240 buses on the roads with volunteer drivers; the armoured cars in this case having to convoy the buses clear of the possible danger areas, and gather them in again at night.

Patrols round the docks area - through Limehouse and Poplar, escorting the Indian Mail out of the Victoria Docks at Tilbury, convoying petrol lorries from Thames Haven to Wanstead, were daily duties which fell to the lot of the company.

There were few areas north of the Thames which did not at one time or another watch with astonishment Rolls-Royce armoured cars gliding through their streets with two steel-helmeted soldiers sitting on the tray of each, armed with cudgels. And with it all, there was an almost total absence of anything hostile - the very occasional remark from some crowd of unemployed was shouted usually more in humour than in anger; the one or two ejaculations from rather savage females reflecting upon the parentage of the military; the single glass bottle which burst like an egg, some yards behind the car it was aimed at - these were the only incidents that occurred as far as the company was concerned.

The impression conveyed to one's mind - by the general demeanour of the crowds and by occasional conversations with strike pickets - was that of a gigantic bubble. No one seemed to have any clear idea of the cause for which they were striking, and no one seemed to have been consulted as to their own wishes in the matter. Consequently, their hearts were not in it; they were merely responding dumbly to some not very clear appeal to their sense of loyalty and comradeship. Nevertheless, the General Strike was in action, but each day its effect was being increasingly neutralised by the response of the country to the Government's appeal for volunteers. This placed the men out on strike in a rather ridiculous position. For under their very eyes the food supplies were running smoothly; the trains, tubes and buses were

carrying full complements of passengers; life generally was very like the normal. The thousands of workers watched serene and cheerful volunteers doing their own job. No man likes ridicule or insult added to injury, consequently there were certain occasions when the strikers were coerced into breaches of the peace, rather by the taunts of others than by the appeal of their cause.

It was all a great big bubble, which was burst by the active will of the people. But the bursting of it might well have been a far more serious affair, had not a very determined show of force been made - *Si vis pacem pare bellum.* How true that was.

Police, mounted and on foot, special constables, infantry, armoured cars, even tanks - in addition to all the volunteers - had appeared and continued to appear in the most populated thoroughfares of London; so that no doubt was left in the minds of possible malcontents as to the nature of the nut they would have to crack before they could wreck the country. And so the bubble burst without a bang, and 'Z' Armoured Cars withdrew to the peaceful precincts of Albany Barracks.[3]

The Royal Tournament at Olympia 1920. One of the attractions was this Mark V** heavy tank, which was six feet longer and seven tons heavier than the original Mark V. Only 25 were ever built, but the crews liked them. The young officer and his crew look extremely smart. TM

The troubles in Ireland. The 17th Battalion was involved in peace-keeping duties in Dublin. This was a 'B' Company Whippet whilst 'A' Coy had armoured cars and 'C' Coy medium and heavy tanks. TM

Above: On parade at Bovington. This Guard of Honour was mounted in March 1928 for the visit to Bovington of HM King Amanullah of Afghanistan. It gives a good view of some of the wooden huts which made up the Tank Corps Depot. TM

Below: The adoption of the beret in 1924, came in for some banter when it was first worn as this cartoon shows. In fact they were ideal headgear for working inside the close confines of a tank and, as they were black, were less likely to show dirt and oilstains! TM

THE ROYAL TANK CORPS UNIFORM.
ANOTHER UNFORTUNATE JUXTAPOSITION.

The 12th Armoured Car Company had been brought back from Ireland for the 1926 General Strike and sent to Lancashire, based at Warrington. It remained there for a few months and then moved down to Bovington. Three years later, in March 1929, it handed over its armoured cars to the 11th Hussars, one of the first two cavalry regiments to be mechanised.

THE BLACK BERET IS ADOPTED

The black beret was officially adopted in place of the field service cap in March 1924, after it had received Royal Approval. The peaked field service cap had been found to be totally unsuitable for wearing in tanks - it didn't fit close enough to the head and the

peak got in the way when the wearer tried to use a gunsight or other vision device, unless he turned it back to front. It also showed the dirt, especially the oilstains. A substitute had been sought during the war and Elles was favourably impressed by the large floppy black beret as worn by the French Chasseurs Alpins, but considered it to be a bit too sloppy, while the Basque beret was far too skimpy. A compromise was eventually produced in the early twenties and submitted for approval in 1923

Left: *The Royal Tank Corps badge which was adopted on 18 October 1923, when the Regiment was granted the title: 'Royal'. Initially, when the old Tank Corps badge was superseded, the newly struck badge had the tank going the same way (ie: facing right), however, this looked wrong on the beret, so a new badge was struck with the tank facing left.* TM

Below: *This splendid photograph shows 'The Father of the Regiment' Maj Gen Sir Ernest Swinton, leaving Buckingham Palace with Batch 'N' – newly-commissioned young RTC officers – after attending a levee there in 1936. It shows both the normal RTC beret and the full dress one* TM

---

[1] Armoured cars of the 17th Battalion had, of course, crossed the same bridge on 6 December 1918.

[2] This rank was abolished in 1921 and replaced by 'Colonel Commandant' which remained until 1928 when the far simpler term 'Brigadier' was revived.

[3] *Tank Corps Journal.*

Chapter 6

THE ARMOURED CAR COMPANIES

FORMATION

When the First World War ended, British armoured cars were operating all over the world, but, with the exception of 17th Armoured Car Battalion, all were crewed by non-Tank Corps personnel. The majority were manned by the men of the Machine-Gun Corps (Motors) which had initially consisted of Armoured Motor Batteries, Light Armoured Car Batteries and Light Armoured Batteries. Later, eight-car Light Armoured Motor Batteries (LAMB) were formed and operated in such places as Egypt, Palestine, Persia and Iraq. The importance of armoured cars in peacetime and their value in what was known as Imperial Policing became more and more obvious as the size of the

army was reduced and the requirements for controlling the British Empire grew. The Tank Corps reaped the benefit of this extra workload with the formation between January 1920 and July 1921 of 12 Armoured Car companies. They were mostly raised at the Tank Corps Centre and then sent out all over the Empire. They absorbed the LAMB and, in 1922 when the Machine-Gun Corps was finally abolished, they became entirely responsible within the army for the manning of armoured cars. Lt-Col George Lindsay (later Maj-Gen.), who in 1921 was sent out to Baghdad to take control of all the armoured cars that now formed No 1 Group, Tank Corps, was a major exponent of armoured car/aircraft co-operation and the highly effective and economic use of mechanised mobility for Imperial Defence.[1]

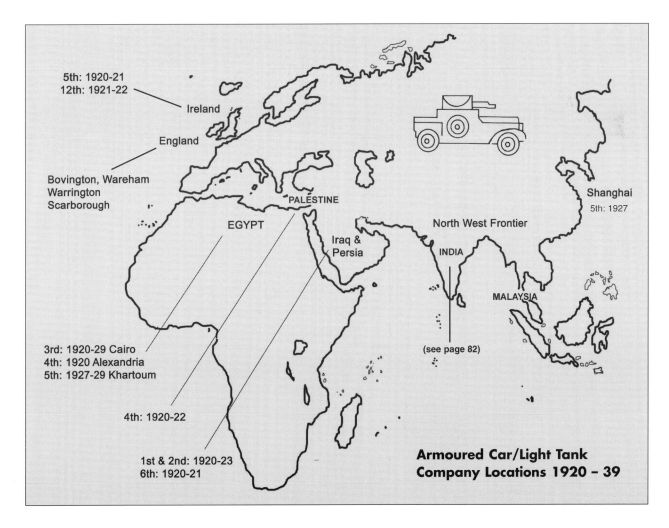

5th: 1920-21
12th: 1921-22

Ireland

England

Bovington, Wareham
Warrington
Scarborough

PALESTINE

EGYPT

Iraq &
Persia

North West Frontier

INDIA

Shanghai
5th: 1927

MALAYSIA

3rd: 1920-29 Cairo
4th: 1920 Alexandria
5th: 1927-29 Khartoum

(see page 82)

4th: 1920-22

1st & 2nd: 1920-23
6th: 1920-21

**Armoured Car/Light Tank
Company Locations 1920 – 39**

INDIA

The greatest concentration of armoured car companies was in India. By the end of 1919 there were, for example, 16 LAMB operating there, although by 1920 this number had been reduced to nine. They operated in three main areas - Southern Waziristan, Peshawar and Lahore-Delhi. Faced with the approaching disbandment of the MGC, army headquarters in India decided to include eight Tank Corps armoured car companies in their post-war establishment. The companies were to be organised on approximately the same lines as tank companies at home. This figure was subsequently reduced to six, but then raised again to eight on the recommendation of the Inchcape Committee in 1922. The original intention was to form the eight companies at Wareham. Four would then proceed to India in the winter of 1920-21 and the other four would follow later, but this programme was never carried out due to policy changes in India and Mesopotamia. The first four companies (7, 8, 9 and 10) were formed and despatched. Nos 11 and 12 were subsequently forrned to complete to six, but only one of these (No 11) went to India, the sixth coming from Mesopotamia, when the RAF took over there. The final two companies (Nos 1 and 2) did not arrive until February 1925, having been re-formed at Bovington in 1924 after being disbanded the year before.

India contained many areas of potential disaffection, from the sparsely populated hill areas of the North-West Frontier to the densely populated urban areas further south. Political agitators were constantly at work and, in addition, there was the continuing Hindu-Moslem bitterness which

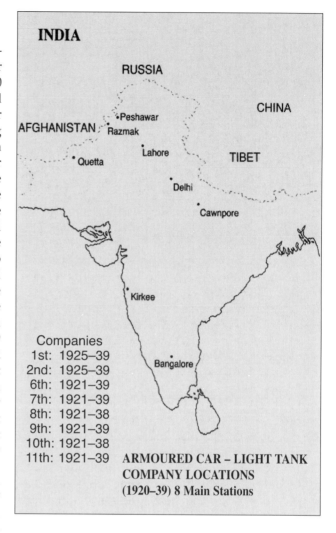

INDIA

Companies
1st: 1925–39
2nd: 1925–39
6th: 1921–39
7th: 1921–39
8th: 1921–38
9th: 1921–39
10th: 1921–38
11th: 1921–39

ARMOURED CAR – LIGHT TANK COMPANY LOCATIONS (1920–39) 8 Main Stations

A patrol of India-pattern Crossley armoured cars belonging to 8 ACC outside the Red Fort at Delhi in the early 1930s. TM

One of the most important jobs of the armoured cars was protecting vehicle convoys in the Northwest Frontier. This armoured car belonged to 8 ACC. TM

provided a constant source of turmoil. In all these troubles armoured cars played their part and thoroughly justified their existence. In many cases their mere presence was sufficient to prevent serious rioting. Their speed, mobility and above all, their efficiency, were of the greatest importance in keeping the peace. The first companies to arrive were equipped with old-pattern Rolls-Royce cars, but during 1921, the Indian Government ordered a number of other armoured cars to their own design, the first being on the 1920 Rolls chassis, but strengthened to carry additional weight in the form of improved armour plate. The 'India Pattern' Rolls had a domed turret with a 'swinging' traverse and an independently rotating hemispherical cupola with protected vision slits. There were four ball-mountings in the turret for machine guns, into which the vehicle's two Vickers .303 MGs could be mounted (either two front, or one front/one rear on opposite sides was the 'norm'). Perhaps the most famous Indian armoured car was *Wedding Bells*, a Rolls-Royce that had started life in France in 1914 and then went on to serve in Egypt (1916), Palestine (1917),

Iraq (1918), South Russia (1919), and all over India from 1921 onwards until 1940. Despite strenuous efforts by Lt-Col Sleeman to have the historic old car shipped back to England it was broken up in Ahmednagar in 1940 and all that now remains of *Wedding Bells* is a cigarette lighter - what little regard we show at times for our all too short history!

ARMOURED CAR ACTIONS

Life in armoured car companies in India between the wars held its share of excitement as these short extracts from contemporary articles which appeared in the Corps magazine show. The first was in a 1937 issue:

The situation on the North-West Frontier of India during the past few months has imposed much work of an arduous and dangerous nature on members of the Royal Tank Corps in India. Gradually, as their capacity for dealing with awkward situations in the difficult circumstances experienced in mountain warfare was realised, company after company has been drafted into that area. Today the bulk of the Corps units in India are on active service…

On one occasion recently where an Indian battalion had got into an extremely critical position, a section of armoured cars was the only

An excellent close-up shot of two India Pattern Crossleys, on manoeuvres. TM

Rolls Royce armoured cars at Data Khel Fort, Waziristan on the NW Frontier, circa 1925. TM

One of the most famous landmarks on the road up to the Khyber Pass was Greenwoods Corner. This photograph was taken about 1925. TM

unit available to afford them assistance. The section commander, ordered at short notice into the battle, and having to make full use of his mobility if valuable lives were to be saved, led his section into the battle area. The situation was rapidly becoming desperate. The tribesmen, always more dangerous-during a withdrawal, were on the point of executing their final rush with their long and vicious knives when the much needed reinforcement arrived. The Section was in action for ten hours in conditions of extraordinary difficulty but by their tenacity and activity were instrumental in saving many casualties to their hard-pressed comrades on foot. For this action the Section Commander was awarded the Military Cross, and one of his men the Military Medal.

One of the most important developments on the North-West Frontier during the past few years has been the construction of high-grade roads over great distances through what was once an impenetrable tangle of precipitous hills. Along these roads wind the MT columns supplying garrisons stationed far inside tribal territory. The engineering feats accomplished by the sappers and miners in constructing these

roads are often stupendous. Steep hills have to be circumnavigated, and deep ravines traversed in seemingly unending succession. In some places the cliff rises vertically for hundreds of feet on one side of the road, whilst on the other side is often a sheer precipice into the bottom of the ravine below.

Suddenly, as the head of a convoy rounds some greater shoulder of rock, the leading vehicle will find its path barred by an unexpected obstacle. At the same time a heavy fusillade of well-aimed fire will be poured into it from innumerable dark figures hidden among the rocks and boulders that clothe these barren slopes. The difficulties that confront a column of MT in such an event can well be imagined. The obstacle bars forward movement, the column in the rear prevent backward movement, there is barely room to pass between a vehicle on the road and the bottomless ravine below. It is a case of fighting it out where one is, and to the armoured cars of the escort falls this onerous duty.

Adequate fire positions can only be secured by slithering past the vehicle ahead or in rear. The standard of driving required is superlative. An error of judgement on the driver's part, even

CSM Bateman, at the Vehicle Park,
Razmak, circa 1935. TM

This line of Rolls Royces was photographed outside the
Armoury of the Calcutta Presidency Battalion Auxiliary
Force. TM

of the smallest fraction, and the armoured car crashes over the precipice to certain destruction below. And all the time the merciless rain of bullets goes on. It is a situation that calls for iron nerve, and a standard of courage as high as that of any wars of the past.

In April 1937, a section of four armoured cars under Lt Alan Browne was escorting a convoy two miles long up the Wana road in Waziristan. Because of the convoy length, the cars were spread throughout and a company of truckborne Indian troops was also spread along it. As the convoy passed through a very narrow and precipitous defile, known as Shahur Tangi, a large group of tribesmen, who had blocked the road, took the escort completely by surprise and opened a hail of well-aimed fire, almost wiping out the infantry company in a matter of minutes. The Section responded with the utmost gallantry, but the narrowness of the road and the number of knocked out trucks made manoeuvre extremely difficult. Nevertheless, by their skill and courage they managed to stave off what would have been a total disaster. They fought grimly for nearly 24

Riots in Peshawar City 23 April 1931 This Crossley,
belonging to 2Lt Synge, was assisting in containing the
riots when it was set on fire. (Ted Gillingham). TM

hours until infantry reinforcements were able to secure the surrounding heights at dawn. Alan Browne was awarded an MC and two of his Section won a DCM and an MM.

In built-up areas life could be just as exciting. Take, for example, the activities of a section of the 1st Armoured Car Company in Peshawar city on 23 April 1930, when there was trouble within the city and reports that the frontier tribes were marching on Peshawar from the hills:

At 10.15am a section of the 1st Armoured Car Company was ordered to proceed to the Edward Gate, taking the District Commissioner of Peshawar with them. This section was commanded by Capt S.J. King, MC with 2/Lt T. M. Synge commanding the rear sub-section. On arrival at Edward Gate at 10.45am, a large and hostile crowd met the cars, and many missiles were thrown at them. The District Commissioner, who was in the leading car with Capt King, wished the cars to proceed 300yds down the street, and they were ordered to do so. A despatch rider, No 7876463 Pte H. Bryant, who was unfortunately with the cars though ordered not to approach the gates if any mob were met, was knocked off his motorcycle and fell under the second car and was killed. The sudden halting of the second car caused the third and fourth cars to telescope before they could be stopped. One car damaged a petrol pipe and became immovable. The leading car halted on finding the second car had stopped, and came back to the second car. The mob were then endeavouring to get at the body of the despatch rider and swarming round the cars. Burning kerosene had been poured on the body. 2/Lt Synge got out to try to help the despatch rider and was at once set upon by the mob. He shot one of his assailants and, finding he could not save the despatch rider, he fought his way with

rounds were again fired and the street was cleared. Subsequently the streets were patrolled and gradually the disturbances died down. 2/Lt T.M. Synge was awarded the OBE for his gallant conduct. It is sad to record that this very gallant officer was murdered in Waziristan near Dargai Oba, on 2 November 1931.[2]

Of course life, even on the North-West Frontier, was not always quite so hectic. Capt. A.J. Holbrow, MSM, TD, served there in the mid-twenties with 11th Armoured Car Company. The company left Lahore in March 1926 and moved its column of 15 Crossley armoured cars, plus support vehicles, to Razani in the North-West Frontier Province. Capt. Holbrow recalled in the *Tank Corps Journal*:

We found Razani Camp so different from the well laid-out newly built barracks we had occupied at Lahore. The company lines consisted of tent tops with stone walls, some of them even had doors and windows. The only building was split up into the company cookhouse, the company dining-hall and the sergeants' mess. The offficers' mess was a double tent with stone walls. The tank park was not enclosed but had overhead cover… The camp was enclosed with a perimeter wall and barbed wire, giving newcomers the impression that it was not exactly a peaceable spot. To add to this feeling one saw the permanent posts on the hill-tops surrounding the camp. The following were the roles of the three sections, changed round weekly:

Duty Section
Standby Section
Reserve Section

The duty section carried out all road patrols and escorts for the week. The standby section was the first to be called out in an emergency, while the reserve section, as its title implies, was the next in order for turnout… At first we found the differing duties very interesting but the novelty soon wore off. The country was very bare and hilly and there were few inhabitants. But one never became unmindful of the need for constant vigilance which was stressed by the occasional bullet from some Wazir in the hills. The minor excitements included wending a way through the convoy of camels or just missing a passing vehicle by 1/1000th of an inch with a drop on your side of 3 to 400ft. One car did finish up at the bottom of the cud when the clearance was less than that quoted above. It might be that a river bed, dry when you passed in the morning, was in spate on your return journey. You might: decide to rush it and occasionally a crew had to climb out through the cupola and remain on the

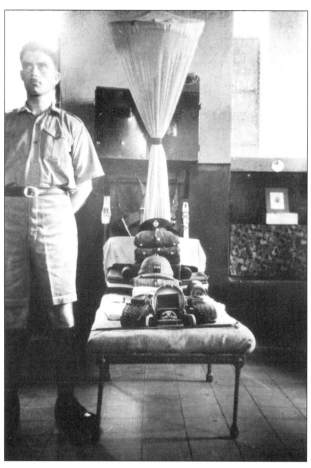

'Stand by Your Beds!' Saturday morning kit inspection of 3 ACC at Mustapha Barracks Alexandria, August 1930. TM

several officials to the police post. The District Commissioner also got out to go to the police post, but was knocked out by a brick on the head.

2/Lt Synge, looking back, saw that his car was on fire and, thinking his men might be in it, he fought his way back to it. He found the crew were out of the car and then went towards the leading car, having to shoot several of the crowd who attempted to stop him. He was saved by the leading car opening fire, the first burst of ten rounds killing several men. The crew of the burning car had saved themselves, two of them reaching other cars and one reached the police post, shooting several assailants on his way thither.

The section commander also had to shoot an Indian who had clambered on to his car. The crowd then retired from the cars, which remained on duty near the gate. At 11.30am another section, under Capt A.H. Gatehouse, MC arrived in support, the crowd having returned and being very hostile. Attempts were made to place a barricade across the road which was charged by a car and broken. Unsuccessful attempts were made to prevent this car returning.

Many of the infantry were being knocked out by missiles thrown from the house-tops, so a few

top until the spate subsided. Towing the Field Cashier's car provided another diversion. We would collect any coal dropped on the road by the steam-rollers - especially welcome when the wood ration was short - Sport was an essential part of life at Razani and we were very well off in that respect. There were two hockey pitches, one football pitch (very stony), three tennis courts and many basketball pitches. We also managed to construct a cricket pitch on the football ground and had several enjoyable games - In conclusion the writer can truthfully say that he enjoyed every minute of his sojurn in wild Waziristan.

EGYPT

Col Alec Dow joined 3rd Armoured Car Company in Egypt in 1927. He went out on an old troopship *City of Marseilles*. As he later recalled:

We were only just within sight of the distant flat shore line of Egypt when I had my first whiff of the unique smell of the country… a mixture of spices, scents and camel-dung, which pervaded the towns, cities and villages and which I came to love and still miss. I was still in charge of a draft

of 50 cavalry reinforcements that I had been given at Southampton so we were in a special coach on the train from Port Said to Cairo. My memories of the journey were of airlessness, as there was no cooling system, and of the ever present dust if one opened the windows, even with the slatted shutters closed. Apart from the non-stop noise of tram gongs, motor-horns and police whistles, I do not remember the two-mile drive out to Abbassia, the barracks and HQ of the Cavalry Brigade and some small units. One thing that struck me at the time was the Military Police Post and barrier at the entrance to the Garrison. I had never seen any such security measure before - now so commonplace and essential at any Service establishment anywhere.

We shared an officers' mess with a Field Company RE and the Cavalry Brigade Signals Company. It was then a modern building with spacious rooms - a delight after the inadequate cold brick huts at Catterick and the old wooden ones allotted to students on courses at Bovington and Lulworth in those days. The 3rd ACC were still equipped with the old 1920 Rolls Royces, though we knew that they were to be replaced with the new 1925 ones. The Company

The Cairo Brigade camp under the shadow of the Pyramids. This large tented camp was put up for the annual manoeuvres in 1928. TM

'Give us a piggy-back!' One way of dealing with a breakdown whilst out in the desert was to lift its front wheels onto the back of an armoured car! This little Ford has been pulled up on the back of a Rolls-Royce armoured car. TM

Commander's staff-car was then a magnificent T Model Ford open-tourer, a glossy green, with highly polished brass-work and white seat and hood covers. After several months on section training, learning my way round the local desert, I was given the job of, in October 1927, taking the last of the old Rolls to Port Said to be shipped back to the UK. The new cars were a great improvement with their high turret and revolving cupola, but they had been fitted with larger low pressure tyres which at times gave steering problems and caused more than one car to overturn. We had three sections in Cairo and one in Alexandria and I was fortunate in being sent to Alex. The section had a small hutted barrack, hangar and car park close to the main barracks occupied by the Durham Light Infantry,

including their own bit of sandy seashore. The DLI could not accommodate our officers, so the policy was to have three unmarried subalterns living in a nearby flat, drawing reasonable allowances. Apart from driving through the main streets of Alexandria to do a bit of desert driving to the western desert, and standing by for civil disturbances, we had little to do. At the same time there was summer swimming and sailing, a good hotel with casino, several good restaurants and cabarets, it was a pleasant life for a fun-loving youngster.

CHINA

During January 1907, 5th Armoured Car Company, stationed at Scarborough was ordered to proceed to China at short notice to join the Shanghai Defence Force to defend British lives and property during the Civil War. Only once did they become involved in a 'shooting war' when a sub-section under command of Lt T.P. Newman MC, DCM, came under heavy fire in Darroch Road as the following extract from a letter home explains:

We have all been seeing plenty of life in the way of hard work, patrols day and night, and have had one or two small shows. Newman's was of course the biggest, he has his right arm smashed-up. He was caught in a narrow road at 15yds range by a machine gun and got three bullets through the driver's observation slit, one of which wounded him, and what with 'splash' and the remaining two, the whole of the crew were hit and the car ditched. Newman got out to get the car out and was hit by another bullet in the same

The 'Garage' in Shanghai may look ad hoc, however, it provided adequate covered accommodation for the entire complement of Rolls Royce armoured cars belonging to 5 ACC. TM

On the streets of Shanghai. A 1920 pattern Rolls Royce armoured car belonging to 5 ACC. TM

This is Rolls H 3830, which was one of Lt Richardson's Section in Shanghai in 1927. It is still in perfect running order at the Tank Museum and is used on special occasions, such as when HM The Queen visits. TM

Sun, sand, date palms and camels, all make a perfect backdrop for this Rolls Royce armoured car, probably somewhere in Palestine. TM

arm, one inch above the first wound. This one broke the bone and put him right out of action. His car was pulled out by the other car of the sub-section (Sgt Tomlinson) and taken back to camp. Wilcox carried on the show for the next six hours, and then I went up with my sub-section and remained on the spot for four days... Things are very quiet now.

…After the show we counted 91 bullet marks on Newman's car.

The sub-section successfully silenced two rebel machine guns.

PALESTINE

The Jaffa Riots in May 1921 involved 4th Armoured Car Company and, in an amusing article which appeared in the *Tank Corps Journal*, one of the company officers gave this first-hand account of their 'crash-out' from camp:

It was exactly 3.20pm when the telephone bell rang. There were only two officers left in camp; one we will call Mr A and the other Mr H.

Mr A answers the 'phone: he picks up the receiver, and hears the following extraordinary utterances, expressed in a type of mixed Dago-Turco-Grecian falsetto voice. Then the voice changed, and in a good comforting English tone another voice said, 'Hallo! Is that Armoured Cars?' 'It is,' says Mr A; 'A speaking.' 'S, speaking,' replies the voice. 'S? S? Who the hell is S, anyhow?' says Mr A, aside to H, forgetting meanwhile to let go the button in the receiver. 'General S, Commanding Blank Brigade,' very quickly comes back over the 'phone. 'Oh yes, sir, very sorry, sir; I did not imagine you would be ringing up, sir; so sorry, sir.' 'Never mind about

This convoy was photographed near Rustamabad in NW Persia, circa 1920. TM

apologising for your lack of manners,' cuts in General S. 'How many armoured cars and Rolls tenders can you turn out at once, there's a' - here the telephone went wrong - Bang - sploch - splutter - 'row' - splutter - splutter, 'Jews, Arabs' - splutter - 'killed, wounded' - splutter, bang - Government House' - splutter - 'report to me at once at my headquarters with as many cars as you can. Understand?' 'Yes, sir.' 'All right, don't waste time.'

A, now fully aware that something has to be done, replaces the receiver in such a way as to show that it is Government property, and rushed off to H.

'H, you old blighter, wake up, we've got a job; there's still a hell of a row at Government House - somebody killing somebody else, and old man N (a most important person) has been slaughtered, and all the Arabs in the country are marching on Jerusalem. We've to turn out with as many cars as we can and report to Brigade Headquarters at once' - all this said in one breath.

Very soon the whole camp was astir, whistles blowing, drivers and gunners rushing madly into the wrong stores in search of the wrong articles, engines being started up and 'konking' out again, and cries of 'That bus of yours full up, Private Jones?' 'Yes, sergeant,' to a lance-corporal. 'Where's my blinking spare parts case?' 'Please sir, Private Wobble, driver of *Repulse*, is gone out.' 'Well, you can drive the damn thing, can't you? Get on with it!' 'Please sir, I've only got two spare tubes.' 'There are about 700 in the stores my good man; for heaven's sake use your brains, and get some.' 'But the storeman is out, sir.' 'Blast the storeman. Get the tubes somehow.' 'You ready, Mr H?' 'No. I'm one gunner short.' 'Pinch that sentry then, he looks capable and, what's more,

he's got a gun which is more than I have.' 'All aboard - right ho - order of march, *Ramillies*, *Repulse*, *Revenge*, *Renown* and *Royal Sovereign* - Blank Brigade Headquarters as hard as you can go.'

And in eight-and-a-half minutes from the receipt of the telephone message, three Rolls armoured cars and two Rolls tenders, fully armed and manned with wondrous crews, some men with and some without coats, one man in running shorts, a sergeant with only one puttee, a lance-corporal with his shirt outside where it should have been inside, and so on pulled up outside the general's house...

Mr A, being the senior officer, was seen disappearing into the general's house garbed in a concoction of wearing apparel in good harmony with that of the men. So we will now transfer our imaginations into the presence of the general. 'Hallo sir!' says Mr A, inanely, really meaning to say 'Section reported present,' or some such military salutation. 'Hallo, my boy!' says the general having been put off his guard, 'how many cars have you brought? You have been very quick.' 'Three Rolls and two tenders, sir.' General S up to this moment had not looked up from a sheet of paper on which he was scratching hasty instructions, and it was about this moment that our Mr A realised that his vestage was not that in which he would normally report to his brigadier. A white cricket shirt open at the neck covered by a graphite and oil-spotted drill jacket, surmounting a very short and even dirtier pair of shorts, with the crowning effort of a soft and very distorted FS cap, and at his lowest extremities a pair of blue and red 'Soccer' stockings, did not exactly add to his appearance or dignity. So when General S did look up, our Mr A was quite prepared for any remarks that might follow. 'Good Lord, you can't go down to Jaffa like that.' 'Jaffa, sir?' says our Mr A, dismayed at a destination he had never contemplated; 'I understood Government House.' 'No, Jaffa - riots started there at one o'clock, and I believe there's the devil of a row going on,' and after a further survey of this wondrously attired individual - 'What are your men like?' 'Much worse, sir.' 'Well, it can't be remedied now, there's no time. Get on down to Jaffa as hard as you can go, and report to Colonel____; he's the governor; I'll see you about your turn-out later; here's your written orders; carry on.' 'Yes, sir,' falters Mr A in sudden fear lest the absence of a sun-helmet at that time of day might be commented on, and hastily reappears in the street.

Despite this rather chaotic start the section acquitted itself very well indeed during the riots which took some four weeks to put down.

RE-EQUIPPING WITH LIGHT TANKS

As explained earlier, the armoured car companies were re-equipped with light tanks in the 1930s. Maj.-Gen Bob Foote, VC, was then serving with 7th Armoured Car Company and remembers the first light tanks to arrive:

In 1930 Sir Philip Chetwood, who was C-in-C India, decided to buy four Vickers Mark 1A light tanks to see if they were suitable for conditions in India, particularly those in the North-West Frontier to protect convoys in that area. Col N. M. Dillon, who was Colonel RTC at GHQ India, was given the task of organising the trials. I was then adjutant 7th ACC at Lahore, commanded by

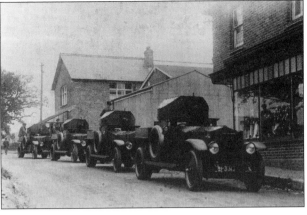

A line of immaculate Rolls Royce armoured cars in the centre of Bovington village (known as 'Tin Town') TM

Major King, and was told to raise a troop to man the tanks on their arrival at Chaklala, which was the repair workshop for the North-West Province. Vickers sent an engineer, a Mr Butler, to assist and we had an RASC major with engineering experience to help from workshops. I took a sergeant and four drivers to look after the tanks and drive them on the trials.

At Chaklala we were able to call on Rawalpindi Arsenal for help in designing the inside stowage and gun-control equipment. We were to take the tanks up to Razmak and carry out trials under frontier conditions. At that time all the convoys had to be escorted by armoured cars and infantry piqueting the hills on either side of the road. The infantry were often attacked by tribesmen as they withdrew from the hilltops. But the tanks could stay on top until the infantry had withdrawn, and stop the tribesmen from attacking them. At the end of the trials I was told by Col Dillon to lay on a demonstration for

More Rolls Royce armoured cars, this time on yet another parade between the wars. TM

Rolls armoured cars of 12 ACC taking part in the King's Birthday Parade at Marlborouch Barracks, Dublin, on 22 June 1922. TM

General Chetwood and all the top brass. He told me to make it as spectacular as possible but as safe as possible as we did not want any breakdowns.

We laid on a demo of climbing in and out of nullahs, knocking down walls, and trench-crossing capabilities. Halfway through the demo Chetwood stopped it and summoned everyone to hear his verdict. We were all very relieved when he said: 'Gentlemen, I think we have seen enough to show that light tanks are obviously very suitable for the North-West Frontier and I am going to order enough to equip two light tank companies straightaway.'

Gradually all the armoured-car companies were re-equipped with light tanks and in June 1936 all companies were designated Light Tank Companies. They would not remain thus for very long and in 1938, the first two light tank companies (8th and 10th) handed over their duties to the mechanised cavalry regiments and were disbanded. One of the last to go was the 6th Light Tank Company, the C-in-C inspecting its final parade in front of the Red Fort at Delhi. A contemporary newspaper report read:

Light tanks of 2 Lt Tk Coy taking part in the Viceroy's Inspection Parade at Peshawar, 1934. TM

On the Bela ground in front of the ancient walls of the Red Fort which had so long been their home, the men of this unit, which in its short life-time has done such notable service, paraded together for the last time. It was an impressive ceremony and one not without a note of sadness.

On his arrival the Commander-in-Chief was received by Major H.C.J. Yeo, Officer Commanding, and inspected the company which was formed up in close columns, 21 tanks and 12 lorries, manned by 109 other ranks, being on parade. The company then formed a hollow square and was addressed by the Commander-in-Chief. His Excellency said that the company had been on service in India for the past 17 years. During that time it had distinguished itself on active service, particularly in the operations in Waziristan in 1937 when its gallant actions and service were suitably rewarded. The unit had also distinguished itself in the field of sport, particularly football. The standard of discipline in the unit stood very high and one of which every man ought to be proud. In his opinion it was second to none. It was a sad thought that a unit like that should be broken up to meet the need of reorganisation but he was sure that wherever each of them might go, he would maintain that very high tradition and remember the happy days they spent with the 6th LTC. His Excellency wished them all good luck.

The Commander-in-Chief then took up a position on the side of the road and the company marched past the line, His Excellency taking the salute.

In Egypt also the tanks were coming. In the case of 3rd Armoured Car Company in 1929 they handed over their armoured cars to the 12th Lancers, provided all the instructors needed to help them convert, and were issued with Vickers Medium Mark IIs in their place. As Col Alec Dow recalls:

They were the first tanks to be used in Egypt and everyone from the GOC downwards took great interest in their performance both tactically, mechanically, and in their fire power. Many experiments and demonstrations were indulged in. On the whole we had less mechanical trouble than we feared, chiefly trackpins, main sprockets and petrol pumps.

Wireless had not by then been fitted and we relied on wooden semaphore signals, later coloured flags for tank to tank communication. Internal communication was at first by 'voice tubes' followed by the laryngaphone - as used then in submarines. Experiments were carried out in various colours for camouflage, including my own tank in pink and black, but all attempts were soon abandoned. More important to us at this time was to overcome the heat inside these tanks

Gen Cassels, C-in-C India, took this farewell parade of the 6th Lt Tk Coy, when it was disbanded at Delhi on 28 February 1939. TM

in summer. In the end the turret and hull were covered by white asbestos sheeting with a ¼ in air gap between the asbestos and the armour.

In 1930 somebody decided to embark on what must then have been the longest distance tank exercise - from Cairo to Alexandria by the desert route and return. No serious mechanial break-down occurred, but some four days were needed for tracks, bodies and sprocket replacements in Alexandria before returning through a blinding sandstorm.

TERRITORIAL ARMY ARMOURED CAR COMPANIES

In 1923 certain Yeomanry Regiments were mechanised and converted into RTC Armoured

Whilst light tanks were supplementing armoured cars abroad, the TA had to make do with much older vehicles. Here a vintage WWI Peerless of the 23rd (London) Armoured Car Company, helps 'Keep the Army in the Public Eye' with a bevy of beauty in the turret – note the solid rubber tyres! TM

Car Companies of the Territorial Army. They were:

> 19th (Lothian and Border Horse)
> 20th (Fife and Forfar Yeomanry)
> 21st (Royal Gloucestershire Hussars)
> 22nd (Westminster Dragoons)
> 23rd (Sharpshooters)
> 24th (Derbyshire Yeomanry)
> 25th (Northamptonshire Yeomanry)
> 26th (East Riding of Yorkshire Yeomanry)

These Yeomanry affiliations ended in 1938 when they reverted to full regimental status and their proper titles. However, the Lothian and Border Horse and the Westminster Dragoons remained affiliated to the RTC.

A GEORGE CROSS FOR THE RTC

Pte Frank Naughton of 10th Light Tank Company was awarded the Empire Gallantry Medal on 1 February 1937 when, with complete disregard for his own safety, he rescued L-Cpl S. Temple from the flooded Indayani River near Moshi on 5 August 1936. In September 1940 this award was superseded by the George Cross by Royal Warrant.

POTTED HISTORIES

The histories of the various Armoured Car/Light Tank Companies can be usefully summarised as follows:

1st and **2nd Companies** were formed in Wareham in January 1920 and **3rd** and **4th Companies** in Bovington two months later, with personnel drawn from the 4th Battalion.

Light tanks and armoured cars of 7 Lt Tk Coy on parade at Peshawar in 1937. TM

The **1st Company** went to Mesopotamia in May 1920, and arriving at Basra the following month, where they absorbed 15 LAMB. This was disbanded on its return to England in February 1923, but was later reformed in Bovington and Lulworth to become the 1st Light Tank Company in 1936. This was, in turn, disbanded in 1939.

The career of the **2nd Company** followed a similar pattern. After a period of service in India it became the 2nd Light Tank Company in April 1933, but was disbanded in 1939.

The **3rd and 4th Companies** were transferred from Bovington to Worgret Camp in May 1920 before moving out to Egypt the following month. The 3rd Company became an Independent Tank Company in 1929 handing over their armoured cars to 12 RL and was redesignated the 3rd Medium Tank Company. In April 1933 they formed the nucleus of 6 RTC.

Meanwhile, the **4th Company** went on from Egypt to reach Palestine in September 1920. After a brief tour of duty the unit was returned to the UK and disbanded in June 1922.

A busy camp scene at the Brigade camp at Hassan Abdul, 1934, with light tanks being worked on in the ad hoc tank park. TM

Light tanks leaving Miramshah Fort in the North-West Frontier Province, July 1938.
Despite the sceptics, they performed very well over the rough terrain. TM

In 1935-36, long before the harmful effects of asbestos were known, trials were held in Egypt to use asbestos cladding
on tanks to reduce the heat levels inside. This Vickers Medium tank belonged to 6 RTC. TM

The **5th Company** was raised in Dublin from 17 AC Battalion in May 1920. Three years later, in March 1923, it was posted to Scarborough. Overseas duties followed, first in Shanghai in January 1927 and then Egypt later that year. Like the 3rd Company, it lost its armoured cars to 12 RL in 1929, becoming an Independent Tank Company, and then forming the nucleus of 6 RTC in April 1933 with 3rd Company.

The **6th Company** was formed in Mesopotamia in August 1920, drawing its personnel from LAMB. The unit was posted to India in December 1921, became the 6th Light Tank Company in 1936 and was disbanded in 1939.

All the remaining units were formed in Wareham and with one exception (12th Company), served in India. The **7th and 8th Companies** were formed in May 1920 from 4th Battalion personnel and reached India in January of the following year. The **7th Company** took part in light tank trials in 1930, became the 7th Light Tank Company in April 1933 and was much involved in relief work after the Quetta earthquake in May 1935. The unit was disbanded in 1939. **8th Company** sent a section to the Malabar Force in October 1921, and was disbanded in March 1938.

9th Company, formed in October 1920, and the **10th Company**, formed three months later in January 1921, both arrived in India in March 1921. In March 1935 they became the 9th and 10th Light Tank Companies before being disbanded in 1939 and March 1938 respectively.

Similarly, **11th Company**, formed in March 1921, eventually became the 11th Light Tank Company, and was disbanded in 1939.

Lastly, **12th Company** was posted to Ireland in May 1922 within a year of its formation in July 1921. It carried out strike duties at Warrington during the General Strike of 1926. Three years later, on disbandment in March 1929, the unit's armoured cars were transferred to 11 H.

Meanwhile, back in Blighty, the NAAFI did a roaring trade in tea and sticky buns! . TM

---

[1] It has to be said that his success with the Armoured Car Companies, especially when working with aircraft, led directly to the RAF making a 'take-over' bid for Iraq where, in 1922, they formed their own armoured car units.

[2] *A Short History of the Royal Tank Corps* published in 1938.

Chapter 7

MECHANISATION AND EXPANSION

TOWARDS MECHANISATION

Whilst the armoured car companies were involved all over the world helping to police the British Empire, major events were taking place at home. Despite the initial post-war prejudice against the tank and mechanisation which pervaded the British Army from top to bottom, it would be wrong to think that no progress whatsoever was being made. Although the remaining Tank Corps units had to make do with old Mark Vs and Whippets from the war, many new designs were being produced for new tanks, especially of the lighter variety - tankettes as they were popularly called which made up for their lack of firepower and armoured protection by being cheap and easy to produce. They had the merit of being adequate training vehicles, despite their lack of sophistication such as not having a rapid means of communication on the move. The first Chief of the Imperial General Staff to be converted to the new gospel was Sir George Milne who, in 1925, declared his intention to mechanise the Army, with the tank in the principal role. To emphasise his point he chose Fuller as his Military Assistant. However, the road would be a long and hard one before this goal could be achieved.

EXPERIMENTAL ARMOURED FORMATIONS

An experimental mechanised brigade was formed on a temporary basis as early as 1921, but it was not until 1926 that it was really decided to go above the level of the tank battalion and to form a larger force, known as the Experimental Mechanised Force, which came into being on Salisbury Plain in May 1927. It comprised tanks, infantry, machine-gunners and artillery. The mixture of armoured and unarmoured vehicles in the formation proved to be very difficult to handle. 1929 saw further experimentation with light tank battalions and the following year the first improvised armoured brigade, containing two tank battalions, plus supporting arms, was introduced. Despite the obvious need for an all-arms team, there was a strong body of opinion, supported by Fuller, that armoured forces should consist almost entirely of tanks, with supporting arms being considered as an unjustifiable hindrance to the speed of manoeuvre of the tanks, although it was recognised that they would need to be attached for particular operations.

The Experimental Force, the ancestor of all future armoured divisions, comprised all available units of the different arms that had been mechanised, viz:

3rd Battalion, RTC - HQ and two companies of armoured cars, one company of tankettes.

5th Battalion, RTC - HQ and three companies of medium tanks.

2nd Battalion, Somerset LI - machine-gun battalion (motorised and half tracks).

In September 1927, Winston Churchill, then Chancellor of the Exchequer, attended a special demonstration laid on by the Experimental Mechanised Force on Salisbury Plain. It was a very significant event because, as Liddell Hart puts it: …'it provided a foretaste of the high-speed indirect approach and encircling manoeuvre that the prophets had forecast'. It was the first time theory was put into practice by an organised force and the potentialities of mechanised speed and manoeuvre demonstrated on the ground. The medium tanks belonged to 5 RTC. TM

9th Field Brigade, RA - two batteries towed (by Dragons), one battery half-tracks and one self-propelled.

9th Light Battery, RA - 3.7in howitzers in half-tracks.

17th Field Company, RE - motorised.

Also in support for many exercises were:

No 16 (Army Co-operation) Squadron, RAF No. 3 (Fighter) Squadron, RAF

Nos 7 & 11 (Bombing) Squadrons, RAF.

For movement the Force was generally divided into three groups, known as: 'Fast', 'Medium' and 'Slow'. The 'Fast Group' consisted only of armoured cars and was expected to travel about 100 miles a day, at an average speed of 25mph. The 'Medium Group' contained the light artillery battery, the sapper

Fortunately, HM King George Vth, our Colonel-in-Chief, shared Churchill's enthusiasm for the Experimental Mechanised Force. Here he talks to Col (later Lt Gen Sir Charles) Broad, whilst looking at a Carden Loyd Mk V from the 3rd Battalion. TM

company and the machine-gun battalion and was set to cover 50 miles a day at 10mph. The 'Slow Group' contained the tanks, both the medium battalion and the tankette company, plus the remaining artillery. A day's march for them was set at 30 miles, average speed being 7mph. Of course there were speed problems within groups, while on cross-country the 'Slow Group' could normally manage a faster pace than the 'Medium Group', but this grouping formed the basis of Standing Orders for the Mechanised Force.

An example of how successful mechanised forces could be against unmechanised forces was given in the manoeuvres of 1927, when they were ranged against a much larger force of infantry (3 Division) and cavalry (2 Brigade). Initially the two forces started 80 miles apart, the larger force then had to push eastwards to secure high ground near Andover some 30 miles from their start line, while the Mechanised Force tried to stop them. Liddell Hart describes the latter's efforts as looming like a cloud on the commander's horizon, which paralysed the horse and foot soldiers. The 'Fast Group' circled around the enemy's cavalry screen - they had travelled 40 miles in the first hour and seized a series of vital bridges unopposed, allowing the rest of the Mechanised Force to get into a flanking position between the enemy cavalry screen and its main body. Lt-Col M.A. Studd, DSO, MC, who took part in this exercise with the Heavy Group, explained how

the Mechanised Force Commander decided to attack with two tank companies, supported by low-flying aircraft:

> This attack got through the hostile screen of anti-tank artillery and inflicted heavy casualties on the infantry. Finally, just before dusk the third tank company was put in. In the semi-darkness it achieved complete surprise and also inflicted heavy casualties on the infantry who were forced to scatter… The attack owed much of its success to the successful combination of tanks and aircraft.
>
> In the end the exercise had to be called off as the larger force could only get halfway to its objective.

THE PURPLE PRIMER

In 1929 the first War Office manual on armoured warfare *Mechanized Armoured Formations*, drafted by Col (Later Lt-Gen) Charles Broad was published. Because of its colour, it was known to all as the 'Purple Primer' and was avidly read, not only by the British Army but also such German armoured enthusiasts as Guderian, who managed to obtain a copy through the treachery of an infantry officer named Baillie Stewart, who was court-martialled and confined to the Tower of London, thereby gaining unwarranted fame as 'The Officer in the Tower'.

FURTHER REORGANISATION

In 1930, tank battalions were reorganised; a close support battery (6 close support tanks mainly for providing smokescreens) was added to each Battalion HQ, while there was one light tank company (32 light tanks, although some were Carden Loyd MG carriers instead of tanks) and two medium tank companies (each of 16 Vickers mediums). The battalion and brigade organisations were to change constantly as training progressed; for example, a complete light tank battalion was introduced into the mechanised brigade.

THE TANK BATTALIONS LEAVE BOVINGTON

While the 1st (Depot) Battalion moved only a short distance down the road from Worgret Camp, Wareham, to Bovington in May 1921, it did not officially become known as the RTC Depot until 10 June 1927. It would be another seven years before the 1st (Light) Battalion was re-formed and moved first to Perham Down and then on to Egypt in 1938.[1] The others moved further afield. 2nd moved to Pinehurst Barracks, Farnborough, in Aldershot Command in March 1921. They would remain there until 1939. 2nd became part of the Experimental Mechanised

A high standard of turnout. This typical picquet outside their guard tent, shows the extremely high standard of turnout maintained by the RTC. A great deal of their two shillings a day pay in the 1930s went towards purchasing Brasso, Bluebell, Blanco and Cherry Blossom boot polish! TM

Brigade, was visited by HM King George V and Queen Mary in 1922 (they would also visit Bovington and Lulworth in the late twenties), and was issued the first new Vickers tanks in 1924. 5th Battalion was the next to move, in April 1922, when they left for Perham Down Camp, near Tidworth in Southern Command. On 10 April 1923, 3rd Battalion departed for Lydd Camp, Kent, in Eastern Command.[2] In November 1923 'B' Company of the 3rd went over to Cologne to relieve 'B' Company of the 5th Battalion. It returned on 26 January 1926, being the last formed body of British troops to cross the Rhine. Last to leave Bovington was the 4th Battalion, which had expanded from a cadre to a complete unit on 1 April 1922. Initially it had moved only to Bovington in June 1925 when Wareham Camp closed down, but later the battalion moved up to Catterick in Northern Command.

1 TANK BRIGADE

In one of the most important developments, 1 Tank Brigade was formed on 1 April 1934. Brigadier P.C.S. Hobart, DSO, OBE, MC, assumed the dual role of Brigade Commander and Inspector of the Corps. His brigade comprised:

> Brigade HQ at Pinehurst Barracks, Farnborough
> 1st (Light) Tank Battalion at Perham Down
> 2nd Tank Battalion at Farnborough
> 3rd Tank Battalion at Lydd
> 5th Tank Battalion at Perham Down

The Tank Brigade fought as a brigade in the Army manoeuvres on Salisbury Plain that year under the eagle eye of 'Hobo', truly the greatest ever armoured trainer. It then served under Maj-Gen G.M. Lindsay, another distinguished officer of the RTC, who commanded the Mobile Force in the 'Mobile Force Exercise' in which, despite the worst efforts of the opponents of armour, it distinguished itself. Nevertheless,the Army prejudice against the RTC and armoured development remained strong, so real progress was painfully slow. The Germans, however, took full advantage of the lessons being demonstrated by the British, and, although they did not form their first tank battalion until 1934, they had three complete panzer divisions by October 1935 and six by 1939. We, on the other hand, did not start to form a true armoured division until 1937 and had but two incomplete ones when war began.

JOINING THE CORPS BETWEEN THE WARS

'Generically, newly-joined subalterns were known as *Warts*, a wart being an unpleasant excrescence on the face of the Regiment.' So reads the opening sentence of a splendid article which appeared in *The Tank* some years ago and gives a graphic description of a young officer on training at Bovington:

On arrival at Bovington the newly joined were immediately put on the 'Square', and there drilled by drill instructors who knew far less about drill than they did. But there were two honourable exceptions to this. One was the Regimental Sergeant Major who was known as 'Tisshup' due to the peculiar noises he occasioned by clearing the phlegm from his throat before giving a command. The other was a Quartermaster Sergeant of the Household Cavalry who, when one of his charges made a mistake, would project his 6ft 4ins on to the square in an attitude of prayer, and on his knees with his eyes turned up to heaven would address the offender in far from biblical terms. One of our favourite amusements was to feign collective deafness as a squad, and continue to march smartly off the square into the moorland beyond it while the instructor got redder in the face and hoarser in the voice. This worked well until one day when the squad was well off the course and into the rough, they heard, close behind them, the dreaded 'Tisshup'. There followed an agonising twenty minutes of doubling over the very rough countryside. After that the squad remained on the square.

Our accommodation had to be seen to be believed. We were housed in a collection of huts known as 'Siberia'. They were neither draught-proof nor rain-proof. The only way to sleep in comfort was to hoist an umbrella or waterproof

Recruits – Various Stages at the Depot.

The New Recruit.   *Stage I.*   *Stage II.*   *Stage III.*

HM King George Vth was never happier than when visiting his troops. Here he is visiting the Gunnery School at Lulworth on 24 April 1928. The first Colonel Commandant of the RTC, Maj-Gen Sir John Capper, can just be seen behind him. TM

sheet above the bed, and to buy a large dog to act as a mobile hot water bottle. Nor did the present mess exist. The mess was a series of interlocking huts, but they were waterproof.

After completing our period on the square, we proceeded to do our elementary D & M and Gunnery courses at what was then known as the Central Schools. The courses lasted two months each. This was long before the days of Methods of Instruction, and of teams who spent their lives going round minding other people's business. The amount of instruction one imbibed depended on one's instructor's personality to a very great extent, and on one's own receptivity. At Bovington our instructor was an excellent wielder of the crowbar and sledgehammer, but during periods of theory, which he learnt by heart, rather after the manner of a museum guide, it was quite possible to steer him on to dirty stories after the first ten minutes of the period, these stories getting bluer and bluer as the period progressed to its salacious end. On the other hand, at Lulworth our instructor was so good that one could not help learning from him. He had an inexhaustible capacity for beer, and the more beer he drank the better he instructed. When the writer went back to Lulworth as an instructor twelve years later he was still there, bless him.

Having spent a period of nearly nine months gestation one was expelled from the womb of Bovington far more conscious of one's shortcomings, insofar as regimental soldiering was concerned, than a newborn babe. The writer was posted to the 3rd Tanks, who were then at Lydd, less one squadron who were occupying a small portion of Germany.

Lydd, as many will know, is a pleasant little village in the south-west corner of Romney Marsh. Between Lydd and Dungeness lies a five-mile wilderness of shingle. This was our training ground. This sounds very dreary, but in fact that part of the country has a strange attraction of its own, and no one ever wanted to leave Lydd when the time came to move on. This was not only due to the countryside but to our Colonel and the Second-in-Command. The former was an awe-inspiring individual to the newly joined, until one got to know the enormous fund of kindness behind the military facade. He had four loves, the Regiment, his wife, his dogs and his horses. What man can want more? The Second-in-Command was also a big man in every sense of the word, with an inexhaustible fund of reminiscences, so much so that we had a duty roster of subalterns to sit up with him after dinner and listen to his memoirs. It was also rumoured that he wore spurs when driving his very ancient Chevrolet. These he used to press into the floor boards with wild oaths when ascending a hill, as he was not quite sure how to change gear.

Training was very simple. One did individual training in the winter and squadron training in the summer. The Regiment was equipped with 1918 pattern Mark V tanks. The majority were male, but our troop had one female tank, which was our pride and our delight. Once a week

On manoeuvres. The crew of this Vickers Medium are making an excellent job of camouflaging their tank during manoeuvres on the Sussex-Hampshire border. TM

Above: *A Vickers Medium Mark II, belonging to 5 RTC fording the River Wylie during an exercise. Some 200 of these 13.2 ton tanks were built.* TM

Left: *This Vickers Medium Mark Ia, belonging to 2 RTC, has had its main armament removed and been turned into a wireless control vehicle - note the large radio mast on the back of the turret.* TM

Below: *'Three Cheers for His Majesty!' Vickers Mediums and their crews of A Coy 5 RTC, celebrate the King's Birthday.* TM

during the summer the whole squadron would make a complete circuit of the training area at an average speed of two to three miles per hour. If one got round without a breakdown it took the whole morning. No one worked in the afternoon, summer or winter, although, as will be seen later, one's afternoons were much more energetic than one's mornings. In the summer we also used to loose off our 6pdr guns at large white targets. This was an astonishingly accurate gun, but of very low velocity. If one had not wined too well the evening before it was possible to see the shell wending its way towards the target. That completed our highest form of training. At the end of September, the tanks were put away into heavy preservation and left in the hangar until the weather became seasonable again the following April. So one passed into the individual training-cum-leave season period or, as our forebears would put it, we went into winter quarters…

But let it not be thought that all life was as easy as this. Our real work began in the afternoon. At that time the Regiment had a cross-country training team much above the average, a boxing team which had to train and be trained in the winter, and a very good athletic team to keep us occupied in the summer. These gladiators were a race apart, they lived in separate barrack rooms; had special rations, and got inside tanks even more seldom than the ordinary mortals.

THE TWELVE DISCIPLES

Before leaving the subject of subalterns it is worth mentioning the first batch of subalterns who were gazetted into the Tank Corps from Sandhurst in 1923. They were twelve in number and became known as 'The Twelve Apostles'. The next batch numbered five and were called 'The Minor Prophets'. Thereafter, no more appropriate Biblical names could be found for subsequent batches. As one of the last remaining Twelve Apostles reflected in a letter to *The Tank*: 'Fifty years of much reflection have failed to convince me personally that we ever earned any right to a Biblical reference.'

TAKING THE KING'S SHILLING

Another article from *The Tank*, written by Mr R.W. Munns, tells of how he joined the Army in 1931 at the height of the Depression, when recruiting centres were able to be very selective.

I was 19 years old when I first visited the Army Recruiting Office in Liverpool. I was attested, swore to serve the King, his heirs and successors, and finally given the King's shilling. Within a short time I had signed on for six years with the

colours in the Royal Tank Corps and recall that I was given two days' pay with ration money, which amounted to about six shillings, and told to report again to the Recruiting Office in two days' time when I would be despatched to the RTC Depot in Bovington, Dorset. I had never been more than 20 miles from Liverpool before, and it was quite an experience two days later to be put on the train at Lime Street Station by the Recruiting Sergeant, bound for London with two other recruits who were going to Woolwich to join the Royal Artillery. My father came to see me off, and after pulling out of the station we settled down to a game of pontoon, which we thought was right and proper for three new members of the licentious soldiery. On arrival at Euston I left my RA companions and, never having been in London before, found it rather confusing to get to Waterloo Station from where the 'Belle', as it was called, left for Bournemouth Central. I then changed to a train going to Weymouth, which stopped at Wool and I arrived about 6.30pm where a single-decker Hants and Dorset bus took me to Bovington Camp. Being late November it was dark and cold and the conductor, who had obviously seen recruits arrive before, was very kind and told me I should report to the Guard Room and as I got off the bus he showed me the way there. It was a few hundred yards from the bus stop, which gave me time to reflect on what lay ahead of me. I was tired, having been on the way since I left home that morning; I was hungry, as I hadn't eaten anything substantial on the journey; and I was cold, as I was dressed in only a threadbare suit with holes developing in the knees. All these things combined made me feel apprehensive as I approached the dimly lit Guard Room where I saw a uniformed soldier wearing a black beret marching up and down the concrete veranda. I didn't realise that I shouldn't have spoken to him when on guard duty, so when I mentioned that I was a new recruit he didn't reply but motioned to the door of the Guard Room, so I climbed the steps from the road, knocked and entered. I found the remainder of the Guard sitting at a wooden table on which were plates of food and mugs of tea, and it made me realise how hungry I was. The room was warm and the Sergeant invited me to sit down and give him some details of myself. Finally he asked if I had eaten and when I told him I had had a sandwich and a cup of tea at Waterloo, he offered me some of their food, including a mug of hot tea poured out of a bucket, saying it was too late to get any food from the dining-room at that time of night. The apprehension that I had experienced earlier disappeared and I felt much better for having eaten some food and sitting close to a warm combustion stove. I was taken by one of

The cup that cheers! Colour Sergeant (later RSM) Sinclair of the 4th Battalion, dispenses cups of char at Catterick where 4 RTC were stationed in the 1930s. TM

the Guard (who I found out later was the stick orderly) to the recruits' hut, where I was handed over to the NCO in charge of recruits.

There was little time for introduction on that evening of 23 November 1931 and I was happy to get some sleep after being shown how to make an Army bed with three mattresses, or biscuits, filled with coir, sheets like sandpaper, and a pillow of the same material filled with straw. I was tired but slept fitfully because of the interruptions by the Guard, and I heard my first reveille sounded on a trumpet at 6.30am the following morning. I washed and shaved along with the others, in the cold water of the annexe between the recruits' hut and the next one. I was shown how to make up my bed and at 7.30am L-Cpl Ferguson marched the five of us to 'B' Company dining-room where I had my first Army breakfast after standing in a long queue. As I remember, it was a piece of bacon with a fried egg, which had a kind of plastic skin over it, with two pieces of bread, a mug of tea and a pat of margarine.

That first morning in Bovington Camp was a new and strange experience, but not unpleasant - it was a fine clear morning and I was impressed with the views of the surrounding countryside. I had been brought up in a city and seen little of the rural beauty of England and I found it pleasing to be in this setting instead of being surrounded by terraced houses, warehouses, docks and hordes of traffic. To the north I could see moorland stretching as far as the eye could see, and to the east and south farmland and woodland, and to the west the camp buildings which made up Bovington, the Royal Tank Corps Depot. I came to have great affection for the area and spent many hours tramping over the moors and woodlands during the time I was stationed at Bovington...

During this build-up period of squad personnel, we were becoming more accustomed to Army life - marching to the dining-room for meals, making beds up in the morning and down after the last parade in the afternoon, cleaning the barrack-room each morning by each recruit tidying his own bedspace, and the room being swept and dry-scrubbed. Cleaning utensils such as brooms, dryscrubbers, etc laid out in regimental fashion on the floor after being washed with soap and water; table tops and forms scrubbed white; personal kit boxes left tidy in front of made-up beds with mug, knife, fork and spoon laid out on top; fireplaces cleaned after the previous night's fire, with black-lead and whitewash; windows cleaned; wash bowls and toilets cleaned in the annexe, and a last minute dusting before being inspected by the NCO in charge…

Before reaching the required number of recruits to form a squad for training, we had been issued with the regulation kit from the RQMS stores. This consisted of two uniforms, one for best and one for everyday use, including the appropriate RTC shoulder badges, small silver-coloured collar badges, (or collar dogs), two black berets with cap badges, two pairs of heavy Army boots, which had to be 'boned' to produce a high polish, two of all underwear, including the rough Army shirts, a 'housewife' - not the flesh and blood type, but a small linen pouch with needles, cottons, thread, wool, etc, for first-line repairs to clothing. Also a mug, knife, fork and spoon, toothbrush, shaving brush, razor, comb, hairbrush and a brass button-stick, a greatcoat, woollen gloves, a short cane with a silver knob on which was engraved the RTC crest and, most important of all at this particular time, two pairs of brown overalls or dungarees, which we wore daily until training commenced. Each day we would be detailed for a 'fatigue', which usually started at 7.30am and continued late into the afternoon. Every day these fatigues would be posted on the company notice board and there was no lack of variety in the work they entailed. The two popular ones were the Sergeants' Mess and the Officers' Mess, as there was spare food to be had, and this was important to a growing nineteen-year-old. These two jobs mainly consisted of washing up the dirty pans, crockery and cutlery after breakfast, morning tea, lunch and tea at 4pm, but occasionally one had to return in the evening to help out with the dinner, which was quite rewarding in the way of left-overs.

The worst fatigue was washing the tins and plates in the main depot cookhouse, and this one was avoided whenever possible. Plates for three companies of men would have to be washed after breakfast and the midday meal - no plates were used for tea, and there was no evening meal. As well as the plates, all the tins used in the cooking had to be washed and some were so large they would have to be placed on the floor, filled with hot water and liquid soap, and cleaned with an ordinary bass broom. Then there were the large coppers in which the vegetables were cooked, the

lids being lifted by a weighted chain. One had to climb inside these monsters to clean them ready for the next meal… Of course, there was the NAAFI canteen and one or two other cafes within the perimeter of the camp, but money was scarce and what wages we received on the Friday of each week was soon spent and didn't last much longer than the weekend. All recruits were paid 14s per week, 4s of which were deducted to cover the cost of haircuts, washing, items of clothing bought from the QM stores, etc., and any credit left in this account could be drawn when going on leave. Of the 10s actually drawn each week, 5s were sent home. Out of the remaining 5s I bought the usual toiletries, white and khaki

Presentation of Long Service and Good Conduct Medals to men of 5th RTC in 1930. Old soldiers would put a safety pin into their tunics onto which the medal could be hung, so that it didn't fall off as soon as they stamped their feet! TM

These light tanks, belong to the 5th Battalion and were ideal training vehicles, being light, fast and manoeuvrable, however, they would prove of little use in combat against better armoured and armed tanks when war came. This column is a mixture of Lt Mk VI and Lt Mk II and it is lined up outside the battalion's newly-built brick barracks at Perham Down, circa 1934. TM

blanco for my webbing equipment, 'Bluebell' polish for buttons and other brasses, boot polish and other small items - the balance, which was not a lot, could be spent on food...

I found the training programme exhilarating for a young fit man with the energy to cope with all it entailed, and despite our constant hunger we were really very fit. None of us had any surplus fat and we were to stand the rigours of that winter, although the hard physical training took up most of our energy.

Each day was a full one and any spare time in the evening was spent in preparing for the following day's parades, cleaning equipment, buttons, boots, rifle, etc, with a roll call each evening at 9.30pm, when all recruits stood by their beds as the Orderly Sergeant walked though the barrack-room checking that everyone was present. Lights out was at 10.15pm, shortly followed by the grunts, groans and snores of the recruits until reveille next morning at 6.30am.

The first five weeks' drill was performed with arms to the sides, this being considered to give the recruits a soldierly bearing. It also indicated to the recruits in the other squads that we were in our first five weeks of training - young soldiers with only a few weeks' service - it being very important to know where you stood as far as

length of service was concerned in relation to other recruits. All RTC other ranks had Army numbers starting with 788, but it was the last four numbers that were important. My full number was 7883086 and any recruit with a number after mine was my junior in service, and all recruits knew who was their senior and who was their junior...

Drill movements on the square were made to represent tank movements in the field and so, as well as learning to march correctly, we also learnt crew drill, which was the formations tanks would use when moving in battle - mainly across country. The squad would be made up into five crews, five men being a crew, one of whom was the crew leader who took up his position in front of the other four, the crew leader of No 1 crew being the Section Leader, as senior soldier of the squad. All movements of the crews were controlled by flag signals given by the Squad Sgt who would stand at the other end of the barrack square, blow a whistle to call the attention of the Section Leader, give him a drill signal by the position of his two flags and the Section Leader would transmit the signal to the Crew Leader, who in turn would indicate with their flags the movement to be carried out, and when everyone knew what the formation change was to be, the

On Salisbury Plain at Perham Down, circa 1933, the 5th Battalion RTC, is drawn up for inspection by the Colonel Commandant, Gen Sir John Capper (on left with his hands on his Sam Browne belt). TM

On the road to Lulworth for open-range firing. Tanks, like these Vickers Mediums, usually moved everywhere on their tracks as they did little damage to road surfaces. TM

Section Leader would drop both his flags to his side at the appropriate time and the change of formation would take place as a drill movement. There were a number of these movements such as Line Ahead, Line Abreast, Trident, etc., and, when done smartly, was very effective and good training for later tank manoeuvres on Salisbury Plain. By this time new appointments had been made in the squad and I had replaced Black and been given the job of Section Leader, which not only involved me in the crew drill but gave me overall responsibility for the good behaviour of the squad personnel when off duty, the cleanliness of the barrack rooms in which we lived, the turn-out of the squad on parades and the marching of the squad to meals in the dining-room and areas of training. I continued to do this job until I left the Depot in October 1932 after my training, on being posted to the 3rd Battalion at Lydd in Kent.

Rifle drill was also part of our training and although the .45 Webley revolver was the personal weapon of the RTC at that time, all recruits had to pass out on rifle drill, which included the usual slope arms, order arms, fix and unfix bayonets etc., after which rifles were handed back into stores and we concentrated on

Good shot of a group of immaculately dressed RTC officers, outside Lydd Parish Church in the 1930s. They were probably from the Third Battalion. TM

revolver drill. There was plenty of opportunity to fire the .22 rifle on the miniature range, which was just behind 'B' Company offices, usually on Saturday mornings when .22 competitions were held and, later, the .45 Webley revolver at the ranges on the moors close by - this weapon had considerable 'kick' when fired and was later changed to a .38 calibre.

So training continued, physical training, drill, education, regimental history and later, MPV (or mechanically propelled vehicles). Lessons and lectures being held in the recruits' wing, which was near the Sergeants' Mess. This part of the training I really enjoyed, learning the intricacies

THE ROYAL TANK REGIMENT

of the internal combustion engine, gear boxes, steering, etc., and later putting it into practice, first driving six-wheeled vehicles on the moors and later on the roads within a 20-mile radius of Bovington. This was very exciting and we were able to visit places like Dorchester, Bere Regis, Wareham, Corfe Castle, Swanage, East and West Lulworth, Wool and, on one occasion, Weymouth.

By the 21st week we had completed all our training at the Depot and only had to do the nine weeks' Gunnery Course at Lulworth. At this point the squad was due for seven days' leave and so we were issued with free railway warrants and returned to our respective homes, much

wiser, much fitter and more disciplined than when we had left six months earlier. I enjoyed seeing my parents and friends again, although my friends seemed different, typical civilians; to me they seemed to be untidy, even sloppy, with little or no apparent purpose in life. In contrast, I felt I was part of something which gave me a lot of satisfaction - certainly more so than before I joined the Tanks, when I had felt at a complete loose end. I could hardly wait to get back to Bovington, knowing that I would be going to Lulworth for nine weeks and this was during the summer of 1932. I think all the recruits of 357 Squad were pleased to be back again, at least there was a purpose in our lives and I found it satisfying to be directed towards that purpose. I was sorry to leave Bovington, but found that Lulworth more than replaced the beauty of landscape that I had left behind. Bovington had been

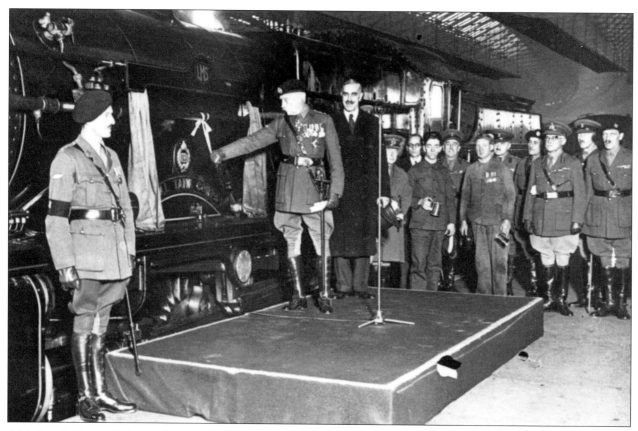

Maj-Gen Sir Ernest Swinton, then Representative Colonel Commandant, christens Locomotive No 45507 as: ROYAL TANK CORPS during a ceremony at Euston Station on 20 November 1937. The nameplate is now on show at the Tank Museum. TM

a new experience for me and I never got tired of walking over the moors, but Lulworth opened up new walks along the chalk cliffs and over the gunnery ranges to Rings Hill, Arishmel Gap, Mupe Bay, Worbarrow Bay, Lulworth Cove, Durdle Door, etc. I never tired of walking over this area, although it was often closed because of firing on the ranges.

Training consisted of learning how to fire a 3pdr gun fitted in a medium tank, with a machine gun fitted coaxially. Using the same trigger mechanism one could fire a 3pdr shell or, by movement of the coaxial lever, a Vickers machine gun. The first few weeks were spent in the classroom stripping and assembling these weapons and competitions were held on how fast the 'lock' of a machine gun could be stripped and assembled - I seem to remember the fastest time was about thirty-two seconds. From the classroom we progressed to the miniature range where 'Rypas' or mock turrets fitted with air guns attached to the 3pdrs, were used to fire at miniature moving targets on huge tables, set out to represent the local countryside with hill, fields, rivers, bridges, etc. It all looked very real from the eye-piece of the gun. The 'Rypa' was made to oscillate and so one had to fire from a moving platform at a moving target, which was good practice for when we did the same exercise with real tanks and guns on the ranges of Bindon Hill.

I suppose there was an element of danger in teaching young recruits to fire a 3pdr shell from a moving tank. Fortunately 357 Squad completed their gunnery training without mishap, but an earlier squad nearly demolished the øfficers' Mess. The 3pdr was fired from a tank on four sides of a square run, each side being about half-a-mile in length. The first side (on the right of the square) ran from north to south, away from the camp and towards Bindon Hill, where all shells were supposed to finish up. At the end of this half-mile the tank turned left - an angle of 90 degrees for the next leg of the run, and the gunner should have traversed his gun 90 degrees to the right to keep the gun pointing down the range. Unfortunately this recruit got a little mixed up and traversed it 90 degrees to the left - the gun was now pointing towards the camp. Worse still he fired, and the shell screamed over the ranges and into the camp, thudding on to the Officers' Mess gardens, just as most of the officers were taking morning tea. There is no record of the comments made by the officers, but the recruit concerned was taken to task and duly reprimanded. Our instructor was Sgt Bastard, ably assisted by our Squad Sergeant and Corporal. From time to time we had visits from Lt-Col J.F. Hope who was CO of the Depot, to see how we were progressing. He would ask questions on

'Look what you've done to our lamp, you'll hear about this from the War Office!' A 1937 cartoon by Colin Campbell, published in the RTC Journal. TM

local knowledge subjects and I well remember not being able to answer one he put to me, and my punishment was to walk to the summit of Rings Hill and back, which for me was a real pleasure. I particularly liked walking over Bindon Hill and down to Mupe Bay, where I learnt to swim. Being summer I did a great deal of walking over the ranges and when it was time to leave Lulworth and return to Bovington I really felt sad at leaving such a lovely spot. So after nine weeks of gunnery we returned to Bovington, having got through our exams with various grades.

Back at Bovington we took up the life as we had known it before, we were relatively old soldiers by now and getting to the end of our training. We did a short period on medium tanks at the D & M Schools and our training was considered complete when we had done a 24hr guard at the same guard room that I had approached so apprehensively nearly twelve months previously.

So ended my training at the Royal Tank Corps Depot, which must have been similar to that of hundreds of other recruits who joined in 1931 - a year which I look back on with happy memories. All the recruits of 357 Squad saw their names posted on Part II Orders as being awarded 3d per day extra for successfully completing their recruits' training. I had recently passed a 2nd Class education exam, which also gave me an extra 3d per day, so my weekly wage increased by 25 per cent from 14s to 17s 6d. Postings were made to all the battalions, and I and three others were posted to the 3rd Battalion at Lydd, Lt-Col Broome. I continued on with company training and battalion training and in July 1933 I was posted back to the D & M Schools, where I spent a very pleasant 4½ years, renewing acquaintance with all the walks on the moors, with an occasional trip to Lulworth where I improved my swimming and tramped the ranges as I had done in the summer of 1932.

HM King Carol of Romania visited England in 1938 and during his visit inspected tanks of both the 2nd and the 4th Battalions at Long Valley, near Aldershot. In the first photograph he inspects a line of Vickers Mediums, belonging to 2 RTC. In the second photograph he is looking at one of the tiny Matilda Mark I, Infantry tanks of 4 RTC. He was accompanied by Lord Gort (on his left), Sir John Dill and other senior officers. TM

TOWARDS WAR AGAIN

By the mid-thirties mechanisation was gathering momentum although Britain lagged far behind other continental armies. The Army Estimates of 1936, for example, contained only £2 million in total for mechanisation. Most of this was to be spent on trucks for the infantry, while less was allowed for tracked vehicles than in the previous year. Brigadier Hobart's annual report gave a graphic indication of the situation:

> ...The Royal Tank Corps has now completely lost the lead in the matter of Numbers, up-to-date Equipment - and now retains superiority, if at all,

only in Maintenance, Organisation and Tactical Methods; and Personnel... As to Numbers. During these last three years our potential enemies have increased enormously their tank corps. In the Royal Tank Corps no such increase has taken place... With only one Tank Brigade, complete training, especially tank v tank, cannot be achieved.

An all too clear indication of the continuing official view of mechanisation was expressed by the Secretary of State for War (Duff Cooper), when he introduced the Army Estimates for 1936. Apologising to the Cavalry for having to start mechanising eight regiments, he said: 'It is like asking a great musical performer to throw away his violin and devote himself in future to the gramophone.'

Fortunately such ostrich-like mentality would be forced to change, but it would leave the British Army woefully short of armoured fighting vehicles when war inevitably came. This is not the place to catalogue the follies of the late thirties, suffice it to say that some progress was made, the Mobile Division came into existence in Egypt in 1938, with 'Hobo' as its commander. It would go on to become the famous 7th Armoured Division, 'the Desert Rats', but sadly the continuing prejudice against its commander would mean him losing his command before they had fired a shot in anger.

EXPANSION AT LAST

In May 1937 the Royal Tank Corps had begun to expand, the 7th Battalion being formed at Catterick Camp on 21 May.[3] A year later, the 8th Battalion was reformed at Perham Down. In 1938 also, as part of the mechanisation of the Army, and in preparation for the war which was even then so inevitable, certain infantry battalions of the Territorial Army were converted into Tank Battalions of the RTC. These were:

7th Bn, The King's Regiment became:
40th RTC at Bootle
10th Bn, The Manchester Regiment became:
41st RTC at Oldham
7th (23 London) Bn, The East Surrey Regiment
became: 42nd RTC at Clapham Junction

6th Bn, Northumberland Fusiliers became:
43rd RTC at Newcastle
6th Bn, The Gloucestershire Regiment became:
44th RTC at Bristol
7th Bn, The West Yorkshire Regiment became:
45th RTC at Leeds

In April 1939, further reorganisation was introduced and the TA doubled its strength, so six more TA Regiments were formed (now RTR) based upon the original six, viz:

46th (Liverpool Welsh) Bn RTR at Liverpool
47th (Oldham) Bn RTR at Oldham
48th Bn RTR at Clapham Common
49th Bn RTR at Newcastle
50th Bn RTR at Bristol
51st Bn RTR at Leeds

Throughout the spring and summer of 1939 the 12 TA Regiments of the RTR trained in the evenings and at weekends, their training culminating at camp in August 1939, where they consolidated their individual training and prepared for war.

FORMATION OF THE ROYAL ARMOURED CORPS

On 4 April 1939, Mr Leslie Hore-Belisha, then Secretary of State for War, announced in the House that the newly mechanised regiments of the Cavalry were to combine with the RTC battalions in order to create a single Corps, to be known as the Royal

War clouds gather. Light Mark VIs of A Coy, 1 RTC, on exercise near Mersa Matruh in the Western Desert, circa 1938. (Author's collection)

A9 cruiser tanks belonging to 1 RTC, passing through the streets of an Egyptian town on their way to the desert, 30 May 1938. Note that the number plates have been 'whited-out' on this photograph, however, one can still see the divisional sign of the Mobile Division on the mudguard (a white circle on a scarlet ground - soon to have a scarlet desert rat superimposed inside the circle - Floreat Jerboa!) TM

Armoured Corps (RAC), with precedence immediately before the Royal Artillery. The RAC would deliberately be far more an 'association' than an 'amalgamation', so as not to offend anyone. It was, as Liddell Hart called it: 'A characteristically British compromise that was designed to cause the least possible disturbance of regimental feelings and traditions, even though it complicated organisations.'

For the time being only the 18 already mechanised Cavalry regiments and the eight mechanised Yeomanry regiments would be included, together with the eight regular RTC battalions and their Territorial battalions. All units of the RTC would keep a corporate existence within the new Corps, becoming Battalions (later changed in 1946 to the Cavalry nomenclature of Regiments) of the Royal Tank Regiment. All RAC recruits would have a common uniform and cap badge, which they would wear in training until posted to their units. A new Pay and Records Office would be established, so personnel would eventually be interchangeable between units; however, this process would not be rushed. Regimental identities would be preserved

and all units of the RA: would keep their old designations, distinctions and badges. As Liddell Hart remarked:

This epoch-making change came just on the eve of the outbreak of war. The Royal Tank Corps thus passed away before it had a chance to fight as such. But what it had achieved since 1923 decisively moulded the shape of the war to come.

---

[1] 1st (Light) Battalion also served in Egypt from 24 October 1935 to 24 October 1936.

[2] 3rd Battalion cadre had gone to Ireland in January 1921, but returned to Wareham in April 1922 and was boosted by the arrival of some 20 officers and 400 other ranks from the disbanding Machine-Gun Corps. Later Battalion HQ joined the unit.

[3] 6th Battalion RTC had already been formed in Egypt on 1 April 1933 from 3rd and 5th Tank Companies.

Chapter 8

BLITZKRIEG

WAR IS DECLARED

Major Dai Mitchell, then a Trooper in the 5th Battalion at Perham Down, remembered the momentous day of 3 September 1939:

I remember little about the build-up to war that summer, but what does remain vividly in my memory is being woken up with a mug of tea on the morning that war was declared - Sunday morning and we had been on the tiles all night! Somebody switched on the radio and that dear old fogey Neville Chamberlain was quacking away. Then the penny dropped, a state of war existed between Great Britain and Germany. Life would never be the same again.

War meant the 5th leaving their comfortable barracks and moving under canvas at Windmill Hill, so that a newly formed training regiment could occupy their peacetime quarters. Tents remained their temporary home for two months, whilst they were brought up to full wartime establishment with reservists and had begun to receive new tanks. 5th still had its elderly mediums and light tanks, but received some A9 and A13 cruisers direct from Nuffields. On 29 October they were put at six hours' notice to move, issued with their mobilisation equipment plus full loads of ammunition, and moved to St Albans to join 2nd and 3rd RTR, forming 3rd Armoured Brigade.[1] The brigade later moved up to the Salisbury-Fordingbridge area and would stay there until May 1940 before going to France. The other three regular RTR Battalions in UK were 4th, 7th and 8th (1st and 6th were still in Egypt), they made up 1st Tank Brigade. The 4th had the distinction of being the first RTR unit to be sent to serve with the BEF in France, leaving UK on 19 September 1939, equipped with 50 Matilda Mark I infantry tanks. 4th spent the winter in Picardy and then in the spring moved to the French tank training area at Pacy-sur-Eure, 60 miles west of Paris. The only other British armour in the BEF at that time were cavalry reconnaissance units, equipped with armoured cars and light tanks. The rest of 1 Tank Brigade remained in England, waiting for the issue of the new Matilda Mark II Infantry tank - later to earn its title: *Queen of the Desert* in North Africa. The 7th went over to France 6-7 May 1940,

together with Brigade HQ, but 8th remained behind. 7th had 27 Matilda Mark Is, 23 new Mark IIs and a few light tanks.

At that time the RTR contribution to the British Army as a whole was far greater than just the eight regular Battalions and the 12 newly formed Territorial Army Battalions (40th to 51st RTR inclusive), because they had also provided the essential instructional staff to train the rest of the Royal Armoured Corps in their conversion to tanks and armoured cars. They then helped to build up the converted units to full strength with RTR reservists, because the Cavalry reservists were of no use until retrained. The RTR also provided a large proportion of the executive and technical staff for these units.

THE TRAINING MACHINE EXPANDS

War was only a few hours old when Parliament passed the National Service (Armed Forces) Act, making all physically fit males between the ages of 18 and 41 liable to military service. By the end of 1939, 727 000 men had registered; by 1940 this increased by a further 4 100 000; and in 1941, another 2 200 000 were called up. This meant an enormous increase in the training organisation, including the formation of eleven RAC Training Regiments in the first year of war. Here recruits received a 24-week concentrated course which prepared them to take their places as crewmen in field units. Men were trained as drivers, gunners, wireless operators, driver mechanics, fitters, electricians, clerks and storemen, in the required proportions as laid down by the War Office. Their first eight weeks were taken up by General Military Training (GMT), which included drill, PT, rifle and pistol shooting, gas training, elementary tactics and introductory lessons in driving and maintenance (D & M). At the end of this period of GMT they were earmarked for a trade, but before starting a detailed training course everyone was given three more weeks of D & M plus a similar period of elementary gunnery. The aim of this extra training was so that they would then be able to join a tank crew in an emergency, no matter what their basic trade. After this, drivers did six more weeks' driving, gunners six weeks' advanced gunnery, while the remainder went to their respective trade schools. The last four weeks of the course were devoted to collective training in

Training in the UK 1939-40. Here infantry train with both old and new tanks - in the background is a pre-war Vickers Medium, whilst in the foreground is a Matilda Mark II, which came into service in 1939 and was soon to win its spurs in France with the BEF. TM

which, with the aid of lectures, sand-table and outdoor exercises, they were taught the functions and handling of the units in the Royal Armoured Corps.

Roger Blankley of Cumbernauld recalled the early training days of 48th RTR thus:

Initial training was carried out in part of Battersea Town Hall. Later a Girls' School at South Side Clapham was taken over as a Drill Hall. Little kit was available and it was not until just before the August Camp that almost every man was issued with a uniform. Even then many went to camp with only an issue of brown over-alls. Vehicles at that camp were a hodge-podge of old trucks, some ancient Vickers Mediums, and a variety of motor-cycles hurriedly obtained and still in the original makers' livery. Driving was on Long Valley, the camp being at Aldershot. The Regiment did return from camp, the call-up coming some two weeks later. After a further issue of more kit at Clapham the Regiment went into civilian billets at Sanderstead, Surrey. We stayed there until early in 1940. During this time more vehicles were issued, the Regiment acquiring its first tank, a Matilda - we were allowed to look but not to touch, mostly it was kept under wraps. The local Golf Club House became the Officers' Mess, the Golf Course the training area, the Church hall the ORs' Mess Hall and for a time meals were ferried in from a large department store in Croydon. Eventually our

own cookhouse was established, this did not please most of the troops as the food provided from civilian sources had been more palatable.

A local beauty spot, a park known as Purley Beeches, became the tank and vehicle park. The Regiment now had a collection of various impressed vehicles: some Bren Carriers, several 30cwt trucks, many of which had mockup wooden turrets and wooden guns. Driving tuition was carried out at Dee's Driving School at Croydon which the Army had commandeered. This was a purpose-built driving school with several miles of concrete roads, and was also used for drill and Regimental parades.

It was at Sanderstead that the Regiment had to contend with a local pacifist cleric who weekly preached against the war and our presence. Also whilst there we were in receipt of a weekly allowance of 5s per man for providing our own mess and personal kit, plus 7s 6d for providing our own overcoats. The 48th had a very high proportion of professional and business men and private transport exceeded military vehicles. The joke about troops being asked to move their cars to allow the squadron commander to park his bike was certainly true.

From Sanderstead the 48th went to Colchester and occupied Sobraon Barracks vacated by the 17/21st Lancers. Here we acquired some two-man light tanks, Rolls Royce engined, with a self-changing gear box. This vehicle had an unfortu-

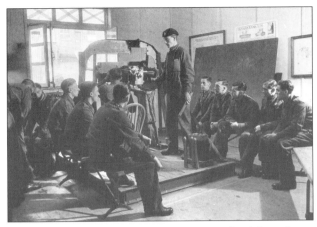

Training methods had to be quickly streamlined in order to cope with the vast influx of conscripts. Here a 2 RTR instructor goes through loading drills on a 2pdr classroom mounting. TM

AFV recognition was essential in order to tell friend from foe before engaging a target. Students had to get used to recognising all types of tanks through their tank periscopes and episcopes. (Author's Collection)

nate habit of changing up but refusing to change down, often with alarming results. In addition, we took over what I believe were Carden Loyd carriers, a small tracked vehicle with a canopy and promptly christened 'Ice Cream Carts', quite fast and of some use for training but having a habit of suddenly deciding to go their own way whatever the driver did. Whilst we were at Colchester, France fell.

BLITZKRIEG

To the BEF it must have appeared that the war had got off to a very slow start as the period known as the 'phoney war' dragged on. After their successes in Poland, the German panzer divisions had much to do before the Blitzkrieg could be unleashed on France and the Low Countries. Sadly, the Allies took little advantage of this period, indeed they were probably

no better prepared to meet the German onslaught when it came than they had been the previous year.

On 9-10 May 1940, only two days after the 7th arrived in France, the Germans struck into Holland, Belgium and Luxembourg. On 12 May, 1 Tank Brigade was moved forward to the Brussels area, the tanks moving up by train. Thereafter they carried out patrolling in front of the French Army in the St Armand Valenciennes area, finally falling back to Petit Vimy. This last move took the 4th 24 hours and had to be completed entirely on tracks, as by then every railway station en route had been dive-bombed. After refuelling, they moved by night to a harbour area on the reverse slopes of Vimy Ridge, arriving about 2am on 21 May. The fields between the Lens-Arras road and the woods in which 4th leaguered were carefully raked, with the result that they escaped enemy air attack. 7th also had to move back by road, but found their journey even more difficult, as the roads were choked with refugees. They were subjected to air attacks en route and again when they reached their leaguer area.

COUNTER ATTACK AT ARRAS

By 20 May 1940 Guderian's panzer forces had reached the Channel, west of Abbeville, leaving the BEF only the ports of Boulogne, Calais and Dunkirk for both supply and withdrawal. Before the panzers could move in to deal with the single British infantry battalion covering this sector, they received an order direct from the Führer to halt and not to cross the Aa Canal. One of the major reasons which prompted Hitler to give this fateful order was a small, but spectacularly successful counter-attack in the Arras area on 21 May, which was led by the 4th and 7th RTR.

Maj-Gen le Q. Martel, GOC 50th Division, had given his orders at 0800hrs that morning, explaining how the aim of the battle was to assault and capture the high ground south-east of Arras, and thus provide a breathing space to enable the BEF to withdraw. Martel formed his small force into two mixed columns, each consisting of a tank battalion, an infantry battalion, a field battery, an anti-tank battery and a machine-gun company. 7th RTR led the right column with 8th DLI while 4th RTR led the left with 6th DLI. Columns were to be about three miles apart and would advance southwards just west of Arras, then turn south-east to capture the lines of the Cojeul and Sensce Rivers in turn.

Unfortunately there was little time left after Martel's orders before the tanks had to leave their leaguer areas, so full details were never passed down to individual tank crews. There was also a desperate shortage of maps of the area, so initially it was a case of troop leaders leading, with the rest of their tanks conforming to their movements. 4th RTR was led up to the start line by 'A' Sqn, thereafter 'B' Sqn (left) and 'C' Sqn (right) took over.

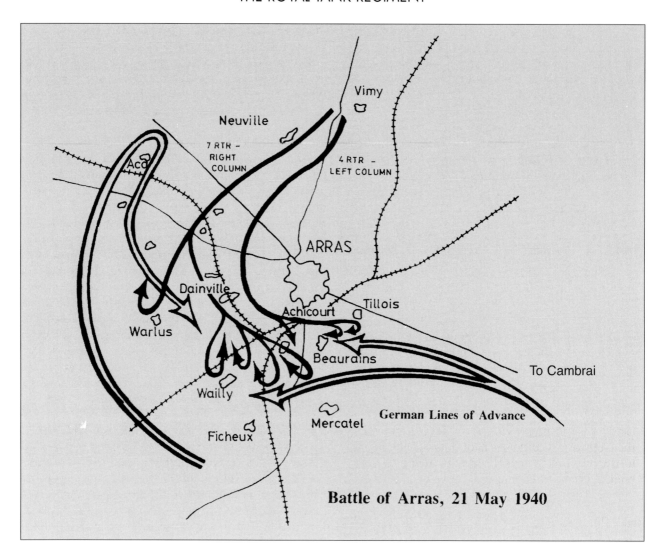

Battle of Arras, 21 May 1940

The first enemy were actually encountered near Dainville at about 1230hrs well before the start line, but were quickly knocked out. By 1345hrs the 4th had reached the start line and were in action again between Dainville and Arras. A large party of German lorry-borne infantry were observed moving along the Doullens-Arras road. It was an ideal shoot for the machine guns of the Matilda Mark Is and great destruction was effected before the 4th pushed on south to cross the railway line which ran parallel to the road.

The battalion was being heavily shelled by field artillery, firing over open sights. This proved to be the best way of knocking out the tanks as the standard German 37mm anti-tank gun would not penetrate the Matilda's thick armour. As the 4th fanned out south-wards after the railway and moved around between Agny and Arras, they came under heavy fire from some 105mm field guns to the south of their line of advance, around Mercatel. A direct hit from one of these guns killed Lt-Col Fitzmaurice (CO 4th RTR). WO III 'Jock' Armit of 'A' Sqn was ordered up to flank the guns and deal with them. Armit later recalled:

On the move to the gun position we struck a sunken road and my driver managed a crossing, but my other two tanks got stuck. I got in touch with the Squadron Commander and told him of the job I had to do, and asked for support for my tank. The squadron had become scattered by this time and were under troop control, so he promised to support me himself. I advanced over a small ridge and ran smack into six anti-tank guns. My .5 machine gun was brought into action and I got two of them before they realised I was on them - the range was approximately 200yds.

The other guns started on me now and one hit the gun housing. This caused the recoil slot-pin of my gun to snap and shook the gun back in the turret, jamming me between the shoulder piece and the back of the turret. I forced the gun back and pressed the triggers of my two smoke mortars, but they did not fire. I found out afterwards that they had been shot straight off. During this time, which was only the space of a minute, they hit my tank about ten times, but none of the hits did any real damage. I quickly made up my mind that the best way out was to back over the crest until I could get my gun cleared, so I gave my driver the order and we slowly zig-zagged back a distance of about 100yds.

I got my gun going again and, thirsting for revenge, I returned to the attack. They must have thought I was finished, for I caught the guns limbered up, moving to another position, and revenge was sweet.[2]

Armit then collected a number of other tanks which had lost their commanders or troops and led them in an attempt to reach some more field guns. At about 1700hrs they had a long and confused action with German tanks and mechanised infantry on the Wailly-Arras road. They never really got to grips with the field guns, but they were able to put some fire down on the artillerymen and by 1800hrs they had all stopped firing. Meanwhile the main body of the battalion was further north, just south of Arras. They took Achicourt and had reached Beaurains by 1700hrs, which was subsequently secured by men from 6th DLI. A small force of tanks, infantry and recce vehicles managed to push on to Wancourt, but that was as far east as they penetrated and were too weak to take the village. The majority of 4th were held up around Beaurains, as Armit remembers:

The situation was terribly confused, with tanks of the 4th and 7th mixed up all over the place with the Germans. I could see a lot of tanks belonging to the 4th, but later realised that they had been knocked out by artillery fire.

July 1941 and an instructor puts his class through its paces on top of a Matilda Mark II, whilst the edge of his trusty blackboard can be seen over to the left. TM

Beaurains was heavily dive-bombed and became untenable for the infantry, while a German all-arms attack came in from the east. 4th were under tremendous pressure, so the Adjutant (Capt Cracroft) hoisted his 'Rally on me' flag. Only 15 tanks could respond and he led them back to Achicourt at about 1830hrs.

The day's action was still not over. In the gathering darkness a heavy tank approached and Cracroft, thinking it was friendly, walked out to guide it in. He only discovered it was enemy when he put his map over the driver's vision slit to stop him! A confused night action followed at close range, but after about 15 minutes the enemy withdrew. 4th were now very short of ammunition and appeared to be surrounded. Cracroft decided to return to Brigade HQ on Vimy Ridge with the remnants of the battalion. Movement was slow as there were so many damaged vehicles and they were fired on by both sides. They got back eventually to the comparative safety of Vimy Ridge and went into a harbour area. Everyone was dog tired.

Sergeant Major Armit, for example, had had to sit on the front of his tank all the way back, slapping his driver's face to keep him awake.

On the morning of 22 May, the 4th took stock. They had only 15 tanks left out of 42 and many of these were damaged - Armit's for example had taken 36 direct hits ('he merited the VC that day,' wrote one of his contemporaries later, 'but, as so often, his action was not observed by anyone senior enough to recommend him'). However, the morale of all ranks was high. They had achieved considerable success against a larger enemy force in their first major action of the war.

Now turning to the 7th. The CO, Lt-Col Heyland had also spent much of the morning at Brigade HQ, not returning until just after before midday. This left only five minutes for orders and no time to brief individual tank commanders. Two sections of Matilda Mark IIs were detached to the 4th, commanded by Major Hedderwick (killed later that day and buried at Beaurains). The 7th were in some confusion as they left for the start line, seven miles away, and did not arrive there until 1425hrs - 25 minutes after H Hour and still without infantry support. En route they had come under fire from elements of Rommel's 7th Panzer Division. They crossed the start line two squadrons up ('A' and 'B').

About 1500hrs the 7th's Battalion HQ ran onto an anti-tank and field-gun position. Both the CO and the Adjutant were killed. Meanwhile, Major King, with what was left of the 7th's Matilda IIs, was following up the lead squadrons, and despite some mechanical problems, kept going and destroyed a number of anti-tank guns near the Doullens-Amiens road. By 1650hrs the pace of the advance was slowing, so 'D' Sqn passed through to take the lead. In fact they had to swing south as, like the 4th, they were suffering from

'Report my Signals!' Classroom instruction on the wireless, which was now a standard fitting in all British tanks. Note that the instructor still wears the pre-war RTC tunic with its brass buttons, whilst his class are all in modern, recently introduced, battledress. Photo was taken at a Catterick or Barnard Castle-based RAC training unit, 31 Oct 1940. TM

On training. Crewmen of 48th RTR, one of the London TA regiments based at Clapham Common, on top of their Valentine I 'Infantry' tank Mark III, which had a three-man crew – commander, driver and gunner. The Valentine II had an AEC diesel engine replacing petrol, whilst the Valentine III's turret was modified to take a loader. From the VIII onwards it was rearmed with a 6pdr gun, while the final XI had a 75mm gun. TM

The real thing. An operator adjusts his Wireless Set 19 in the turret of his tank. The 19 set was the most widely used British tank radio during the Second World War and was three sets in one: 'A' set - long range to squadron and regiment, 'B' set - short range within the troop, and 'IC' - within the tank. TM

the attentions of field and AA guns firing from the area of Mercatel. 'D' Sqn crossed the Arras-Amiens road south-west of Beaurains, and knocked out four enemy tanks plus groups of infantry and anti-tank guns.

As they pushed on to the south they came across '88s' used as anti-tank guns for perhaps the first time in the war. Major John King described the incident:

Driving on, another anti-tank battery was met and knocked out, mainly by Sergeant Doyle who was

with me in his Matilda. He charged straight at the gun under intense fire and ran over it. On emerging, his forward tool box was on fire, his turret jammed and his periscope shattered. Shortly after this I came upon the extreme left 88mm gun, but before it could open fire I speeded up to gain cover in a sunken road. I motored on down this to the end and then swung the tank so that the jammed turret would bear on the target, and put in a burst of machine gun fire to disturb the Germans' aim. Almost simultaneously, Doyle arrived on the scene and decisively relieved the critical situation by knocking out the 88. But this was almost the end of our run because, shortly after, my tank caught fire inside and we had to bail out; and Doyle, trying to push on, was knocked out by a field gun firing from Mercatel.

Sergeant Doyle was later awarded the DCM for his gallantry.

By 1800hrs the 7th found themselves under increasing enemy pressure from both air and ground, and were eventually ordered to withdraw to Petit Vimy and to rally near Brigade HQ. They reached their harbour area about 2300hrs and found they had lost 16 Mark Is and 10 Mark IIs. 4th and 7th Battalions were now so depleted that they had to be amalgamated for the remainder of their time in France. Their achievements at Arras were remarkable and had it not been for the presence of the enemy artillery round Mercatel, they might have achieved even more. General von Rundstedt, the German C-in-C, wrote later:

BLITZKRIEG

A critical moment came just as my forces reached the Channel. It was caused by a British counter-stroke southwards from Arras on 21 May. For a short time it was feared that the panzer divisions would be cut off before the infantry divisions could come up to support them. None of the French counter-attacks carried the threat of this one.

Liddell Hart comments:

It may well be asked whether two battalions have ever had such a tremendous effect on history as the 4th and 7th RTR achieved by their action at Arras. Their effect in saving the British Army from being cut off from its escape port provides ample justification for the view that if two well-equipped armoured divisions had been available the Battle of France might also have been saved.[3]

The 'Back to 1914 Brigade' had much to answer for.

3RD RTR AT CALAIS

The 3rd were in 3 Armoured Brigade of the 1st Armoured Division (with 2nd and 5th), stationed at Fordingbridge. They were the first tanks of that division to go to France and were sent to Calais on 21 May 1940, in support of 30 Infantry Brigade, in order to honour the Prime Minister's promise that: 'Calais should be fought to the death.'[4] Major Bill Close, MC was then the Troop Sgt of 3rd RTR Recce Troop. He remembers that there were many hitches unloading the tanks at Calais as the cruisers were not only packed at the bottom of the ship, with the light tanks on the deck above and the scout cars at the very top, but the ammunition, spare parts, radio accessories, etc had been 'tucked away in any odd corner that suited the mate's displacement requirements'. Liberal quantities of mineral jelly had been spread everywhere (to prevent corrosion), while the absence of any mechanical machine-gun belt fillers added to the chaos, so there was some delay as the crews worked throughout the night, but eventually everything was unloaded, the guns were cleaned, and the tanks made ready for action. As the light improved Recce Troop was ordered to find the enemy. Bill Close recalls:

We split into two groups of five vehicles. The Troop Commander led one up the coast towards Gravelines and Dunkirk. I set off with the other in a southerly direction to search the area around

A column of A9 Cruiser Mark Is, led by the Close Support version, which mounted a 3.7in howitzer and was only found in squadron HQs. The A9 saw service in both France and the Western Desert, but was considered to be too slow and lacking in armour for the cruiser role. They also needed a six-man crew as there were two separate machine-gun turrets, one on each side of the driver. TM

Another column of tanks on training in the UK, these are A10 Cruiser Mark II, which had thicker armour than the A9, but was still as unreliable and had an even worse performance due to its extra weight. TM

The Cruiser Tank Mark IVA, also known as the A13 Mark II, was produced in 1939 and saw service in France and the Western Desert. TM

Guines. When we left the battalion, men were sitting in the dunes painfully forcing rounds of ammunition belts, blistering their hands and breaking their nails. Others were cursing ill-fitting machine-gun barrels.

It was another cool misty morning and we got our first close look at Calais as we drove up streets of red-brick houses where bakers were opening their shops. Further on we saw the first refugees, some camping by the roadside and others heading towards the town. We had seen plenty of newsreel scenes of the Spanish Civil War but the haggard looks, the crazy transport, lorries, prams, push-carts, bicycles piled high with household goods, were a shock all the same. French soldiers sometimes tramped past shouting something but we couldn't stop to find out and wouldn't have understood if we had. Enemy planes flew high overhead and the crowd increased its rate of shuffle.

We drove along the side of a canal part of the way and a few miles out of town the refugees thinned out. With some relief I spotted the first formed body of troops I had seen, vehicles hidden under the trees by the side of the road. They were eating. Some had mess tins in their hands. I signalled to the section to halt and raised my binoculars. 'Oh Christ, Billy, they're Germans! I can see the black crosses on the tanks.'

There was a flash, a bang, and something rasped noisily overhead. Another flash, bang

and rrrasp was followed by a solid thump some way behind. I had been standing and sat down quickly. The enemy had sited anti-tank guns to cover the road during breakfast. Let's get out of it. Quick!'

Bullets cracked on the cobbles ramming home the personal nature of the affair. I thought: 'My God, it's me they're trying to kill... me...' This wasn't like random bombing when you might be unlucky. This was with murderous intent. Someone had watched our approach, taken aim through a graduated sight, got us in his cross wires and pressed the trigger. Billy remained unruffled. He reversed coolly and deliberately until we were at right angles to the ditch which ran alongside the road, then bumped over it into a field of half-grown crops.

The two Dingos (Daimler Scout Cars) immediately behind us were doing the same but tipped over, either hit or because they had taken the ditch at too sharp an angle, and lay there, wheels spinning. No one got out. Of the remaining Dingos I could see nothing.

Fear was now replaced by anger. We had no radio and it was our job to get back as fast as we could and report what we had seen. Then we'd show them. 'Get going, Billy!' We bumped over the field with soil flying all around us.

The Germans were having no problem with their machine-gun ammunition. A shallow valley offered shelter and we fled up it. Everyone had been looking for light armoured forces. I reckoned we had found them. But 'light'?

The CO showed obvious irritation when I gave my report, as if I was personally responsible for the loss of two and possibly four of 'his' Dingos. To make matters worse there was no news at all of the rest of the Recce Troop under the Lieutenant. I was told to stand by, and parked near HQ. The

Valentines of 48 RTR are seen here exercising in Suffolk just before the regiment moved up to Scotland and was re-equipped with Churchills. TM

RSM told me the Colonel had every right to be touchy as he was getting a string of contradictory orders... In the early afternoon we advanced towards Boulogne, my orders being to stick behind the CO's HQ tanks in case I was needed. Once again we drove through crowds of refugees. Half-an-hour later the leading elements swung off the road to investigate suspicious vehicles beside a wood. One of our top commanders got to within pistol range before enemy tanks were identified.

It did me good to see our cruisers in action. They were mainly A13s, racy looking tanks with four big road wheels on each side and a 2pdr gun for main armament. You could reach 40mph on firm ground. The long days spent on the ranges on the Dorset coast paid off and soon half-a-dozen German tanks were ablaze. The armour of the A13s - up to 30mm - seemed able to keep out the

enemy shells. Only when the German field guns joined in did the scene change.

The panzers crept nearer and our squadrons began to suffer. One of the A10s, ugly brutes with box-like turrets and a 3.7in mortar, instead of a two 2pdr, began to burn; a track was blown off another cruiser, the gun on the Colonel's A13 was shattered. We withdrew over the crest of a ridge and at dusk took up position around a small wood. German bombers flew overhead but ignored us and dumped their cargoes on Calais where the drifting smoke was growing thicker.

About 2000hrs a staff car appeared from the direction of the town, an officer's red band clearly visible. The wearer had a long conversation with the colonel and when he left the adjutant, Capt Moss, came over and told me my vehicle had been placed at the disposal of Brigadier Nicholson who had been sent over from England to take

Looking more like men from Mars than conventional soldiers, these crewmen of 'B' Sqn, 3 RTR, were on anti-gas training at Wadmans Coppice on Salisbury Plain, in 1939. TM

Cambrai celebrations still took place in wartime whenever possible. Here men of 40 RTR from Bootle, celebrate at Crowborough in November 1941. They would sail for the Middle East six months later, with the 46th and 50th as part of 23rd Armoured Brigade. TM

overall command at Calais. He had arrived that afternoon but when he tried to raise the colonel on the net he was told to get off the air as the CO was 'trying to fight a bloody battle'. The Colonel had no idea at that time who he was talking to.

We followed the brigadier's car back to Calais. As we pulled away, Billy Barlow nodded towards three bundles covered by groundsheets. Boots stuck out from under them. 'Who are they?' I couldn't say. As they were from tank crews we must both have known them. Nearly all of them had been at Lydd. 'What'll happen to them?' I wasn't sure. We'd never practised burying the dead during exercises on Salisbury Plain. I was not long at the Citadel. After I'd made a couple of journeys the brigadier said simply; 'I don't think you can do much more here, sergeant. If you want to try to make it back, it's all right by me.' Then he added: 'Colonel Keller has no further use for you.' When I asked about the Dingo he gave a little grin and said: 'I shan't be needing it again.'

I realised something must have happened but couldn't very well ask what. I wished Brigadier Nicholson good luck, saluted and made off. There was no sign of the despatch rider. The Brigadier must have realised then that the chances of getting away were fast disappearing. He'd been told on the morning of the 24th that evacuation had been agreed 'in principle' but another signal received late that night said the French were against it. He was told to fight on for the time being. Of these matters I knew nothing as I headed for the Gare Maritime. Things had worsened since we left and more

4 RTR in BEF. One their way up to Amiens by rail are these Matilda Mark Is of 4 RTR, who together with 7 RTR were the first RTR battalions to serve in France. TM

Excellent photograph of tank crews belonging to the Fourth, preparing their little Matilda Mark Is for action. Dreadnought *and* Dolphin, *together with Matilda Mark IIs of 7 RTR, did extremely well against the German panzers at Arras on 21 May 1940.* TM

Belgium, 1940. Matilda Mark Is carrying out training exercises in Belgium during the 'Phoney War' period of late 1939-early 1940. TM

Hurried track maintenance on this partly camouflaged A13 cruiser, in a small French town in Normandy, as they withdrew back to the Channel ports. TM

burning and abandoned vehicles blocked the roads. The Dingo carried a box of six grenades and I slipped one of these under the bonnet to set it alight before continuing on foot.

I don't know where the little ship came from or what she was called, and I've wondered since if she was a trawler mentioned in one account of the battle as having brought an important message for the naval detachment at the Gare Maritime. What I do remember is that they were pulling up the gang plank as I ran down the quayside. Those of us on deck lay flat as we steamed away, to avoid being blown overboard at the last minute. Shells were splashing quite close and once clear of the smoke we could see the flashes of the enemy batteries on the ridge above Coquelles. Destroyers were firing back while zig-zagging to avoid the Stukas queueing

up to dive on them. Once or twice ships vanished under clouds of spray but emerged with their pom-poms blazing away. Near misses blew bits of metal off our superstructure, gashing some of the men, but in mid-Channel the air activity died down.

Ships from the other ports in France had been landing troops at Dover and the quay was packed. Salvation Army vans were dispensing tea, ambulances were crawling through the crowds, there were nurses, policemen, Redcaps, people pushing chocolate into your hands and giving you cigarettes. No one asked what was happening back there though the artillery fire could be plainly heard. I was shoved into a train for Aldershot with a lot of other weary soldiers and, still wearing the revolver I had never drawn, fell fast asleep. I never did get my BEF ID card.

Two A13 cruiser tanks being unloaded at Cherbourg on 23 May 1940, when 2 and 5 RTR landed there to join 1st Armoured Division. TM

Prime Minister Winston Churchill chose to wear an RTR beret and badge when he visited the Vauxhall Motors Test Ground. TM

Men of 5 RTR rest on the dockside at Plymouth after their evacuation from France. TM

---

[1] The original Tank Brigade of 1934-38.
[2] Quoted in a short history of 4 RTR published 1980.
[3] *The Tanks*, Vol 2.
[4] The rest of 3 Armoured Brigade came over on 23 May and joined 2 Armoured Brigade which had arrived a little earlier. 1st Armoured

Division then fought a number of engagements in the Somme area to take pressure off the stranded BEF. They were finally withdrawn through Brest and Cherbourg, having had to destroy most of their remaining tanks and transport.

Chapter 9

WAR IN THE DESERT

REGIMENTAL INVOLVEMENT

The scene now changes from Europe to North Africa. Between 1940 and 1943 Britain, with the help of Commonwealth forces and later the Americans, fought a series of bitter campaigns, initially against the Italians and then against the Germans and the Italians. The battles raged backwards and forwards through North Africa, from Egypt through Cyrenaica and Tripolitania twice, and then finally, in 1943, on into Tunisia where the Axis forces eventually surrendered. The Royal Tank Regiment played a major role in all these campaigns, 19 of the 24 RTR Battalions taking part at one time or another. The main battlefield was the Western Desert, which stretched some 1400 miles from Alexandria to Tripoli. It was rightly described by one German General as being both a tactician's paradise and a quartermaster's nightmare, yet it held a special fascination for those who fought there. The men who served 'Up the Blue' will never completely forget what it was like be they:

...in shops or offices or factories, or by the fireside or in the garden at home, sometimes they will pause and remember, and their thoughts will take them back to the great days of long ago and far away - to the Western Desert and the Eighth Army and the old Matilda, to the sand and the dust and the smell of diesel and bivouacs under the stars, to Sidi Omar and Knightsbridge and Sidra Ridge, Derna and the Trigh Capuzzo, to Sidi Muftah and Tobruk - memories of a great adventure and a gallant regiment - and memories of those of their comrades for whom the desert is a resting place for ever.[1]

This is how one RTR desert warrior wrote in *The Tank* about his impressions of soldiering in the Western Desert in 1941:

Who will ever forget those dark, perishing cold desert nights? Sleeping beside your own vehicle with everything packed in case of a move at a moment's notice. Covered by the tank sheet, with only your head exposed, you would hear the wind whistling through the track plates, you could feel the icy dampness settling on your face

and you would subconsciously hear the slow pacing of the sentry-go. Maybe you would have kipped-down for only two hours when suddenly a rude shake would bring you to life. It was the sentry to tell you it was time to do your turn or to tell you that the Squadron Commander wished to see you immediately. And whilst you were sitting up and putting your boots on, you would see over the horizon coloured Verey lights being put up by some German patrol.

Sleep, hot food and mail meant everything towards maintaining morale. 'Miranda' was our code word for 'brew-up' and as we stood round the brew-can in greatcoats, scarves, woollen gloves and balaclavas, waiting for the precious water to boil, we would exchange news about home, smoke cigarettes, and the Tank Commander would place himself so as to hear messages that might come over the W/T. Usually the head-sets for this purpose would be hanging down the side of the hull. 'Mirandas'

Lt Mk VI in desert. Two light tanks of 1 RTR 'Up the Blue'. The regiment had a full-complement 58 light tanks and was part of the Mersa Matruh Mobile Force, which then formed Mobile Division and then became the world famous 7th Armoured Division - 'The Desert Rats' as they were called after their divisional sign. TM

Excellent shot of the crew of a Light Mark VI 'brewing up'. It is probably early morning, hence their balaclava helmets. These were needed (and greatcoats!) as it was perishingly cold at night in the desert. TM

were not always so successful. On many occasions Jerry demanded attention before 'Miranda' was completed in which case the water was hurriedly poured back into the container and saved for another time. But on all occasions we kept a tin of bully, butter and issue biscuits on top of the wireless set and the operator would make himself responsible for supplying the rest of the crew as we went along.

In those days of hard living, not knowing what the next day would bring nor where it would find us, there was tremendous understanding between officers and men. Officers lived on their tanks, gave a hand with the cooking (if there wasn't a conference being held), with the general maintenance, and took their turn at doing sentry. In this way they really did get to know and understand their men individually. But at all times discipline had to be maintained to its highest degree and familiarity was dealt with accordingly. For this the Troop

Commander depended to a large extent upon his Troop Sergeant. A good Troop Sergeant meant everything to the Troop Officer. Orders are orders and it was up to him to see that they were carried out without question; without delay, for delay in action might well have fatal results.

FOX KILLED IN THE OPEN!

Italy entered the war on 10 June 1940, at a time when Britain stood alone. Their armies in North and East Africa were ten times as large as those of the British - over half-a-million men as compared to only 50 000. Events were to prove that sheer numbers do not always win battles. The quality of the British troops, typified by the Mobile Division, now renamed 7th Armoured Division, which contained both the 1st and 6th RTR, was to prove far too good for the unfortunate Italians. From the outset, the British under General Sir Archibald Wavell, C-in-C Middle East, took the initiative, continually harassing the much larger Italian Army under Marshal Graziani and inflicting over 3500 casualties in the first three months of operations, for the loss of just over 150. Towards the end of June, the Italians began to move forward to the frontier between Libya and Egypt, but it was not until 13 September that they summoned up sufficient courage to cross it. At about this time further reinforcements reached Wavell, including both the 2nd and 7th RTR, the former equipped mainly with A13s, while the latter had Matildas, the first to arrive in the Middle East. In December 1940, the Western Desert Force, under General O'Connor, began an offensive against the Italians who by then had reached as far into Egypt as Sidi Barrani. In a series of well-executed encircling moves, O'Connor's forces pursued the enemy relentlessly westwards capturing the strongholds of Sidi Barrani, Bardia and Tobruk. By early February it was clear that the Italians were set to pull out of Cyrenaica completely unless something could be done to prevent their flight and destroy their forces before they could escape. Wavell flew forward for consultations with his field commanders and a daring plan was decided

Matilda Mark II of 7 RTR refuelling and carrying out urgent maintenance in the Tummar area after the capture of Nibeiwa Fort. TM.

upon to send elements of 7th Armoured Divison across the desert to get behind the Italians and cut them off well to the south of Benghazi, while the rest of the British forces, including 6th Australian Division, continued to harry them. There followed an operation which Liddell Hart described as 'one of the most daring ventures and breathless races in the annals of the British Army'. The RTR played a prominent part in this venture, as both 2nd and 6th were now in 4th Armoured Brigade leading 7th Armoured Division's attack, while 1st RTR was in 7 Armoured Brigade in divisional rescue.

2nd was sent off as part of the cut-off force and arrived in the ambush area of Beda Fomm late on the afternoon of 5 February, after completing a difficult journey across 150 miles of virtually uncharted desert in under 30 hours. They joined a flying column, commanded by CO 11th Hussars, which had been despatched earlier to Sidi Saleh. The Italians arrived to find their retreat blocked by the small British force and the subsequent bitter fighting lasted until 7 February, during which time the 2nd alone accounted for 79 Italian tanks. Topper Brown was a gunner in the 2nd and knocked out 20 enemy tanks during the battle. He later wrote:[2]

My recollections of Beda Fomm start with the 36hr run across the desert area… The terrain we crossed to cut off the Italians was terribly rocky. As we approached Beda Fomm my commander (Lt Norman Plough) told me to shoot up an enemy staff car, but the range was too great and the tank was bouncing about all over the place - whether I hit it or not I don't know, but some of my tracer certainly surrounded it. We then joined the rest of the squadron…

It was quite dark now and after some time my commander told me that we had to go out to spike some deserted enemy guns; this was going to be my job. We mounted and advanced along the convoy of enemy trucks. When we got to the end we saw two Italian M13 tanks stationary and we approached them from the side until we were about 15yds away. The operator, Taff Hughes, was then ordered to get the crews out. I offered to set them up with my 2 pounder, but Lt Plough rejected this, because the flash would have shown up our position.

Tpr Hughes, a miner's son, then in his early twenties, takes up the story:

I crawled up past them and got behind them. The first thing I did was to try a handle on the side of the first tank. I tugged on it but I couldn't move it. Later I learned it was a revolver port. I went around the back of the tank and over the top: it was still firing. I tapped my revolver on the cupola of the tank. This officer heard it. He shot

'Fox killed in the open.' The ignominious defeat and surrender of the entire 10th Italian Army was brought about by the expertise of tank crewmen such as Lt Norman Plough's crew, seen here before the battle with their A13 cruiser. His gunner, Topper Brown, knocked out at least 20 enemy tanks. (Author's collection)

up and as he came up he was right on the end of the barrel of my revolver - and he never stopped - he just shot out!

I took his gun off him and motioned him to stand away. Another two popped up, they couldn't understand why their commander had left, you see. I got them all up then, one at a time. They were frightened and I thought I'll try this with the next one. They were still firing. I did exactly the same thing again and I got away with it. I had a bit of trouble getting the driver out. He took a bit of coaxing but he knew what I meant. My gunner was supposed to give me covering fire but was firing over my head. He was frightening them to death. I marched them down this piece of road back towards our tanks. On the road there was this big naval gun which had been mounted on wheels. I was marching them past and there was an Eyetie officer in a beautiful powder-blue uniform with gold braid everywhere. I said to him 'fall in' and there were some objections from him, but I made him march back with his hands on his head as well. My tank commander saw me coming back and I was loaded with their guns and bars of Nestles chocolate they had given them to me and they were on about their bambinos and whatnot. The message went back to my Colonel and then to the Brigadier. These two tanks were a new type and we had never captured any of them before. The following morning we destroyed that column; we wrecked 80 of their tanks with about 20 of ours.[3]

Elfred Hughes thought no more of the incident, but was later awarded the Distinguished Conduct Medal for his bravery.

Back to Topper Brown:

Tanks in Line! Matilda Mark II – known as the 'Queen of the Desert' (until the more powerful German tanks arrived). This lineup belonged to 4 RTR, hence the tank names began with 'D'. TM

This old Matilda II certainly deserved the title 'Queen of the Desert' as it had been in action almost constantly from early 1940, when it first reached Libya, until 1943, when this photograph was taken. The commander Lt Joe Sweeny and his gunner Cpl Garrett were in 42nd RTR, Ist Independent Tank Brigade. TM

It rained very heavily for most of that night - my duty was the second half of the guard and I was soaked, even wearing my greatcoat. We were hull down behind a low rise and just as it began to get light Lt Plough suddenly said: 'They're here, reverse!' Whilst the driver (Cpl 'Barney' Barnes) was reversing I managed to get into my gunner's seat and the next thing I saw as I looked through my sights was an M13 about 30yds away, coming straight towards us. Without thinking I pulled the trigger of the 2pdr but I didn't even see any tracer. I thought: 'Oh my God, I've missed.' I gave it another one, but just then one of the crew climbed out of the top so I shot him. Daylight shone through the hole made by my first shot - was I relieved! We were so close that the tracer hadn't time to light up. Another M13 came up almost alongside it so I hit that one as well; knocking both out took less than a minute.

Practically all morning we never stopped firing at wagonloads of infantry or tanks. I haven't a clue how many enemy I killed, but it must have run into hundreds. We definitely had a score of 20 M13s at the end of the day… At times we were getting overwhelmed and had to keep withdrawing to the Pimple. One time we came around the right of the Pimple and stopped. My orders were to traverse left and I then saw at about 600yds an M13 coming towards me on absolutely flat ground. Just as I was about to fire Taff said, 'There are only two rounds left.' I cursed but fortunately hit the tank with both… We had started out with 112 rounds of 2pdr, 97 in the racks and 15 extra… We then went back for more ammo - I was also nearly out of .30, so you can understand the amount of firing I had done.

Next thing we were back in the thick of it again. I can honestly say that I didn't at any time feel scared; this I attribute to being so busy, also to the calm commands of my commander. We literally didn't have a quiet moment all day. If we weren't firing at guns or tanks we would pull up behind a wagon full of infantry and just pour dozens of Besa into the packed wagon. They simply didn't have any idea, or maybe they were petrified. I can recollect each tank I knocked out quite vividly, also several of the infantry wagons. When we pulled back after dark it was sheer relief. My eye ached with the strain of looking through the telescope for about 13 hours without a break.

Eventually the Italians had had enough and surrendered their entire force. For a total of nine killed, fifteen wounded and four tanks knocked out, 7th Armoured Division had destroyed the entire 10th Italian Army, taking over 20 000 prisoners, including six Generals, 216 guns, 112 tanks, 1500 lorries and immense quantities of arms, ammunition, equipment and stores of all kinds. It is no wonder that Anthony Eden coined a new version of Winston Churchill's famous phrase, when he said: 'Never has so much been surrendered by so many to so few!' O'Connor's message to Wavell, simply read: 'Fox killed in the open.'

THE AFRIKA KORPS ARRIVES

The German view of the lull following the destruction of the Italian 10th Army, as expressed by General Warlimont, a leading member of Hitler's staff, was as follows:

We could not understand at the time why the British did not exploit the difficulties of the Italians in Cyrenaica by pushing on to Tripoli. There was nothing to check them. The few Italian troops who remained there were panic stricken and expected the British tanks to appear at any moment.[4]

Wavell, however, had other problems. A few days after the victory at Beda Fomm, it had become necessary to switch his main strength to Greece, leaving only a token force to hold the enemy in Cyrenaica. The ill-fated expedition to Greece and Crete ended in tragedy when the Germans invaded Greece in strength on 6 April 1941. The British were soon forced into a 'Dunkirk-type' disaster with 3rd RTR once again having to leave behind all their tanks, after fighting as bravely as they had done in France. In all, over 12 000 men were take prisoner. A detachment of the 7th fought equally well in Crete, but with the same unfortunate result.

Thus the opportunity to clear the Italians from North Africa was wasted, and on 14 February Rommel's Deutches Afrika Korps landed in Tripoli and immediately seized the initiative. In a whirl-wind advance which lasted for only a month (24 March to 25 April 1941), they retook the whole of Cyrenaica, and crossed the Egyptian border reaching as far as Buq-Buq on the coast. Only Tobruk remained inviolate, but was surrounded by Rommel from 11 April onwards. The RTR was well represented in the mainly Australian Tobruk garrison, which included elements of the 1st (less one squadron), the 5th and 6th (mainly minus their tanks, so they acted as 'mobile infantry' until the initial crisis was over, when they were shipped back to Egypt for re-equipping), while a squadron of the 7th (equipped with Matildas) was landed on 19 April. Despite all his efforts Rommel failed to capture Tobruk, the handful of British tanks playing a vital role in its epic defence.

There followed two abortive operations on the part of Wavell to recapture lost ground and relieve Tobruk: *Brevity* in May and *Battleaxe* in June. Both ended in failure, with many tanks of the 2nd, 4th, 6th and 7th being knocked out in a series of heroic but tactically unsound operations. Both sides then spent the rest of the summer licking their wounds and building up their strength for another onslaught.

It is April 1942 and these tankmen of 44 RTR are 'washing their smalls' in a few pints of precious water. Keeping clothes clean was always a difficult problem, especially when water was scarce. TM

Wavell was relieved of his command and replaced by General Sir Claude Auchinleck, who resisted Churchill's repeated urgings to attack again whilst he built up his forces. The Desert Army (soon to be called the Eighth Army) received large numbers of reinforcements, which included 1st Army Tank Brigade comprising the 8th, 42nd and 44th RTR. 8th RTR was equipped with Valentines, while the 42nd and 44th, who were the first Territorial battalions to see action, had Matildas.

CRUSADER

The aims of Auchinleck's November offensive were to trap and destroy the enemy forces in Eastern Cyrenaica and to relieve Tobruk, which was still holding out despite continual pressure. Ten RTR Regiments took part in *Crusader*, viz: in Tobruk there was the 1st, 'D' Sqn 7th and the 4th (from October 1941), which formed 32nd Army Tank Brigade; the assault was led by three armoured brigades – 4th, 7th and 22nd - with 2nd and 6th RTR in 7th Armoured Brigade, and 3rd and 5th RTR in 4th Armoured Brigade; the 8th, 42nd and 44th were in 1st Army Tank Brigade, while the rest of the 7th was used in a deception role or for tank delivery.

Crusader was a bitter, hard-fought operation in which both sides lost large numbers of tanks. The human cost was equally heavy and the Regiment lost many of its best young tank commanders and their experienced crews in four weeks of non-stop bloody fighting, beginning with the battle of Sidi Rezegh, probably the largest tank battle the British had fought so far.

One of the young tank troop leaders, David Ling, (later Major, MC) of 'A' Sqn 44th RTR, had portions of his diary for that period published in the *Tank Magazine* some years ago. They included this graphic description of what every tank commander dreads, namely, being knocked out:

The whoosh of a shell close to my head surprised me and I redoubled my efforts to find a target. There should have been a trace of the gun after firing. Dust should have been kicked up and - whoosh, whoosh. Where the hell was the damned thing?

I was reporting to Stump Gibbon, who commanded the squadron, that an invisible gun was disturbing my tranquillity when the next effort of a singularly poor enemy gun-aimer was successful and from a range of 100yds he succeeded in hitting me on the fourth attempt.

The well was reminiscent of Alice's, only it was blacker, of greater girth and infinitely deeper. In falling down it I was glad that I was not turning over but kept a reasonably even keel as I sped on my downward journey. I was lying on my back facing upwards and should, by all the laws of nature, have seen an ever-decreasing disc of white daylight as the well's rim receded. But there was no daylight; all was blackness and I fell with an even but fast speed.

I wondered if there was a bottom and whether I would be brought up with a jolt but this did not worry me and I did not believe it would happen. Probably I would be gently slowed up. After all, to be stopped instantaneously after such a fall

Crusaders moving up to forward positions. The Crusader became the principal British tank in the desert from the spring of 1941 and first saw action in June 1941. (Author's collection)

must kill one and that was ludicrous because one cannot be killed twice and I was already dead.

Of that there was no doubt in my mind and it was in fact the only lucid truth I knew. I was dead, positively dead and presumably speeding to wherever dead people go. I had no knowledge of why I was dead or how I had died. I merely accepted it as a commonplace fact and one that should give rise to no excitement, speculation or regret.

I was dead and I didn't seem to mind. I was aware that this was the beginning of a new journey and I remember reflecting that death after all wasn't so bad as I had imagined and there did not seem to be any reason to be afraid of it. Fortunately the thought did not occur to me to compare the remarkable similarity between this fall and that of Lucifer from Heaven.

The humming which had started as a soft whisper grew to a gentle murmur and the moon had pushed its way through the clouds, becoming faintly visible and then growing slowly to a pearly brightness. I was still falling when I became aware of a star close to the moon, that was ruby red. Its brightness drilled into me boring away the shroud of black that encompassed me and simultaneously revitalising my easy death to uncomfortable life.

The star was the radio's warning light while the moon dissolved and took the shape of the illuminated tuning dial.

I lay still, as clarity, sanity and reality came back. I was comfortable and in no pain. I knew now that I was huddled on the floor of my tank, that we were not moving, that the engine had stopped and that my last clear memory was an urgent call on the radio that some big gun was trying to hit me. Obviously it had. It was black inside and the turret and the air was full of black smoke. With difficulty I peered across the 2ft of space separating me from the face of Cpl Hill. We must have received shocks of equal intensity for he also was beginning to move. I reached to him, clutched his arm and groped his face; and he returned my grip.

'Are you all right, Hill?'

'I'm all right, Sir - are you all right?'

'Yes, I'm all right.'

I did not ask the same of Tpr Bucket, my expert and lovable gunner who used always to make my biscuit bergoo and brew my char. He could impart to those warming concoctions a flavour which, like the shining efficiency of his guns, others could not match. Now slumped across his little adjustable seat he sprawled backwards and downwards. His head split in twain, was poised over my chest while his hot blood poured over and through me, a black glistening stream from the back of his crushed skull. His suntanned face turned half sideways was closed and white with death, shining clearly in that black murk. I remember I struggled to get up and Hill struggled also. We were entangled and I had to move Bucket. I remember I stretched up my arm to push him forward and away - and that two of my fingers went through the hole in his skull, into the warm softness within. I wiped my hand on my blood-drenched clothes.

The good soldier is the well-trained soldier. That is why the Hun is good and why the Guards Brigade better. Their training is more thorough and longer. The good soldier has less need to think because a textbook answer presents itself to him on most awkward occasions - automatically and without efforts. My training was thorough. Years of drill, learning and manoeuvres had fitted me for just this moment. I wish I had been a worse soldier for then I could have applied reason and acted very differently from the way I did. As it was, I repeated my text-book teachings. I was a commander and being out of action it was my duty to dismount and assume command from another tank. As simple as that.

I told Hill of my decision. And then I remembered my driver, Cpl Ennaver, for the first time. In contemplating our own troubles we had both forgotten him. We both yelled to him and he, also returning from the land of Nod, assured us he felt fine. He tried his engines and they burst into life. This was grand and made me feel less like the proverbial rat in the sinking ship. With instructions to them to turn about, and after sighting through the periscope my nearest tank, I bid these two adieu and awkwardly clambered out.

The warm sun, the bright clear air, the hard clean ground on which I toppled and crumbled, contrasted dazzlingly with the black cylinder smelling of hot oil from which I had emerged. The world was startlingly clear and vivid, filling me with elation. Picking myself up and gathering around me my wet greatcoat I stumblingly started on the run to Sgt Bleadon's tank. He was my troop sergeant, and on another day and in another battle I was to see him stained and grimy with his left eye nearly gouged out and resting quivering on his cheek bone while he tried desperately to thumb it back.

The distance between our two tanks could not have been more than 150yds, but ever growing as his tank slowly pulled away and into the battlefield. My period of unconsciousness after the hit must have been brief, for Bleadon's tank during this time had moved no more than 300yds. Feeling a little panicked I ran too urgently and without looking. I stumbled continually in my straining effort to make more speed. Once I fell headlong. My fears were merited and I had but covered half the distance when the sis-sis-sis of machine-gun bullets about my feet told me that the obvious, if I had only paused to reason, had happened. An eternity and boundless space separated me and the safety of my objective, and I redoubled my desperate attempt in what seemed so forlorn and pathetic a hope.

That some unseen mind guided me, that some invisible will encircled me, only can explain the impossible fact that I gained the side of the tank without a single hit registering on me. Although it cannot be denied that I must have presented a most comical sight to the enemy, a mad Englishman swaddled in the thickest woollens on what was now a broiling day, careering and tripping in crazy fashion between tanks in a desert battle, and that this sight may have affected his aim, I prefer to believe Fate protected me.

A VICTORIA CROSS FOR THE REGIMENT

The *Crusader* operation brought the Regiment its first Victoria Cross of the war. It was won by Capt 'Pip' Gardner, MC, of 4th RTR, shortly after the breakout frorn Tobruk. He had been sent with two tanks to help a pair of armoured cars belonging to the King's Dragoon Guards which were out of action and under heavy fire. His CO, Walter O'Carroll, gave this account of what happened:

They raced down the long desert slope as fast as they could, abreast, with 100yds or so between them. Crossing a ridge they saw both cars, being used as it were for target practice by the enemy, with a slow deliberate fire… and occasional bursts of machine gun. The closer of the two was the chief target. Ordering the second tank to

Taken just before the action which resulted in Capt 'Pip' Gardner, MC (on left with hands in pockets) being awarded the Victoria Cross. The others in the photograph are fellow 4 RTR officers: Lt Dick Simpkin, Maj Alan Roberts and Lt Paul Gearing, whilst seated on the Matilda Mk II is Sgt Boniface, MM. TM

1 RTR crews bombing up their A9 cruisers during a range practice in Egypt. Although the early British standard main tank armament was only 2pdr, it was a highly accurate, quick firing weapon with a good performance and could deal with most Italian tanks. TM

make a wide circuit to the left, Gardner raced his tank up to the stricken car …

While the 'stand-off' tank manoeuvred about and kept up a sustained fire on the enemy position, Gardner, dismounting from his tank, started detaching his tow-rope with a view to towing the car away. The one along the side of the tank was jammed, so he set about the rope at the rear. On detaching the free end, Gardner signalled to his driver, Tpr Robertson, MM, to turn about - but this of course upset the gunner who had to traverse his turret as the tank turned. Tpr Richards (the wireless operator) serving the gun, and with headphones still on, looked out of the turret to see what was going on, and was instantly killed. L-Cpl McTier (the gunner) finding his gun empty, looked round and saw what had happened. He now had to leave his gun and get Richard's body clear so that the turret could traverse - no easy task in the confined space of a Matilda tank. He managed it, however, and then took his place in the turret, looking out in his turn for instructions from Gardner, who was lifting Lt Beame of the KDGs, who was wounded and lying outside his car on the ground, into the car again. The tow-rope was

now secured, and Gardner was signalling to McTier to direct the driver to move, when a bullet struck him in the leg, fortunately not breaking it. Meanwhile the tow-rope tightened as Robertson moved the tank and then suddenly parted - probably shot away. McTier's face was now bleeding from splash off the turret as bullets bounced about round him, though it was not until after the battle that he found this out. At the time he thought it was sweat - some of it was! Gardner now, despite his wounded leg, returned to the car, lifted out Lt Beame, and staggered back to the tank, half carrying and half dragging him. McTier was back at his gun, loading and firing it as hard as he could by himself, in order to give some distraction to the enemy while Gardner hoisted the badly wounded officer onto the side of the tank. Again he returned to the car but found there were no other survivors and, signalling McTier to warn the driver to advance, he scrambled back to the tank and clambered up beside the wounded officer, receiving a bullet in the arm as he did so. McTier then ordered the driver full speed and, reloading his gun with another belt of Besa, kept up fire on the enemy position as the gallant little party withdrew.

TRIUMPH BY NIGHT

The arrival of the German 88mm gun in the desert completely destroyed the invulnerability of the Matilda. Brig 'Boomer' Watkins, commander 1st Army Tank Brigade, with two Matilda regiments (42nd and 44th RTR) and a Valentine regiment (8th RTR), realising the serious disadvantage that his slow moving under-gunned Infantry tanks would now suffer, decided that the only way to enable them to close with the enemy was under cover of darkness - a revolutionary concept at the time. For several months, whenever operational committments permitted, he had the regiments attacking dummy enemy leaguers and positions in the dark, having first had to navigate their way to their objectives. Despite the difficulties of night navigation, they soon became skilled in this new art, especially 44th RTR (Lt-Col Bill Yeo)

On 25 November 1941, the 44th put in a brilliant night attack to open the way into Tobruk, from Bel Hamed to El Duda, in support of the New Zealanders. The breakthrough achieved, at the cost of a single infantryman killed and no tanks hit, they joined hands with the 1st. Tragically, Bill Yeo then learned that his son, the 1st's Adjutant, had been killed in Tobruk that very day.

A month later, on 31 December, Bill Watkins was ordered to support the South Africans in a daylight, head-on attack against the formidable, heavily armed fortress of Bardia. He at once protested the sheer folly of such an operation and, reminding the Corps Commander of Bill Yeo's brilliant success at El Duda, proposed that he should put in a night attack against the flank of the fortress with two regiments and South African infantry support. This was agreed and he was given command of the attack. Six breaches in the wire and anti-tank ditches were created by gallant Sapper parties and 8th RTR, followed by the 44th, led the assault. Despite problems caused by the terrain and the width of the frontage to be covered, the attack was a complete success; 8000 prisoners, including 2000 Germans and 35 heavy guns were captured at a cost to the Brigade of only three tanks destroyed and 35 damaged, six men killed and 20 wounded. It had indeed been a triumph of professionalism, good training and courage, shattering the myth that tanks could not fight at night.

Crusader ground to a close as the year ended, with Rommel withdrawing his forces back to El Agheila, his starting point eight months previously. Both sides had suffered grievously and were happy to lick their wounds and to build up their strength for the next round.

ROMMEL STRIKES BACK

History was to repeat itself far more quickly than anyone imagined, when Rommel launched his second onslaught only a bare three weeks into the

Tobruk in flames soon after its capture in January 1941 from the Italians. A 7 RTR Matilda flies a captured Italian flag as it passes a long column of prisoners. TM

New Year. He had received much-needed tank rein-forcements and was determined to seize the initiative before the British could ready themselves for Operation *Acrobat*, which Auchinleck hoped to launch in mid-February. Rommel caught the Eighth Army off-guard, with much of its strength back in reserve or being refitted. The battle-weary 7th Armoured Division had, for example, been replaced by the newly arrived 1st. Within three days the DAK had reached Msus, almost annihilating 2nd Armoured Brigade on the way, which lost 70 tanks between 21 and 23 January. Benghazi was captured a few days later and by 2 February the triumphant Afrika Korps had pushed the British back to the Gazala-Bir Hacheim line where they began to run out of steam, so the front stabilised itself for the next three months, while both sides once again built up their strength. The Gazala line was based upon a series of infantry-held strongpoints, or 'Boxes' as they were called, with deep belts of wire and mines in between. The tanks were supposed to be able to both support these 'Boxes' and at the same time manoeuvre between them to deal with enemy armoured penetrations. The outcome was that they fell between two stools and were unable to achieve either task effectively. In addition, the complacency and incompetence of some senior commanders did not help. By June 1942 the British had nearly 850 operational tanks, of which 167 were the new American 'lease-lend' Grants, as compared with some 560 Axis tanks, half of which were Italian. However, they were tactically badly handled and Rommel was able to destroy them piecemeal.[5] The opening phase of the battle was described in *The Tanks* by General 'Pip' Roberts, who was then commanding 3rd RTR. His battalion was in its battle positions and was able to inflict a fair number of casualties with their brand new Grants:

We had been going about 10 mins and the light squadron was about 2000yds ahead, when they reported a lot of dust and unidentified movement three miles to their front. Perhaps the 8th Hussars. Then a report from Brigade came through that the Indian Motor Brigade just east of Hacheim had been overrun by tanks about 3-4hrs before. Perhaps it's not such a Sinbad[6] after all!

We continue to move forward slowly, closing up on the light squadron and looking for a suitable hull-down position. 'Gosh! There they are - more than 100. Yes, 20 in the first line, and there are six, no, eight lines, and more behind that in the distance; a whole ruddy panzer division is quite obviously in front of us! Damn it. This was not the plan at all… where the hell are the rest of the Brigade?' However, no indecision is possible because no alternatives present themselves. 'Hullo, Battalion - Orders: 'B' and 'C' Sqns (Grants) take up battle line on the small ridge 300yds to our front. 'B' Sqn right, 'C' Sqn left. 'A' Sqn (Honeys) protect the right flank from an outflanking movement and try to get in on the enemy's flank - leave one troop on the left to keep in touch with 8th Hussars who should be coming up on our left at any moment.'

The Grant squadrons were instructed to hold their fire until the Boche tanks were within 1200yds or had halted. Meanwhile our gunners, the famous Chestnut troop had heard the situation on the wireless and were going into action close behind us… The leading enemy tanks had halted about 1300yds away; all our tanks were firing, there was no scarcity of targets, certainly two of our tanks were knocked out, but the enemy also had losses. I could see one tank burning and another slewed round and the crew 'baling out'… 'Peter (my adjutant), tell Brigade we are holding our own but I do not anticipate being able to stay here for ever, and suggest that 5th Battalion should come up on our right, they would prevent us being outflanked and might get a good flank shoot at the enemy.' However, it appeared that the 8th Hussars thought it would be a good idea if the 5th Battalion came up between the 8th Hussars and ourselves; the 8th Hussars were fighting a battle in their original leaguer area against a large number of enemy tanks and had not had time even to get into battle formation. Our instructions were to hold on as long as possible.

Pip Roberts had to intersperse his radio conversation with orders to his crew:

…'Peter, tell Brigade we cannot hang on here much longer, either there will be nothing left or we will be cut off, or both. Driver, advance slightly into line with the other tanks. 75 gunner, enemy tank straight ahead receiving no attention - engage. First shot over - come down half-a-tank

height. Good shot - that got him - same again. Hullo! there is a dashing Boche on the left, he has come right forward against 'C' Sqn who have withdrawn a little - just the job for the 37mm. 37 gunner traverse left, traverse left - on; enemy tank broadside - 500 - fire! 37 gunner - good - have a couple more shots and then get ready with the coax.'

But 'C' Sqn on the left are all going back, or what is left of them. 'Hello 'C' Sqn - what's the matter – you're going the wrong way. 'Sorry,' replied 'C' Sqn Commander, 'but I can't see a damn thing with blood in my eyes, and all my periscopes are smashed. I think the same thing has happened to my other remaining tanks. Also. I have no more ammunition.' 'OK, well done - carry on.' It was found out afterwards that this tank had had 25 hits on it.

But the situation was now getting serious… On the right, 'B' Sqn seemed to have three tanks still firing, but they obviously could not have much ammunition left; no sign of the 5th RTR coming up on either our right or left. There are certainly 20 Boche tanks knocked out in front of us, if not more, but if we are to reorganise at all we must go - and pretty quickly.

3rd managed to extricate themselves, refuel with ammunition and petrol and rejoin the battle.

Space was always very limited in a tank, especially in the A9 which had a crew of six. This led to the need for stowage on the outside of the vehicle. This is clearly a newly-arrived crew as the solar topees were never worn by hardened 'desert warriors', whilst stowing bedding on the front glacis plate was inviting trouble, as it would have 'brewed up' very easily and might have then set the tank on fire. TM

Artist's impression of Lt-Col Bob Foote, DSO, winning his Victoria Cross, at the head of 7 RTR. TM

A SECOND VICTORIA CROSS

There followed eight days of the heaviest tank fighting of the desert war in an area rightly called 'The Cauldron'. The bravery and discipline of the tank crews was personified by Lt-Col (later Maj-Gen) 'Fairy' Foote, DSO, who was then commanding the 7th RTR and was awarded the Victoria Cross for his outstanding courage and leadership over the period of three weeks (27 May to 15 June 1942) when he was, as his citation explains:

> …always at the crucial point at the right moment and over a period of several days he gave an example of outstanding courage and leadership which it would be difficult to surpass. His name was a byword for bravery and leadership throughout the brigade.

Typical were his actions on 13 June, when he was ordered to delay the enemy so that the Guards Brigade could be withdrawn from the Knightsbridge escarpment. When his leading tanks had been destroyed, Bob Foote reorganised the remainder, going on foot from one tank to the next, under continual intense artillery and anti-tank fire, calmly encouraging his crews to fight on. As it was essential not to give ground, he put his own tank in front of all the others, where he could be seen plainly by everyone, despite his tank being badly damaged by shell-fire and all its guns being knocked out. By his magnificent example the corridor was kept open and the Guards Brigade was able to withdraw.

The Gazala battle inevitably ended with the British being forced to withdraw out of Cyrenaica. Tobruk was invested once again, but this time the South African garrison was forced into an early surrender. 4th and 7th RTR, who had been supporting the South Africans, were all but wiped out, the surviving tank crews fighting on as infantry when their tanks were knocked out. Sadly, both our Victoria Cross winners, Bob Foote and Pip Gardner, were taken prisoner after breaking out and trying to evade capture.

There followed the battles of El Alamein and then Alam Halfa, truly the major turning point of the desert war in which, as always, the RTR played a full and important part. As Kenneth Macksey points out in his short history of the Regiment:

> Up and around Alam Halfa Ridge, the key to the Alamein defensive position, there sat three armoured brigades, commanded by Royal Tank Regiment Brigadiers, Roberts, Custance and Richards, all under command of a Royal Tank Regiment General, Gatehouse. As members of these Brigades there were 1st, 3rd and 5th Royal Tank Regiments. They were getting ready for the last defensive battle to be fought before the Eighth Army took the long road back to the west along the desert coast road.[7]

THE TIDE TURNS

About six weeks before the most famous battle of the desert war, Jake Wardrop of the 5th RTR wrote in his diary:

> It was now about 8 September 1942, the last throw of the dice had failed and we settled down to get ready for the big push. The divisions were grouped into formations, there were three corps in the Eighth Army, and General Montgomery visited every unit in the desert. About this time a big decision was taken which was worthy of note. The 5th Battalion had been on the desert since March and it was thought that they were sick of it, so one day a parade was called and

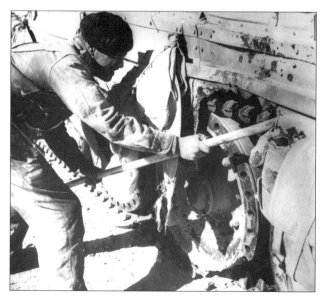

A driver's work is never done. 'Track bashing' was a constant chore, adjusting the track and ensuring that nothing was preventing it from turning properly. Here a driver uses a crowbar to bend twisted metal away from the track. The damage was clearly caused by an enemy shell. TM

First of the American tanks in the Western Desert was the little M3 light, which began to arrive in July 1941. Armed with a 37mm gun, it had a top speed of 36mph and earned the nickname 'Honey' (British official name was Stuart), as it was so reliable and well-liked by the British crews. This crew from 5 RTR are celebrating Christmas 1941, plus their Honey and a plum pudding! TM

'Captain Reilly-Fowle' a cartoon character from the wartime Daily Mirror adorns the side of this Sherman Medium M4 tank, belonging to 'B' Sqn, 5 RTR. The Sherman was undoubtedly the most successful of the American tanks to see service in the Western Desert. There were some 285 in British service by the Battle of El Alamein in October 1942. Some of this crew are wearing the American-style crash helmets which came with the tank, but were not much worn, the crews preferring their berets. TM

The first American medium tank to reach the Western Desert (on Lend-Lease) was the M3 Medium Grant - a special version of the M3 Medium Lee which had special requirements to suit British crews (eg: it was not so tall so less conspicuous and had room in the back of the enlarged turret bustle for the radio). Its main armament was a 75mm gun in a side sponson – this crew are loading up with ammunition thought the sponson door. TM

Fearless put it to us. He gave us the choice of going to Cairo and missing the push or staying on the blue and taking part in it.

He mentions General Montgomery who had taken over the Eighth Army and was in the process of revitalising his command.[8] Jake had a very high opinion of Monty, who wore a Royal Tank Regiment Other Ranks beret, complete with the RTR cap badge alongside his General's badge, ('the means by which I came to be recognised throughout the desert' is the way Montgomery himself described it) and also of 'Fearless' Jim Hutton, who had taken over command of the 5th during the Gazala battles:

Just about this time we had a new CO Lt-Col Hutton known to one and all as Fearless Jim. He was young for a CO, about thirty; he had the MC and bar. He had been wounded twice and he must have been one of the greatest guys who ever joined the Army. He was always well up in his tank giving orders on the wireless in a nice pleasant voice, just like the announcer reading the news. The lads would have done anything for him and gone anywhere with him - if he had said we were going to make a frontal attack on the gates of Hell, they would have been off like a shot.

The choice made by the men of the Fifth was therefore not surprising, as Jake goes on to explain:

At the end of his speech Fearless asked us to step forward if we wanted to stay and the whole battalion took a pace forward. There was no turning back then. It was a great outfit, everyone of them had been in the push since it started and were prepared to go on again. We had good officers, of course, the very best and we respected them as fighting men. Every one of the majors had been in through the summer. Fearless had been in the 3rd Tanks and had been wounded at Knightsbridge and was back for more and everybody was raring to go.

EL ALAMEIN

Jake Wardrop gives this description of the opening of the El Alamein battle:

By about 9pm on the 23rd, everybody had closed right up to the minefields. At ten the barrage opened up all along the line. There were infantry attacks in many places and the tanks were to

push through about four in the morning to reach the other side just as the light was breaking. Stanley, George and I were on the same tank now, the Major's, and we had a bottle of Gilbey's Spey Royal that night to keep out the cold. None of us slept, we were all a bit excited. About four in the morning we pushed off and got through the three minefields with little trouble. There was some shooting back and forwards and a couple of tanks were on fire, but we had to carry on until the open ground was reached. We had been travelling in line one behind the other, but when we reached the open ground we opened out into a semi-circle and pushed on as fast as possible. There was a slight hitch as another minefield was encountered, some of our tanks went up on it and

Famous arrival who changed the fortunes of the British and Commonwealth forces in North Africa, was Lt-Gen (Later Field Marshal) Sir Bernard Montgomery, GOC Eighth Army. He took to wearing an RTR beret and badge, which soon became his trademark. TM

A Sherman at speed in the desert kicks up a lot of dust which can been seen for miles, so it was a dead giveaway. The externally-mounted machine gun is the famous .50cal Browning, which was and still is, widely used. TM

Monty was kept well supplied with tea by his crew, from 6 RTR. The tank he used was a Grant which is now on show at the Imperial War Museum. TM

'Sunshields'. One way to disguise tanks was to fit them with canvas screens that made them look like lorries. There were also screens for lorries to make then look like tanks! (Author's collection)

The Battle of El Alamein, 23 October 1942. A column of tanks moving forward to the minefield breaches, whilst the devastating artillery barrage is in progress. TM

they were told to sit tight and shoot it out for a bit at any rate. To our front there was some high ground with guns on it and as day broke they could see us and started to give us a lacing with everything they had.

The Fifth were of course not the only RTR Battalion to take part in the El Alamein battle, in fact there were ten battalions there - the 1st, 3rd, 5th, 8th, 40th, 41st, 45th, 46th, 47th and 50th, together with elements of the 6th RTR, 42nd and 44th who were under direct command of HQ Eighth Army, with 'B' Sqn 6th RTR providing HQ protection, while the other two squadrons were equipped with Scorpions (Matildas fitted with rotary flails for mine sweeping).

The battle lasted for two long weeks, until 5 November, when a breakthrough was achieved and the Afrika Korps was forced to begin their stubborn, fighting withdrawal back to Tripoli. Alamein was undoubtedly one of the most important battles of the war and set the Eighth Army on their victorious advance through Libya. They covered the 1400 miles to Tripoli in 90 days, an incredible 16 mile-a-day average, despite the terrain, weather and the Africa Korps' skilful delaying action. The RTR was well in evidence, the 1st, 5th, 40th and 50th RTR all being among the first troops to enter Tripoli. It was during this advance that the 40th was given the title of 'Monty's Foxhounds'. They had fought without rest, except for short spells of maintenance, for the entire campaign, being the armour which had formed Monty's northern spearhead. Their Valentines, hardly built for speed, had travelled thousands of miles on their tracks in the forefront of the Eighth Army.

Their nickname is said to have originated when an infantryman, seeing the 40th pushing through again, turned to his pal and said: 'The hunt's on again, here come Monty's Foxhounds!'

THE FIRST ARMY JOINS THE BATTLE

Just over two weeks after the Eighth Army won the battle at El Alamein, the Germans had to face a new threat to their rear, in the shape of the Allied Torch landings on the coast of Algeria and Morocco on 8 November 1942. Then the war moved on to Tunisia with the Churchill tanks of the British First Army in action for the first time. The Churchill had had a disastrous start in life when used in August 1942 on the ill-fated Dieppe raid and had not been considered suitable for desert warfare, due to its weight and slowness. However, in the difficult mountainous country of Tunisia it was to prove its true worth. The Allies were so keen to keep the Churchills' arrival secret, that the men of 51st RTR who, together with the North Irish Horse and 142nd RAC Regiment, made up 25 Army Tank Brigade of First Army, had to hide their black berets in the kitbags and sail out wearing khaki side-caps and plastic Royal Artillery badges!

Their first major action was later described as one of the most remarkable stories in the history of the Royal Armoured Corps. It involved 'A' Sqn 51st RTR as part of an all-arms group, in a reconnaissance-in-force operation some 5½ miles north of El Aroussa to Steamroller Farm, with the task of discovering the enemy's strength. As a result of this action Capt (later Maj) 'Gin' Hollands was awarded an immediate DSO to add to the DCM he had won in 1940. Hollands was commanding 1 Troop but was in fact riding in a 5 Troop tank *Adventurer*, to which he had transferred after losing a track. Hollands recalls the action:

The crew of this Sherman wanted to wish everyone a Happy Christmas in 1942! TM

Major Ted Hadfield deployed his dozen-plus Churchills in the usual two waves with the infantry riding on the tanks of the second wave. Probing slowly forward in the close country, it was not until 1600 that the force came into the area of Steamroller Farm where the valley opened out. Pushing Nos 1 and 4 Troops forward to take up suitable fire-positions, Major Hadfield deployed 2 and 3 Troops from the second wave on the left to protect that flank of the attack and avoid bad-going. Suddenly, the Tuesday afternoon quiet was noisily dispelled by the whiplike crack of A/T guns sited in the farm and surrounding wadis; the infantry hastily deployed and went to ground, No 1 Troop's 6pdr guns opened up in reply and soon a heavy fire-fight was in progress. Tracks clattering and clanking, 2 and 3 Troops waddled forward to take the infantry onto the objective as they had done in so many exercises back in Britain.

Suddenly and without warning the air was filled with noise as Stukas came hurtling out of the sky to release bombs that burst in an irregular pattern round the tanks; simultaneously the German A/T gunners redoubled their fire. When the dive-bombers had left, it was seen that two tanks had been knocked out - that of Capt G.C. Franklin ('A' Sqn second-in-command) and one in 2 Troop. The A/T guns had accounted for others so that only nine tanks remained; 1 and 2 Troops with one each, 3 Troop and Sqn HQ with two each, and 4 Troop still intact on the right but badly held up by wadis.

Although the squadron had knocked out some of the A/T guns and silenced mortar positions beyond the farm, the British force was in a difficult position and the German defenders were justified in thinking that they had held them off. At this point Major Hadfield

received positive orders that he had to 'get on at all costs' - force a way past Steamroller Farm and destroy the enemy on the high ground beyond. Perhaps forgetting that 1 Troop was down to a single tank, Hadfield ordered Lt Hollands (Acting Capt) to take his troop forward, so *Adventurer* rolled forward onto the road and, with no infantry support, set off alone for the head of the pass. Its driver, Tpr John Mitton, could see very little ahead on either side because his driving compartment was set far back from the forward trackhorns, nevertheless he saw enough to write a vivid account of it a few days later. This is how he recalled the battle:

Dropping feet first through the cupola and nearly massacring the crew, Capt Hollands gave the order to advance. Moving forward I found the ground pretty difficult, scrub, rock and very little if any cover. Moving on half-a-mile or so I stopped, not by an order, but because on passing through a patch of bushes the ground fell away, heavily bushed, farther than I could see through the visor, and rising to the opposite slope, which seemed miles away. Clearly impassable. Could I get down? Over the intercom: 'No! Driver, reverse!' Inch by inch, I backed away. The German ants opened fire from across the wadi. I wished for four reverse speeds at that moment. 'Driver, right. Speed up, broadside on to the wadi and the ants.'

I was told next day that the German gunners hit all around us. I didn't know it then, I just kept moving as fast as possible, crossing the road, round through the trees of a farm, then out into the open and on to a road. The road ran up hill then weaved left and sharp right. Taking this corner in third gear, I drove round and stopped dead.

I appeared for a few seconds to be facing a barricade of greenery blocking the road, surmounted by a big black hole. It was in fact an 88 not more than 30yds away, if that, set up on the left verge. Peering through the visor, I saw a flash of white faces and the hole vanished in a red sheet of flame, blinding me for a moment. The tank rocked, a sound of falling kit in the turret. The right-hand junction box and roof fan had dropped as the shell grazed the turret, taking half the back bin with it. 'We're hit! Traverse right!' over the intercom, 'Right!' in a shout 'not left!' The turret was at 20-to-6 and Mick (the gunner) was struggling to free a jammed 6pdr round which had slipped out of its rack.

Once again the hole vanished in another sheet of flame, but missing us completely this time. During these hectic seconds Hank Howson, the front machine gunner was calmly reloading a new Besa belt as though on range practice. Closing its rear cover carefully, he cocked the gun, laid and fired. The tracer streaked into the greenery, then climbed lazily into the air and vanished. The gun crew ran. We had knocked out our first 88! The intercom was deafening as Capt Hollands shouted for the Bren gun, so I pulled past the 88 muzzle, just in case, and waited. The Bren fired one round and stopped. 'Tommy Gun!' - with which he fared no better, firing one burst and jamming. Hollands was now fighting mad. Throwing the Tommy gun after the fleeing Germans, he shouted for grenades, and stood half out of the turrent throwing them.

Again I moved forward as ordered. Directly in front was a running mass of grey figures. All guns fired, bowling them over and over until nothing moved.

'Gin' Hollands continues:

It was here that we spotted our second 88mm which was on the right of the road below the crest of the hill, and although it did not, to our knowledge, fire at us, we quickly disposed of the crew. It was at this point when we were at the top of the pass and having disposed of two 88 A/T gun crews that I radioed for tank and infantry support but was informed that neither were able to get through, Jock Renton having heard my request for assistance on the radio asked the Sqn Commander for permission to join me. This was given and Renton came to the top of the pass and then we sat picking targets. The only unfortunate creature was a horse behind a camouflage net which moved, once too often.

Back to John Mitton again:

Directly in front of us was a slit trench, covered by a camouflage net and from it emerged a German helmet, face and shoulders, with a rifle and grenade-thrower attached. Taking a snap shot upwards, he ducked back into the trench.

A muttered curse over the intercom, then 'Who the * * is firing at me?' from Hollands. I pointed out the German in the slit trench. Mick, traverse left, on, see him, right fire!' The Besa burst was right on the target. 'Stop, traverse right, continue firing... ' During the next few minutes the German fired three times at Hollands and twice at the tracks. After each shot Mick swung back and fired, using two belts of Besa and four armour-piercing shells low down. On

Tripoli 23 January 1943. These Valentines of 40 RTR drove into the city at first light, others to arrive on the scene very soon afterwards were the 1st, 3rd, 5th and 50th. TM

Another surprise for Rommel's Afrika Korps was the arrival of the British Churchill tank, fitted with a six-pounder gun. Here, a column moves up through the dust across Tunisia. The Churchills did extremely well in the mountainous area and proved their worth in such actions as that of 51 RTR at Steamroller Farm. TM

the fourth AP the trench seemed to vanish in a cloud of smoke and dust, the net flapping wildly, breaking free from the blast of the AP. As dust settled, the German crawled out, stood dazedly looking at the tank turned, slowly, dropped his rifle and staggered away. Hollands ordered, 'Stop, firing! He deserves to live.'

Two tanks (Panzer IIIs) came into view lower down the valley, and although we both used our 'special' AP we were unable to set them on fire, but the crews bailed out and were given a burst of Besa fire.

Inside was pretty thick by this time, having been closed down from 1000, and it was now 1900. During this time we had fired 21 rounds of AP and 23 boxes of Besa, most of the empty cases still remaining with their attendant packing strips and loose rounds, Hank and myself half deaf by blast.

At this point came the order from OC Sqn to retire. Infantry held up. Two tanks burning, squadron in bad shape. Unable to consolidate. Capt Hollands gave the order, 'Destroy everything.' Here was a gunner's dream. The echelon of soft vehicles, 27 in all, laid up in orderly array, backs down, towards us. Mick rang up on the intercom, 'See that Staff Car, Johnny, well watch me let its tyres down.' He was as good as his word; next a 3-ton Bedford, a burst of Besa into the petrol tank, a lick of flame up the cab, igniting the camouflage net and in seconds a roaring inferno.

Lt Renton was up alongside, also firing and adding to the general din of explosions and crackling flames as petrol and ammunition blew up. To get further gun depression I was ordered

to swing left, sideways to the slope, the gun moving to 3 o'clock. The vehicle park was now well ablaze, and we commenced to retire, well satisfied that Jerry would not be able to use that lot again. Starting down the hill we came up in rear of a second 88, and fired two rounds of AP into the breech at point-blank range, fixing it good and proper.

Down the reverse slope, the wireless failed completely. Hollands, seeing that I was moving away from the road, jumped out of the turret and sat on the front and guided me with his hand in front of the open visor, shouting directions through the open driver's hatch. On again in third gear, then the engine stalled. I pressed the starter, the lights grew dim, but no engine roar. Stalled with flat batteries in the middle of the enemy positions.

Meanwhile the other Churchill was safely on its way; Lt Renton saw Hollands' frantic hand signals when his own tank turned a bend in the road. He immediately stopped and hurried back to help *Adventurer*. Renton seized his Bren and rushed to meet Hollands. Unfortunately he left the LMG in the way of his own tank and it backed right over it! 'Don't just sit there,' yelled Hollands, 'do something.'

The crew of *Adventurer* uncovered the rear towing shackles and tied the rope, despite MG bullets spattering the Churchill. Renton was the only casualty, injured by a mortar bomb before he dropped down inside his turret cupola.

The first tug on the tow rope and the engine roused to life. Faster moved the front tank, still towing. Knowing I couldn't stop to unhitch, I revved hard and braked. The tow rope stretched and parted. Speeding up I overtook the other tank going flat out down the hill until stopped by a burning Churchill, the flames roaring out in great gushes, half across the road. A grimy figure darted out seemingly from nowhere, and ran up to the visor. It was Sgt Rowlinson. 'Jump on,' I yelled. 'I can't' he replied, 'I have two badly wounded men over there, and can't leave them. You'll have to help me.' Getting out, Baines was the first placed on board, and laid on the tool box. Harrison was placed on Renton's tank which had pulled up behind us. From then on it was a straight run back to the squadron lines, where our story was told with disbelief until acknowledged three days later by the infantry, who finally got through, confirming greater damage than we had claimed.

The German battle group holding Steamroller Farm had heen badly shaken by the two Churchills. An intercepted radio message from their commander Hauptmann (Capt) Schirmer, to Oberstleutant (Lt-Col) Walther Koch (CO of the Parachute Hermann Goering Jaeger Regiment) reported that he had been attacked by 'a mad tank battalion' whose tanks had scaled 'impossible heights' and caused him losses that made withdrawal imperative.

For his daring, single-handed attack, Hollands was awarded an immediate DSO in the field. Lt Renton received an MC, Sgt Rowlinson the DCM, while Tpr Mitton and another tankman received Military Medals.

ONE LAST COMMENT FROM 'GIN HOLLANDS'[9]

Any reader of this action would no doubt be entitled to ask: 'How could a seasoned German gun crew of an 88mm A/T gun, fire two rounds at a range of about 30yds and fail to destroy a 40-ton Churchill tank and its crew of 5?' Here I would remind the reader of how Hank Howson (the front MG gunner) reacted when, coming round the bend in the road, he was confronted with an 88mm A/T gun firing at us. He kept a cool head and his gun firing at the enemy gun and crew during this critical period when we

Tunis 8 May 1943. Churchill tanks in Tunis, drive past welcoming crowds. (Author's collection)

were first hit and it was sufficient enough to have caused the German gun aimer to miss with his second shot. There is absolutely no doubt in my mind that the action of Hank Howson saved the lives of all the crew that day. It is a matter of personal regret that, although I have tried many times to trace Hank Howson, I have never been able to do so, as I feel he should have had his action recognised.

ON TO TUNIS

1st and 8th Armies linked up with the transfer of both 7th Armoured and 4th Indian Divisions to First Army in late April, to make a joint convergent offensive aimed at enveloping and destroying the German forces in Tunisia. Tunis was reached by the Desert Rats on 7 May 1943. Fittingly two RTR Regiments were poised to enter the city first, as George Stimpson of the 5th recalled:

That morning the 5th were on the high ground overlooking Tunis and 1st RTR were more or less level with us, on sightly lower ground. After a while - I think we had had breakfast - the order was given to charge down the valley and take the city, a mass of white buildings in the green valley below. About 100 tanks in line abreast charged flat out down the open slope, until the close country forced them to take to the roads. 5th RTR were the first to do this and got to a junction just before the 1st, who then had to wait until the 5th had passed. As 'B' Sqn, who were leading, got near the outskirts of the town, armoured cars of the 11th Hussars tried to overtake them, but 'C' Sqn, who were behind 'B', deliberately blocked the way until we were well past the sign which said 'Tunis'. I believe the 11th Hussars and the Derbyshire Yeomanry agreed to call it a dead heat as to who entered Tunis first - but they didn't ask anyone else! They may have been first into the centre of the town, but 5th RTR were first past the post and therefore first into Tunis. In fact I was standing by the sign, with one foot in Tunis, when the Cherry Pickers went in![10]

THE END IN AFRICA

From Tunis, 12th and 48th RTR moved up the Cap Bon peninsula, mopping up the remnants of the Axis armies and taking large numbers of prisoners.

Five days later, just before midnight on 12 May 1943, the Afrika Korps surrendered. In his congratulatory message to the Eighth Army published on 14 May, Monty recalled the stirring words of Winston Churchill in his speech at Tripoli in February 1943, 'I MARCHED AND FOUGHT WITH THE EIGHTH ARMY.' No one could be prouder of their record in North Africa than the Royal Tank Regiment who were awarded 19 battle honours, more than during any other campaign, encompassing every stage of the Desert War.

Victory in North Africa came on 13 May 1943, when the last remnants of the once-proud Afrika Korps were forced to surrender to the Allied forces. (Author's collection)

---

[1] The 'Epitaph' to the Short History of 42nd Royal Tank Regiment.
[2] *Desert Rats at War, North Africa* by George Forty.
[3] From *South Wales Echo*, as published in the *Tank Magazine*.
[4] *The Tanks*, Vol 2.
[5] Rommel had remarked to one captured British officer after Sidi Rezegh: 'What difference does it make if you have two tanks to my one, when you spread them out and let me smash them in detail?'
[6] *Sinbad* had been the code name given to a recent British reconnaissance in force, to test enemy reaction, so it was wrongly assumed by Division that this was what the enemy was now doing.

[7] *To the Green Fields Beyond* by Kenneth Macksey.
[8] General Alexander had also replaced Auchinleck as C-in-C Middle East.
[9] 'Gin' Hollands is one of only two RTR officers to be awarded both the DSO and DCM in the Second World War. The other was Major Jim Cornwell, now living in Australia, who won his DCM with 3rd RTR at Gravelines on 24 May 1940, and his DSO commanding 'B' Sqn, 12th RTR in Italy during August and September 1944.
[10] *Desert Rats at War, North Africa* by George Forty.

Chapter 10
OTHER THEATRES OF WAR

In addition to the main theatres of war in the Middle East and North-West Europe, units and sub-units of the Royal Tank Regiment were involved in a number of smaller, but nevertheless important, campaigns all over the world during the Second World War.

EAST AFRICA (SEPTEMBER-APRIL 1941)

Two RTR squadrons took part in campaigns in Italian East Africa: 'B' Sqn, 6th RTR, were sent to the Sudan in mid-September 1940, while 'B' Sqn, 4th RTR, took part in the successful campaign to liberate Eritrea in 1941. In one operation in the Sudan - the attack on an Italian fort at Gallabat on 17 October - just three light and five cruiser tanks of the 6th were mistaken by the Italians for 'forty tanks, most of them heavy ones', so it is not surprising that GOC Sudan praised their work and *élan*.

'B' Sqn, 4th RTR, was part of a mechanised column known as *Gazelle* force which stormed through the Eritrean mountains to take Keren, Asmara and, eventually, Massawa. As well as their battle achievements the squadron gained an enviable reputation for serviceability, managing to keep their 26-ton Matildas moving and fighting for over 800 miles of rough and rocky terrain with the loss of only two tanks from mechanical breakdowns. P.K. Barrington recalled some of his experiences there in the *Tank Magazine* thus:

The campaign was well under way to the south when the first four tanks of the squadron came under orders of Brigadier F.W. Messervy in a force known as *Gazelle* and it was part of the strategic planning that *Gazelle* should break through the Agordat defences to the Keren Road and spearhead the advance through Keren and Asmara on to the port of Massawa on the Red Sea.

The town of Agordat was well protected by the natural fortifications of Mount Lacquetat to the west of the approach road, and the Cochen Mountains to the east. A projection of Cochen, known as Gibraltar, jutted onto the plain which separated the two main structures. The enemy forces were deeply entrenched across the plain and the mountains on either side were bristling with machine-gun and artillery emplacements. The whole forward area across the plain was further protected by a double-banked barbed-wire entanglement in front of the trenches, and the enemy observation posts - high in the mountains - had a commanding view of our forces as we prepared to attack their positions.

On the night of 2 January the tanks, together with a troop of Bren carriers from the Camerons, lined up abreast of the plain, while the Indian infantry began the assault on Lacquetat and Cochen. Four days later, after a bitter struggle in which our infantry suffered very heavy losses, the high peaks were conquered. On 31 January we advanced on the plain, the tanks crushing the wire and overrunning the trenches, scattering the colonial defenders with bursts from their coaxial machine guns. The Royal Fusiliers fanned out to the left of the plain while the Camerons tackled Gibraltar to the right with fixed bayonets and, reaching the top of the peak, they spotted a formation of Italian tanks in a valley on the other side. The Matildas pressed forward, turning right into the valley. The Italian tanks opened fire, but their shells bounced off our armour. Our formation advanced, blasting AP shells clean through the Italian armour, and in just a quarter-of-an-hour the enemy formation, consisting of nine medium and two light tanks, was completely destroyed. They were no match for our Matildas, and we never again encountered a single Italian tank for the duration of the campaign.

The way was now open across the plain, strewn with the bodies of dead colonial defenders, to the Keren Road, leaving the town of Agordat to be occupied by our forces. One of our tanks - that of Sgt 'Lofty' Grant - struck a mine, but the blast did little more than 'scorch' the skirting flaps, which were then difficult to open. We did however, manage to free him.

On 1 February as we reached the road beyond the plain, an enemy column was seen retreating through the Cochen Gorge and two of our tanks set off in pursuit. They had covered 12 miles before being forced to abandon the chase at a steel-structured bridge across a dry river bed - the Ponte Mussolini - which had been blown by the retreating Italians. The road through the Gorge was littered with dead bodies; burnt-out and abandoned vehicles caused minor hold-ups.

The squadron was now at full strength as we waited for the bridge to be repaired. Brigadier Messervy was none too happy about the time being afforded the Italians at the stronghold of Keren, our next objective. On the afternoon of 2 February our 26-ton Matildas safely negotiated the bridge and began the 45-mile journey to Keren.

We had covered about 30 miles when one of our tanks developed trouble in one of its engines. Having checked all the obvious things - fuel supply, pump, injectors, compression - we tried in vain to get it started, so a decision was taken to abandon it and press on with 15 tanks to Keren. A few days later I returned with a truck to strip the abandoned tank of many parts which could be useful as spares. I was not amused at the sight of three vultures perched on the turret as I swung the truck round in a cloud of dust. To my relief they took off, and I sweltered in the heat of the day to dismantle as much as I could.

Barrington goes on to tell of the battles for Keren and Asmara and the final 60-mile advance to Massawa which they reached in early April:

There were more road blocks to be cleared before we finally reached the outer defences of the port. The Italians seemed to be set to defend their positions when our Matildas broke through the defences and got inside the perimeter. The end was in sight, and although there was still gunfire until late in the morning, the battle was virtually over. We entered the town to find about 30 ships scuttled in the harbour. It was now 8 April 1941, and within a few days a channel had been cleared through the sunken ships to enable another ship - the *Takliwa* - to enter the harbour. Our 15 Matildas were loaded aboard and we again set sail for Suez and North Africa... The Eritrean terrain was most unsuited to tank warfare, but 'B' Sqn, 4 RTR gave good account of itself ... It has been said that the tank battle at Agordat was the turning point of the campaign.

GREECE AND CRETE (MARCH-MAY 1941)

Mention has already been made of this abortive campaign in the spring of 1941, which sadly achieved nothing other than to seriously weaken our forces in the Western Desert.[1] 3rd RTR in 1 Armoured Brigade Group was part of this force, landing at Piraeus on 11 March. They were equipped with old A10 tanks previously belonging to 5th RTR which had badly worn tracks - the source of many problems. Their initial mission was to assist in guarding the Florina Pass between Greece and Yugoslavia but they were soon forced to withdraw due to heavy enemy pressure. Liddell Hart quotes from one battle report of the amazing sight which confronted the 3rd when the enemy attacked:

> ...enemy infantry, with anti-tank guns, in extended order on a front of 1200yds, who marched forward steadily, as though on parade, to their objective; it was a brave sight, if somewhat foolhardy in its method. The Besa machine guns stopped them at 400-600yds and forced them to dig in.

Hampered by disorganised Greek troops and crowds of refugees, the 3rd fought a difficult and costly withdrawal action against the Germans and by the time they reached Trikkala they had only five tanks left and a few days later there were none. On 22 March the tank crews were regrouped into four infantry squadrons equipped with B Echelon vehicles and machine guns from broken-down tanks. They fought on bravely. Eventually, on 27 April, just 12 officers and 180 men of the Regiment were embarked with the other remnants of the British force, in two destroyers HMS *Hotspar* and *Isis* and sailed for Crete under continuous air attack. Subsequently they completed their voyage back to Alexandria in an ancient Greek ship which had not been to sea for 27 years and had no food on board! Despite the difficult circumstances of the campaign, the 3rd had managed to inflict many casualties on the enemy during the arduous retreat.

Half a squadron of 7th RTR in Matildas took part in subsequent operations in Crete, mainly being used for airfield defence against the enemy parachutists. By 25 May all the tanks were out of action and three days later they were ordered to evacuate. Most of the personnel managed to reach Egypt safely, after many adventures and hardships en route.

BURMA (FEBRUARY-MAY 1942)

Between February and May 1942, 2nd RTR, as part of 7 Armoured Brigade, was involved in the first campaign in Burma, having sailed from Egypt in January 1942, together with the 7th Hussars. Both regiments had been re-equipped with American M3 light Stuart tanks. They had been destined originally for Malaya, but were diverted to Rangoon after the surrender of Singapore. The campaign was little more than a fighting withdrawal, in which 7 Brigade acted as rearguard for most of the way. Fighting was bitter and confused, with the problems of Command and control in difficult terrain, being partly offset by the sheer blood and guts of the soldiers, who had to fight against an enemy superior in everything but courage.

'B' Squadron were first to be unloaded at Rangoon on 21 February 1942, and just over a day later were in action some 70 miles away against infiltrating Japanese. During the following eleven weeks,

An M3 light tank belonging to 2 RTR in the depths of the Burmese jungle in 1942. Despite the difficult conditions, 7th Armoured Brigade did a wonderful job as rearguard during the withdrawal through Burma. (Author's collection)

Are they really going to eat it?! Living off the countryside is one thing, but… (Author's collection)

Eventually the tank crews had to make a long and dangerous trek through the jungle to India, mostly by night, hiding up during the day to dodge Japanese patrols. They reached freedom eventually and lived to fight another enemy, being then sent to Italy. (Author's collection)

the tanks covered over 2400 miles with little maintenance, in terrible conditions, yet it was not until 6 May, only five miles from the Chindwin River and not far from the border with India, that the first three tanks had to be abandoned through mechanical breakdowns. Typical of the close-quarter jungle fighting which was the feature of the campaign is this extract from the reminiscences of Major Arthur Fearnley, MC, then a young troop leader in 'A' Squadron, who was sent to rescue the Brigade Commander of 63 Infantry Brigade together with three of his battalion commanders and a small number of Brigade HQ staff, out of Pegu which was surrounded by Japanese. They managed to get into the town without hindrance but it took Fearnley two hours to persuade Brigadier Wickham to leave. Eventually he agreed, but then refused to travel in one of the tanks, preferring to use two Indian scout cars. One of the Brigade HQ staff said he would like to travel in a tank and so shared the small turret with Fearnley, who now takes up the story:

It was about midday that the small column set off southwards down the road. The column consisted of Sgt Barnes's tank leading, followed up by my tank, then the two scout cars, with my corporal's tank bringing up the rear. About half-a-mile south of Pegu, the road passed under a rather narrow bridge. All was surrounded by thick jungle. Immediately beyond the bridge appeared a British truck slewed across the road. Sgt Barnes stopped his tank and asked me on the radio what he should do. 'Carry on,' I said, 'there seems to be enough room to get through on the left.' Sgt Barnes approached the gap, the rest of the convoy following. As he reached the opening, heavy machine-gun firing broke out. The leading tank, having passed the obstruction, continued down the road. We had just passed the obstruction when my tank lurched off the road, down the embankment and came to rest in the bottom of the ditch on the left-hand side with the engine stopped. After that, complete silence. I could not understand what had happened. I looked out of the small metal-hinged flap on the left side of the turret; by now of course my head was well inside. I saw two Japanese soldiers on their hands and knees crawling away into the undergrowth. I poked my revolver through the opening and fired at them. Whether I hit either of them is doubtful. I then shouted to Cpl Macdonald: 'Fire your Browning.' 'What at Sir?' he said, 'Never mind what at, just fire the bloody thing!' I shouted. He fired a few bursts and then fell back against the turret. 'Have you seen this sir?' he said and showed me a very nasty-looking hole in the upper part of his chest from which blood was oozing.

It was only now that I looked down through

As they withdrew, their tanks had to be destroyed south of the Chindwin River. Only one tank - an M3 light belonging to the 7th Hussars - was rafted across the river in 1942. It returned to 'fight another day' as a command tank in the Indian 7th Light Cavalry Regiment. (Author's collection)

Japanese hand-grenade lobbed through the open top. Seconds were desperate.

I squeezed through the very narrow gap between the turret floor and the top of the forward hull, pushing Ross's body to one side to do so, then I sat in his lap. How thankful I was for those short weeks of training in driving a Stuart tank in England; I knew exactly what to do. I said a little prayer to myself and pulled together the two switches in front of me to start the engine. Nothing happened. After a few seconds I realised the tank had stopped in gear. I depressed the clutch and kicked the gear lever into neutral. Pressed again the two switches. Never have I been so thankful before or since to hear an engine roar into life. Then I discovered another hazard … The driver of a Stuart tank looked forward when closed down through a bullet-proof glass panel. This one was completely shattered and opaque; one bullet, or maybe more, had pierced the glass and penetrated Ross's eye.

I shouted across to Bossom (my operator) sitting alongside me: 'Can you see through your visor?' 'Yes,' he said. 'Then you'll have to guide me out.' Bottom gear engaged and, guided by Bossom's instructions, we climbed the embankment and got back on the road. Immediately heavy firing broke out. We could hear machine-gun bullets spattering the tank on all sides. Along the road we went until, on negotiating a bend, Bossom said: 'There are two trucks end to end completely blocking the road.' 'Right,' I said, 'we're going to hit them. Steer me into the left-hand one.' A juddering crash. Again we came to a halt with the engine stopped. This time she started easily…'

the base of the turret at Tpr Ross, sitting in the driver's seat. I saw with horror that the back of his skull had disappeared. Now the full implication of the position became clear. Somehow we had to get out of this situation. I knew what had to be done. I had to drive the tank. My passenger and I struggled to get poor old Ross out of his seat. It was quite impossible. The position of the driver, low down in the hull of the tank and with no room in the base of the turret to get any purchase on him, made this attempt a waste of effort. Still dead silence. I became increasingly aware that the next likely happening would be a

Malta. From 1940, No 1 Independent Troop, RTR, was stationed in Malta, with four Matilda Mk II 'Infantry' tanks and two Mk VI light tanks. Note the strange camouflage pattern to match the houses and stone walls of the George Cross island. TM

Fearnley managed to force his way through the gap he had created and they moved off again southwards. The next hazard was the tank filling with choking smoke, but he didn't stop to investigate, as machine-gun bullets were still hammering on the outside. Eventually they reached the rest of their squadron.

> I opened the hatch and practically fell out. I suppose I must have looked an awful sight. My overalls were spattered with blood from head to foot. Smoke was pouring out of the tank and I was badly shaken. 'You can get out now Bossom,' I said. 'I can't, sir,' he replied, 'there's something wrong with my leg.'

Bossom had been wounded by a bullet which had shattered his right leg. The tank was festooned with the cores of armour-piercing machine-gun bullets which had penetrated part of the way through the armour and remained stuck in, about ½ in deep.

> …We had a dead driver, a gunner with a severe chest wound and a wireless operator with a shattered right leg… but such is the resilience and organisation of a tank unit that within an hour I had a new tank, a new crew and we were back in business.

Sadly, the Brigadier and the three COs Fearnley had rescued from Pegu had all been killed during the ambush. On approaching the Chindwin River, the tanks had to be destroyed as there was no means of getting them across. Orders had been given that they must not be burnt since that might cause 'alarm and despondency', so they were drained of oil and then run until the engines seized. Destruction was then completed with sledge hammers, having first recovered radio sets and machine guns. From then on the tank crews had to march out on foot. As one soldier wrote later:

> Eventually we were organised for marching. Everything had been sorted out in real infantry style, and off we went in our various platoons and formations, up hills and down valleys, till we reached the now famous River Chindwin. I was lucky enough to catch the last ferry boat, but the others had to cross the best way they could. Somehow or other all made it, and off we went again by fairly easy stages to the frontier and safety. Shall I ever forget those aching feet and sore back, the lying down with a soaked shirt at all times of the night and morning, the rising before dawn, chilled to the marrow; then, just when things seemed to be going all right, the endless rain. Had it not been for staunch comrades and true, I should still be out there or my body would.[2]

Operation Husky, *Sicily, July 1943. A Sherman belonging to 'A' Sqn, 50 RTR, comes ashore on a crowded beach during the mainly unopposed landings on Sicily, 10 July 1943. Three RTR battalions were involved - 44 RTR of 4th Armd Bde, 46 and 50 RTR of 23rd Armd Bde.* TM

SICILY (10 JULY-16 AUGUST 1943)

While this campaign was merely a preliminary to the Allied landings in Italy, it was still a separate operation which followed on just two months after the surrender of the German and Italian forces in North Africa. Three RTR battalions were involved: the 44th of 4 Armoured Brigade, which was to support 13 Corps, and 46th and 50th RTR of 23 Armoured Brigade supporting 30 Corps. 40th RTR, the third regiment of 23 Armoured Brigade, could not be re-equipped in time to go to Sicily. The Eighth Army formed the right wing of the Allied landings on 10 July 1943. The Italian coastal divisions disintegrated without firing a shot, while their field divisions surrendered *en masse* almost as soon as battle was joined, thus the only effective opposition was from the German forces on the island. By 13 July, British forces had cleared the south-east of Sicily and advanced some 40 miles up the east coast. The armour was being employed in small packets, to support the infantry in the difficult, scrubby and rocky terrain dominated by Mount Etna. Most movement was confined to the roads - tactics that were very difficult to come to grips with after the free-ranging operations of North Africa, but good training for Italy where the conditions would be similar. The British armour had been re-equipped with Shermans in place of their ageing Valentines, the new tanks being superior in nearly every respect except for their tendency to burst into flames when hit by enemy fire. This led to the Sherman earning the unfortunate nickname of the 'Ronson Lighter' - because it was guaranteed to light first time! The Germans had a number of their lethal 88mm anti-tank guns, plus some Tiger heavy tanks, which proved very difficult to winkle out of ambush positions on the narrow roads and tracks, which threaded their way through the orange groves of the foothills.

All three RTR Regiments saw a great deal of action. Early on, 5 Troop, 'C' Sqn, 44th RTR, knocked

Lt-Col Bob Lindsay briefs some of his officers of 44 RTR, just before an attack in Sicily, July 1943. TM

Another officers' briefing in Sicily, this time at the side of a Sherman tank. TM

out a covey of tanks and captured the Divisional Commander of 34th Napoli Division and his staff. The 5 Troop's total 'bag' was one divisional general, 3 brigadiers, 4 staff officers, 59 ORs, 8 tanks, 6 guns, 29 trucks, 4 staff cars and 5 motorcycles! Some of the toughest fighting was undoubtedly against German paratroopers who, in the close country, stalked and sniped at the tanks continuously. They were excellent shots, as the history of the 50th recalls.

> Their marksmanship was constantly to be feared; they shot men clean between the eyes and tank commanders were shot in the hands when only these were exposed on the edge of the cupola.

The fighting was both hard and exhausting. In one action involving 'A' Sqn, 50th RTR, the infantry they were supporting had failed to flush out the enemy from an area of close country and suddenly a battery of 88s opened fire at point-blank range, knocking out all six tanks of the two leading troops. Five burst into flames immediately. Lt M.O. Waddell earned a well-deserved Military Cross, when he went forward under fire in his scout car and rescued eleven survivors from the burning tanks. On another occasion 'B' Sqn 50th lost nine tanks protecting infantry in close-quarter fighting. 25th Armoured Brigade history sums up the battle for Sicily by describing it as: 'the hardest, the bloodiest and above all, the most disillusioning campaign in which the brigade served during the war.' They lost 25 out of a force of 95 tanks in the short campaign.

One interesting innovation which came in during the Sicilian campaign was the introduction of composite rations (known as 'Compo') as the history of the 44th relates:

It was at this period also that the rations took on a 'new look'. Whereas previously the staple diet had been bully beef, biscuits, meat and vegetables, jam and tea, there now arrived fascinating boxes containing all that was required for so many men for so many days. One of these boxes issued to a tank crew would last them for three or four days and contained stews, steak pudding, suet pudding, tinned fruit, boiled sweets, cigarettes and even tea and sugar ready mixed with milk in powder form. This issue, known as 'compo rations' was, needless to say, greatly appreciated.

GREECE (OCTOBER 1944-JANUARY 1945)

The RTR was to return to Greece towards the end of the war, when the German occupation forces withdrew in October 1944. 23 Armoured Brigade, still comprising 40th, 46th and 50th RTR, formed part of the British contingent. 40th and 50th were temporarily converted to infantry before leaving Egypt, while the 46th was split up, with 'B' and 'C' Sqns - still with tanks - joining the other two regiments, and RHQ and 'A' Sqn being equipped with armoured cars. The force was initially welcomed with open arms and immediately split up

A Sherman of 'C 'Sqn, 50 RTR gives covering fire to a street patrol in Athens during the fighting in Greece in December 1944-45. Initially they were the only tanks operating there, but were later joined by 46 RTR. TM

A Sherman of 46 RTR gives covering fire for a group of paratroopers who are getting ready to cross the street, during bitter hand-to-hand fighting in Athens. TM

Athens again, more street fighting and more difficult and dangerous work for the tanks and paratroopers during the ELAS rising. TM

and sent all over Greece, to help with the preservation of law and order. Unfortunately this wide dispersion meant it was extremely difficult to react effectively when the Communist-controlled ELAS rose in armed insurrection. 23 Armoured Brigade was responsible for internal security in Athens and all of Attica. Fighting was confused and sporadic, but there were a number of fierce attacks on the outposts. By 5 January the worst of the fighting was over, and a squadron of 46th RTR took part in the pursuit of the ELAS command of Thebes, where they were forced to sue for an armistice.

One interesting task given to 50th RTR involved Capt Barry O'Sullivan's troop which was sent to Salamis Island. His party of 30 men had taken control before the ELAS rising, so they were able to arrest the rebels before they could raise trouble. They controlled the distribution of food and fuel, policing the island with 200 dockyard workers whom O'Sullivan had raised and armed as police.

The prestige of the British force was extremely high among the 20 000 inhabitants and they managed to prevent any attempts by ELAS to get onto the island, instituting boat patrols and repulsing two attempted landings.

Before they left Athens to return to Egypt, the Brigade was visited by the Supreme Commander Mediterranean Theatre, Field Marshal Alexander, who told them that he realised how difficult it had been for tank men to fight without their tanks, but that if Britain had not taken action then there would have been large-scale massacres all over Greece: '…a good, stout-hearted Brigade on the spot prevented this and the Greek people are grateful to you.'

---

[1] However, it can be argued that the abortive campaign caused the Germans to delay *Barbarossa* (the assault on Russia) and this had a major effect on the outcome of the war.
[2] *Seconds Out* by Kenneth Chadwick.

Chapter 11

ITALY

PREPARATION

As the Regiment rested at Homs with the remainder of 7th Armoured Division, Jake Wardrop of 5th RTR wrote in his diary:

About the beginning of August we started to equip again; the campaign in Sicily was drawing to an end and we all had a pretty good idea where we would be going next... The tanks with big mileages were taken away and we got new ones, tracks were renewed and things started to move. I got a Sherman and the crew was Stan driving, Carlo - machine gunner, Jimmy - 75pdr, and the old Pathan Woody - operator. We did some shooting and 'Sure-Shot' Jimmy blew the targets to pieces at any range. All the old hands were there again. The ones who had sworn that

they were finished after Tunis, the bugle blew and they were off to war.

In addition to individual training and re-equipping, they had to be trained to fight in close country and also had to practise for their coming seaborne landing, as Wardrop recalls:

Two chaps came from REME one day and gave a demonstration of how a Sherman could be water-proofed to drive in 6ft of water. They fitted a cowling over the air intake, extended the exhausts to stick up in the air, plugged everything up with putty and pitch, and sealed down the driver's and machine gunner's flaps. It was then possible to drive in right up to the turret which they did one Sunday morning. We all turned up to cheer or laugh, depending on

Invasion practice in North Africa. Before attempting a seaborne landing on the coast of Italy, the invasion force had to practise both the waterproofing of vehicles and the tactics of a 'wet' landing. Here a Sherman medium tank leaves the open bow door of a landing craft somewhere on the North African coast near Homs, June 1943. TM

whether it was a success or not and just in case, a tow rope was shackled to a tank on the beach. It was a huge success; the tank reversed right in until the water almost went into the turret, then came out forward. They did it once more for good luck and the experiment was over. Within a week all the tanks in the battalion had been treated for taking to the water except for some finishing touches which were to be done in the Tripoli area... On 27 August the tanks were packed, the work was finished and we were ready to go. It was great, the lads were frisking around like dogs with two tails, our spirits had soared sky-high again. That day the canteen came and by the old ruse Stan, George and I got five each of beer, which was better than nothing. We had a little party for a farewell to Homs, that delightful seaside resort.

THE LANDINGS

On 3 September 1943, the same day as the armistice was signed with Italy, the invasion started with a virtually unopposed seaborne assault across the Straits of Messina from Sicily, followed on 9 September by another in the Gulf of Taranto, which also involved troops of the British Eighth Army. On the same day, the US Fifth Army met strong German opposition when they landed in the Gulf of Salerno. The RTR was well represented in both armies and RTR units continued to serve in Italy until final victory, a total of twelve battalions being involved at one time or another - 1st, 2nd, 5th, 6th, 8th, 12th, 40th, 44th, 46th, 48th, 50th and 51st.

The first RTR unit to land was the 40th RTR at Salerno, where they took part in the initial assault, together with the Greys, supporting 46th and 56th Divisions. Four days later 5th RTR landed, followed on the 22nd by the 1st, both regiments being part of 7th Armoured Division, which spearheaded the advance towards Naples through the Vietri Gap, near Mount Vesuvius. They pushed on until they reached the Volturno River on 10 October, when two squadrons of the 40th were embarked into LCTs and put ashore on the northern bank at the river mouth to take the enemy from the rear. A similar stratagem was tried again at the next river line, the Garigliano, but this had to be abandoned as the beach was too heavily mined.

Tanks of 22 Armd Bde halted in the morning mist just outside Naples. They were part of 7th Armoured Division and had landed at Salerno with US Fifth Army during Operation Avalanche which had begun on 9 Sep 43. First RTR unit to land there was 40 RTR and four days later 5 RTR. TM

7th Armoured Division was pulled out of Italy to train for 'D' Day, just before the Garigliano was reached, the 1st and 5th embarking for the UK on 20 December. This left just the 40th with 10th Corps for the eventual crossing of the Garigliano in mid-January 1944. The Regiment is unlikely to forget that winter of ice, snow, sleet and torrential rain, as they continued their slow, slogging advance up the west coast. At the end of January, 50th RTR was sent over from the Adriatic coast to rejoin 23 Armoured Brigade in the Garigliano bridgehead, then in March the complete brigade again went across to rejoin the Eighth Army on the east coast.

The fighting on both fronts in Italy was as difficult and dangerous as any the RTR has ever had to face. With the Italians out of the reckoning, the Germans buckled down to a tenacious and determined defence, in countryside which always favoured the defender. The craggy mountains running down the central spine of Italy had many closely cultivated ridges running away at right angles down to the narrow coastal plains. The streams and rivers in between these ridges had cut their way deeper and deeper into the soil of the plains so that they formed an ideal series of natural tank obstacles and lines of defence. Space does not permit a detailed account of all the battles fought by the men of the 'forgotten' Eighth Army who, very unfairly, became known as the 'D Day Dodgers', when the war in Europe stole the headlines. However, here are a few battle stories which at least give an accurate 'flavour' of the fighting there.

CROSSING THE SANGRO

The battle to cross the River Sangro and break through the strong German defences was typical of the winter operations of 1943-44 and shows how the weather and the bad going could, at times, affect the battle even more than the enemy. 50th RTR were in support of 8th Indian Division at the time and played a major part in the operation. Their initial task was to cross the river and then to form up on the escarpment to the north within a bridgehead to be established by 78th Division. The Indians would then break out on a two-brigade front with 'A' and 'B' Squadrons, 50th RTR, each supporting a brigade. Once they had secured their objectives, the rest of 4 Armoured Brigade would pass through and roll up the enemy defences from the rear, eastwards towards the sea. During the planning and recce phases continuous rain fell, which made the task of getting across the river and up the escarpment more difficult daily. After much patrolling it was decided that there were only two suitable tracks up the escarpment; however, confirmatory foot recces were impossible as 78th Division was unable to secure the bridgehead. The 50th had been increased for the river crossing by ten extra tanks which they took over from 46th RTR,

A Sherman of 'B' Sqn, 5 RTR, negotiates a narrow street in Rafati, north of Naples. During the Italian campaign, twelve RTR battalions would be involved at one time or another. TM

giving them a strength of 61 - one can imagine the headaches for the squadron commanders, trying to find the men to crew them, but eventually they managed. The first crossing attempt took place on the night of 19 November, 50th RTR's history giving a vivid account of the problems they encountered:

At 2100 hrs Major D.P. Venn, MC, returned to RHQ and informed the CO that, as had been expected, the majority of the tanks were stuck in the river bed at H443905. Twelve tanks of 'A' Sqn (Major E.T.W. Jenkin, MC) had got through and were presumably at Paglietta (just south of the town). Wireless silence being in force, this could not be confirmed. The other two regiments of the brigade were following on the same route. By morning all three regiments, less 'A' Sqn's twelve tanks, were piled up in the river bed area, a pathetic sight. Luckily, the enemy air did not observe the dire plight the brigade was in.

78th Division had, by this time, managed to get a brigade across the river to form a bridgehead, and on 21 November a second order was received by 50th RTR for 'A' Sqn to attempt again to get tanks over to support the bridgehead troops:

A troop was sent down. One tank got bogged on this side of the river, a second got over but could get no further. Another tank was sent, and this got over, but blew up on a mine while attempting an alternative route. The attempt was then given up. The tank strength was being gradually whittled away due to this bogging, but the loss was considered acceptable by higher authority owing to the

This 5 RTR Sherman was called Emanvee (Meat & Vegetables) *after the tins of M&V in the ration packs. It is passing an Italian farmer with his ox-cart on the road to Aversa, north of Naples, October 1943.* TM

tactical situation. On this date, 20 tanks were off the road, due to this reason... 'B' Sqn (Major R. Garratt) was ordered down to the river line and a troop commenced to cross. The troop got over, but the ground on the far side was so soft that they got bogged. 'B' Sqn harboured at The Mill, where they stayed until they finally crossed.

This day the initial attack was altered - the axis of advance for 8th Indian Division was changed. They were now to advance up the line of the road to Mozzagrogna, a key position in the Corps plan. 17 Indian Infantry Brigade were given the task of capturing this objective with 'B' Sqn in support. 21 Indian Infantry Brigade were to swing to the right, with 'A' Sqn, to secure Li Colli Ridge. The follow-up of 4 Armoured Brigade was unchanged. Repeated patrols were made on the line of the river to try and find suitable crossings for tanks. Outside efforts having failed, Maj J.C. de F. Sleeman (then acting CO) decided to construct one himself. This crossing utilised the main Paglietta-Mozzagrogna main road as far as possible. All that was required was four hours' bulldozer work on the far bank. Unfortunately, no RE work was undertaken the first night, and 24 hours were lost. During the night 25-26 November the RE work was excellently carried out, but there had been rain in the mountains during the day and a rise of 4ft in the water recorded, just as the RE's work was completed. This spate of water altered the current from the middle of the river to the far bank, and made the crossing impassable.

One tank of 'B' Sqn was tried across it at 0300hrs, but stuck and was drowned, blocking the bulldozed gap. Attempts were again made by 'B' Sqn at other places along the river, but all failed

owing to the wet ground, two more tanks being bogged. The next morning, the CO asked for Bailey bridges, but the materials and personnel would not be available for the following night. An alternative route was then selected. The whole attack was now dependent upon the success of our efforts to get tanks over. These efforts were ceaseless, but on every occasion, just when things seemed to be going well, something happened to throw them out of gear. 8th Indian Division were quite prepared to put the attack in, with the proviso that they could get their supporting weapons, ie tanks, anti-tank guns and mules, over the river. There had been no consistency in the weather during the whole of the planning stages. The rain held off just long enough on many occasions to enable final plans to be made, and then down it came and everything had to be redone. This could be seen from the fact that 8th Indian Division issued four operation orders prior to the attack.

A successful crossing was finally achieved on the afternoon of 26 November and the next phase of operations, the break-in battle, started on the 27th. Undoubtedly the bad weather had proved to be a more difficult opponent than the enemy. The Regiment had a total of 31 tanks bogged at one time or another, plus 15 put out of action by mines, and one completely drowned.

The 50th pushed on and was involved in the hard fighting north of the river; the next extract from their history gives a good example of the personal bravery of their tank commanders:

Lt K.J. Pillar led the attack on to the objective, where he was dealing effectively with machine-gun and mortar positions which were holding up the infantry. In manoeuvring for position near the top of the ridge, and while still ahead of the leading infantry, Lt Pillar's tank was hit by an enemy tank about 400yds to the north-east. Without hesitating, he continued to advance and fight his tank. It was hit a second time, putting the gun out of action. Lt Pillar gave the order to bale out and he and three of the crew succeeded in getting to the ground in face of heavy MG fire from the enemy tank and infantry MG and mortar positions. One of the crew who baled out was wounded. Lt Pillar, in spite of the exposed position and intense fire which was being directed on them, dressed the wounded man and carried him to a more sheltered position. Lt Pillar then realised that the driver was still in the closed-down tank and, on hearing that he was wounded, he advanced alone to the tank, which was still under short-range AP fire from the enemy tank and in danger of being set on fire at any minute. While climbing onto the tank it was

A Sherman medium tank belonging to 40 RTR, crossing the River Gargliano in mid-January 1944. TM

hit a third time, the force of the impact throwing Lt Pillar to the ground. Undaunted and completely ignoring his personal safety, he again climbed on the front of the tank and began to open the driver's hatch. As the hatch was being opened, he was killed outright by a fourth AP shot.

Lt Pillar's troop originally consisted only of two tanks. The other tank (Sgt E.G. Taylor), which was covering Lt Pillar, was also ahead of the infantry. At this stage the infantry were running short of ammunition and temporarily fell back some 200yds to await further supplies. Sgt Taylor therefore was left well forward entirely single-handed, facing a ridge over the top of which he knew were enemy tanks. He held his ground with extreme calm and continued to fire at enemy positions, keeping his CO informed of the situation. When a second troop reached him to give support, he dismounted and by crawling some distance he located three of the crew who had baled out of Lt Pillar's tank, and assisted to dress one who was wounded. They told him that Lt Pillar had returned to the tank to attempt to get the driver out, but had not been seen since. In fact Lt Pillar had been killed in this attempt. Sgt Taylor continued crawling to the knocked-out tank, but realised that it was hopeless to try to get to it, as the enemy tank still had it covered. He therefore returned to the crew and assisted them back to his own tank, put his supporting troop leader in the picture and brought back the wounded man on his tank.

Of course it wasn't always mounted action. No tank man likes to be operating outside his vehicle, but on many occasions this was necessary, as was the case in this next account:

To ensure that his squadron would arrive at their correct location Lt G. Keohane was ordered to accompany the infantry on foot, to recce a route for the tanks and to find out where any diversions or mine-clearing work was required. Keohane took two of Recce Troop's carriers as far as possible and then dismounted with a manpack radio - a No 38 set - to keep in touch with the carriers who would then pass back the information to RHQ via the more powerful vehicle 19 set.

The history of the 50th records his adventures:

Soon after leaving the carriers, the 38 set was put out of action and runner became the only means of communication. The infantry attack was successful, but pockets of enemy resistance were left behind and Lt Keohane constantly ran into groups of enemy on his recce. Whilst examining a track, he ran into the crew of a 75mm anti-tank gun who were in the process of spiking their weapon before abandoning it. Lt Keohane dived for cover as the enemy took up their arms, but as he was planning to take them on, two worked round and captured him. He then struggled for some time and made as much noise as possible, and was successful in attracting the attention of a Mahrattas section, who were mopping up. Some time was lost in establishing his identity. Lt Keohane, however, succeeded in leading this section and eventually took all the enemy prisoner. By this time, heavy mortar fire was falling on the road, and it became impossible for the sappers to continue sweeping for mines. Lt Keohane, realising the importance of his task, went forward and was able to satisfy himself that the road was clear of mines and capable of

Above: *This Sherman belonged to 50 RTR of 4th Armd Bde and is seen here moving up to the River Sangro in December 1943. In the background are the Maiella Mountains.* TM

Left: *A Sherman belonging to 2 Troop, 'B' Sqn, 44 RTR also of 4th Armd Bde, halted at the Sangro River crossing.* TM

carrying tanks. Two of the Mahrattas section accompanied him after his first misfortune, as escort, and at this stage one ducked quickly to avoid mortar shrapnel and unfortunately his bayonet wounded Lt Keohane in the leg. Lt Keohane carried on, completed his recce, and in pain walked back to his carrier and gave a concise report to his Squadron Leader. He returned again to the forward infantry, established their position, and when the tanks arrived, was able to lead them into their battle position with a minimum of delay.

HELL'S HALF-ACRE

On 21 January 1944, 46th RTR, which had been operating in the Garigliano Valley, was withdrawn, moved to Castelmare and embarked into LSTs. They sailed for Anzio, arriving at the beach-head on the 22nd. The landing was unopposed, but the enemy soon reacted and rapidly the assault force found itself facing a semi-circle of 10 German divisions. The fighting in the beach-head, which became known as 'Hell's Half-Acre', was some of the bloodiest of the Italian Campaign. 46th RTR not only supported the infantry throughout the operations, but also spearheaded three of the mobile columns which eventually achieved the breakout five long months later. These extracts from the diary of 'A' Squadron, 46th RTR, deal with a typical early day in the beach-head:

22-23 Jan: The Sqn commenced to land at 1600 on 22nd and by 0900 23 January it was completely assembled in area 'DOG'.

24 Jan: Sqn moved to 'RED HOUSES'. Sqn CO informed that the squadron had been placed in support of the Guards Brigade and that it would form part of a 'mobile column' which was to proceed the following day along the Anzio-Albano road. Enemy tanks were known to be in the area of Carroceto village.

25 Jan: The leading elements of the column - 3 carriers Grenadier Guards and No 1 Tank Troop (Lt Dodd) - passed over the flyover bridge (862286) at 1715hrs without incident. As the carriers approached the road junction at 862298 they were engaged by enemy small-arms fire from the general direction 850300. This was immediately engaged by the tanks (HE 75mm and Browning) and effectively silenced. From this point the tanks were placed in the lead. As the leading tank approached the railway bridge at 865326, enemy infantry were sighted on the bridge and were immediately engaged with small-arms fire, but not with any marked success owing to the height of the bridge and the adjoining embankment, which provided the enemy with excellent cover. At this juncture, the road immediately under the bridge was observed to be mined, with trip wires on either side. An RE party was detailed to remove these obstructions but they were driven off by concentrated enemy

small-arms fire and mortars. The leading tank (comd - Sgt Herbert) was accordingly instructed to ease his tank forward through the mines and unfortunately he lost both tracks. A platoon of Guards was then brought forward to cover the REs and the bridge was finally taken by a company of Guards - the tanks giving full support and successfully eliminating very heavy mortar fire which had been coming from the direction of the station. Immediately the road was cleared of mines, the OC instructed No 2 Troop to push forward into the village in advance of the infantry. The leading tank (Sgt Chadwick) was fired upon from the right (it was afterwards discovered that this part of the road was covered by an enemy tank from the 'Factory' area) immediately it left the cover of the bridge, but it reached the village successfully although the remaining two tanks could not make it. Sgt Chadwick proceeded through the village and disposed of a 50mm anti-tank gun at very close range and, at the request of the infantry, gave all the houses in the immediate vicinity a thorough 'dusting' with 75mm. Several enemy infantry were seen making for the factory area. The OC now sent No 4 Troop into the village to cover the infantry 'follow through' into the factory area and No 3 Troop were also sent to take position

Churchills belonging to 'A' Sqn, 51 RTR, at the Gothic Line in September 1944. They are on a hill overlooking the River Foglia and are waiting to attack. TM

The Eighth Army's advance on Ferrara. Infantrymen clamber onto a Sherman to begin the final advance through the Argenta Gap. TM

A GEORGE CROSS FOR THE REGIMENT

On 23 July 1944, Lt St John Graham Young, RTR, who was then serving with the Central India Horse, was in command of a patrol ordered to occupy a hill. At about 2200hrs as the patrol neared its objective, explosions were heard at very close range. Young thought they were under mortar fire and ordered a withdrawal to the previous bound but, while they were doing so, more explosions were heard in their midst. Young realised that they had run into a mine-field and at once ordered everyone to stay still until daylight - it was a moonless night and the country was both scrub arid broken.

After about two hours one of the patrol, who had been wounded and was now in great pain, started calling for help. Young immediately began to crawl forward, telling everyone else to stay where they were. He went forward, probing in front with his fingers and managed to find and render safe three Schu mines. Getting closer, he realised that he had to alter course slightly and, as he did so, knelt on a Schu mine which blew off his right leg. Immediately he told the patrol he had been wounded but that everyone was to remain where they were. He then continued to crawl towards the wounded man, whom he found unconscious, and applied a dressing to the man's thigh which had been shattered by a Schu mine. It was now about 0100hrs.

Until almost 0600hrs, when the Regimental Medical Officer found him, he continued to command his patrol. He was then sitting up giving orders to his patrol, indicating the way and supervising the evacuation of wounded. He lost consciousness soon after 0600hrs and died that evening. His citation for the George Cross says:

> Lt Young, by crawling forward into an area he knew to be thickly mined, in order to help one of his patrol, showed the greatest personal courage and contempt for danger. And later, throughout the long period of five hours from the time when he was wounded to the moment of losing consciousness, this young officer, by his inspiring leadership, cheerfulness and disregard for pain, maintained complete control of his patrol. It was a direct result of his determination to the end that the remaining members of the patrol reached safety. In thus laying down his life, Lt Young showed that he understood the limitless responsibilities of a leader and that, with a great heart, he accepted them.

THE SENIO ASSAULT

The war of patrols, static shoots and feints, which the winter of 1944-5 and the exigencies of other theatres had compelled, was now over. With the whole weight of Allied power ready for the assault, 48th RTR prepared for its last battle. The troops rallied in

covering enemy interference from the left flank. The infantry shortly afterwards reported that the factory was in their hands.

At 1530hrs Lt Wingate and Lt Wells were wounded simultaneously whilst conversing outside their tanks. Lt Triffitt took immediate control of No 3 Troop and Sgt Williams No 4 Troop. At 1600hrs the tanks were required to assist the infantry in a set-piece attack on two houses flanking the road on a forward ridge at 870336. The houses were mortared heavily for 10mins, smoke was put down on the left flank by the Medium Regiment and No 3 Troop moved forward along the road followed by our infantry. As the tanks approached the crest they deployed to the right and fired on the two houses. Enemy were seen to leave in utter confusion. No 4 Troop followed the infantry and deployed left to afford flank protection.

The infantry were able to dig in almost immediately and at last light reported that they were completely satisfied and that their anti-tank guns were in position. At dark, the squadron was withdrawn into leaguer at 864302.

Tank state: 1 tank damaged track
               1 tank damaged sprocket (AP)
               1 tank damaged transmission (HE)

Casualties: Lt Wingate (subsequently died),
               Lt Wells and Sgt Herbert

Waiting for the mules. Italy was the one European theatre where the Allies used pack transport animals in the mountains. Here a Sherman has to wait for some slower road users to get clear in the outskirts of a small town. TM

Bagnacavallo on 3 April and occupied a concentration point just outside the town on 5 April. As tension on both sides mounted, every evening brought a fresh display of rockets, mortars, nebelwerfers and HE, though these were fortunately, mainly directed outside the Regimental concentration area. On 8 April the tanks moved to a forward area and the following day the assault against the Senio positions began. 'B' Squadron, 48th RTR was committed from the evening of the 9th and at 1900 took up action stations. One troop went forward in support of flamethrowers operating against the river banks. In the darkness the rest of the squadron awaited the signal to advance. This is how the advance was described in the souvenir number of their *'B Line' Magazine*:

10 April: Tanks advance at 0420 and at 0500 cross the Senio, being the first armour to do so. By dawn the whole squadron had made a substantial advance into territory which, until a few hours previously, the enemy had held for six months. The tanks are operating in the Lugo area and little opposition is encountered until 1615hrs when the enemy is engaged. Self-propelled guns and other large calibre pieces are in evidence. The harbour to which the squadron repairs in the evening is swept by Spandaus.

11 April: Two troops of tanks leave the harbour at 0420 to lay covering fire for an infantry assault. Harbour is shifted; a Tiger tank opens up at long range without causing any damage.

12 April: Another move in the small hours (0400) and the troops make contact with their infantry. In the evening, tanks and infantry cross a canal and enlarge the bridgehead on the other side. A cautious advance of some 2000yds ensues

during which houses and other potential gun sites are sprayed with fire. It is close country intersected with lines of vines. The tough wire supporting the vines wreaks considerable minor damage to mudguards and exterior fittings of vehicles. One tank loses a track while negotiating an irrigation ditch. Light is failing when the squadron, moving in line ahead, makes a dash through hitherto unpenetrated country and enters San Patrizio. A number of prisoners are taken during this 'swan'. When the town has been secured, two troops, with infantry aboard their tanks, are despatched to prevent demolition of canal bridges two miles ahead. Their mission is successful, a bridge demolition party is shot up and prisoners taken. The rapid advance has thrown the enemy into confusion, and back in San Patrizio an SP gun is obliged to surrender to the squadron commander.

13 April: While the remainder of the squadron holds San Patrizio, the two detached troops guard the bridges while enemy panzers shell from the far bank. The stonking intensifies during the day and one tank comes under heavy AP fire.

15 April: The squadron concentrates near San Patrizio, remaining there for two days. On 17th it proceeds 15 miles to join up with the infantry.

18 April: Reveille is 0330 and, while still dark, tanks advance two miles with infantry aboard. Spandau fire necessitates disembarkation of infantry. As the squadron skirts Argenta, prisoners are taken. By 0800hrs the enemy suddenly opens up with mortars, Spandaus and AP fire from concealed AP guns. The Churchills engage the points of fire and for the next three hours endure bitter shelling. Under this barrage several tanks are hit and brewed up. There are casualties. By noon the situation is somewhat easier. Tanks which have been pinned down return under cover of smoke and rally, with the exception of one troop which has pushed on and is holding an area with a small group of infantry. The squadron now musters only four battleworthy tanks.

21 April: Replacement tanks arrived at first light on 20th; the following day the reconstituted troops make a rapid six-mile move to meet their infantry. At 1630 the push is on again. Enemy delaying action is determined, mortaring is heavy and prisoners are taken at this stage. The rate of advance greatly increases under cover of darkness, engaging targets en route, the squadron initiates a swanning movement which continued until 0330 on the 22nd. Twenty miles have been covered overnight and the tanks' spearhead is within three miles af Ferrara. At 1400 infantry and tanks advance to the canal in front of the town. Progress is checked as the

bridge is found demolished and a Tiger tank covers the approach. The squadron's leading tank is hit repeatedly and the crew injured. On the following day troops re-form east of Ferrara and prepare to continue the advance. An approach march of 11 miles on the 25th brings the column to within 800yds of the Po. Features of this march are the number of enemy prisoners and horses passed on the road and the thick dust.

27 April: The tanks are on the move at three in the morning and advance through heavy rain, thunder and lightning to the Po. Vehicles are ferried across the river one at a time, a procedure which causes considerable delay, but ferrying continues throughout the night and by dawn on the 28th the whole squadron is across. The tanks proceed to Revigo, where troops spend a night in billets. Shortly after noon next day the squadron advances to the Adige River and, after an hour's wait owing to congestion at the hastily constructed bridge, crosses the river and, pushing on with all speed, reaches Brenta Lungo near Venice, accomplishing the 50-mile march in 5½ hrs.

2 May brought news of the unconditional surrender of the enemy in Italy and on 8 May, the day of the official announcement of the capitulation of Germany, the squadron rejoined the rest of 48th RTR at Stanghella, just north of the Adige. This is how the *'B Line' Magazine* closed its story:

Tanks! Cross, insatiable beasts which demanded slavish attention, which wallowed in filth and devoured vast quantities of sustenance - and yet, for so long virtually our homes and the focal points of our endeavours. Tanks, spitting rapid death or thundering measured destruction; tanks - a lurching column of them, more massive and more formidable in the African moonlight, or decked with vineleaves and branches, advancing in carnivalesque procession among the Apennine foothills. The distant clatter of tracks in an Algerian olive grove, the angry glow of red hot exhausts in the night. And dust spirals of dust, blankets of dust, moving clouds of dust, surmounted by black berets. Vivid impressions of darkness relieved by graceful arcs of tracer fire, or dispelled by flares and burning dumps. Ships - Landing craft on Loch Fyne; troopships bursting with human cargoes; swaying hammocks; cursing and loss of equipment. Fishing craft off Riccione, and Venetian gondolas. Trucks - endless convoys, creeping up fissures in the Atlas mountains, winding through Tunisia, exploring every route from Taranto to Turin: ammo trucks, petrol trucks, liberty trucks. Prisoners - hundreds of thousands trudging the roads and filling enormous compounds. Rain and wind - the hot sirocco which scorched Cap Bon and Penthievre. Exotic shrubs and fantastic reptiles, scorpions and centipedes and the infuriating cigale. Inoculations, drill parades, guards, fatigues - Ah! The enchantment dies...

We disperse and go our ways. From time to time, God willing, we will meet; perchance we will see our own transitions to sedate and greying citizens reflected in each other. But when this happens we will not be thinking of what we are then but of what we were during the testing time of active service, and we will delve into the wealth of experience which is ours. The remembrance of these things, the fellowships and the hardships will not fade away; and while remembrance endures the squadron will live on.

A 2 RTR Sherman threads its way carefully through the streets of an Italian town. TM

Tankies enjoying some R&R in Venice.
(Author's collection)

Chapter 12
PREPARING FOR 'D' DAY

EXPANSION OF THE TRAINING MACHINE

The expansion of the training machine which began in 1939-40 continued apace throughout the early years of the war, leading to a massive effort to prepare the invasion force for 'D' Day. In all this training it is impossible to divide the RTR effort from that of the remainder of the Royal Armoured Corps, although it was considerable, because of the sound methods of training and the reserves of trained officers and men which the Regiment had built up before the war. The expansion was enormous as it had to cope with the training of over 190 Regular, Territorial and wartime-formed units of the RAC, not to mention two regiments of Household Cavalry, the seven of Foot Guards that were converted to armour,

plus the Commonwealth and foreign contingents such as the Canadians, Czechs and Poles.

From early 1941, D & M and gunnery training courses had to be run, not only on the numerous British-built AFVs but also on the newly arriving American tanks, such as Stuarts, Grants and Shermans. It soon became necessary for Training Regiments to specialise - hardly surprising when there were no fewer than 42 different AFVs in British Army service in 1943-44! A selection system had also to be developed that earmarked a man for a particular type of AFV even before he started training, then ensured that he was trained exclusively on that type and, finally, that he was posted to a unit so equipped. From July 1941, when the Americans started to arrive in the UK, most of the RAC Training Regiments had to move up north in order to make room for the US

'Speed the Tanks!' All over Great Britain throughout the war years, there were continual parades and other events to boost civilian morale and to raise funds for the war effort. Tanks were always very popular. This parade was held in Bath in 1941, the Home Guard, who can be seen in the background were led by a Matilda Mk2 tank and a Daimler 'Dingo' scout car. TM

The Prime Minister was everywhere! In the first of these two photographs he is climbing up steps to inspect one of the new heavy tanks that bore his name - the Churchill. In the second, he inspects a complete regiment of Churchills on parade with their RTR crews. TM

forces, although those stationed at the Army AFV School (Bovington and Lulworth) remained in situ.

From 1943 onwards, the main task of the training machine was to help get the invasion forces ready for 'D' Day. It was a rush job, not made any easier by cuts in training manpower in order to make up field force units, and by the withdrawal of trained instructors from the AFV School for continuation and specialised training in units. The AFV School was the

most important part of the training machine, being the birthplace of all doctrine for RAC training, because it was so well equipped with both trained instructors and proper facilities.

Lt-Col Tony Blad, MBE, late RTR, joined the Army in May 1943 and was trained at 58th Training Regiment, Bovington Camp. He writes:

The huts (as I remember) were joined together in pairs with a corridor running between them containing the washing facilities. The outside of the barrack rooms was sandbagged. The huts were scrupulously clean inside. We slept on double-tier bunks, reveille was at 05.45, washing and shaving was in cold water. The furniture in the barrack room consisted of a 6ft trestle table and two wooden benches which were cleaned by scraping the surfaces with a razor blade until they were white. There was a stirrup-pump and fire-bucket, also a coal bucket but as all these items had to be kept clean and smart they were never used. Nobody ever contemplated lighting the round stove which would otherwise have heated the premises.

The keen young soldiers spent the next six weeks learning the basic skills of military training, drill, the rifle, the Mills grenade and the Bren gun. We were also taught the Boyes anti-tank gun which was by then obsolescent, if not obsolete. There were lessons on gas which were given by a sergeant who was known as 'Phosgene Pete'. Knowledge of chlorine and mustard gas did not seem to have engendered a sense of humour in this otherwise efficient instructor and we treated him with considerable respect…

At the end of the six weeks the majority of the intake moved down to the 58th Training Regiment at Stanley Barracks. The Regiment was responsible for training recruits for the Royal Armoured Corps in the skills needed by tank crews and it was said to be particularly geared to the training of potential NCOs and Officers. The first three weeks were spent in General Military Training which was an extension of the work at 30 PTW but we now wore the RAC badge. Then began our proper training with five weeks of Driving and Maintenance.

It was an extremely good course which included basic instruction on vehicles followed by wheeled-vehicle driving, classroom instruc-tion in tank details and tank driving. The wheeled-vehicle driving instructor was a some-what stout corporal who played the saxophone and had a much better sense of humour than the majority of corporals whom we had contacted so far in our training. Driving a Crusader tank made one feel a bit special even if there was only a qualified 'f. good' on one's training report.

The accommodation was in the familiar wooden spider blocks where the same high standards of cleanliness were maintained as had been instilled in the Primary Training Wing. Bedding was folded and blocked each day and a complete set of webbing was blancoed, polished and laid out. All clothing had to be marked with one's Arm Number and occasionally there was a full kit check with every item of equipment presented and displayed in accordance with time honoured-custom and in the correct order: knife, fork, spoon, razor, comb and lather brush…

The discipline was extremely strict. Troopers stood to attention when speaking to NCOs and only high standards of turnout were accepted. Everyone leaving barracks reported to the Guardroom and was inspected before 'booking out' and it was not unknown for men to be told to return to their barrack-room and clean their buttons, brasses or beret. A great deal of time was spent in ironing knife-edge creases in our battle dresses. Those who did leave the barracks had to book in at the Guardroom on their return and present themselves to the Guard Commander who, one hoped, would write SPD (sober and properly dressed) against the appropriate name in the book with the time of return beside it to confirm that one was not late. As the nearest pub was 2½ miles away, the pay extremely low and there was no transport, it was most unlikely that anyone returning to camp would be drunk.

Part of the four-week gunnery training was completed in Bovington but the firing took place on the Lulworth Ranges and it was during this time that the trainees were housed and fed in Park Camp. It was a fairly scruffy collection of huts and fortunately there was a compensating reduction in the need for spit and polish… On the ranges, we fired the 2pdr gun mounted in Valentines. This main armament was elevated and depressed using a shoulder-holster and was, at this time, nearly, if not quite, obsolete. We also fired the 6pdr and, amongst the machine guns, a Bren gun mounted on the turret with a system of springs intended as an anti-aircraft weapon We fired on Bindon Hill against an aeroplane silhouette which moved in a straight line on the moving target track - even so, it was extremely difficult to hit.

Four weeks were spent in Wireless Training wrestling with phonetic alphabets, radio procedure, the Morse Code and the No 19 Wireless Set. It was a change to be away from the dirty jobs associated with the tank park and, to a lesser extent, the Gunnery Wing. Those who learned about the 19 Set were special, for it needed constant attention to keep it working properly, tuning and retuning using the 'penny screws' and readjusting the variometer. The morse test

HM King George VI also carried out many visits and inspections. He too is about to climb onto a Churchill. However, this was one of the earliest models, which had a 2pdr gun in the turret and a three-inch close-support howitzer in its nose. TM

Training of course had to continue at ever increasing speed and intensity, preparing for the 'Second Front'. Here an instructor gets his class to recognise and deal with faults on the BESA machine gun, which was the standard British coaxially-mounted tank machine gun. TM

was at eight words a minute - although it was never entirely clear, then or later on, why the subject was taught.

Throughout the course there was plenty of drill and PT. The physical training staff were not over-popular especially one of the more senior ones who inspected the troop for cleanliness before training and on occasions carried a cotton-wool pad dipped into methylated spirits which he applied to the necks of those he deemed to have not washed. The PT itself was active and energetic and we were all extremely fit.

THE ROYAL TANK REGIMENT

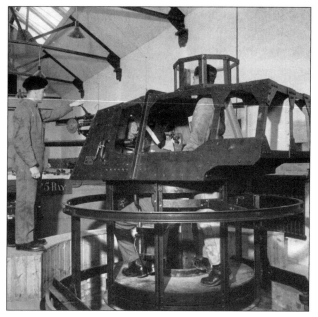

More sophisticated training devices were also introduced to make training more realistic, like this gunnery device which had an air gun fitted beside the real gun which was activated by the gunner's controls, so that, for example, the trainee gunner could engage moving targets. The cutaway portions of the turret meant that the rest of the class could see what he was doing throughout the practice shoot. TM

The final part of the course was Collective Training which consisted of a tactical exercise with carriers, simulating tanks, each carrier with a crew of four. There was also a 50-mile bash, a sort of old-fashioned yomping. The troop was divided up into sections and taken to some forgotten place 50 miles away and set off with maps, and kit and food with the aim of returning to Bovington within 48hrs. There were occasional 'tactical' incidents on route but the main task was to complete the journey. The arrangements at night were to be at our own initiative. At one village we stopped and asked whether they had a place where we could shelter and before long permission had been given for the local chapel to be opened and, moreover, the boiler was lit. When you are young, fit and tired, there is no better place to sleep than under a chapel pew with one's back against warm pipes.

HOBO'S FUNNIES

Sir Winston Churchill, in his history of the Second World War, wrote about Maj-Gen Sir Percy Hobart who, in 1941, he had brought back from obscurity to command the newly forming 11th Armoured Division:

Monty also visited the training establishment – here he is talking to some of the senior instructors at the Armoured Fighting Vehicles School at Bovington Camp. TM

Maj-Gen P.C.S. (later Sir Percy) Hobart, was the commander of the 79th Armoured Division which contained all the full range of 'Hobart's Funnies' - amazing specialised armoured fighting vehicles which would have a tremendous effect upon the outcome of 'D' Day. TM

166

One of the most important of the 'Funnies' was the DD tank, which, with its screen raised, could swim ashore and thus give direct close support to the assaulting infantry. The propellors which ran off the engine can be seen at the rear of the tank below the screen. TM

Another was the Sherman 'Crab' mine clearing vehicle, which could clear a path through an enemy minefield, using its flails which rotated on a drum mounted in front of the tank. (Author's collection)

I am quite sure that if, when I had him transferred from a corporal in the Home Guard to the command of one of the new armoured divisions, I had instead insisted upon his controlling the whole of the tank developments, with a seat on the Army Council, many of the grievous errors from which we have suffered would not have been committed.

Hobo was a great trainer of armoured troops, as he had already proved before the war on Salisbury Plain and again in Egypt with the Mobile Division. However, it was to be his later work with specialised armour 'Hobo's Funnies' as they came to be called, which was the pinnacle of his career. In 1943, aged 57, after being robbed of the chance to command 11th Armoured Division operationally on the grounds of

being too old, he was switched instead to the newly forming 79th Armoured Division, and given the task of preparing the specialised armour which would spearhead the invasion.

When Hobo was charged with the task of creating 79th Armoured Division he began with a blank sheet of paper in January 1943. Eighteen months later his 'Funnies' had been conceived, designed, developed and produced, whilst the doctrine for their use was evolved and the units trained. They would not only carry out their initial task of defeating the German beach defences, but would continue to be of inestimable value for the rest of the war. From start of finish the whole project would be minutely controlled by that great dynamic soldier. The story of 79th Armoured Division is surely one of the most remarkable achievements of the Second World War.

TYPES OF SPECIALISED ARMOUR

In the initial stages there were four main types of specialised armour in the division:

Swimming tanks, known as DD tanks, Duplex Drive being the method of propulsion conceived by the fertile imagination of Nicholas Straussler; flotation was by means of a collapsible canvas screen which could be erected around the tank to make it into a small, open-topped boat, then quickly removed when shore was reached. *Mine-clearing tanks*, like the earlier Matilda Scorpions as used in the desert, but now based on the ubiquitous Sherman; the Sherman Crab, developed in 1943, was a great improvement on the Scorpion and proved to be the most effective wartime way of gapping a minefield having the added advantage of being able to retain the use of its main armament, except when actually flailing. *Armoured engineer assault vehicles*, known as AVREs as they were manned by the Royal Engineers. *Tankborne searchlights* known as CDLs (Canal Defence Lights), which was a top secret device designed to blind the enemy during night attacks. Sadly, it was the only specialised armour not to be given a chance to show its true worth during the 'D' Day landings. It was, however, used to provide artificial moonlight during the crossings of the Rhine and the Elbe.

Later, these first four types were joined by:- *Kangaroos*, which were a basic form of armoured personnel carrier for infantry, made by simply taking the turrets off Canadian Ram tanks; *Buffaloes* which, as their name implies, were tracked amphibious landing vehicles (LVTs) which had been originally developed for the US Marines to use in the Pacific; finally, there were the *Crocodiles*, Churchill tanks fitted with lethal flamethrowers, which rapidly proved their worth and were much in demand.

43rd Royal Tank Regiment worked from June 1943 until 'D' Day as the 'Backroom Boys', doing experimental work on the various equipments which

Tank training of a more conventional kind was also essential, especially for those British armoured regiments, which had given up their Shermans for the lighter, faster, but not so well armoured, Cromwells as seen here, ploughing their way across a training area. TM

'Practice makes perfect'. Unloading Churchill tanks from landing craft in a very muddy estuary, was excellent training for all, especially after the debacle at Dieppe in 1942. This time there must be no mistakes. TM

Planning was vital. Here Monty has a briefing from Brig (later Maj-Gen) Nigel Duncan who commanded 30 Armd Bde in 79 Armd Div. Gen Hobart's hat is just visible! 30 Armd Bde's main task was mine clearance. (Author's collection)

the Division was developing and then instructing other units in their use, as the weapons became fully developed and put into service. This invaluable work kept them in UK, so they did not have a chance to join the invasion forces. At the start there were only a few RTR units serving in the Division, although the Regiment did provide a large number of the officers and men in the various headquarters, including for example, Brigadier (later Maj-Gen) Nigel Duncan commanding 30 Armoured Brigade (Flails). 11 RTR, 42nd RTR and 49th RTR, made up 1 Tank Brigade which took on the CDL role, but as they were not used for their correct task, the 11th was later re-equipped with Buffaloes (in October 1944) and the 49th with Kangaroos for the APC role. 7 RTR was part of 31 Tank Brigade and was equipped with Crocodiles, while the reconstituted 4th (formerly 144th RAC) led the attack across the Rhine in Buffaloes, on the night of 23 March. The CO (Lt-Col Alan Jolly - later General Sir Alan) carried across the same historic Tank Corps flag which 17th Battalion had flown while entering Cologne via the Hollenzollern Bridge over the Rhine in 1918. Perhaps the most unsuspecting RTR unit to become a 'Hobo's Funny' was the 44th RTR, who were converted to DD tanks in just ten days and then performed most gallantly and effectively during the Rhine crossing. Their history comments:

> The crossing was made on a two-squadron front, with 'A' Sqn right, 'C' Sqn left… Both exits had by this time been completed and soon the river was full of tanks looking rather like floating hip-baths drifting downstream. Over half of 'A' Sqn was waterborne when the enemy started shelling

the tanks as they were entering the water. One tank was hit as it left the shore and sank like a stone, but luckily all the crew abandoned ship and made the shore safely. They now have a swastika flag emblazoned on it 'First to the bottom of the Rhine 2 Baker'. The last tank of 'A' Sqn was hit as it was going down the runway into the water, but it managed to reverse out and retired for patching.

They managed to get sufficient armour to the far bank to make a major impact on the battle, Commander 12 Corps later commenting:

> There is not the slightest doubt that the presence of DD tanks on the far bank so early in the proceedings did, in my mind, materially contribute to the enemy break-up on the line of the Rhine.

It is quite certain that 79th Armoured Division played a vital part in the success of the 'D' Day landings and continued to play an important part in the final stages of the war. Just before the Rhine crossing, the Division comprised five brigades of 17 regiments, a total strength of 1566 tracked AFVs and 21 000 all ranks, as compared with the 350 AFVs and 14 000 all ranks of a normal armoured division. Liddell Hart rightly describes them as the 'tactical key to victory', while Nigel Duncan in his book about the Division, captures their jaunty mood thus:

> The inverted triangle with its ferocious Bull's Head, the divisional sign of 'Hobo's Funnies', was better known and more widely distributed in Second Army's area than any other. Inspired by its divisional commander, it pursued its way with gaiety tempered with the resolution to be defeated by no difficulty whether of Nature's or man's creation.[1]

TOWARDS 'D' DAY

In addition to 79th Armoured Division there was of course a vast Allied armada getting ready for the Normandy landings. Among these forces were 1st and 5th RTR, both in 7th Armoured Division, which had been brought back from Italy to add a leavening of experience amongst the many untried units who would shortly receive their first blooding. They would be the first RTR armoured regiments to go ashore a few days after 'D' Day and would be in action by 8 June. The third unit to land would be 44th RTR, then the 3rd, 7th and 9th. The build-up to 'D' Day varied little between units, so this extract from the 44th's history is relevant to all:

> At first we had absolutely no vehicles. Gradually these came in and then a trickle of tanks grew to

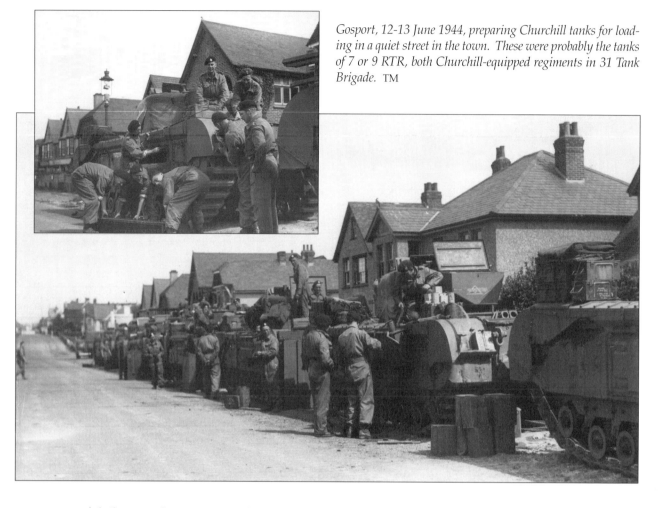

a stream of daily arrivals. Ever since the war we had had diesel-engined tanks. The new ones now being given to us were petrol-engined Shermans. We eyed them with the utmost misgivings, strongly suspecting they would prove to be under-engined and highly inflammable if hit in action. This disappointment was partly balanced by the new 'Fireflies'. These were Shermans with 17pdr guns fitted - highly secret at this stage; at last a gun which one could trust to get its teeth really deep into any German tank it met. At the end of March we went to Kirkcudbright tank ranges to fire our new tanks - and how rude they were about our shooting! Then in April we started to do training schemes... With May came a quickening of the tempo.

We began to suffer from visits and inspections. We soon found we had got all our tanks, vehicles and wireless sets. All these had to be thoroughly checked over. Round after round of ammunition had to be stowed away. We had to change the tracks and lastly there was the waterproofing to be done. By now we were up to full strength in men and equipment.

...On 4 June the first elements of the Regiment started to move out of Worthing towards the port of embarkation. The previous days had been a nightmare of hard work. It had seemed impossible to complete all that had to be done in time, but somehow all was done. There was no question of concealing the movement of the Regiment from the citizens of Worthing, so as the long columns lined up to cross the start point for the march there was seen many a touching farewell. Amid tears and cheers we pulled out on the road for Portsmouth. Here we got caught up in the great machine which churned us up into ship-loads and moved us steadily forward whilst we added in sequence further bits and pieces to vehicle waterproofing. After several delays, due to weather and other reasons, the main body of the Regiment sailed from Gosport on the evening of 8 June, 48hrs later than expected.

This fine TA Regiment had not only fought with distinction in the Western Desert and the various campaigns in the Mediterranean theatre, but had now become widely regarded as one of the outstanding armoured regiments of Monty's 21st Army Group,

---

[1] *79th Armoured Division Profile Book* No 3 by Nigel Duncan.

Chapter 13

INTO EUROPE AND ON TO VICTORY

FIRST ACTION

The 'Funnies' apart, it was 22 Armoured Brigade of 7th Armoured Division which contained the first RTR Regiments to see action in Normandy. These were 1st and 5th RTR. They landed the day after 'D' Day and were in action by 8 June, helping to clear out pockets of enemy between the British and American beach-heads. An initial armoured thrust was then made towards the south, but proved unsuccessful and the Division suffered its first heavy casualties in the Villers-Bocage area. 44th RTR landed next on 9 June with 4 Armoured Brigade. In the period following the initial landings this brigade was taken over by Brigadier (later Field Marshal) Mike Carver of 1st RTR. They were followed on 14 June by 144th RAC in 33 Independent Armoured Brigade, who would later become the 'reborn' 4th RTR. Next to land, on 17 June, was 3rd RTR who were part of 29 Armoured Brigade in Maj-Gen Pip Robert's 11th Armoured Division. Roberts had commanded the 3rd RTR and 22nd Armoured Brigade in North Africa and was, at 37, the youngest divisional commander

in the British Army. Finally, a few days later, came the 7th and 9th RTR, both Churchill-equipped regiments in 31st Tank Brigade.

For many tank commanders and crews this was their first taste of fighting after months of intensive training. The initial action of 'A' Sqn, 7th RTR, was described in a privately published diary, and is typical of those early engagements with the German panzers. The 7th had embarked on 18 June, but got caught up in the severe gales which lashed the beach-head area, and did not finally get ashore until 21 June. Two days later, while enjoying some much better weather near St Gabriel, they were told that they were to move that night as part of 2nd Army's first attempt to break out of the bridgehead. The plan was for two brigades to break through the encircling enemy at Cheux and then for 11th Armoured Division to go through the gap and on towards the Odon and Orne rivers. The diary explains:

'B' and 'C' Sqns moved off with, as objectives, the villages of Cheux and Haut du Boscq to the west. 'A' Sqn was to act as reserve and, when both

Coming ashore on the Normandy beaches was not always achieved without incident. This little Stuart V, belonging to RHQ 5 RTR, got rather wet whilst it was landing on D+1 and had to be recovered. TM

From DD into gun tank. Once the Sherman DD tanks were ashore they could let down their canvas swimming screens and use their main armament normally. This line-up of DDs was actually photographed much later in the war and belonged to 44 RTR just after they had crossed the Elbe in 1945. TM

move attracted to the two troops the entire fire of the Hun and three tanks were penetrated almost immediately. Although one 88 and the Panther were accounted for, a sharp battle ensued before things quietened down. Shortly afterwards four Mark IVs appeared from a wood over to the west and, despite intense fire from Churchills, Honeys and Shermans of the 11th Armoured Division, they all succeeded in reaching the shelter of the next wood unscathed.

By this time Cheux and Haut du Boscq had been cleared and 'C' Sqn were breaking through trying to reach the Odon crossing against fairly heavy opposition. The order was then given for 'A' Sqn to go through Cheux to seize its objective. The remaining tanks waddled through the streets midst gutted and burning houses and then spead out to cross the open country beyond. Not till they started going up this hill was there any opposition. This came from Spandaus and snipers. The advance was nearing the crest when a well-known crack was heard - luckily a miss - but a prelude to a ghastly game of hide and seek, with the Churchills one side of the crest and Panthers and Mark IVs the other. The only consolation was that at that range the British 75 could penetrate and before long brewed up a Mark IV. Lt Barratt's tank was then knocked out by a Panther and he himself, along with L-Cpl Cairns and Cpl Murray, were killed. Shortly afterwards Capt Webb's tank was hit on the turret by HE, blinding both him and his gunner. The crew managed to bale out, just before an armour-piercing shot followed. The order to stick it out at all costs was not necessary. After

villages had been taken, was to pass through to take the '100 contour', a high ridge further south, overlooking both villages. The squadron divided into two, two troops going round Le Mesnil Patrie to the west, the remainder to the east. These latter ran across the edge of a minefield, losing two tanks with tracks off. All efforts of the crews to bale out were frustrated by sniping which went on until late in the day. The other two troops raced across the cornfield, down what was to become the best known highway in Normandy - Cassino - and from there up to the ridge overlooking Cheux, where the rear half of 'C' Sqn was being engaged by 88s and a Panther firing from the woods to their right rear. This

Prepare to advance! The tank on the right is a Crusader AA Mark II which was a Crusader III with the normal turret replaced by one mounting a twin 20mm Oerlikon cannon. TM

Breakout and on into the bocage. Cromwells belonging to 7th Armoured Division thread their way though the difficult and dangerous bocage, an area of sunken roads and high hedgerows, where an ambush was to be expected around every corner. (Author's collection)

Off the beaches and into the bocage. Infantrymen dig their fox-hole close beside an M4A2 Sherman near Rauray. TM

another hour's snap shooting whensoever a target appeared, the Boche tanks withdrew. The last half of the battle had not been improved by blinding rain, and as dusk came tank commanders were not sorry to pull back to Forward Rally just north of the Oban-Cassino crossing. Before the battalion leaguered for the night a Crocodile flamed the hedges round the field and 40 Huns came out.

That day we lost five tanks knocked out and three on mines. We became a squadron of ten tanks and wiser and more sober men. We had lost some of our best officers, NCOs and men in a few hours after years of intensive training.

THE BOCAGE

That attempted breakout was frustrated, as had been 7th Armoured Division's earlier thrust. The country-side was known as the bocage - small fields and orchards surrounded by thickly hedged banks inter-spersed with sunken roads. Ideal countryside for the defender and very difficult for tanks as these two short extracts from 'A' Sqn 7th RTR's diary show:

After advancing half-a-mile through this, with the leading tanks poking their noses gently through the hedges before bounding to the next one, the only incident reported was an encounter with a Panther - not seen until within ten yards but then luckily brewed up. Just after this the leading tank reversed hurriedly as an 88 just missed it. Infantry in the area told us that they had been pushed out of Brettevillete and that what had just fired was a dug-in Tiger, which was supported by a 75 A/T gun. To add to the general discomfort it was discovered that several Panthers were prowling about in the woods 300yds in front.

As the diary later pithily puts it:

It is not good for morale to awake at 2 o'clock in the morning and to hear a Panther prowling about some 300yds away!

We then moved into the field in which the two 'B' Sqn tanks were still burning, leaving two troops as outer flank protection. One tank moving up to a gap saw in the opposite gap a Panther with its gun - a large black hole - pointed straight towards it. A quick look along the vane sight and a snappy '300yds fire!' was answered by the gunner with 'But I can't see anything'. A well-placed kick however and his foot went down with good results. Two more followed with the speed of a Bofors. The crew relaxed slightly.

The main battlefield in the fighting on the Odon was known as Hill 112. This was the ridge to which the 7th RTR diary extracts refer. It was the scene of the fiercest and bloodiest fighting in the bridgehead. Even the soldiers of 2 SS Pz Corps, who were denying the feature to the 43rd (Wessex) Division, said later that they had never encountered such fighting in Russia. 7th and 9th RTR supported the Division and fought magnificently, but at heavy cost. Even the heavy armour of their Churchills gave little protection against the 88mm and 75mm of the Tigers and Panthers which abounded in the area. A Churchill tank now serves as a memorial to all who fought and died on Hill 112.

BREAKOUT AT LAST

At the beginning of July seven-and-a-half of the eight panzer divisions which the Germans had brought

Above: *Moving into action in Normandy. This Churchill is kicking up plenty of dust as it trundles across the fields at its maximum speed of 12.5mph. It was taking part in Montgomery's new offensive which was launched on 18 July 1944.* TM

Left: *And this is what it would have been like for the driver. This view of his back shows him using the steering levers to control the tank.* (Author's collection)

into Normandy were still engaged on the British front as they continued to fight around Caen, while the Americans prepared for their breakout. Progress was 'slow and sticky' and there were heavy losses in battles such as the one for the Bourgueous Ridge. A 'more ambitious undertaking' was now planned - Operation *Goodwood*, which would involve all three armoured divisions (7th, 11th and Guards Armoured) in a new thrust towards Falaise. 3rd RTR were in the thick of this fighting and typical of the courage displayed by their tank crews was that of Sgt Frederick Kite. Already the holder of the Military Medal, he was to win two bars to his MM in under a fortnight. The commendations for his two awards read thus:

This NCO was commanding a troop in 'A' Sqn during the actions on 18 and 19 July, near the village of Bras. At all times he displayed a very high standard of leadership, dash and personal courage and was an excellent example for the remainder of the squadron. When the squadron was held up by two enemy tanks and two 88mm guns on the high ground at Bras, Kite, by clever use of the ground pressed forward under heavy anti-tank fire and knocked out one enemy Mark IV, one Panther and one of the 88mm guns, and held on to his position under extremely trying circumstances. This allowed the remainder of the squadron to get forward into better positions. During both days of action Sgt Kite displayed the highest standard of leadership, initiative and personal courage.

The second commendation reads:

On 3 August 1944 at Le Grand Bonfait, Sgt Kite was commanding one of several tanks on the edge of an orchard, the duty of these tanks being to support a company of infantry. This position was counter-attacked by enemy infantry and at least one Tiger and four Panther tanks. The enclosed nature of the country enabled these tanks to approach within 400yds. All the other tanks in the vicinity of Sgt Kite were hit and set on fire, but despite this he maintained his position. He assisted in the correction of our own artillery fire thus preventing the enemy infantry forming up with his tanks for an attempt to advance on our position. Sgt Kite kept his own tank in action and secured at least five hits on enemy tanks at short range before his own was hit and he himself was seriously wounded. Sgt Kite showed the greatest personal courage and his example of remaining in action against odds that were very much against him was an inspiration to all. He undoubtedly helped to a considerable degree to beat off this attack on a feature of great importance. Sgt Kite was the only soldier in the Secon World war to be awarded three military medals.

In Harbour
by a Member of 11th Armoured Division

In the misty moonlight of the winter night
A metal door clangs loudly, harshly shut;
The rutted, wheel-tracked field is dewy white
With lines of shadowed black in every rut.

Faint lights glow here and there; red, yellow, green
And somewhere men are singing tunelessly.
Life's at its lowest ebb and each machine
Is lifeless, cold; but ceaselessly
The wireless hums and whines and patient men
Keep weary watch for some far-distant station
Which breaks the earphones' rustling now and then
Demanding answers: 'What is your location?'
'Report my signals': 'OK': 'Say again.'

The air is chill and to the tired eye
The dark seems granular, seems to consist
Of specks which eddy subtly in the sky,
Intangible, like some ethereal mist
Which flees the fixed and concentrated gaze
And then by stealth as subtly reappears
When the eye's focus shifts and always stays
Too short a time to kill the childhood fears
The mind retains of dark and flitting shapes,
Imagined forms of vague and loathly things:
But when to end these dim imaginings,
The brain's unsheathed, each haunting one escapes:

The body, clumsy with the sober gloom
Of sleeplessness, feels prisoned by the walls
Of iron grey - the bare, accustomed tomb
Which is the convict's cell: and then there falls
Obliquely through the narrow vision-slit
The sun's first ray, than these poor lamps more bright.
The dust which settled softly in the night
Whirls up and dances in the slanting beam
And then the cramped interior, warmly lit
Through the now open door, begins to gleam
With ruddy light, dismissing as a dream
The hours just past, the morbid reveries
The introverted eye had judged to be
Reality and now can clearly see
With day's far truer sight as mockeries
Which only (like the stars) can shine so bright

By contrast with the blackness of the night.
Now day has come, the calm and leisured tread
Of time must change abruptly, in its stead
The rush and hurry, the excited shouts
And racing engines claim the eye and ear
And night has been repulsed, with all its doubts
Life suddenly seems sweeter than one dared
To think it could, the issues crystal clear.
We think of all the boredom we have shared,
The waiting for this chance, our hearts are light
And now the time, the longed-for moment nears
The dreaded moment, too, our hopes and fears
Have centred on, the chance to prove our worth
The chance to earn our right to this dear earth
Which now may see us die, which gave its birth,
At last the moment's here, at last the chance:
'Start up!' 'Stand by.' 'Be ready to advance.'

THE DRIVE TO AMIENS

While the battle of the Falaise pocket was in its final stages the uncommitted 1st Corps on the British left was ordered to take advantage of the situation and push on towards the Seine. It was given 7th Armoured Division for this purpose. The advance was slow, with every bridge and culvert blown, while off road movement was as always hampered by the bocage. Meanwhile the 2nd Army had mounted a northwards drive, Supercharge II, 30 Corps being ordered to establish two armoured divisions in the Amiens area with the utmost speed. 3rd RTR led the right-hand column of 11th Armoured Divison in this advance to the Somme, with Major Bill Close's squadron at the 'sharp end'. He later wrote a description of the advance which is included at some length, because it typifies all the danger and excitement of

This young Frenchman has attached himself to a tank crew in Viencourt (probably their Cromwell Doreen *belonged to 1 or 5 RTR), as they pause for a quick meal during the advance through the Somme.* TM

General view of the beach at Walcheren, where on 1 November 1944, Buffaloes of 11 RTR took part in a two-pronged amphibious assault during the clearing of the Scheldt estuary, to open up the port of Antwerp. TM

this type of armoured operation. He writes:

Eight o'clock on an overcast evening and the battalion was busily refuelling and replenishing its ammunition. The men were weary and wanted to get their heads down. Permission had been given to make a brew, and a mug of tea was pushed into my hands. I was glad of it. It was cold and a thick drizzle was falling. 'Orders, sir.' They were simple. 'Pack up and be ready to move in figures three zero.' We were to drive on Amiens at 30mins' notice. Late that afternoon Horrocks had seen the divisional commander and proposed a moonlight march to seize the Somme bridges. There had been some doubts about the RASC reaching us with petrol and supplies but they'd made it. 'Your squadron will lead, Bill,' said the CO. 'Don't let anything stop you.' By then it was raining hard. Amiens lay more than 20 miles away through enemy-held territory. There was no moonlight.

A wet day. Maj (later Col) Tom Craig sensibly uses a brolly to keep off the rain as he makes his way across Holland in his Cromwell. He was at the time OC 'B' Sqn, 1 RTR. TM

The head of the column was at the village of Fontaine Bonnelieu. It consisted of a troop of Shermans followed by my HQ tank and the rest of the squadrons. Then came the Rifle Brigade company in half-tracks and lorries and the other tanks and infantry… Rain was streaming from the hulls of the Shermans as I walked down the line to make sure each tank commander knew what was expected of him. About 10.30, in pitch darkness, the advance began. All preparations had been made. It was up to the drivers.

Huddled in their turrets, the commanders studied their maps by the shaded light, headphones humming, and felt the water trickling down their necks. Operators tinkered with the radios and the 75mm gunners, having checked and rechecked their ammunition stocks, hunched in their seats, damp and weary behind their useless sights. They could afford to relax slightly. For the drivers there was no relief. In front of the first Sherman stretched an unfamiliar road, sometimes reflecting the pale sheen of distant searchlights. Hatch open and head out, the driver could only stare into the darkness and obey instructions. The head poking out of the hatch on the other side of the turret; belonged to the co-driver manning the .30 machine gun. If there was any trouble they would be the first to suffer. For the drivers following it was a question of maintaining the required distance and keeping their eyes on the dark shape in front. Unlike performing elephants, we had no tails to hold; nevertheless, the circus was going to town.

A mile passed without incident. And another. The headphones' drowsy hum was broken by a crackle. The message was 'Push on…push on.'

A line of hills appeared silhouetted in the soft blue glow of the far-off searchlight, still sweeping the sky. 'Keep going…press on…' The driver of Sugar Two, the lead tank, steering sticks in his hands, maintained speed.

Things began to happen at the first and only crossroads between our start point and the outskirts of Amiens. Sugar Two reported a column of horse-drawn artillery and limbers on the road, too close to engage effectively with his guns. 'Okay Sugar Two. Motor through them. Run over anything that gets in your way. Out.' Soon we came across splintered wreckage and writhing mounds by the side of the road. Vague shapes were stampeding over the fields. 'Keep going. Press on…' The word went monotonously from the general to the brigadier, from the brigadier to the CO … to me… to Sugar Two… to the driver with the chilled face and strained eyes: 'Keep going…'

Two miles further on, with visibility down to 20ft, a Volkswagen appeared directly in front of the lead tank. The commander, with the constant urgings ringing in his ears, ordered his driver to speed up and overtake it. The little car skidded wildly and was crushed. Though the passenger was killed the driver managed to clamber out, and as the Sherman manoeuvred free of the wreckage, began to stammer and shout. When it dawned on him that it was no panzer that had hit him, he burst into hysterical laughter and stumbled wildly down the column. The sound of automatic fire came faintly through the night as the engines revved again.

More humming…more crackling. Sugar Two was having quite a night. A large object was parked across our route, half blocking it. 'Sugar Two…am engaging enemy tank on the road in front of me…Sugar Two out.' The column slowed. In every turret there would be a spark of interest, gunners shifting their positions, radio operators twiddling knobs afresh.

From my turret I saw three flashes in quick succession send shadows racing across the dripping fields. Inky darkness closed over us again, only to be routed by a ball of orange and yellow flame which scattered fiery fragments over a wide area. Heavy concussion indicated the enemy tank was carrying a full load of ammunition. Sugar Two had fired three rounds of solid shot from 20ft and quickly reversed. Three men, who had probably been asleep,

This Churchill Mark VII, photographed at Lichtenvoorde after the Reichwald Forest battle, belonged to 'B' Sqn 9 RTR, at that time part of 34 Armd Bde. Its name was Inspire V. TM

Grabbing a hasty bite before remounting their Cromwell, this crew belonging to 'B' Sqn, 1 RTR, is just about to take part in Operation Blackcock, *designed to clear the area between the Meuse and the Roer. Conditions were appalling, however, at least the crew are wearing the heavy one-piece tanksuits, which kept the wearer fairly dry. Note the commander's binoculars, their pistols, and the envious looking radio operator on wireless watch in the turret!* TM

Lt Crockett, IO of 3 RTR in his Humber scout car, which was slightly larger and heavier than the Daimler 'Dingo'. Behind him is one of the new A 34 Comet cruiser tanks, which were issued to 11th Armd Div in March 1945, although a few did get there by the end of December 1944. TM

Crossing the Rhine, 23 March 1945. Lt-Col Alan Jolly (later Gen Sir Alan), then CO 4 RTR, proudly flew the original Tank Corps flag that had first crossed the Rhine at the end of the Great War. Here it is raised on his Buffalo by the RSM. TM

11 RTR made some 1900 round trips across the Rhine in their Buffaloes, however, their most distinguished visitor was undoubtedly Winston Churchill, who crossed on 26 March 1945. 'I congratulate you and your Buffaloes' said the Prime Minister and presented the unit with one of his famous cigars! TM

scrambled out of the wreck and ran a few yards before it blew up. It was quite the biggest and best explosion we had seen for some time…

About three miles from Amiens we pulled off the road to close up. Squadrons were starting to straggle. Brew cans were quickly produced but hardly had the first mugs of tea been gulped down than we were ordered to 'make all posible speed'. I put another troop in the lead to give Sugar Two a break.

What they say about the cold light of dawn is true - it does help to concentrate your thoughts. Though the appearance of German transport going about its normal early morning business implied the enemy was still unaware of our presence, I felt this incredible state of affairs couldn't last. We engaged target after target. The countryside was littered with burning wrecks, alive with running figures. Somewhere the alarm bells must be ringing; maybe the night trek was going to prove to have been the 'easy bit'. The idea of plunging into an unknown town didn't appeal to me at all. I remembered Calais only too well. Of Amiens I knew only it had given its name to a big battle in which the Tank Corps played a leading part in the Great War. We'd already passed one or two British military cemeteries.

After four years of occupation, during which its goods yard and the surrounding rail network had been regularly bombed, the city was run down. Clattering over the uneven paves, past patches of waste ground, rows of dingy houses and dilapidated factories, I thought: 'What a place to die for.' The driver and co-driver had already closed their hatches and I sank further into the turret. Too many tank commanders had been shot in the head.

Some armed men standing on a corner signalled us to stop. A number of Brownings swung in their direction. They turned out to be Resistance fighters from a well-organised local maquis. I asked them anxiously about the best way to 'Le Pont'. They said they could show me but did I know there were about 4000 enemy troops in the city, some of them with anti-tank guns?

At this stage my squadron consisted of ten tanks. Noel Bell, who came up to confer, said, rather plaintively, that his company strength was 70 riflemen. We decided, nevertheless, that as the rest of 3 RTR and the Rifle Brigade were coming up we would push on…the lead tanks being covered by the others. Road blocks are useless unless they are substantial and well defended. The enemy had been given no time to organise himself and at the first barricade all eyes looked for the opposition.

Bang! The enemy gunner must have been nervous. His shot demolished a hardware shop and before another could be fired the position had been smothered in .5 Browning fire. An abandoned lorry and a couple of carts were swept aside by a Sherman and we moved on. Impressed by this success, excited maquisards climbed onto the back of the tanks, pointed out the way and known enemy positions. The buildings got taller and the back of my neck grew pricklier, but gradually, shooting now and then, we worked our way to the river. And there it was. A large bridge. Deserted. I scanned the houses on the distant bank through binoculars but saw little sign of activity. The people of Amiens were sensibly lying low. So was the enemy.

The first Sherman crossed the bridge in quick time, reported no opposition and was promptly reinforced by the rest of its troop. I prepared to join them. 'Driver advance…' We emerged from the shelter of a side street, increased speed and were climbing the approach road when, only a few yards away, the bridge was enveloped in smoke and collapsed noisily into the river. Reversing hurriedly into cover, we waited for the dust to clear. I told the troops on the other side to take up an observation position and saw their exhaust smoke vanish among the silent houses. It was just after 7am.

ON TOWARDS THE RHINE

The pursuit was now on in earnest, with the armoured divisions well to the fore. France and Belgium lay virtually wide open. 11th Armoured Division covered a staggering 340 miles in just six days, the 3rd spearheading their entry into Antwerp on 3 September. 7th Armoured had equal success further north, covering over 200 miles through France and Belgium to liberate Ghent on 5 September. All were pressing towards the Rhine hoping to link up with Montgomery's daring airborne assault at Arnhem, which sadly failed. It was soon realised that a winter campaign would be necessary in order to build up for the final massive assault over the Rhine and into the Fatherland. In the meantime, the Scheldt estuary area had to be cleared if Antwerp was to become a major Allied supply port. The 'Funnies' once again took a major part in operations, when men like Sgts William Malcolm, Edward Milton and Tpr Stack, all of 11th RTR, were awarded Military Medals for bravery. Malcolm's citation is typical:

Men of an armoured personnel carrier unit, equipped with RAM Kangaroos (de-gutted Canadian Ram tanks capable of carrying an infantry section inside with armoured protection) look as though they are about to do some 'de-gutting' of the hens they have 'acquired'! They are probably from 49 RTR, who formed the 49th APC Regiment and were invaluable during the exploitation into Germany. TM

This NCO commanded an LVT which together with five other LVTs and four Weasels was loaded on an LCT. His LVT was second vehicle off on landing. The first LVT was going ashore when a shell hit the Weasel next to Malcolm's LVT. A terrific blaze started and all vehicles had to be evacuated. Malcolm, quickly appreciating a difficult situation, gathered his crew and got back on to his LVT, which was now well ablaze. He managed to get it through the LCT door and into the sea where it eventually foundered. By his gallantry and quick action he not only enabled two more LVTs to land, but also undoubtedly saved many lives, as if his vehicle had been left any longer it would have probably blown up as LVTs were carrying a lot of ammunition and explosives. The effect of his example did a lot to maintain calm.

While these operations were taking place, 7th Armoured Division were further to the north-east around Tilburg and S'Hertogenbosch. In this latter area the 1st gained two DCMs in the same day - 30 September 1944. One was awarded to SSM Robert MacGregor, MM, who was commanding a troop of tanks ordered to attack Middelrode village in conjunction with a section of carriers and an infantry platoon.

As soon as the advance started, the enemy brought down heavy observed shellfire on the attacking troops and after 300yds the infantry and carriers were brought to a halt by MG fire. Realising that the whole attack was in danger of being held up and knowing full well the risk attached to advancing in close country without infantry support, SSM MacGregor moved forward with his troop, destroyed the MGs holding up the infantry and an A tank gun which he met face to face at 50yards' range and reached the centre of the village. The infantry then came up and SSM Mac-Gregor moved to a position from which he could shoot the enemy withdrawing from the village and observe the enemy's main position. He remained in this position under continuous shellfire, mortar fire and sniping for seven hours directing artillery fire onto the enemy guns. During this action his troop destroyed two A/Tk guns and 2 MGs, took 20 PW besides killing a number of enemy and forcing 200 to withdraw. This WO's coolness, courage and judgement were entirely reponsible for the success of this action and had it not been for his leadership and handling situation, both his own troop and the infantry would have undoubtedly suffered severe casualties without reaching their objective.

Sgt Jack Moat was in command of a Sherman tank during an action to clear the enemy from the village of Corso; he was in a position of observation directing artillery fire, when his tank was hit by heavy, accurate mortar fire:

Sgt Moat was hit in the head with splinters from a mortar bomb which burst against the aerial and the tank refused to start up. Sgt Moat then climbed out

One of the most effective of Hobo's 'Funnies' was the Churchill flamethrower, seen here in action near Belsen concentration camp. Known as the 'Crocodile' its bow-mounted flame gun had a range of some 80-120 yards and a full trailer held sufficient flame fuel for 80 one second bursts. (Author's collection)

Two Comets passing through Wesel, the commander of the front one is Maj Watts. The main armament – a 77mm – brought Comet on a par with most German tanks . It even looked like a smaller edition of the Tiger. (F. Rigby)

11th Armoured Division Comets pushing on through the debris of a German town towards final victory. TM

spirit and cool courage were an inspiration to his troop and by his action he opened the way for the advance to continue.

Tanks in line[1]
(To the tune of *Tales from Vienna Woods* by Strauss)

Tanks, tanks, tanks, in line
Sweeping up towards the Rhine.
The First, the Fifth, the Skins the Guns,
We're out to bugger up the Huns.
Cromwells, Honeys, Fireflies too,
A floating punch to see us through.
The Engineers with Scorpions
And troop of Bofors,
Half-a-dozen loafers
And the Navy, nice and wavy,
RAF umbrella, nothing could be sweller,
Deutschland, here we come - run, run.
The First are always at the front,
'C' Squadron picked to bear the brunt.
The 'iron ring' well at the back,
The Sergeant Major's thrown a track.
The fitters then will do the trick,
But only with their usual tick.
The 88s are banging,
The 95s are wamming.
Major Dingwall's slanging
Tank Commanders hazy,
Operators lazy.
Office staffs are playing,
Tank crews are saying
'It's about time we had a brew - too true.'

and attempted to hitch the tow rope of another tank on by himself. He was unable to do this so he collected two members of his crew to help him, both were killed by mortar fire while attempting to fix the rope and Sgt Moat finished the job himself. By this time a Spandau had opened up on him as well as the mortar fire, so he climbed back on his tank and engaged the Spandau himself with his Browning and destroyed it. He then ordered the tank to be towed away and went forward on foot to try and deal with the mortar OP. He located the OP and captured it himself taking 12 PoW. This action put a stop to the mortar fire and undoubtedly saved many lives. This NCO's aggressive

As the spring blossoms burst forth victory is in sight. This Cromwell, belonging to 7th Armoured Division, crosses a railway line near the village of Sustedt, a few miles from Bremen. TM

A tank crew's work is never done. Here spare crewmen of 3 RTR tighten the track of a Comet. Spare crews were held at A1 Echelon. Note the mixture of cap badges, including a Gloucestershire Hussar and a Royal Armoured Corps 'Mailed Fist'. (F. Rigby)

Another constant chore was 'bombing up' with fresh ammunition. Here they replenish with 77mm armour piercing rounds. The Comet could carry 58 rounds for its main armament. (F. Rigby)

ACROSS THE RHINE

The winter campaign was a busy one during which the Germans tried their major counter-thrust through the Ardennes, that so nearly came off. It was also during this winter that the latest British tank started to arrive, the Comet, which would help pave the way into Germany and final victory. Before that could happen, however, the Rhine had to be crossed. Four RTR Regiments would play leading roles in the crossing on 23 March 1945: the 44th in DD tanks, the 4th and 11th in Buffalo LVTs and the 49th in Kangaroos and CDLs, giving 'movement and direction' lighting. The honour of carrying across the Tank Corps flag was given to CO 4 RTR, Lt-Col Alan Jolly (later General Sir Alan) who recalled the crossing in his privately published history of the 4th entitled *Blue Flash*:

> ...Precisely at 9pm, under a starlit sky, the leading Buffaloes climbed down the steep, stone facing of the river bank and churned their way across the Rhine. Everyone has his own memory of these occasions; the river smell of weeds and mud will strike a chord with some, the Jocks' mournful rendering of Annie Laurie will be remembered by others. There was no opposition to speak of. That was to come later when the infantry experienced bitter fighting in Rees. Only the odd mortar shell sent up a spurt of water from the river without doing any harm.
>
> At four minutes past nine the leading Buffaloes grounded on the far bank and the infantry scrambled out to collect themselves for

the advance inland. Among the first to reach the other side was the 'Flagship' in which the CO was flying the flag which had once led the British Army across the Rhine. This Buffalo was commanded by Lt S. Millership and members of the crew were L-Cpl W. Davies (driver), Tpr W. Marsh (gnr), and Tpr J.J. Tyler (operator). The flag was so tattered that it threatened to disintegrate in the breeze, so it was only unfurled for the last part of the journey. As soon as it had safely returned to the home bank it was taken to Bn HQ from where it was despatched the next day by liaison officer to 21st Army Group with a message that it had once more been in the van of the British crossing of the Rhine.

THE ECHELON

This is perhaps a good place to pay tribute to those unsung heroes of all armoured regiments - the Echelon. The jobs are far from glamorous, but without their constant support the tanks would soon grind to a halt. Here is how the 'A' Sqn, 7th RTR diary described their echelon at the time of the Rhine Crossing:

> The work of this most essential part of any squadron is necessarily less colourful than the more spectacular role of the tank troops; but in such a happy squadron as we were, each department appreciated the work of the other. There were always the good-humoured cracks about the boys who were lucky enough to be in the rear

when things were flying around, but the tank troops were never let down, and the rivalry between the two departments was always most healthy.

As we had to be self-contained, the LAD at RHQ, was decentralised and to us came a detachment consisting of AQMS Keillor and eight Craftsmen. Other attached personnel included a detachment of RAMC in a half-track and a battery charging lorry in which rode Sgn Tatlow and his driver. We also had our own DR, whose main job was conveying tank states and sitreps back to advance HQ for onward transmission to Div HQ.

By some means or other SSM Robinson also acquired a motorcycle and it was found invaluable. He seemed to get great delight dashing around on it, whatever the weather, and did some excellent work.

We still had only one water-truck, which meant that when the squadron was split, Cpl Anderson had an extra busy time looking after both halves. The cooks and their utensils were divisible and some went with each half-squadron when it was necessary. In all, the Sqn Echelon consisted of 33 vehicles of various types.

By the time that the assault was made on the Rhine we were all teed up and everybody full of enthusiasm for our new role. The tanks moved out of harbour to cross the Rhine early in the morning of 25 March. Later the same day a

skeleton echelon received orders to move up to the Rhine and to cross the bridge at the earliest opportunity.

This skeleton echelon consisted only of the petrol, ammunition, nitrogen, and of the flame-throwing fuel lorries. The remainder, under the able and experienced command of SQMS Mist, remained in harbour until the Rhine bridge was less congested. We moved up to the marshalling area during the late afternoon and were shepherded into a large wood where we were told to wait…

We remained in this wood until approx 4 o'clock in the morning and during the night we witnessed some of the heaviest Ack-Ack fire any of us had ever seen whenever a Jerry plane came over in an attempt to destroy the bridge, which was still under construction. Eventually we received orders to move down to the river, and after crawling behind streams of other vehicles, had the thrill of crossing the Rhine at 0800 hours. On the other side of the river we moved inland a few miles until we came to a 'T' junction where the traffic from both Class 16 and Class 40 bridges converged. The congestion was like Derby Day. We pulled off the road into an orchard where we brewed up and SSM Robinson went off in search of the tanks.

Thanks to good signing he soon found them and learnt that they were expecting to go into

On the streets of Hamburg. This photograph of a Sherman Firefly, which mounted a 17pdr gun, was taken on Adolf Hitler Platz, the day after the unconditional surrender of the city on 3 May 1945. Its wilting camouflage looks strangely out of place amid all the concrete. It belonged to 5RTR whose CO – Lt Col Rea Leakey, DSO, MC, was one of the regiment's heroes of World War Two. TM

Just before the war in Europe ended, the new A 41 Centurion Mark I medium gun tank came off the assembly line and six pro-duction models were rushed out to Germany in May 1945. However, they did not arrive until after VE Day. Main armament for the Centurion Mark I was the 17pdr (cf the Firefly). Trials then took place and the tank proved to be a resounding success. TM

action almost at once. The squadron was going to operate in two halves, but for the time being the echelon was to remain in one packet. During the afternoon we were summoned to refuel the OC's half-squadron. At this stage the bridgehead was so small that all the traffic was confined to one third-class road, so progress was painfully slow. To make matters worse, heavy rain fell and it was not long before this road was a quagmire and the sides crumbled away in many places.

We were pleased to learn that the first action had been successful, with no casualties. After darkness we were guided by Lt de Groot in a scout car to where Capt Pearson's half-squadron were harboured and required refuelling. This was an even more tedious process, making our way to them in complete darkness and on an even worse and more congested road. It was nearly dawn before the echelon returned to our base in the orchard.

There is one aspect of the work of the echelon which is often overlooked. There are many hours during the day whilst the battle is on when the drivers and co-drivers are doing nothing yet cannot relax because it is never known when they may be required. Eventually the order is received to move up, usually towards dusk and the heavy work starts. The nitrogen bottles are no light weight to throw about, nor indeed are the drums of flamethrowing fuel, and once the tanks are refilled the lorries then have to be driven back over congested and bad roads, perhaps several miles to the RASC dump, where a complete load is taken on again. The result is that frequently it was well nigh dawn before anyone could think of a few hours' sleep.

The second day over the Rhine we moved forward to the area in which the airborne troops had landed two days previously. The sight of the gliders and crashed aircraft which were strewn over the countryside was one which can never be forgotten. On this day the residue echelon under SQMS Mist crossed the Rhine and harboured a mile or so from where the rest of the echelon

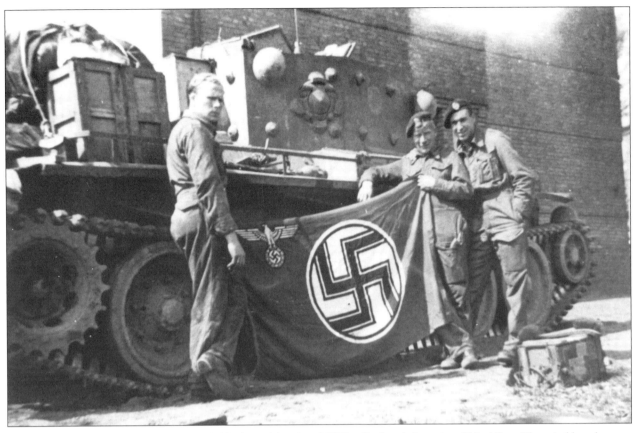

'Gotcha Adolf!' An RTR tank crew - probably from either 1 or 5 RTR - display their captured Nazi flag. The mind boggles over what else they have liberated - note the crates on the back decks. TM

were. The 10-ton Fodens were not good off the metalled roads and consequently their uses were limited and often restricted our choice of harbours.

When the breakthrough occurred and we were left behind, we all rallied into one harbour, centred around a crashed Dakota. We were all tired and dirty and were glad to have a wash and sleep and brush up. It was Easter time and Padre Preston visited us and conducted a very impressive service which was well attended.

Soon we were on the move again. This time to join the Canadian Army on the left. Long marches followed during which time, many live pigs, chickens and rabbits were acquired; Tpr Walters' bottle lorry was always conspicuous by the number of hens which used to ride on the bottles, never making any attempt to escape. In the echelon we had several experts with the knife and many were the meals of pork chops, fried eggs and roast chicken that were eaten. Cpl Caswell and the other cooks were always most helpful in preparing any extras…they were equally as tired of cooking corned beef or M & V as we were of eating them. Our appetites seemed insatiable when living in the open all the time.

Tank crews were always glad to see the echelon arrive because it usually brought a letter

from home or maybe some much-needed cigarettes. Our journey through Holland was so well received by the population that we were reminded of the days in Normandy following the breakthrough.

THE LAST LAP

Once they were across the Rhine in force then the enemy were incapable of offering any effective co-ordinated resistance and all the divisions were able to 'crack about in the plains of North Germany and chase the enemy from pillar to post', as Field Marshal Montgomery had ordered. Osnabruck was captured by 3 April, Hannover by the 7th, Bremen on 27 April and Hamburg finally surrendered on 3 May. En route, POW and slave labour camps were liberated and the prisoners released. There was great devastation in the towns and cities from Allied bombing, which made vehicle movement very difficult. As one eyewitness reported:

Now we were getting into the really flattened sectors of the city. Huge bomb craters and massed rubble blocked the road while the tram wires, straggling at all angles across the streets, were a formidable obstacle too. Many a tank commander going forward with head out of

Still wearing his RTR beret and badge, Field Marshal Montgomery reads the surrender terms to the German delegation, in a tent on Luneburg Heath, some 25 miles south of Hamburg, on 4 May 1945. TM

cupola was nearly decapitated. It took a long search to find our way through, but by the evening all objectives were in our hands and the infantry engaged in detailed searching of buildings, factories and workshops. That night we leaguered amongst the infantry in the city but there was little sleep. The whole night long, drunken celebration of our arrival was continued by the liberated slaves.

The enemy now sued for peace and on the morning of 3 May a surrender delegation appeared before General Sir Miles Dempsey, Commander of 2nd Army. Field Marshal Montgomery signed the Instrument of Surrender at 1820 hours on 4 May, capitulation being effective from 0800 hours the following morning. Once again a 'war to end all wars' had been fought and won in Europe, with the Regiment playing a major part on all fronts. Armour ended the war, having earned the major share of the credit for the Allied Victory. The tank had firmly established itself as the main weapon of decision of the land army.

FRIENDSHIP THAT WILL NEVER FADE

In six years we have come to know our colleagues more intimately than a man knows his own brother. We have worked with them, played with them, fought with them, eaten, slept and bathed with them - never a moment's privacy for 24hrs a day, seven days a week. We have seen them at their best and at their worst, in good times and bad. Surely friendships which have survived that supreme test need never be allowed to fade.[2]

Now it was time to think of peace.

---

[1] This song was written by the late Capt H.M. Stephens, MC, of the Royal Tank Regiment.
[2] Taken from The *'B' Line Souvenir edition* published by the Cedar Press of Hounslow for 'B' Sqn, 48th RTR.

SECTION IV

Chapter 14

THE UNQUIET PEACE (1945–1959)

REGIMENTAL ROUND-UP

The Regiment had finished the war with battalions spread all over the world, so this chapter begins with a résumé of their locations and the moves they made shortly afterwards. Germany contained the largest proportion of the Regiment, in what was now known as the British Army of the Rhine (BAOR). The 1st (in Berlin) 3rd, 4th, 5th, 7th, 9th, 11th, 44th and 49th all ended the war in Germany. The 9th, 11th, 44th and 49th were rapidly disbanded as the Army was 'slimmed down' to peacetime proportions. Army Order 42 of 1946 authorised an important change of nomenclature from 'Battalions' to the Cavalry term 'Regiments', so from now on reference will be made to '1st Royal Tank Regiment', (abbreviated to '1 RTR'), etc. 4 RTR was one of three RTR regiments earmarked to fight in the Far East against Japan (together with the 8th and 43rd) but moved instead to Palmanova in Italy in August 1946. Those Regiments left in BAOR settled down to peacetime soldiering in the difficult conditions of war-ravaged Germany, with large numbers of their experienced soldiers being replaced by National Servicemen. National Service would continue until the 1960s, providing the Services with the manpower needed to fulfil their worldwide commitments. It brought into the Army a wonderful cross-section of characters - from public schoolboys destined for top jobs in industry and commerce, to ambitious mechanics and artisans; from professional sportsmen,

doctors and dentists, to unskilled labourers, spivs - even burglars and layabouts - although it is true to say we were luckier than most Corps, in that the RAC as a whole took only the best. All were conscripted and, as an article in *Soldier* magazine put it:

> ...each one played his part in watching over the interests of his home and country, each one coming to terms with Army life in his own way and leaving his mark.

The next large group of Regiments was in the Mediterranean area, namely, 2nd, 6th, 8th, 12th, 48th and 51st in Italy; 40th, 46th and 50th in Greece. The 2nd ended the war in Italy, but moved to Austria on 15 May 1945 and spent some time on operations against Yugoslav insurgents, before settling down to occupation duties, which included rounding up the German SS men living in the area around their base at Klagenfurt, but returned to Italy in December 1945. The following year 2nd moved again, this time to BAOR (Luneburg). The 6th remained in Italy until July 1947, when they moved to Egypt with 4 RTR who had replaced the 2nd at Palmanova. The 8th had more moves than any other RTR at that time, going from Italy to UK in 1945, UK to Austria in 1946 and then on to Palestine, by which time they had travelled over 8000 miles in one year! Sadly the remaining Regiments, 12th, 40th, 46th, 48th, 50th and 51st were all disbanded by mid-1946.

Whilst the barracks in Germany which the British Army of the Rhine now occupied, were generally of a high standard, those in the UK left much to be desired. For example, 2 RTR was stationed at Haig Lines, Crookham, near Aldershot, from the late 1940s until the early 1950s, and as this view through the main gate shows, they were vintage wooden huts.
TM

Winston Churchill inspected his 'Dear Desert Rats' at the British Victory Parade in Berlin, 21 July 1945. 22 Armd Bde at that time comprised 1 and 5 RTR (who are on the far side of the road) plus 5 Innis DG whom the PM is driving past in this photograph. TM

INDIA

The only Regiment to go to the Far East in order to fight against the Japanese, was the 43rd. They had been re-equipped with CDLs and sailed for India in June 1945, to become part of the Allied Land Forces, SEAC, which were preparing for the invasion of Malaya. When Japan surrendered, the 43rd reverted to India Command and did good work in an internal security role, helping to quell riots in Bombay and Calcutta. They were disbanded in 1947, having in the meantime become 2nd/43rd RTR, as the new 43rd RTR (TA) had formed in England. 7th were withdrawn from BAOR at the end of 1946 and sent out to India in early 1947. Brigadier Reggie Wood recalls those days:

We arrived from England in January and were stationed at Sialkot - a small station in the Northern Punjab. As soon as we had settled in we began to look round to try and get a picture of the political situation. We had an opportunity to do this as we had arrived without vehicles and it was some time before they were issued to us... Our vehicles began to arrive and we, who had been equipped with Churchill flamethrowers, found we were to get 30 GMC armoured cars, and 24 Stuart Mark VI light tanks. We were given a free hand as to how the Regiment should be organised. After some consideration three mixed squadrons were formed - each with two armoured car and two light tank troops. A troop in either case contained three vehicles... Our first practical experience of Internal Defence came suddenly on 11 March - long before we felt we were ready and while we still had only very few armoured cars. We were having a Sqn Commanders' conference when an agitated voice

on the phone asked us how many armoured cars we could turn out for operations and then ordered us to send them to Rawalpindi by 2pm the next day. We hastily collected the nine cars we had, made up a composite squadron and despoiled all three squadrons to give it the most suitable echelon transport - 4-wheel drive Dodge 15cwts. Most of the armoured cars had not fired a shot, so next morning before each car formed up it drove onto the 30yd range and tested its guns.

The events leading up to this sudden summons showed how quickly a storm might blow up anywhere in the Punjab. A gang of Muslims had decided on the systematic destruction of all Hindu-owned homes and hotels in Murree - a hill station near Rawalpindi. They planned and carried out this operation most efficiently. The smoke of burning houses in Murree appeared to be the signal for a general flare-up of communal feeling in the villages round Rawalpindi. Muslims fell upon Hindu minorities with the utmost ferocity and horrible orgies of cruelty took place. The method adopted to check this outbreak was to deploy troops in small detachments, to establish a sound system of communications and to carry out an intensive programme of patrolling at irregular intervals so that troublemakers could never be sure when they would be interrupted. It was also necessary to give Military Commanders much wider discretion as to what action they could take in the event of trouble... We were only forced to open fire once to disperse a crowd. Infantry units opened fire many times during this period both to disperse crowds and at curfew-breakers. We had been able to avoid firing for two reasons - the quietening effect that the presence of tanks or armoured cars had on troublemakers and the fact that our type of patrolling was more prevention than cure.

The 7th eventually embarked for theUK in September 1947, with the remnants of the 2nd/43rd RTR in the same ship. As Ken Macksey explains in his Vol 3 of *The Tanks*, those whose departure had been delayed told horrific tales of the bloodshed in the Punjab when the British left, the Indian troops being quite unable to prevent it as their units turned against each other.

...The hearts of those who realised what had happened were heavy. Yet this was but the first step in the long retreat from Empire that was to follow.

REBIRTH OF THE TERRITORIAL ARMY

April 1947 saw the rebirth of the Territorial Army, and many of those who had served so gallantly with the TA battalions in the war rejoined. They provided,

Field Marshal Montgomery inspects the immaculate tanks and crews of 1 RTR in September 1945. He is accompanied by the CO, Lt-Col (later Maj-Gen) P.R.C. Hobart, one of the RTR's great Second World War heroes. TM

together with a small Regular Army input, an ideal framework on which to build nine splendid Regiments, six RTR and three Yeomanry, all of which were affiliated to regular RTR Regiments. The permanent staff (normally one or two regular officers and some dozen other ranks ranging from RSM to storemen) came from the regular affiliated Regiment. The full list of Regiments was:

months, NS men did a further four years with the TA, but when full-time service was lengthened to two years, then part-time service was reduced accordingly, so that the total served was still 5½ years. National Servicemen thus provided a number of well-trained soldiers, although the AFVs on which they served in regular and then TA units did not always match up. They also brought with them some

Unit	Location	Regular affiliation
40th (The King's) RTR	Bootle	1 RTR
41st (Oldham) RTR	Oldham	3 RTR
42nd RTR	Clapham Junction	8 RTR
43rd (Northumberland) RTR	Newcastle upon Tyne	7 RTR
44th RTR	Bristol	5 RTR
45th (Leeds Rifles)	Leeds	6 RTR
Lothians and Border Horse Yeomanry	Edinburgh	4 RTR
2nd County of London Yeomanry (Westminster Dragoons)	Westminster	2 RTR
3rd/4th County of London Yeomanry (Sharpshooters)	St John's Wood	2 RTR

The Territorial Army Regiments were honoured by their home towns. Here, the Mayor of Oldham, Alderman Herbert Webster JP, accompanied by Maj-Gen W.H. Stratton, GOC NW District, inspects 'B' Sqn 41 RTR, when the Regiment received the Freedom of the Borough on 17 July 1954. TM

Many of the soldiers were volunteers, but Regiments were made up to full strength with National Servicemen, who completed their part-time service with the TA. Initially, when full-time service was 18

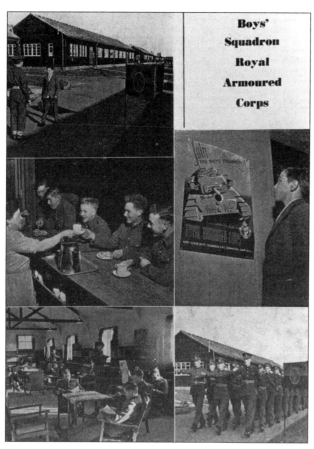

The Boys' Squadron, RAC, was formed in January 1952 and would later become the Junior Leaders Regiment RAC. Just as with the pre-war boy soldiers who first came to Bovington in January 1920, the Boys' Squadron and JLR were an excellent source of first-class recruits. TM

Also formed in the 1950s was the 1st (Berlin) Independent Squadron, RTR, one of whose Comet tanks is seen here during an exercise on the Grunewald Training Area, Berlin, in 1957. TM

headaches, especially for the permanent staff. Most were sensible and well-behaved, attended their statutory number of drill nights and annual camps without any fuss. The minority however had to be disciplined, sometimes by 'subterfuge'. I well remember, as a young TA adjutant, unashamedly concocting a plot with my CO and RSM. If an NS man failed to attend for camp we would write him a nice letter, explaining that because he hadn't come he had missed a free exchange of uniform and personal equipment. However, if he would please come along on the next drill night in uniform, we would then be able to completely refurbish his gear. When the unsuspecting offender arrived he would be collared by the RSM, marched in front of the CO and charged for missing camp. The charge sheet having been read, he would be asked if he would accept the CO's award or go to Court Martial. Invariably they chose the former, little suspecting that we had an escort from the guardroom of the Guards Depot at Pirbright in the wings. Two weeks 'inside' under a Guards Provost Sergeant was enough to persuade even the most persistent offender that he would do well not to miss another camp!

TA training was extremely thorough and culminated in the annual training. Here are some extracts from a contemporary article taken from the *Tank Magazine* and entitled 'A Fortnight in the Field':

...Redland is at war with Blueland. Across the air the electric message comes - the situation is no better, it is much the same. It has been the same now for decades; sometimes, as local fighting flares up on Salisbury Plain, or more recently on Luneburg Heath, Redland will gain a temporary advantage; sometimes Blueland will. Sometimes their brave allies, Northland, Southland, Eastland and Westland, will shoulder the burden. No one thinks of referring the dispute to the Hague Court of the United Nations, the battles are fought relentlessly to the last paragraph, generals hold searching inquests into their conduct, and then the respective armies pack up and go home.

...Leaving the road, we bump over rough cross-country tracks to The Rings. It is from these little round coverts that the tanks of the -th Royal Tank Regiment (TA) set off earlier today. Strictly speaking they are not the tanks of the -th RTR; they have been borrowed for the duration from a training pool. Not that the -th RTR haven't got any tanks, because they have; but if all their tanks were placed end to end they wouldn't be enough to equip one squadron let alone the whole Regiment; and besides it seems hardly worthwhile bringing them down from Newcastle, where the Regiment normally lives, when the country around Salisbury Plain is virtually one large tank park... A tank snorts up the bank towards us and comes to rest a few yards from

'Goodbye to Blighty!' B Sqn, 3 RTR marching through Bovington Camp - they are passing the Tank Museum - on their way to Wool station, on the first leg of their journey to Hong Kong, May 1949. They will go by troopship from Southampton. TM

our car. From its open turret projects the top half of a cheerful sergeant who hails the Adjutant in a broad Northumbrian voice. 'They're stuck up there,' he says, easing his wireless headset off. 'Can't get forward at all.' The Adjutant introduces us all round. The sergeant is a clerk in the Inland Revenue; but he spent his war with the -th Royal Tanks and rejoined them again as soon as he could after his demobilisation.

His obligations to them are 30 drills a year and 14 days in camp; but in practice he gives the Regiment more of his time than the legal minimum would exact. They run, he tells me, a cricket team, and a rugger team, and a soccer team, and a hockey team and a golf team. There are training weekends from time to time too. 'I like it, you see,' the sergeant explains.

The rest of his crew are rather young. They pop out from various holes in the tank - the driver, the co-driver, the wireless operator. They are all volunteers; everyone in their particular Regiment, the Adjutant explains, is a volunteer with one exception, a National Serviceman doing his continuation training, and he is likely to be a volunteer any moment, especially if he enjoys his camp. 'Will he enjoy it?' 'Well, we work them hard,' the Adjutant says. 'They've been up every day for the past week at five in the morning, and they don't get in as a rule till after eight; and then they've got maintenance to do but they seem to like it.' The tank crew confirm this. 'We've got 98 per cent of the Regiment in camp,' the Adjutant adds with justifiable pride. The Sergeant has just climbed out of his turret and opened the back of his tank to display the engine and gearbox, which he obviously loves like brothers, when across the air comes an electric message and the wireless

operator calls to him. 'Says we've to close on him,' he reports. 'OK,' says the Sergeant, 'Wilco out,' says the operator. The engine roars into life, an ostrich-plume of white smoke emerges from the exhaust and the tanks roll on.

...'How,' we ask (in the mess after the battle is over) 'do you reckon these chaps compare with Regular soldiers?' The Adjutant puts his drink down with an emphatic gesture. 'If I had to go into action tomorrow,' he says, 'I'd rather go with these chaps than anyone else in the entire Army.' 'May we quote on that?' we ask. 'You certainly may,' the Adjutant replies expansively. And so, having taken the precaution of publishing neither his name nor that of his Regiment, we gladly do.

AREAS OF GROWTH

The early 1950s saw the formation of two important units. The first of these was the Boys' Squadron RAC, in Bovington in January 1952. Its aim was to train future WOs and NCOs for the Royal Armoured Corps. Boys joined between 15 and 16 and normally spent two years with the squadron, after which they enlisted at the age of 17½ with the Colours for either 12 years, or 8 and a further 4 with the Regular Army Reserve. The course was designed to provide a wide background of military and academic knowledge to boys who were to become leaders, the syllabus being roughly divided into one-third general education, one-third military training and one-third sports and games. Major Barry O'Sullivan, RTR, was its first OC and the squadron was granted regimental status in 1958. It went from strength to strength to become the Junior Leaders' Regiment, RAC, and produced high-class recruits for all the RAC Regiments, until its disbandment.

Churchill tanks of 'C' Sqn 7 RTR leaguer up in 'Compo' Valley, Korea, during the bitter winter weather of 1950-51. They were part of 29 Bde and the first RTR unit to serve in the Korean War. TM

A brew-up will always cheer you up. Two crewmen of 'C' Sqn, 7 RTR, making a brew in Korea. Note the NCO is wearing the 29 Inf Bde flash. TM

The next unit to serve in Korea was 1 RTR with Centurion Mark IIIs. Here an immaculate 'honour guard' of the 1st with the flag of the Republic of South Korea. TM

The other unit to be formed in the 1950s was the 1st (Berlin) Independent Squadron, RTR, which was formed in November 1951, under Major Rollo Campbell, DFC, at the time of the Berlin Blockade crisis. Its role was to provide armoured support to the British independent infantry brigade in Berlin. As a result of the rundown of the Army in 1956-57, the squadron was disbanded on 12 October 1957, its last parade taking place on the Olympische Platz in front of 2000 people. It would be re-formed six years later, only to be disbanded once again in November 1965.

DEFENDING THE EMPIRE

The Regiment was involved in helping to police the far-flung parts of the Empire, both in the Middle and Far East. In the latter area, there was a potential threat from newly emergent Red China on the Crown Colony of Hong Kong, so it was decided to bolster up the garrison with tanks. The 3rd were the first RTR unit to serve there in August 1949. Their place was taken by the 7th in 1952, who stayed until November 1954. Three years later, in June 1957, the 1st did a stint in the Colony, until May 1960. Not only did 3 RTR have its main body in Hong Kong, but it also had an element in Malaya. This was because of the lack of a tank firing-range, until the discovery of a suitable area in North Malaya, at Kedah. A contemporary article from *The Tank*, telling about the range and its 15-mile training area, contained an interesting report of operations against the Chinese Communist bandits, in which tanks were used for the first time, to support an attack on two bandit camps with both main armament and machinegun fire. Much was learnt about the use of tanks in jungle conditions. As the article says:

The experience gained within a space of three months by the Detachment of 3rd Royal Tank Regiment in Malaya has shown conclusively that, however slow the progress, tanks can be driven over almost any type of terrain except swamp and thickest jungle.

KOREA

On 25 June 1950, the North Koreans crossed the 38th Parallel, which divided their country from neighbouring South Korea, and invaded in considerable strength. American forces in Japan, representing the United Nations, went immediately to their aid, while an all-nation UN force was being assembled. Britain was the first country after the USA to send troops to Korea, elements of 27 Infantry Brigade arriving on 28 August 1950. From July 1951, the British and Commonwealth troops in Korea were formed into one unique division - the Commonwealth Division, in which the RTR was well represented. The first RTR unit to serve in Korea was 'C' Sqn, 7 RTR. On 29 July 1950, while the Regiment was at Bovington Camp, it was ordered to mobilise an armoured

THE UNQUIET PEACE (1945–1959)

Excellent shot of a 1 RTR Centurion Mark III in its firing position. Note the ammunition bunker, close at hand for immediate replenishment during action, also the clothes line to the rear! (Lt Col Peter Massy)

squadron equipped with Crocodile flamethrowers as part of 29 Independent Infantry Brigade. They were being sent from UK to support 27 Infantry Brigade sent from Hong Kong. In addition to the Crocodile squadron there was to be a complete armoured regiment of Centurion tanks (initially 8th King's Royal Irish Hussars), plus an Armoured Reinforcement Group.

At that time 7 RTR was split with one squadron guarding an air base in Norfolk, and another at Gosport equipped with amphibious tanks. The Regiment was under strength and contained many National Servicemen, who were ruled too young to go to war (this rule was later changed). It was decided to re-form 'C' Sqn and to transfer in all available regular soldiers from the other squadrons, then to make up the shortfall by recalling Regular Army reservists. In addition, the BBC broadcast an appeal for volunteers to join up for 18 months' service in Korea, and those who responded were known as 'K' Type Volunteers.

Under the command of Major Jack Pettingell, the squadron landed in Korea on 17 November, after the tide had turned against the North Koreans, and it was expected that the war would be over by Christmas. However, on 25 November, 180 000 Chinese troops launched a massive offensive against the UN forces near the Yalu River and forced them to withdraw. In bitterly cold weather, destroying vast dumps of stores on the way, the entire Eighth US Army - as the UN Force was called - was forced into a headlong retreat. By then 'C' Sqn, which had moved north towards the Korean capital of Pyongyang, was forced to withdraw and moved into a defensive position in rear of the Imjin River. At that time they made up half the British armour in Korea, as all the Centurions had been withdrawn to Japan

because they were reckoned to be too secret to risk in battle, leaving only the 8th Hussars Recce Troop of 12 Cromwells! Lt (later Major) Bryan Clarke recalled a typical action at that time, involving his troop and two tanks of SHQ, which had been ordered to clear a pocket of enemy out of a village in the middle of a defended area into which they had infiltrated. The ground was intersected with narrow, frozen streams and ditches, and was overlooked by enemy infantry positions on the surrounding hills. The tanks had to move in single file along the narrow track leading to the village. Clarke recalls:

> As I was in the leading tank I think I fired more than the others and I was getting very short of ammunition by the time both my guns fell to pieces in the middle of the battle! Sgt Dowling then took up the lead and did a lot of shooting as well... I was never conscious of anything coming back, but I recall trying to shoot at a machine gun with my Bren (from the top of the turret) and having difficulty making up my mind whether to show myself or whether safety was the better part of valour. We wreaked terrible execution... The only anti-tank weapons they had were long bamboo poles with a very crude explosive charge tied to the end, and which on rare and brave occasions they would ram against the side of the tank.

The village was retaken, but later everyone had to pull back to the south of Seoul.

By mid-January the front had been stabilised for the winter along the 38th Parallel, but the Chinese launched a spring offensive on 22 April. By the end of the month they had been contained at great cost to both sides -the Chinese alone lost an estimated 70 000

Good shot of the author's tank on the Hook, illuminated by flares during a night engagement. His tank was also fitted with a searchlight which provided night illumination until shot out. (Author's collection)

Entrance to a typical bunker where the tank crew slept when not on duty. Built with the help of local Korean labour, they could withstand most shellfire.
(Author's collection)

men. There were many epic feats of courage, including the famous stand of the Gloucesters. Once again the enemy ran out of steam, the UN were able to resume the offensive and to force them back across the now well-trodden 38th Parallel. From then on the battle became a static contest, vaguely reminiscent of the First World War, with lines of fortified positions on opposing hills, and both sides patrolling into No Man's Land in between. Tanks were used as mobile pillboxes, dug into the hills, with their crews living in bunkers close by. 'C' Sqn sailed for home in October 1951, having never fired their flamethrowers in anger, but having shown that the Churchill tank was ideal for such conditions, especially in the soft paddy fields.

The next RTR unit to arrive was 1 RTR, who landed in Korea in 1952. They took over from the 5th RIDG who had earlier replaced the 8th Hussars. The

Regiment was boosted with many volunteers from other RAC Regiments, plus an entire squadron from the Canadian Armoured Corps. Life in the line was so like that of the trench warfare in 1914-18, that this account of a day in the line in Korea, taken from 1 RTR's *Korean Journal*, could well have been written in 1916 rather than in 1953:

'Wake up, sir, it's three o'clock. Time to get up, sir.' The troop leader yawned and stretched, then hastily slipped his arms inside the bedroll as the cold night air licked them. 'Right-O, Kemberry, I'll be out in a few minutes. Would you please light the candle' - then, as the other did so and left: 'Thanks.'

The quivering flame of the candle lit the inside of the hutchie - a square hole carved deep into the side of a Korean hill. It was just long enough for a bedroll, and 2ft wider. Within reach of the occupant was a drip-fed fire, consisting of an ammunition box, a fuel pipe leading to it, and a chimney of 20pdr cases rising from it up through the roof.

In a quick movement I reached over, flicked the tap on and dropped a match in the flash pan. After a few minutes of luxurious last-minute rest, the air inside lost some of its fierce bite and I put my outer clothes on. Combat jacket and windproof trousers were followed by a balaclava, three pairs of gloves, another pair of socks, a furry hat and a parka.

Switching off the petrol and blowing out the candle to avoid the ever-present danger of fire, I stepped outside, and stood still for a few minutes to let my eyes become accustomed to the darkness. It was a clear moonlight night, with an icy wind blowing hard from the north. Everything seemed still, though there was an angry grumble from artillery in the distance, and an occasional stacatto burst from harassing machine guns. To my left I could hear the steady hum from the charging engine in my tank. I moved quietly towards it, and was challenged by a figure from the shadows.

'Halt! Goal,' it hissed.

I stopped abruptly and whispered 'Post,' the current password.

'OK, sir, everything is pretty quiet.'

'Off you go, then. Good night.'

'Good night, sir.'

I slipped into the weapon pit and looked down into the valley. My gloved hands ran over the Bren and I checked that the magazine was full. There were several boxes of grenades and I made sure that these were primed. Some which were resting on the ground had to be prised free from the earth, frozen hard since they were moved earlier in the night.

The tanks of the troop were dug deep in pits,

in the right-hand side of the largest hill of the area, Point 355. This was known by our American allies as Little Gibraltar, or 'Hell Hill'. Looking back over my right shoulder, I could see my own tank just a few yards away, its bulk partly hidden by the pit. The generator had been switched off, but the high-pitched buzz of the wireless-set was audible. The wireless crackled as a message came over it, and I heard my own operator answering a routine call.

I saw a movement a little way away, and as a figure approached, challenged him. It was the relief who would be on with me until the dawn. I beckoned to him to take the first shift in the turret, and he disappeared inside. When he was satisfied with the wireless and everything else, he dismissed the previous sentry and his head and shoulders reappeared in the turret as he joined me in keeping observation, the meantime checking the operation of the Browning machine gun mounted atop the turret.

We stared out into the re-entrant below, which ran down into the valley, scrutinising each shadow carefully, for the Chinaman is an excellent patroller. We faced north and the wind cut into my exposed parts. The hood of the parka one moulded carefully into the position from which one could see most and expose least. Peering out into the dark, however, one's eyes soon watered from the freezing wind, and after a while they would play strange tricks. One night my fellow sentry tiptoed over and whispered he could see a bear.

To my right a heavy machine gun opened up and the tracers appeared from behind a hill, soared gracefully, and disappeared as they burnt out, each in the same place, like a chorus appearing, gliding across the stage, and disappearing as abruptly as they had come. A few seconds later the sound would reach me, and then the tracers would reappear, sound and sight alternating.

As my feet became cold I stamped them and kicked against the side of the pit. Although wearing two pairs of socks and the 'cold wet-weather' boots issued by the Army, with plastic insoles inside them, and standing on straw to insulate my boots from the frozen ground, the icy cold had still seeped through and was creeping into my toes. One wriggled one's toes all the time while standing, and this slowed up the freezing process. I glanced at my watch and found that I had done my turn in the pit, and so took over the set from the operator, who climbed out. Within the turret the lower part of one's body was out of the wind at any rate, and gradually recovered but all too soon it was time to emerge again.

A Vickers machine gun opened up on my left, from higher up the hill, and this time the tracers

When Her Majesty Queen Elizabeth II succeeded to the throne it was necessary to alter the regimental badge, redesigning the crown to make it a 'Queen's' crown. This is the present version, made of Staybrite material, which was taken into use on 13 January 1953. TM

put me in mind of the lit-up hoardings that one used to see in London, publishing the news abroad to all and sundry. Soon these became fainter, and harder to see as the east became lighter. Once more I was privileged to see a beautiful dawn break in Chosen - 'The Land of Morning Calm'.

When it was really light we stood down, handing over the 24hr wireless watch to another tank. Those who had just come off guard slept while the others prepared breakfast. When this was ready I ate it eagerly, for the fresh air had given me an appetite. This morning it consisted of a tin of ham and Lima beans, heated, and an egg with some bread. I found the ham in the last mouthful of beans, and it tasted excellent. A thick brew of tea restored my spirits, and I went outside to boil some ice for washing. Last night it had not snowed, but everything was frozen, and the previous fall of snow lay hard.

A little later in the morning I walked over to see my right-hand tank, about a quarter-of-a-mile along the front. My troop was in support of the Australians, and as I passed I saw the Diggers doing various jobs, or sleeping after patrol, or simply chaffing one another in their usual good-humoured manner. My troop sergeant's tank was supporting the 1st ROK Capitol Division, and I entered a company area of theirs. I had quickly acquired an admiration for these plucky determined little fighters, and they in turn were very appreciative of tank support. During the night a Korean patrol had located a mortar position and, having reported it, this tank of mine was destroying it. When we achieved direct hits, followed by secondary explosions, the ROK delight knew no bounds, and they bounced up and down clapping their hands in glee, and shouting 'Number One!' - an expression denoting great pleasure.

I found the crew in great heart, and we chatted for a time, while they pointed new diggings and recounted anything of local significance which had taken place during the night. Walking back to my tank I found some Diggers sitting round passing the time of day with my crew. As a general rule the Australians were a little older and more self-reliant than our fellows, although often their platoon commanders were young. I had no wish to serve with better soldiers.

In the meantime other members of my crew had been keeping the front under observation, and one of them had spotted a wireless aerial. I computed the range from my map, and opened fire on it. We hit it, snapping it in two, but evidently it was near some headquarters, for a few days later it had been erected again. The inevitable followed, and it once more disappeared.

Leaving observers, we made our way down to the cookhouse of 'Dog' Company, and there had a hot lunch cooked from fresh rations. As I walked back a shell screamed overhead and buried itself in the ground beyond me, throwing up a heap of earth, and sending shrapnel singing by. I dived into a nearby trench and awaited the next. The arrival of these shells is sudden and surprising; something like the emotional impact of being in a passenger train when an express, with its steam whistle screaming, hurtles past in the opposite direction. If one can hear the whistle one is soon able to tell a 'comer' which is going to be a near one, from one that is going to drop 100yds away, and one takes precautions or not accordingly.

Listening for the next, I heard it coming in a little nearer the tank and, as it landed, sprinted to the next cover; and so by leaps and bounds reached the tank itself and hopped inside, closing the cupola lid as something landed nearby, then started to send back an accurate report of the incoming fire. Having sent back this report, we opened up on all known enemy observation posts, seeking to silence the guns by discomforting the OP crews. The most effective way of doing this was to put a shell into each slit, in the manner of posting a letter. This we did and the shelling became desultory and finally ceased.

As evening drew on, the local company commander informed me of the coming night patrols and, as I could be of practical assistance in one, I chatted with the patrol commander, a young Australian officer, and we planned effective support. Before last light I ranged on a particular supply trench that the Chinese used at night to bring up rice and ammunition, and also on one spot to which the patrol hoped to lure the enemy. We carried out this ranging in the middle of a general 'shooting-up' of trenches, position, OPs etc, in order that the enemy might suspect nothing. Then as the sun set, we stood to.

While dinner was cooking we fired intermittently at the supply trench, breaking up the intervals between shots and occasionally firing two or three in quick succession to harass those bringing up supplies then I handed over to one of my crew while I ate.

As the patrol in which I was particularly interested was not going out until nine o'clock, I lay down for an hour's rest, while the other tank carried on the harassing. I wrote out the day's events and then relaxed. I was soon asleep.

My rest, however, was to be short-lived, for I was woken abruptly by a shell landing close by, and shaking dirt from the roof on to my face. I sat up spluttering, and dressed quickly. As more and more came in, landing methodically round us, it was obvious that they were gunning for the tanks again. I went outside and instinctively ducked as an 'in-swinger' hailed its approach. Without waiting for its partner, I hopped into the tank. As it was nearly nine anyway, we stood by to await the patrol, the while listening to the wireless net on which we were operating. More shells followed and a jarring crash accompanied by fumes told us that we had received a direct hit. I took a quick look round to see whether there was any serious damage and, finding none, hopped in and continued to listen.

The shelling eased up and we opened the cupola lid to have better observation. All seemed as quiet as is normal. Then, down in the valley below, a burst from an Owen gun preceded a fusillade of firing in which one could distinguish the fast chattering 'Burp gun' of the Chinese. Little flashes appeared and the sound of grenades exploding was carried to us, and cries - perhaps of pain or fear - were audible. Then silence, followed again by an outburst of firing. All at once the deep cough of enemy mortars was heard and, ages later, it seemed - the flash of them landing followed by the familiar crump. A few minutes of silence followed and I was beginning to wonder whether the commander's set had been damaged when a message crackled over the air, electrifying us by its urgency.

'Hullo Buck Rogers Dog One-Nine, Starlight One Zero Now. Over.'

I answered: 'One-Nine Wilco Out,' and, before

I had finished, the first round had been fired by the gunner, who was ready for this. A few hectic and strenuous moments followed as one round after another sped on its way. When we had fired them, I reported so over the wireless, and the cryptic message came back: 'One-Nine, successful. Thanks, out.' The trap had been sprung!

By now the moon was up, and the patrol made good time back, reporting in at a quarter to eleven. As the guard alternated each night, I and my fellows were to come on at twelve, so we left the tank and went to bed. As I lay down to sleep I heard the tank engine starting up, to prevent it freezing, but nothing could stop me and I was soon asleep. Another day in the line was over.

The most important action fought by the Regiment during their tour in Korea was in May 1953, when the Chinese made an attack in strength onto the Hook positions, held by 1st Bn The Duke of Wellington's Regiment which tank troops of 'C' Sqn were supporting. As the *Korean Journal* of 1 RTR relates:

On 20 May there was a marked increase both in enemy patrolling and shelling on the left sector and it soon became evident that the Chinese were building up to a major attack on the Hook salient… Throughout the day of 28 May all tanks were subjected to heavy shelling by 105 and 122mm guns, as well as were all front line infantry positions in the Hook area. At approximately 8.30pm the Chinese launched their first attacks and were soon engaging the forward infantry positions on the Hook. By 11pm these positions had been captured by the enemy, but after a counter attack by the reserve company they were once more in our hands. In all, four separate attacks were put in on the front of the 'Dukes'. With the exception of the one which gained a temporary footing in the forward position on the Hook, all were halted in front of the FDLs. Throughout the action the tanks of 'C' Sqn engaged the enemy and inflicted heavy casualties on them - 504 rounds of 20pdr HE, 22 500 rounds of Besa and 4500 rounds of Browning were fired. The tanks themselves averaged five direct hits from shells and mortars and all tank searchlights were shot out early in the action. It is estimated that during the action 10 000 mixed shells and mortars fell on the forward positions. The enemy casualties were estimated to be 250 killed and 800 wounded.

Sgts John McFarlane and A. Wallace were awarded well-deserved Military Medals for their bravery during the action. The ceasefire came on 27 July and shortly afterwards the 1st withdrew to Gloucester Valley where they remained until sailing for Egypt in

A Centurion of 6 RTR, coming ashore at Suez, in support of the Commando Brigade as part of Operation Musketeer, *the Anglo-French operation mounted against Nasser's Egypt.* TM

December 1953. They were replaced by 5 RTR, for whom the unexpected end of the war had come as rather an anti-climax. Nevertheless, they buckled down with a will to constructing the new 'Kansas' line and practising once a month to occupy it at four hours' notice. The 5th left Korea and sailed for Cyrenaica in late December 1954.

SUEZ ADVENTURE

Capt Peter Berry wrote in an article entitled 'Suez Adventure' which was published in *The Tank* in 1957 and began:

> How many soldiers at Catterick in June 1956 would have believed that by December they would have fought an action with completely strange equipment in a very unusual role?

In the article he told how he, together with one other officer and 32 soldiers, had been moved hastily down from Catterick to the School of Amphibious Warfare in Devon, there to form No 1 Landing Vehicle Tank Troop RAC and learn how to operate Buffaloes (LVT III), in which 11th RTR had crossed the Rhine. Fortunately they had Capt R. Butler, MC, RASC, as their instructor who had served with 11th Battalion during the Rhine crossing and at Walcheren.

> We quickly had to alter our driving techniques as 'swimming' through surf and in the sea is very different from driving a Centurion across country!

After an all too short 10-day course they emplaned for Malta, where they met up with the Commandos whom they would be carrying, plus their 16 LVTs which had been sent out from UK.

> During September and October we took part in landing exercises on the beaches of Malta and

6 RTR Centurions advancing through Port Said, November 1956. After Nasser nationalised the Suez Canal, the British/French/Israelis mounted Op Musketeer, *which went very well until 'diplomatic negotiations' took over and UN forces replaced them.* TM

live firing exercises off Filfla, the Naval Gunnery Range. In the four months we spent with the Commandos exactly half our time was afloat in landing ships and craft and we soon developed Naval routine and jargon... Very quickly 'Stand Easy' and 'Out Pipes' replaced 'NAAFI break' and 'Fall In' in our vocabulary.

They were of course to be part of the amphibious assault on Port Said which would be carried out by the Commando Brigade, supported by 6 RTR, as part of Operation *Musketeer*, the Anglo-French operation mounted against Nasser's Egypt after he had nationalised the Suez Canal. Many other troops were at one time going to be employed, including 1 RTR, who were loaded at Portland, while the 6th loaded at Plymouth; plus 5 RTR, then serving with 10th Armoured Division in Libya. In the event, only 6 RTR and 1 LVT Troop would be involved in the action. Peter Berry recalled his part in the assault thus:

> On November 6 at 0415hrs the bow doors opened and we clambered down the ramps into a calm sea two-and-a-half miles off shore immediately west of the Port Said Breakwater. Any apprehension we may have felt a few moments earlier was immediately dispelled by the familiar scene around us. As one Commando in my vehicle remarked, 'Just like an exercise off Filfla.' Our previous training had been so realistic it was difficult to realise that this was the assault. Immediately ahead of us lay two LCAs who were to lead us in. HMS *Daring* was firing her naval guns on to the coast on either flank, the outline of which we could just see in the lightening sky.
>
> We quickly formed up and followed the LCAs (Landing Craft Assault) which were to take us in to a position from which we could identify our particular beaches. As we advanced, HMS *Daring* kept abreast of us, firing broadsides, while we scanned the horizon for our landmarks. At last we could see the spire of the Mosque which was immediately behind our beach. I then waved the LCAs away and we formed into line abreast and made at maximum speed for the shore.
>
> So far the enemy had offered no opposition. I was beginning to feel that this was too good to be true and that at any moment the coast ahead would erupt with Egyptian guns. However, when we were about 200yds from shore four Sea Hawks appeared out of the smoke and made strafing runs on the beaches and bathing huts. How air support inspires confidence.
>
> As soon as the last aircraft had pulled away, the Commando Bren gunners opened up from the vehicles on to the bathing huts and beaches. Exactly 20mins after leaving the ships we were

4 RTR in Egypt. Two Comets belonging to 4 RTR are seen in the tank park at Shandur, 1947. They continued to serve there until 1953, when the 1st came back from Korea and took over. TM

touching down on the beaches. At this stage two machine guns opened up from the Breakwater but they caused no damage and were quickly silenced. Some Egyptians were seen to abandon positions round the bathing huts and run. Obviously they had been expecting us to disgorge our Commandos 50yds or so from shore, but when we merely accelerated out of the sea they thought better of it. (An LVA swims at five knots but as soon as the tracks touch the beach it can accelerate to 15-20mph in a very short space.)

We crossed the beach with our hearts in our mouths, but fortunately it had not been mined and we were soon disgorging the Commandos on their first objective, the block of flats on the seafront.

While the Commandos were winkling out Egyptians from strong points in the houses, the beach-head seethed with activity as the build-up began. Air Liaison and Naval Surface Support Observer teams came ashore and began controlling the support, meanwhile the Commando Mortar Troop 'bedded in' their base plates. Twenty minutes after we landed we were relieved to hear the familiar noise of Centurions once more, as 'C' Sqn, 6th Royal Tank Regiment, waded ashore.

Also listening to 'C' Sqn landing was CO 6 RTR, Lt-Col Tom Gibbon, who later told of the landing in a letter to General Nigel Duncan, then Representative Colonel Commandant:

We watched 'C' Sqn go in in their LCTs to land 20mins behind the Marine Commandos. The Naval and air support on the beaches was impressive but completely obscured our view of the battle. 'C' Sqn waded ashore unscathed and dry which says a lot for their waterproofing work as they off-loaded into about 6-7ft of water! They had a bit of trouble getting rid of their ironmongery as the wiring had deteriorated in Malta and we had had to use it again as no replacements had arrived. However, they got it off quite quickly with the usual persuaders - a sledge and a crowbar!... 'C' Sqn both led and supported the Commandos through the town on two separate and parallel axes - one down the harbour past Simon Arzt and the other down Sh Mohammed Ali from the Governorate to the Station. They dealt with three anti-tank guns and quite a number of MGs, most of which were sited to fire down the side streets. There is no doubt that the speed of movement at this stage down Mohammed Ali completely upset the defence. Two or three rocket launchers were collected

Amalgamation of the 4th and 7th RTR. The amalgamation parade was held at Hohne on 3 April 1959 and taken by Maj-Gen Bob Foote, VC. Here he inspects part of the new regiment, accompanied by the CO, Lt-Col E.R. Farnell-Watson. TM

2 RTR in BAOR. Cpl Bryson on the Sterling range during a Regimental three-day event held in 1959. The Sterling SMG was now the standard tank crewman's personal weapon. 9mm in calibre it had an effective range of about 200m. TM

on the way but they did not succeed in hitting the tanks.

'A' Sqn had quite a job getting past 'C' Sqn and the commandos down the waterfront, pretty closely followed by RHQ. 'B' Sqn did not get off until later, being the last LST in and had to be held in the area of the beach for want of room. On getting onto the golf course and away from the built-up area, 'A' Sqn tried to cut across country to the main bridge leading to the Canal causeway but found the ground very treacherous

and bogged four tanks in quick succession. They were also attacked by one of our own airstrikes, but luckily got away scot free except for a couple of 20mm through the side plates and bins.

The operation which had started so spectacularly soon fizzled out into weeks of diplomatic negotiations, before the UN forces came to take over the policing of the Canal Zone. The Sixth and No 1 LVT Troop made the best of the unpleasant conditions, keeping order in Port Said. The most disgruntled group was undoubtedly RHQ of 1 RTR who did not disembark until 13 November after all the action was over and were then ordered back to Malta after only a few hours ashore! Had they been put ashore as originally planned, just seven hours behind the Commando Brigade, then they 'would have been at Ismailia and Abu Sueir by the cease-fire,' claimed Brigadier Sleeman.

AMALGAMATIONS

Towards the end of 1957 the Army Council released information on the regiments that would be lost in the run-down of the British Army. The Royal Armoured Corps was destined to lose eight Regiments (six in Phase 1 and two more in Phase 2) three of which would be RTR. In Phase 1, the 3rd and 6th would be amalgamated, as would the 4th and 7th. Phase 2 would include the amalgamation of the 5th and 8th. The first of these amalgamations to actually take place was that of the 4th and 7th, a happy combination, because the 7th had originally been formed on a nucleus from the 4th, while the two Regiments had fought together in such epic encounters as the Battle of Arras in 1940. The amalgamation parade, which was held at Hohne on 3 April 1959, was taken by Maj-Gen H.R.B. Foote, VC, CB, DSO, then the Representative Colonel Commandant, who had of course won his VC in the Western Desert when commanding the 7th. He had also been Adjutant of the 4th in 1937, when one of its squadrons was detached to form the 7th. It was reported in *The Tank* thus:

The Parade took the following form: The foot parade was devised in two parts, the first to present the two old Regiments and the second to present the new amalgamated Regiment to the Inspecting Officer. It commenced with the two Regiments marching on from opposite sides of the square, to form up in line, the Fourth on the right and the Seventh on the left. A hot sun in a blue sky shone down on the blue-clad ranks, and gave emphasis to the movement of white-gloved hands on Sten guns as General Salutes were given for the Commander-in-Chief, for the Colonels Commandant, Royal Tank Regiment, and finally for the Inspecting Officer, Maj-Gen H.R.B. Foote, VC, CB, DSO. After General Foote's inspection the two Regiments marched past in column of squadrons to the tune of their

respective marches, the 'Blue Flash' and 'Waltzing Matilda'.

With the Regiments back in their positions their old flags were lowered for the last time, by TQMS Mitchell for the 4th and by SQMS Chesher for the 7th; a moving moment as the band played 'Auld Lang Syne'. The physical symbol of amalgamation came now, as the Regiments marched solemnly towards each other in slow time and merged squadron into squadron. Lt-Col F.R. Lindsay, DSO, MC, left the parade ground, and the second part of the parade was under way. This was now the new 4th Royal Tank Regiment, under the command of Lt-Col E.R. Farnell-Watson, MC.

The 3rd and 6th amalgamated at Sennelager on 31 October 1959, the parade being taken by a former Commanding Officer of the 3rd, Lt-Gen Sir Harold Pyman, KCB, CBE, DSO, who was then a Colonel Commandant, RTR. The 3rd and 6th had much common history, having been brigaded together in 1917, when they were still known as 'C' and 'F' Battalions, Tank Corps. Later in 1917, they were the first units to receive the new Whippet tank. In the Second World War they had fought side by side at Sidi Rezegh and Alamein, while more recently, at

Comet tanks of 7 RTR in the hills above Kowloon in 1953. They had taken over from 3 RTR (who served there 1949-52) and would stay until 1954. Finally 1 RTR would serve there from 1957-60 and a single sqn from 1965 to 1966. TM

Suez, 3rd reservists had served in the 6th. The well-known airstrip at Sennelager was the chosen parade ground, with the old windmill, which stands beside the strip painted in Regimental colours. A mounted, armoured parade took place, sadly in mist and rain. Amalgamation of the 5th and 8th was to have taken place in December 1959, but was postponed at the request of the Supreme Commander of Allied Land Forces, Europe, because he wished to slow down the reduction of British units stationed in Germany.

The reduction of the Territorial Army was even worse. 1956-57 saw the 42nd, 43rd and 45th RTR (TA) revert to the infantry role while the 40th and 41st were amalgamated to form the 40/41 RTR (TA), and the 44th amalgamated with the North Somerset Yeomanry to form the NSY/44th RTR. As Col Mike Jeffery wrote in the 50th *Anniversary Souvenir,* published in 1967:

How any nation can afford to lose so much 'know how' and goodwill is beyond comprehension but it has happened. The problem could be discussed *ad infinitum* but all that need be said here is that

St Peter's upon Cornhill became the Regimental Chapel in September 1954. This is one of the Regimental Memorial windows. The Standards of disbanded RTR Regiments are laid up there. TM

the Royal Tank Regiment will never forget their friends in the Territorial Army nor cease to recognise the great contribution that they made to our short but eventful history.

A REGIMENTAL CHURCH

In September 1954, it was decided to adopt the beautiful Wren church of St Peter-upon-Cornhill as the Regimental Church and the first Regimental Service was held there on 21 October 1954. Thereafter, on a date as close as possible to the anniversary of the first tank action at Flers (15 September 1916), a yearly Tank Memorial Sunday has been held. It was also in 1954 that the Regimental Collect[1] was used for the first time:

Almighty God, Whose perfect love casteth out fear, mercifully grant that Thy servants of the Royal Tank Regiment may Fear Naught but to fall from Thy favour; for His sake in whom Thou art well pleased, Thy Beloved Son, Jesus Christ, our Lord.

Some six years later, on 21 October 1960, a Regimental Memorial Window was unveiled. Under the window are all the Regimental badges, carved in oak. The Standard of the 5th Royal Tank Regiment was laid up there, together with the old Standards of the 1st, 2nd, 3rd and 4th, which were presented by HM The Queen in 1960. Subsequently, the Standards of the other amalgamated Regiments have been laid up there.

A REGIMENTAL HEADQUARTERS

Although certain RTR annual events - such as Old Comrades' dinners - had been regularly held in London since the end of the Second World War, it was not until 1959 that the Army Council agreed to the setting up of a small Regimental Headquarters for the RTR in London, at Elverton Street, SW1, in part of the Westminster Dragoons' drill hall. The Regimental Colonel and a small staff have operated from these premises ever since, dealing with such Regimental matters as dress, promotion, finance, appointments, discipline, property, commissions, bands and major social functions. RHQ RTR was to remain at Elverton Street for nearly 30 years and, at the time of originally writing this book, was scheduled to move down to Bovington in the spring of 1988.[2]

REGIMENTAL RECRUITING

As National Service came to an end, the late 1950s saw the change to area recruiting for all the RTR Regiments. No longer would we recruit haphazardly all over the UK but, rather, specific areas were to be allocated to the Regiments so that TA affiliations could be strengthened and recruiting put on a more business-like footing. The split was as follows:

5 RTR in the RAC Trg Bde at Catterick, 1958. Brig Denis O'Flynn, inspecting 'B' Sqn at a canter, with the CO Lt-Col (later Col) Peter Hordern and RSM Merry bringing up the rear. TM

6 RTR on parade in Munster, motoring past the saluting base during the Coronation Parade in June 1953. 6 RTR were in Portsmouth Barracks and 2 RTR in Swinton Barracks, as part of 6th Armoured Division.
(Author's collection).

7 RTR taking part in the Queen's Birthday parade in Kowloon, Hong Kong, in 1953, when they still had Comets. TM

Regular Regiment	TA Regiment	Affiliated Recruiting Area
1 RTR	40/41 RTR	Lancashire, Cumberland, Westmorland.
2 RTR	Westminster Dragoons	Middlesex, Hertfordshire, Essex, Kent, London, Norfolk, Suffolk, Cambridgeshire, Huntingdonshire & Bedfordshire.
3 RTR	NSY/44 RTR	Cornwall, Devonshire, Dorset, Somerset, Bristol & Cheltenham.
4 RTR	Lowland Yeomanry	Scotland.
5 RTR	NSY/44 RTR	Yorkshire.

STANDARDS AND BATTLE HONOURS

In the late 1950s HM The Queen approved both the award of Battle Honours to the Regiment and the design of Standard, upon which selected Battle Honours would be emblazoned. This was a notable development in our history, because the award of Battle Honours is traditionally confined to those Regiments which carry a Standard, Guidon or Colours. The type of Standard chosen was similar to that carried by Dragoons, with the Regimental badge as its central feature. All Standards for the five Regiments would be identical, except for the unit designation (eg 1 RTR) which would appear in two of the corners. Of the many Battle Honours awarded to the Regiment, which are shown in full on page 256, only a limited number could appear on the Standard - 10 from the First World War, 10 from the Second World War, with Korea making the 21st. The first Standards were presented to the Regiment at Buckingham Palace in 1960.

---

[1] Composed by the then Rector of St Peter's, The Rev Douglas Owen, who was Padre of the 4th from 1938 to 1941.

[2] It has now moved into its new location.

Chapter 15
THE END OF EMPIRE (1960-1969)

5TH AND 8TH AMALGAMATION

The third and final amalgamation affecting the Royal Tank Regiment at that time, namely that between the Fifth and Eighth, took place at Fallingbostel on 1 July 1960. The parade was taken by General Sir John Crocker, GCB, KBE, DSO, MC, then Representative Colonel Commandant, RTR. It took the form of a dismounted inspection, march past, amalgamation and advance in review order, followed by a drive past of the Centurions and Conquerors of the new 5th Royal Tank Regiment. In his address, General Sir John Crocker recalled the histories of the two Regiments, their traditions and achievements, thus:

> These individual loyalties and this pride in the good name of one's own particular unit have ever been the foundation upon which the fighting qualities of the British Army has been built. They are the stuff which has given the British soldier the strength and resilience for which he is famous and which has been the envy of our friends and the despair and undoing of our foes. Today, we have seen in the symbolism of this parade, these two loyalties joined and, far from conflicting, each bringing its own notable contribution and merging into a common loyalty to the new 5th Royal Tank Regiment.

STANDARDS PARADE

Some 2500 spectators, all past and present members of the Regiment, their wives and children, were invited to watch HM The Queen, present Standards to 1, 2, 3, 4, 5 and 40/41 RTR and Guidons to the North Somerset Yeomanry/44 RTR and the Westminster Dragoons. The combined parade for their consecration and presentation was held in the gardens of Buckingham Palace at midday on Thursday 27 October 1960. There were eight Regimental Detachments on parade, each of three officers and 27 other ranks, under the command of Lt-Col Hugo Ironside, while the music was provided by the combined Cambrai and Alamein Bands. The consecration was performed by the Chaplain General to the Forces, the Venerable Archdeacon Neil. In her address afterwards, The Queen spoke of her grandfather's part in embodying the Royal Tank Corps in the

The third amalgamation of the post-war period was between 5 and 8 RTR. It took place at Fallingbostel on 1 July 1960, Gen Sir John Crocker took the parade and is seen here inspected the new 5 RTR, accompanied by Lt-Col (later Gen Sir Allan) Taylor, who commanded the amalgamated regiment. TM

Regular Army and of being its Colonel-in-Chief.

> Your motto is *Fear Naught* and I am confident that you will be as true to it as those who served before you.

ARMY'S NEW GUIDED MISSILE UNIT

On their return from three years in North Africa, Cyclops, 2 RTR, were chosen to become the first air portable anti-tank squadron in the British Army. Stationed on Salisbury Plain while the rest of the regiment went to Northern Ireland, Cyclops took over their new role in 1962, being armed with Malkara, a wire-guided missile mounted on the one-ton Hornet vehicle. Major (now Maj-Gen) John Allen was its first commander and recalls those days:

> The essential training problem in the squadron was to achieve the right balance between many quite different skills and qualities: the essential physical fitness and spirit of élan necessary for continuation parachute training (and, indeed, for service in the parachute role); the skill of GW

Standards Parade, 27 October 1960. Her Majesty The Queen, our Colonel in Chief, presented Standards to each of the five Regular RTR Regiments and Guidons to the three Territorial Army Regiments in the gardens of Buckingham Palace. TM

That evening, the Regiment held a ball in honour of Her Majesty and Prince Philip, at the Hyde Park Hotel. TM

Controllers and their reserves, including daily simulation training; ensuring the serviceability and reliability of the missile system through conscientious care and servicing; maintaining an adequate number of currently qualified platform riggers and checkers; and finally, undertaking proper tactical training, including training with the parachute battalions. These very varied skills demanded very different qualities in the same individuals and it required much thought and planning to get the balance right. We certainly had plenty to do!

In March 1963 I handed over command of Cyclops to Major (now Maj-Gen) Ian Baker and assumed command of 2 RTR in Omagh. By that time, we had two troops operational and the remaining one was well on the way to being so. Fortunately I was able to maintain contact with the squadron by visits to Tidworth and to exercises conducted by the squadron in Libya and elsewhere.

I found the whole period involved in converting Cyclops to the parachute GW role immensely challenging, stimulating and enjoyable. The role attracted a very high-grade type of officer and soldier and it was a real pleasure to work with them. Except during the initially high rates of failure at 'P' Company, morale was exceptionally high. Long after Cyclops and 2 RTR had relinquished the role, it was interesting to see how many parachute badges remained in the regiment and that the wearers retained that rather special quality associated with those who have gone through that mill.

In the first half of 1965, Cyclops, by now formally part of 16 Parachute Brigade, handed over the role to a composite, reconstituted RAC squadron (based on the special Reconnaissance Squadron RAC which had had an SAS-type role) and returned to undercommand of 2 RTR in the armoured role. Nevertheless, a number of Cyclops men remained with the new Parachute Squadron: indeed, for some time thereafter, 2 RTR had more men in that squadron than any other RAC regiment.

STRANGE SOLDIERING

The only RTR officer to be awarded the DSO since the Second World War in times of so-called peace, is Major (now General Sir Richard) Dickie Lawson, who gained his award whilst serving on secondment to the Royal Nigerian Army in 1962. He was on the staff of 3 Nigerian Brigade when he was sent to the Kasai Province in the Congo as part of a UN force trying to restore order there two years after the Belgians had seceded. It was while attempting to rescue some missionaries from among the warring factions that his remarkable story begins. Lawson set

Left: *Everyone in the squadron naturally had to be a qualified parachutist. Here one of the troop leaders checks harness. They did not jump in RTR berets but rather the normal paratroopers helmets.* TM

Below: *Members of Cyclops 2 RTR, formed the first Parachute Squadron RAC, in 1962, their OC being Major (later Maj-Gen) John Allen and his second in command Capt (Later Gen Sir Antony) Walker. They are standing in front of the Malkara-carrying Hornet - and adaptation of the 1 ton armoured vehicle.* TM

out to fly in a light aircraft to Kongolo in North Eastern Katanga in late January, landing at a nearby airstrip on the 23rd. He writes:

As it was unwise to leave the plane on the ground in hostile territory, I sent it back to Luluabourg and started to walk towards Kongolo.

It was a nature ramble with a difference. I avoided looking into the elephant grass at the edge of the airfield but I could see movement out of the corner of my eye. A feeling down the back of my neck told me that people were coming up behind. When I eventually looked round there were some 800 soldiers and half-naked tribesmen who were closing in. Each was pointing a weapon. One was even trying to aim a 2in mortar from the hip. The picture they presented was both frightening and ridiculous. In all fairness I was more frightened than amused.

2 RTR in Cyrenaica 1959-62. They were the last RTR Regiment to serve there having been preceded by 5 RTR (1955-57) and 6 RTR (1957-59). Here a Saladin armoured car crew poses beside the ruins of the ancient city of Cyrene. TM

Major (later Gen Sir Richard) Dick Lawson is seen here briefing crews of the Berlin Independent Squadron, during an exercise in the Grunewald training area, Berlin, 1963. TM

Cpl Brown of 4 RTR and his Ferret in Wadi Taym during the Radfan operations of 1964. Mines were a constant source of trouble, especially for the Ferrets. The terrain was very similar to the North-West Frontier. TM

Then I felt a sharp stab in the middle of my back. I wheeled round and struck a man standing close behind me with an arrow in his hand. He appeared to lose his balance and fell down in an ungainly heap. He was dressed in a pair of ragged shorts and a feathered head-dress. We both looked at each other and he suddenly started to giggle. Then everyone was smiling and laughing and some pressed forward to accept a handshake. A most extraordinary business! I had not meant to hit him; it is just that I break out into an uncontrollable fit of temper when someone touches me from behind.

I have made a fool of myself before because of this failing, but this time it had broken the ice. The crowd lost their immediate desire to shoot their little stranger. A few hours later, after a series of antics more of the music-hall stage than the military procedures prescribed in the text books, it was possible to persuade them to let me take the missionary out of Kongolo. Within three days he was safely back in Brussels.

Elated by the success of my music-hall approach at Kongolo, I was unwise enough to try

This 'Beau Geste' type fort at Ataq on the edge of the Empty Quarter, was the base for George Forty's 'A' Sqn, 4 RTR for three months in early 1964. They garrisoned the fort and patrolled the surrounding tribal areas. TM

On patrol until the end of their tour. Saladin armoured cars and Ferret scout cars halt during one of their last patrols, just before leaving Aden in 1964, bound for the Far East. TM

again to rescue some missionaries and nuns from a village behind the Katangese lines. This time it was a failure: with a Nigerian Officer, Major Conrad Nwawo, I was trapped in the village and beaten unconscious with rifle butts. How we avoided being executed was a miracle, but it taught me a lesson, I had tried to to be too clever.

Lawson modestly does not add that, after a long parley he was able to secure the release and evacuation of the missionaries and nuns, and saved Nwawo from execution. The car provided for his return journey broke down and he had to complete the journey on foot. As Macksey says in Vol 3 of *The Tanks* it was 'a march fraught with all kinds of perils, through country which was hostile in almost every respect'. Lawson went on to command the newly re-formed Independent Squadron, RTR, stationed in Berlin, from March 1963, until it was once again disbanded in late February 1965.

COUNTER-INSURGENCY OPERATIONS

During this decade the final rundown of the British Empire took place, with the Army playing its part in keeping the peace between warring factions and those who wanted the British out just that much quicker than we were prepared to go. The RTR was heavily involved, which had a striking effect on regimental moves, with regiments' detached squadrons serving all over the world outside Europe, in Aden, Cyrenaica, Cyprus and the Persian Gulf in the Middle East; Borneo, Brunei, Hong Kong, Malaya and Singapore in the Far East. Unfortunately space does not permit the detailing of all these activities. Instead, the author decided to choose one regiment which was serving in BAOR in early 1963 and returned there just three years later, having served in

both the Middle and Far East. That Regiment was 4 RTR and the story of those three years began in late 1962. This account was written by Brigadier Bryan Watkins who was, in 1962, CO 4 RTR:

In the autumn of 1962, the Fourth Royal Tank Regiment was warned for service in Aden, and the Gulf in the following year. The Regiment was widely dispersed at the time with Regimental Headquarters in Hohne, APC squadrons in Celle and Lemgo and a tank squadron in Berlin. Each squadron was a self-contained entity and the basic family structure of a normal armoured regiment simply did not exist. For example, we had no Headquarter Squadron and so no regimental system for logistics - the APC squadrons had their own EMEs and LADs and the Lemgo squadron had one of the two quartermasters with it. Something like nine years in Germany had produced a very efficient and happy unit but also one that had forgotten pretty well everything about the realities of active service soldiering - as most of the officers and senior NCOs were quite prepared to admit.

Our role was to be that of the Middle East Armoured Reconnaissance Regiment, with two squadrons in South Arabia and one in the Gulf at Sharjah. In South Arabia we would be providing one squadron to support the Federal Regular Army of South Arabia and one for Internal Security in Aden State. The Sharjah squadron would support the Trucial Oman Scouts and have a secondary role of providing the medium reconnaissance element of the screen for the British plan to support Kuwait against invasion. The Commanding Officer 4 RTR was the Screen Commander. As General Sir Allan Taylor would say, one did not have to take size ten in hats to

From Aden and the Persian Gulf, 4 RTR went on to the Far East in 1964, with RHQ in Seremban and squadrons in Singapore and Borneo. They were embroiled with Indonesian infiltrators in Borneo and here a patrol from 'C' Sqn drives through Serian, a typical kampong, at milestone 24, on the road from Kuching. TM

4 RTR were later followed by H Sqn of the 5th in 1966. Here a scout car of 'H' Sqn, drives across a wooden bridge. TM

work out that we faced a formidable task in uprooting the Regiment from Germany, completely reorientating our military ideas and coming together once more as a unit - although even now, the future would clearly involve us in all the problems of dispersion - and dispersion in situations which did not offer the 'mod cons' of the 'cushy' life of Rhine Army. Furthermore, there was clearly going to be a problem about our families, since no more than a handful would be able to accompany us. As if all that were not enough, our new role involved raising and training our own light aircraft flight.

After a hectic period, training the two armoured infantry battalions how to command and drive their own APCs, the 4th spent an even more hectic training session in Scotland, learning how to use their armoured cars and scout cars in counter-insurgency operations, and then flew out to the Middle East in August 1963. Watkins takes up the story again:

'A' Sqn 4 RTR arrived in Aden at the beginning of August to take over the Western Aden Protectorate role, with the rest of the Regiment arriving some days later. Almost on the day they arrived, Ian Galloway's troop was sent up to Beihan on the Yemen border and immediately found themselves in a near battle situation. The task of the squadron was to provide armoured car support to the Federal Regular Army of South Arabia. This was achieved by detaching individual troops to work with the FRA battalions at Beihan, Ataq, Mukeiras and Dhala. The squadron was equipped almost entirely with Ferrets which were normally deployed by air unless they were being used to escort FRA or even civilian convoys - usually to Dhala or Ataq and Beihan.[1] When Galloway and his troop arrived by Beverley at Beihan, they were rushed forward to the border area in their newly acquired vehicles (which, in this instance included two Saladins). Within hours, Galloway was asked whether he could engage a heavy machine gun which had been a nuisance strafing the camp of the battalion he was to support. By great good fortune, the troop had laid down fixed lines for the 76mm guns of their Saladins before night had fallen. Driving straight out to the prepared fire position, Galloway zeroed his gun on the aiming post, put on the range and bearing of the target on his fire control equipment and engaged - with immediate effect. As 'J' (Sidi Rezegh) Battery RHA had consistently failed to knock out this gun, Galloway's early success was met with tremendous acclaim by the FRA and, as far as they were concerned, 4 RTR were already 'top of the pops'! This was a real stroke of luck for the Regiment, all the more gratifying as the system of fixed lines employed had been taught within 'A' Sqn by George Forty, its commander, who had learned the trick in Korea with 1 RTR. Time spent on training in Scotland had not been wasted.

After this auspicious start, the Regiment's induction went along a little more slowly, with 'A' Sqn deploying troops to the other up-country stations already described and 'B' Sqn, under Alastair Mathieson, providing the escort for a Dhala convoy or two, to get the feel of the job. Aden State was fairly quiet at this time, so the Regiment was able to concentrate on settling in, sorting out a far from satisfactory vehicle situation and learning all there was to know about the Western Aden Protectorate. Up in Sharjah, Tom

THE END OF EMPIRE (1960–1969)

Welch's 'C' Sqn found itself 1200 miles from the Commanding Officer (good news!) but with a collection of Saladins and Ferrets which were no more than eight per cent battleworthy, though fortunately they quickly discovered that the main problem was seized suspensions, clogged with salt-laden sand, which only needed a quantity of grease and some vigorous bouncing over a rocky strip of desert to free them. This done and the cars liberally painted with red lead to counter the effects of the salt on all their metal surfaces, they were soon ready to learn the tricks of desert driving and navigation. The heat up in the Gulf was such that the troops could literally fry an egg on the armour at midday and motoring became impossible, because the petrol was vaporising in the carburettors, often forcing the crews to wait until the cool of the evening before they could get moving.

Back in Little Aden, a Regimental Operations Room was set up under the Signal Sergeant (Sgt Harvey) which kept a net open to all stations 24hrs a day, 365 days in the year. Very soon the value of morse began to show as distant troops strove to get through the difficult radio conditions. Jim Alexander's Regimental Light Aircraft Flight and the Beavers of 256 Sqn Army Air Corps (under whom our flight worked) were on constant call to answer demands for assistance from the outstation…

As is so often the case in these situations where a measure of dissidence exists, there was always a risk of vehicles getting mined and so mine patrols were a big feature of the troop's lives, especially in the border area beyond Beihan and, later, in the Radfan, but even in Dhala and Mukeiras a close watch had to be kept. The Radfan operations developed fairly gradually with 'B' Sqn getting involved in the first instance. After the arrival of 39 Infantry Brigade, the whole scope of the affair was stepped up and the demand for armoured cars increased. At the same time the internal security situation in Aden began to cause some concern. Just to complicate matters, the time had come for 'A' Sqn to relieve 'C' in the Gulf and for 'B' Sqn to take over the up-country role from 'A'. I had a good think and realised that, in the short term, we needed four weak squadrons instead of three. This would mean taking a squadron commander who knew the form to command a skeleton headquarters at Thumeir, the base of the operations, and rotating troops from the other squadrons through his hands. Recalling 7 RTR's 'D' Sqn, I decided to put the need for a 'D' Sqn now to good effect. I can only say that this marked the end of the 4 RTR/7 RTR rivalry and the experiment worked like a charm, thanks in no small part to Alastair Mathieson, who commanded, and Sergeant Major 'Chalky' White (an old 7 RTR hand), both of whom were

A young troop leader of 5 RTR briefs one of his crew during an exercise in BAOR. TM

decorated for the excellence of their work. You do not get many MBEs going to Squadron Sergeant Majors, and Sergeant Major White's was well deserved (as was Alastair's Military Cross). A tough, highly professional soldier of the old school, he had a master touch with young soldiers, who would do anything for him, without him ever having to raise his voice.

When I formed 'D' Sqn, it was clear that there would have to be a few more NCO Troop Commanders to replace various young officers who were getting redeployed to necessary jobs within the organisation. Fortunately, it was a matter of policy with me that at least two troops in each squadron would be commanded by NCOs, so we already had a number of high-class men with troop-leading experience. I looked through my regimental list to pick these men and suddenly realised, as I weighed them up by merit, that virtually all my 'stars' were ex-Junior Leaders - proof positive, to me at least, of the value of the system. I well recall being pressed for 'just one more troop' for Thumeir and going to the radio to call Beihan where there were two troops of 'B' Sqn under the command of a Staff Sergeant. Perhaps unfairly, I asked Sgt Rathmell whether he thought he could make the journey to Thumeir by 'road' across the desert, as there were no aircraft available. This meant a four-day journey which

211

With the Royal Monogram on raised bridgelayers, Her Majesty The Queen has just inspected the Regimental Mounted Review, held at Reinsehlen, Germany, on 14 July 1967. All five Regiments were represented together with the Cambrai and Rhine Bands. TM

normally involved an infantry escort to picquet the heights through the mountainous area south of Ataq. 'Leaving 2300hrs' came the reply. Three-and-a-half days later, a dusty figure reported to me on the airstrip at Thumeir - half a day ahead of 'bogey' for the journey. When I had congratulated the troop on their achievement, I said 'Right. Go and get your heads down and be ready for the mine patrol at 0500hrs tomorrow.' 'But we're ready to go on patrol now,' came the reply and they were. That little story typifies the spirit of the Regiment at that time.

In August/September 1964, the 4th left the Middle East and flew out to the Far East, with detached squadrons in Sarawak (Borneo), Brunei and Singapore, and the rest of the Regiment in Seremban, on the mainland of Malaya. The squadrons in Borneo had to face the threat of invasion from Indonesia, supported by the local CCO (Clandestine Communist Organisation). So 'A' Sqn found itself again performing the same types of tasks as they had carried out up-country in Aden, with armoured car troops strung along the frontier in support of infantry bases. In addition to their operational tasks they were also fully engaged in 'Hearts and Minds' operations to encourage support from the local population who lived deep in the jungle. This often involved foot patrols, as Cpl Lennie Kew of 'A' Sqn recalled in the *Tank Magazine*:

If any of you shudder at the thought of boots and blisters, then you must believe, as I once did, that nothing but pain and misery can come from covering distances of over a mile without the aid of mechanical transport. Since arriving in British

Her Majesty arrives for the Mounted Review, 14 July 1967. TM

Borneo, or to be more correct, Sarawak, I have found that this is not altogether true, and in covering various distances, in areas where vehicles could not possibly move, my fellow 'Tankies' and I have found that although foot patrolling is not always exactly easy, it can nevertheless be very interesting, and often very amusing. In order to indicate what some of these patrols can be like, I will endeavour to describe one in particular, in which I recently took part; it was a short one, and took place on 12 January and was scheduled to last about five hours.

It consisted of myself as leader, three troopers of our detachment, our civilian interpreter (bearer of a strange unpronounceable Dyak name, and known to all as 'Pete') and last, but no means least, PC Harold Muda, a very genial, but highly efficient policeman. Our task was to visit three kampongs which lay south of the main road which connects Bau to Kuching.

At 09.30hrs, travelling in a Saracen APC we called at the Bau police station to collect our constable and, having done so, about 30mins' driving found us at the point where we were to de-bus and continue on foot. Having fixed magazines to our weapons, arranged an order of march, and briefed the patrol on our task and its *modus operandi*, away we went into the ulu. The footpath was well defined but, because of recent rain, very muddy, and a few minutes later we had lost the sound of traffic and could well have been 20 miles from a road by our surroundings. We soon reached the first signs of habitation, a large, but shabby, Chinese-style house on the edge of a small rubber plantation but, not wishing to stop the patrol so soon, I gave order to push on.

During the next 20mins we passed about six such dwellings, each set in their own little rubber or pepper garden, and all being guarded by at least three very noisy dogs. At the end of this 20mins we reached our first objective, Kampong Beninyau Baru, where I called a halt and through our interpreter asked the way to the headman's house… As often happens on any day other than a Sunday, the Tuan Kampong was unfortunately away tapping his rubber. Since there were none of the menfolk in evidence and the women only concern themselves with the problems of feeding and rearing their usually large families, we left the kampong, amidst waves and friendly shouts from the children and mothers.

After ensuring that we were on the right track, since the maps of the area are not entirely reliable in this aspect, we pushed on towards our next port of call, Kampong Peninyau Lama. The track immediately became narrower, and soon diminished to a muddy way, obviously not heavily used, and led us into even rougher going. Although the way never became really tough, we had now to test our agility by skipping across small streams, balancing across narrow bamboo bridges and picking our way through small areas of rather odorous swamp…

Several hours and some 20 miles later they returned to their 'trusty Saracen' and headed homewards.

THE MOUNTED REVIEW BY HER MAJESTY

There was no shortage of splendid parades in this decade. The highspot was undoubtedly the Mounted Review at Reinsehlen held on 14 July 1967, when our Colonel-in-Chief reviewed the Regiment. All five Regiments were represented with 2nd, 3rd and 4th who were all then serving in BAOR, together with the Cambrai and Rhine Bands, at full strength, while the 1st was represented by 'A' Sqn who were then serving in Berlin and 5th by their 'H' Sqn. The Centurion tanks, Saladin armoured cars and Ferret scout cars of the five Regiments were led by a Heavy Mark V tank and a Rolls-Royce armoured car from the Tank Museum, while at the rear was a single new Chieftain main battle tank. Overhead flew the Sioux and Skeeter helicopters of the Air Troops of the 2nd,

Valete 5 RTR. Gen Sir Alan Jolly, then the Representative Colonel Commandant, inspects 5 RTR at the disbandment parade at Wolfenbutel on 20 November 1969. TM

For a while Recce Regiments were fortunate enough to have their own Air Troops. This one belonged to 2 RTR and is seen here with an old Skeeter (on right of photograph) and the replacement Sioux. The photograph was taken about 1968.
TM

3rd and 4th. Her Majesty closed her address after the parade with the words:

> I am deeply impressed by today's Review. I know how much work and preparation is required to bring together such a concentration of men and armoured vehicles and I congratulate all of you on the smartness and efficiency which does credit to your Regiment. You have my heartfelt good wishes for the years to come.

DISBANDMENT OF THE 5TH

As the Representative Colonel Commandant General Bill Liardet wrote, shortly after the Mounted Review:

> It was nothing short of tragic that so shortly after an outstandingly successful weekend in BAOR we should hear that, as part of the Government's planned reduction in the Armed Services, the 5th Royal Tank Regiment are to be disbanded… The news is a bitter disappointment to us all.

There followed in November 1969 four separate disbandment ceremonies, which began on 14 November with the presentation of a painting to the City of Leeds, to mark the fact that 75 per cent of the Regiment were Yorkshiremen and that a great proportion of them came from the Leeds area. On 16 November, the Regimental Standard of the 5th was laid up in the Regimental Church, where it now hangs on the north wall and with it the Standard Bearer's Belt which had been presented by the City of Leeds.

On 18 November the 5th held a 'Farewell to Wolfenbuttel' parade to mark their two very happy years serving in the armoured car role there. Finally, on the 52nd Anniversary of the Battle of Cambrai, the last disbandment parade was held in Northampton Barracks, Wolfenbuttel, which closed with the 5th driving off parade for the last time to the tunes with which the Regiment had particular associations - 'Waltzing Matilda' and 'The Happy Wanderer'.

AIR TROOPS AND AIR SQUADRONS

This is perhaps a good place to cover the subject of fixed and rotary wing support for the Royal Armoured Corps. Now of course all aircraft are centralised under Army Air Corps control. However, for a decade or so in the 1960s, RTR Regiments, in line with the rest of the RAC, had first Air Troops, and then Air Squadrons, as an integral part of the regiment when performing the armoured reconnaissance role. Initially these aircraft were fixed-wing Austers but later these were exchanged, first for the Skeeter helicopter, and then for the more advanced Sioux. The main task of these aircraft was to give another dimension in the reconnaissance role, but they proved invaluable on many other occasions, especially when carrying out counter-insurgency operations.

---

[1] In fact the squadron did have two troops of Saladins, one each at Beihan and Dhala.

Chapter 16
THE SEVENTIES AND EIGHTIES

NORTHERN IRELAND

Although the troubles in Ireland have their roots deep in history, the Tank Corps was not actually involved until January 1919, when the 17th Armoured Car Battalion arrived in Dublin from the British Army of the Rhine. The following year it was decided to form No 5 Armoured Car Company and for the next six years armoured cars assisted the police in maintaining law and order, until the last armoured car company (No 12 ACC) was moved to Warrington in May 1926. In the late 1960s the troubles began again in earnest and by the summer of 1970 a particularly vicious guerilla war was being fought between the police and military on the one hand, and the Irish Republican Army on the other. There were RAC armoured reconnaissance units serving in Northern Ireland but the operational requirement called for more infantry units rather than more armour, so began the practice of withdrawing Corps troops from

BAOR - OP BANNER as it was called (namely, the use of other arms in the infantry role). 4 RTR was the first RTR Regiment to become involved when, in October 1970, two squadrons of the 4th joined the 15th/19th Hussars Group and served in Ulster from July to December 1971. Since then, RTR Regiments have taken their turn in Northern Ireland, either as complete regiments or in squadron groups, eg:

1 RTR - 'A' and 'C' Sqns Jan to May 1972; complete Regt May 1973 to Nov 1974; complete Regt May to Sept 1977 (with part of Regt in armoured recce role and part on OP Banner); 'A' Sqn Maze Prison May to Sept 1981; 'B' Sqn Maze prison Nov 1986 to Jan. 1987.

2 RTR - Badger and Ajax respectively, Sept 1973 to Jan 1974 and Jan to May 1974; Regt complete May to Sept 1975 and May 1979 to Nov 1980; Ajax HMP Maze Guard Force in 1983.

3 RTR - complete Regt Jan to May 1973, and again Sept. 1974 to Jan 1975.

Visit of HRH Prince Charles to 1 RTR. The Prince drove one of their new Chieftain tanks after rapid instruction from Sgt Watkin, and under the eagle eye of the Squadron Commander, Maj Tony Weeks. (Maj T Weeks)

The troubles in Northern Ireland were a continual 'running sore' and all the Regiments took their turn to serve there. They had to get used to using 1-ton armoured 'Pigs' instead of tanks which were never used in the province, and to the wearing of riot gear. TM

Manning Vehicle Check Points (VCP) was one of their tasks. Here Cpl James and Tpr Riding of 'C' Sqn, 1 RTR, man one in Omagh, in 1974. TM

Cpl Dobson and friend. This photograph was taken during a street patrol in 1975 and featured on the front cover of Tank *and in the national press. It was a powerful comment on being on active service amongst one's own countrymen in the troubled province.* TM

4 RTR - 'A' and 'B' Sqns with 15th/19th, July to Dec 1971; then in 1976 and 1978 the complete Regt spent four one-month OP Banner tours (first at the Maze prison, then in Belfast).

Major Tony Weeks, MBE, was commanding a squadron of 1 RTR in 1972 and found himself turned into an infantry soldier. He writes:

The first RAC unit moving to Ulster from BAOR (July-December 1971) comprised the 15th/19th Hussars RHQ and two squadrons, plus two squadrons of 4 RTR. They were followed in 1972 by the 13th/18th Hussars Group, including two squadrons (designated companies) of 1 RTR - 'C' Company (Major A.L.P. Weeks) going to Lurgan some 20 miles from Belfast and 'D' Company (Major N.M.S. Moriarty) to Long Kesh with the task of guarding internees. The period in Ulster was preceded by intensive infantry conversion training at the BAOR Sennelager Training Area. So realistic was this preparation that more injuries were suffered there than in Northern Ireland! It ended with a full-scale training riot in the local transport barracks, with tempers frayed and self-control at a premium.

The 'Lillywillies', as the group was called (a corruption of the 13th/18th Hussars' nickname and 'My Boy Willie'), arrived in Ulster in January 1972. 'C' Company in Lurgan was immediately faced with the problems of Belfast on a mini scale - a majority Protestant population where all civic appointments from Mayor to dustman were excluded to Catholics, a peace-line tension point between Protestants and Catholics and sprawling Sectarian council estates becoming 'no go' areas at the slightest provocation.

Life was busy and if the company was not patrolling or on stand-by quick reaction, it was sleeping. The notorious 'Bloody Sunday' confrontation between the Catholics and the Parachute Regiment, resulting in a number of deaths, had a dramatic 'spin-off' throughout Ulster. In Lurgan, cars and lorries were burnt, barricades erected setting up 'no go' areas, and troops confronted by stone-throwing crowds. Riots had become a public spectacle and a release from boredom for the inhabitants of Lurgan. Tiny children, clutching their mothers' hands in the midst of stone-throwing youths, often became the victims. Ever present was the danger of sniper ambush and shortly afterwards the squadron leader and sergeant major patrolling the infamous Kilwillkie housing estate were indeed ambushed and their escort wounded.

Frequently, house-search operations were launched, usually at first light, with sections arriving simultaneously at several houses with the object of catching the IRA napping. The house was surrounded, a short warning given before bursting in on the surprised occupants whose reaction might lead to a volley of abuse or, more off-putting, finding the kettle already on for tea. A similar operation launched in the Kilwillkie estate at the unusual time of late afternoon lasted all of five minutes before dangerous rioting crowds intervened.

Most soldiers welcomed the change from routine BAOR life and, perhaps surprisingly, quickly adapted to the job of foot-slogging infantry. Being cooped up in an old linen factory at Lurgan was not ideal, but the high level of activity compensated for the discomfort. Occasionally a discotheque was arranged and, unlike Germany, there was no shortage of female volunteers - mothers and daughters all joined in.

Back in Long Kesh, 'D' Company had the unenviable task of ensuring that there were no escapes, though these boring duties were varied for most of the soldiers by arranging attachments to other units throughout the Province.

Space does not permit a complete rundown of every Regiment's service in Ulster, so I have chosen 1 RTR's tour in 1973-74 as a typical example and will illustrate it with extracts from the Regiment's notes which appeared in subsequent issues of *The Tank*. On their arrival they had this to say about their new home:

A small town (May 1973) In the county of Tyrone there is a sleepy little county town which, at first sight, seems to the casual passer-by much the same as any other small town in any other remote part of the United Kingdom. That is, until he comes across the small barricade of sandbags sheltering a little police post which restricts all access to the High Street; there pedestrians only may go, for no car may be left unattended in the street at any time. Apart from that there is little else to distinguish the town from its regional counterparts; although the observant visitor might perhaps notice that the policemen always walk in pairs, and he may even pause to look at the occasional window which has been boarded up.

The inhabitants seem humorously placid - going about their daily business in a manner that seems to brook no incursions upon their long-established rural habits. It rained a lot in that part of the world, and when it was not doing that it usually chose to blow very gustily. The buildings were mostly made out of slate-grey coloured local stone which gave them a sombre, but not quite majestic, appearance. Even the Courthouse at the top of the High Street was redolent of the authority of another generation, and did not seem to exude quite the same aura of purpose now as it might have done then.

This was once a garage in Lurgan until it was blown up by the IRA. SSM Briggs and Sgt Webb of 'D'Sqn, 1 RTR, inspect the debris, during their tour of duty there in 1972. TM

A Ferret belonging to Ajax, 2 RTR, moves out on patrol during their tour of duty January-May 1974. TM

Long Kesh. As well as patrols, etc, RTR Regiments were also involved in guarding prisons - such as Long Kesh. Here Maj (later Brigadier) Nick Cocking leaves Long Kesh, plus dog handler and a very useful looking four-legged guard! TM

THE ROYAL TANK REGIMENT

Night patrol in Portadown. A trooper of 4 RTR on night patrol during their tour in Northern Ireland, provides yet another evocative photograph of the 'Troubles'. TM

Scimitar CVRs on winter training with the AMF(L) in Norway. (Crown Copyright)

In Omagh, for that is the name of the town, a new regiment has arrived to try and keep the uneasy peace. They are determined to succeed - only time will yield the results.

A BEM for Tpr Woolley All ranks of the regiment were delighted and proud to learn of the award of the British Empire Medal to Tpr D.G. Woolley. The action which led to this award took place on 11 December at the RUC station at Belcoo, in County Fermanagh. The police station was attacked from across the Eire border by a number of terrorists. Ignoring the rocket blasts and small-arms fire, on his own initiative Tpr Woolley ran to his Ferret scout car, drove it unaided to the side of the building and engaged the terrorist position 300 metres away. Later inspection of the terrorist positions by the Gardai confirmed that the fire brought down by Tpr Woolley had been very accurate. His actions certainly contributed to the terrorists breaking off their attack and will do much to deter future attacks. At 19 years of age Tpr Woolley has been a member of the Regiment for 11 months. However, his bravery and initiative are in the highest traditions of the Regiment and the Service as a whole.

'A' Sqn (December 1973) A week before Christmas 'A' Sqn found itself back on operations in Area 'M', after spending three weeks off duty. From the start the squadron was kept busy maintaining surveillance over a series of obstacles, which had been set up some time earlier on a number of unapproved crossing points on the Fermanagh-Monaghan border. These obstacles are intended to impede the

movement of terrorists, arms and explosives between the Republic and Ulster and consist of concrete dragon's teeth and craters. On 23 December a considerable crowd gathered at an obstacle and attempted in vain to construct a road by-passing it. Frustrated at their inability to successfully complete this all but impossible task, the crowd turned its attention to the Security Forces in the area. A hail of stones followed which necessitated the employment of a small riot squad to keep this rowdy demonstration in check. The efforts of the riot squad, aided by the onset of a chilly sunset, resulted in the crowds dispersing before any casualties occurred.

Over Christmas the squadron found itself on duty, providing guards for Lisanelly Camp and St Lucia Barracks, as well as for the outstations at Belleek and Belcoo. In addition, the squadron also carried out several routine patrols, including a helicopter patrol on Christmas Day. However the reward for this work over Christmas came when the squadron enjoyed a week's stand-down over the New Year. A substantial proportion of the squadron was able to get back to England for part of the stand-down period.

The first week in January saw the squadron back in Area 'M' and once more involved in protecting border obstacles. A second demonstration occurred at one of the crossings, but the crowd made so little impression on the concrete dragon's teeth with picks and shovels, that it was not necessary to employ the Security Forces in dispersing the demonstrators. On the following day several members of 'A' Sqn had a narrow escape when a command detonated land mine exploded near a party who were carrying out a routine clearance of a stretch of road near the border.

The first two weeks of the squadron's tour of duty in Area 'L' contained a couple of interesting incidents.

'A' Sqn joined forces with a company of 1 DERR and a squadron of REs to block several more border crossings, this time on the Fermanagh/Leitrim border. During this operation several gunmen opened fire across the border at the sapper team working on one of the blocks. Elements of 1 DERR returned the fire and scored two hits, one of them at a range of 900m.

A further shooting incident occurred at Belcoo where the RUC station is garrisoned jointly by the regular Army, the RUC and the UDR. The IRA launched an intense but ineffective attack on the building with rockets and small arms. The SF returned the fire but were unable to observe whether any hits were scored. Apart from these two cross border actions, the period in Area 'L' has seen a number of other incidents. These include the tragic murder of Pte Jamieson, 6

Field Marshal Lord Carver with his newly-completed portrait. With him are Lady Carver and the artist, Michael Noakes. (Photographers International)

UDR, near Trillick, and a retaliation shooting incident when a number of Protestant gunmen indiscriminately machine-gunned a Catholic pub in the village, wounding three innocent people.

'C' Sqn (October 1974) Four 'C' Sqn soldiers had a lucky escape from death on 10 October when their Land-Rover was blown up by a culvert mine near the village of Cooneen in Co Fermanagh. The bomb, which contained an estimated 300lbs of explosive, blew the Land-Rover onto its side and made a crater 3ft deep.

Cpl Tom Gaskell was driving the vehicle with Cpl Ray 'Wilf' Bradley in the passenger seat, with Tprs John Riding and Derek Leek in the rear. None of them recall hearing the explosion, but Cpls Bradley and Gaskell remember looking at each other as they flew through the air. On landing, Cpl Bradley found himself pinned to the ground and shouted to Cpl Gaskell to get out.

'I can't,' came the reply. 'Undo your… seat belt; it's easier!' rejoined Cpl Bradley.

Once out, with the help of Tpr Riding and a rifle used as a lever, Cpl Gaskell managed to prise Cpl Bradley from underneath the vehicle. Unfortunately, the latter's trousers were on fire and these had to be ripped off. We hear he is making a good recovery from gravel rash on his backside!

Within moments of all the soldiers getting clear, the petrol tank blew up along with the ammunition. This did not deter Cpl Gaskell; with great calmness he organised first-aid for his comrades, kept civilians away, and marshalled an RAF Puma helicopter which transported them to Erne Hospital.

Although you might think this was enough, there was more excitement to be had on the last operational tour in St Angelo. Assault Troop, led by Sgt Jim Stanley, watched the downfall of the

Designed by Alex Styles of Garrards, the Crown jewellers, this silver statuette of a Chieftain crew in action, was presented to Her Majesty on her 25th Wedding Anniversary, which coincided with the 55th anniversary of the Battle of Cambrai. Her Majesty graciously decided that it should be held for her by the RTR. It was therefore held annually, by each of the Regiments in turn. TM

29th Customs Post at Belleek. The IRA's demolition squad deftly removed the 29th original, which is now serving Dundalk, Sligo and Bundoran.

Belcoo, not to be out-done, organised a showdown with their friendly neighbourhood gunman. This obliging gentleman turned out to say goodbye to Lt Bede Strong and 2 Troop. Having fired 20 rounds of Armalite at the Land-Rover from 10yard range, he was voted the most disgraceful shot in Ireland.

One Troop has lurked quite successfully at Belcoo, eating Cpl Alfie Jessop's curried rabbit and occasionally going out to do 6hr VCPs thereby keeping the neighbourhood firmly under control.

Four Troop is literally Four troop, there being only four operational soldiers left since the 'Battle of Cooneen'. The remains of the Land-Rover commanded by Cpl Wilf Bradley and Cpl Tommy Gaskell have been returned to the Kinnegar to be buried! The vehicle was shovelled into the back of a 4-tonner.

Three and Five Troops have been particularly quiet and so have their areas of Kesh and Kinawley. Sgts 'Minty' Rose and 'Tug' Wilson have been languishing on numerous occasions in

the mess at St Angelo, beer in hand, telling the new arrivals to pull up a sandbag.

The fitters have been kept hard at work repairing vehicles for handover and generally keeping the squadron on the road.

SHQ under temporary management or mismanagement of Lt Derek Quinn-Hall and S-Sgt Terry Smith, is running as smoothly as ever with some prompting from the father-like figure of Major Andrew Jones. SQMS McKeever comes in once in a while to get his civilian clothing allowance form signed. He is ably assisted by Tprs 'Sooty' Steele and 'Geordie' Gallagher.

Final Comments (Nov 1974) After a year-and-a-half in the province it would be very difficult not to quote a few statistics of our operations:

Incident Summary, May 1973-November 1974

Explosions	Cleared by ATO	Booby trapped	Total
Car	14	4	40
HGV	1	Nil	3
Proxy	7	Nil	12
Bags/cases etc.	24	2	72
Letter bombs	5	Nil	9
Land mines	7	2	14
Culvert mines	7	1	13
Incendiaries	2	Nil	33

Rocket attacks	Rockets fired
8	33

Mortar attacks	Mortars fired
3	25

Shootings	Casualties	Casualties by explosion
37	SF killed 9	killed (3 by terrorist
	SF wounded 9	action, 1 accident) 4
	Civ killed 11	VSI 1
	(inc IRA)	SI Nil
	Civ wounded 13	Injured 24

Arrests 23

Finds:

Weapons:		Explosives:			
Rifles	8	Anfo	4572lb	Blast bombs	24
SMGs	3	Coop	766lb	Pipe bombs	2
Pistols	13	Gelignite	70lb	Incendiaries	7
Mortars	3	Nitrate	25lb	Unidentified	
RPG7	1	Illegal explosives 550lb			
Shotgun	1	Fertilizer 3 bags			

Bomb-making equipment:
No 6dets   114   Ammunition:3109 rounds
Sump fuse 286ft
Cordtex   453ft

Perhaps the most significant feature of our tour, however, is not reflected in the figures above and that is the dramatic drop in the level of incidents compared to the first few months. It must be said that for this we cannot claim all the credit or even any definable proportion of it; the UDR and the RUC continue to make inroads into terrorist activities. However, the Regiment has been part of a team doing endless hours of VCPs and operations in the foulest weather, but seeing Tyrone and Fermanagh creep back towards normality has made it all worth while.

BOMB OUTRAGE IN LONDON

Even RHQ was not safe from terrorism and, in the early hours of the morning of 1 November 1971, a bomb exploded at the door of the Royal Yeomanry entrance to 1 Elverton Street. The explosion blew off parts of the door and scarred it, also shattering windows on both sides of the street but there was no internal damage. Statements in the press attributed the bomb to the 'Angry Brigade', while the IRA denied involvement, although *The Tank* felt that it might be a misplaced compliment by them in recognition of the work being carried out at that time in Ulster by 'A' and 'B' Sqns of the 4th!

PIPES AND TARTANS FOR THE 4TH

4 RTR took two logical, yet revolutionary, steps in cementing bonds with its recruiting area in the seventies, by managing to penetrate the 'Tartan Curtain' so successfully as to be allowed both to wear a tartan and to form a highly successful Pipes and Drums. In 1971, Lt-Col (now Maj-Gen) Laurie New was commanding and, with the encouragement of the officers' and sergeants' messes, ordered a Pipes and Drums to be formed. He was fortunate in gaining formal authority from a family friend, the head of the Clan Rose of Kilravock, to take the Hunting Rose tartan into regimental use in February 1972. This was the plaid to be worn by the pipers and drummers. Two months later, Pipe Sergeant Elder of the Royal Scots Dragoon Guards, agreed to transfer to the 4th and set about forming a regimental Pipes and Drums, with the aim of being ready to undertake public engagements in two years and to play before our Colonel-in-Chief in four years. They achieved everything asked of them, undertaking their first public engagement in 1974 and playing before Her Majesty at the Sennelager Review in 1977. They were officially recognised and established by the Army Board in 1979.

Listen to the Band! The Rhine Band, together with the Pipes and Drums of 4 RTR, in Edinburgh during the Evening News *Centenary Cavalcade in May 1973.* TM

A bevy of Chieftain main battle tanks on training at Soltau in 1977. TM

OUR FIRST FIELD MARSHAL

The first officer of those initially commissioned into the Regiment to reach the rank of Field Marshal, also to hold both the appointment of Chief of the General Staff and Chief of the Defence Staff, was Field Marshal Lord Carver, who was promoted Field Marshal on completing his tour as CDS in 1977. Lord Carver, the Duke of Wellington's great-great-great-great nephew (and his 'spiritual heir', as Henry Stanhope described him in *The Times*), served for 41 years in the Regiment, winning a DSO and MC in North Africa and a bar to his DSO in Italy. He commanded the 1st in 1943, became the youngest Brigadier in the Army in 1944 (aged 29) but then had to revert to his peacetime rank of acting Lt-Col when he left 4 Armoured Brigade in 1947. His post-war career was spectacular to say the least, from GOC 3rd Division in 1964, to CGS in 1971 and CDS two years later. A number of other RTR officers have reached senior positions post-war, including Sir John Crocker (Adjutant General), Sir Harold Pyman (DCIGS), Sir Alan Jolly (QMG), Sir Richard Ward (Chief of Personnel and Logistics), Sir Allan Taylor (Deputy Cin-C UKLF), Sir Richard Lawson (C-in-C AF North) and Sir Antony Walker (DCDS [Commitments]).

OPERATION BURBERRY

One of the strangest jobs ever undertaken by members of the Regiment occurred during the Fire Brigade Union strike in 1977-78, when they became temporary firemen and, for example, 'B' Sqn 3 RTR took on for a hectic six weeks the task of fighting fires in the city of Edinburgh. Between 1200hrs on 7 December 1977 and 0952hrs on 18 January 1978, their antiquated 'Green Goddess' fire engines were called out 449 times, 79 of which were false alarms or hoaxes, 73 were 'out on arrival', but the remaining 297 were all fought successfully. As Capt (now Lt-Col) Rod Brummitt wrote in *Tank*:

Though our training was fundamentary, our experience at the beginning nil and our equipment archaic, I think we can be justly proud of our achievement in Edinburgh. Of course we have caused more water damage than the firemen would have done, and made our share of mistakes. However, with the assistance of the police and the advice of the Fire Officers, we achieved our aim of saving life and putting out fires.

WORLD TRAVEL

Despite the fact that the major role in the seventies and eighties of the Regiment, was and still is, in concert with the rest of the British Army, to provide strong conventional forces in Europe in order to provide a realistic deterrent against possible aggression in Western Europe, there are still chances for units and sub-units to serve abroad. The most widely visited location as far as the armour is concerned has to be the Suffield Training Area in Alberta, Canada; an area so isolated that it was once considered for nuclear testing! Norway has provided another interesting training ground, especially for members of the Allied Command Europe Mobile Force (land), the highly mobile, multi-national force, designed to respond to trouble on the flanks of the NATO area. Peace-keeping operations in Cyprus with UNFICYP have provided a welcome change from the 'Op Banner' type of keeping the peace, while the regular changing between the armoured and armoured reconnaissance roles in UK and BAOR, plus the occasional tours at home as RAC Centre Regiment or running the ABTU at Catterick, have all added to the variety of tasks which the RTR soldier of the seventies and eighties could expect to perform. Some of the following extracts from *Tank* give a 'flavour' of these places and happenings.

3 RTR's visit to Suffield in 1976 was reported in their local West Country newspaper and *Tank* thus:

Tank men from the West Country flew across the Atlantic and most of Canada for a series of live-firing exercises on a bleak prairie training ground almost half the size of Devon. About 350 all ranks of the 3rd Royal Tank Regiment are based at Tidworth. The Regiment recruits traditionally in the West Country, and formed part of an 800-

Goodbye to the Centurion. On 22 July 1974, four RTR veterans assembled to say a proper farewell to the last Centurion Mark XIII then in service. The crew comprised (L to R in turret) Maj Bert Starr, Col Eric Offord and Lt Col (QM) Ken Hill, with Maj Dai Mitchell in the driving seat. They fired off the last 105mm APDS rounds at the RAC Gunnery School, Lulworth and, as was reported in Tank 'despite their tears of nostalgia, the old hands each hit the target.' It was a fitting way to say goodbye to a tank which came into service back in 1945 and has been used operationally by many nations all over the world. TM

strong battle group for the exercises. The group was commanded by Lt-Col Chris Dick of Dartmouth, who is Commanding Officer of the 3rd Royal Tank Regiment. His second-in-command is Major Jeremy Williams of Torquay.

The exercises were held on the 1000-square-mile British Army training unit at Suffield, Alberta - an area so isolated that it was once considered for nuclear tests. It is 150 miles east of Calgary, and the nearest town of any size is Medicine Hat, some 30 miles away. Almost featureless prairie, treeless and undulating, makes an excellent battle-group training-ground and enables the tanks, artillery, mortars and infantry to fight battles in very realistic conditions where live firing can take place. The 3rd Royal Tank Regiment's contribution to the battle group was two squadrons, each of 15 Chieftain tanks, a recce troop of eight Scimitars, regimental headquarters, which acted as battle group HQ, and support personnel including A1 echelon...

I flew out to Calgary for the final exercise in the series, and I marvelled at the sheer size of the prairie as I was driven down the trans-Canada highway to Suffield. Well out of Calgary there was nothing but almost flat prairie as far as the eye could see. Little gophers played at the roadside, a family of fox cubs gambolled, oblivious to the traffic, and we saw a few deer and cattle. There was little else and the camp at Suffield was

6 Tp, 'B' Sqn, 1 RTR wearing their UN berets and badges, with their white painted AFVs at Pergamos Camp in Cyprus, after completing a patrol in the Nicosia area. February 1975. TM

Scorpion CVR(T) belonging to 1 RTR cross the River Weser via an M2 bridge, during Ex Mizzen Mast *in 1977.* TM

simply a stark row of huts. They were comfortable enough and the food was excellent...

The final exercise was Exercise *Ramilles*, during which the battle group had to advance down a corridor up to six kilometres wide and over 30 kilometes long. In earlier exercises the battle group had pushed back the 'enemy', who was struggling to hold ground and was reported to be in a demoralised state...

Scimitar reconnaissance vehicles led the advance, keeping several kilometres ahead to send back intelligence reports. They engaged isolated 'enemy' targets with their 30mm cannon, but Col Dick sent forward two combat teams when the 'enemy' was encountered in strength. Both tank squadrons faced major battles early on in the day and artillery, tanks and infantry made a co-ordinated attack on 'enemy' tanks and infantry in a strong position on high ground. By the middle of the first day, the sappers were committed to finding a safe route through a minefield. When they had taped a path, the advance continued with the 'enemy' continuing to lose ground.

An armoured command vehicle kept me close up behind the batle and Lt Elliot-Square explained the various manoeuvres as they took place. The tank gunnery was impressive to watch and there was a very high rate of hits. The Chieftains' 120mm guns were ranged with rounds from a .5 machine gun and shells were fired with devastating effect.

The advance continued into the evening until a second minefield was encountered. Sappers, covered by infantry, began the long task of clearing a path, first of anti-personnel mines so a bridgehead could be established and then of the heavier anti-tank mines. Their problems did not end there. A road had to be cut through a hilly feature and explosive charges, the first of 300lbs, were laid and fired before earth-moving machinery was brought into play. While the engineers worked throughout the night, many others were able to grab a few hours' sleep before moving off at first light.

Sgt Chris Jeffery, 29, a native of Perranporth, was commander of the armoured command vehicle in which I travelled most of the time. He

The RTR Memorial at Beaurains, near Arras. Maj-Gen Roy Dixon, the then Representative Colonel Commandant, at the unveiling ceremony of the memorial. The inscription reads: 'To the Glory of God and the Memory of All Members of the Royal Tank Regiment who fought here in May 1940.' TM

managed to get hold of half-a-dozen eggs and skilfully turned out a breakfast of poached-egg sandwiches - the eggs cooked in the vehicle's electric pressure cooker. He followed this with tinned bacon sandwiches and coffee and after that we were all ready for another day of bumping noisily over the prairie.

Col Dick was 'killed' during a battle on the second morning and Major Williams took charge of the final phase of the advance. The 'enemy' was established on a hill and, from a helicopter, I watched the bombardment by artillery, tanks and mortars before the infantry moved up in their armoured personnel carriers.

The 'enemy' was vanquished, the exercises were over after more than two weeks in the field and there remained only a 3hr slog over muddy tracks back to the barracks at Suffield. That evening the battle group started cleaning up their tanks and vehicles ready for the handover to the next group to arrive at Suffield, for the exercises continue throughout the summer months each year.

Capt Philip Skinner of 4 RTR, reported on his troop's involvement with the AMF(L) in 1982:

In August 1982, 15 Troop 4 RTR came back from BAOR to UK, to inherit its role as the close reconnaissance troop of the British Infantry battalion committed to the Allied Command Europe Mobile Force (Land). AMF(L) is a multi-national, highly mobile but lightly equipped field army with its headquarters in Heidelburg, Southern Germany. Designed to act as an immediate and flexible response to any build-up of tension on NATO's flanks, the AMF would deploy before hostilities commenced to demonstrate that if the threatened area were to be attacked this would be considered tantamount to an attack on all NATO countries…

After taking over their Scimitars and getting them ready for the rigours of the Arctic, the troop moved to Southampton docks, boarded the *Dana Ventura*, a 'RoRo' vessel, and sailed to Southern Norway. Skinner continues:

A week's intensive training in survival and cross-country ski techniques immediately began; the Norwegian Army officer attached to the company assisted our small nucleus of seasoned instructors. The confidence of living in snow acquired by us all, we were able then to concentrate on working up for the battalion training exercises with our vehicles. Sadly, CVR(T) has a severely limited cross-country performance in snow and for the winter months it is effectively confined to the roads and 'Volvo tracks' (lanes compressed into the snow by Volvo snow-track vehicles). The lack of perforated sprockets and idlers - which have only just been issued for the vehicles - meant that the danger of throwing a track was ever present even when executing the simplest of off-road manoeuvres and as a consequence our recce role was inevitably severely limited. Used, as we were, to a highly mobile role in Denmark and BAOR, we had to content ourselves with acting in the advance as fire support vehicles - a less demanding but vitally important role for which Scimitar, fitted with a Rarden gun of outstanding accuracy, range and a high rate of fire, is well suited. Furthermore, the vehicle optics (superb in Norway's dry atmosphere) and II sights proved to be of immense benefit to a dismounted infantry battalion sited in defence. In addition to OP and close support work, the troop was extensively involved in route clearance, security and marking tasks, rear area security and, even in extremis, troop-carrying roles. Our engine decks were highly sought after always by the hapless infantry wherever we went - offering them an opportunity to dry out their sleeping bags, equipment and thaw out their frozen feet…

Dramatic view of 1 RTR Chieftains in their hangar at Tofrek Barracks during the winter of 1986-87. TM

A new tank makes its appearance. 2 RTR was the first RTR Regiment to be equipped with the new main battle tank, the Challenger 1, seen here going through its paces on exercise in BAOR. TM

A 3 RTR Chieftain belonging to 'A' Sqn, negotiates the infamous 'Dust Bowl' on the Soltau Training Area. Despite initial powerpack problems when it was first introduced, by the 1980s the tank was much improved with a far more reliable engine. TM

The phase in Southern Norway completed, the troop drove back to the port of Granvin at the beginning of March to sail north to participate in Exercise *Cold Winter*. Immensely important politically, it is a co-ordinated exercise featuring US and Canadian Airborne and Marines, elements of Brigade North, Norwegian Army and 3 Commando Brigade and is set in a secluded valley south of Nørvik.

Quite the most horrible period of the exercise was to come when for some 36 hours the temperature rose above freezing point and we experienced persistent rain and drizzle and thawing snow. Our

carefully sealed vehicles soon acquired the characteristics of sieves, and to a man we were all drenched as a consequence - inevitably after the thaw the temperature dropped markedly, involving us all in potentially extremely dangerous situations in moving AFVs. Mercifully our spare kit remained dry in our bins - our infantry counterparts were not so lucky and many suffered.

The exercises completed, the troop was recovered to the ship and on 18 March our long voyage home began. Once back in Tidworth and exposed to the rigours of the Warminster cycle we deployed immediately again to the field in our new wildly

Breaking leaguer. A squadron of Chieftains break leaguer during training in BAOR. (Author's collection)

Lt Roberts and his troop at the Brandenberg Gate in Berlin, August 1974. Interestingly, although 'A' Sqn, 4 RTR was in Berlin at that time, the troop was all from 'B' Sqn, 3 RTR, who were on an exchange with the 4th. TM

inappropriate camouflage scheme on Exercise *Quick Flash* - a combat team commanders' practical exercise. We could not help but feel mildly nostalgic for the unique style of soldiering we had all been enjoying over the past months.

Service in Cyprus, and the sunnier climes of the Mediterranean, awoke more poetic memories in 4 RTR's Tank notes in early 1984:

Looking at the Forecast of Events for 1984 a genuine chill has run down the collective spines of 'B' Sqn's sun-hardened Near East veterans. Troop training in February on Salisbury Plain, Rabbits Run, Phantom Bugle and Castlemartin, all names from a dim and not too distant past, have returned to tax us in our last days in Cyprus. As the warm (70°F) late November, early December days begin to speed past, thoughts turn to Flight Lists, MFO packing, PREs, handover programmes and the frantic dash to do everything we should have done in the past five months.

Even in our last months, events in the Eastern Mediterranean have continued to keep the UNFICYP squadron alert and aware of our closeness to some of the more important incidents going on in the world. UDI by the Turkish North came unexpectedly to keep the United Nations on its toes and to provide more political initiatives for the politicians, whilst events in Lebanon were watched with keen interest. But almost all our memories and experiences of six months in Cyprus as the UN Scout Car Squadron will be happy ones and none of the squadron would have missed this once-in-a-career opportunity to do something so entirely

different from working with Chieftains in the English and German countryside.

Many will remember the long dusty patrols at the height of the summer, winding through the foothills of the Troodos in the Danish sector of the buffer zone; visiting the OPs along the way, with breakfast of home-made bread and coffee at D35 whilst watching the dawn rise on the Mediterranean from the mountain top vantage point. Or driving along the well irrigated fields of the British sector, through citrus groves laden with fruit. The patrols along the Nicosia green line in the Canadian sector that twists and turns through narrow divided streets and below the walls of the old city. Glaringly white hills stretch out on either side of the long miles of rough track in the Swedish sector as it weaves past minefields and through villages that give way in the east to the chokingly dusty track that peters out in the sea on the Austrian line.

THE STANDARDS PARADE, 12 JULY 1985

Probably the most spectacular event of recent years was the presentation of new Standards to all four Regiments by our Colonel-in-Chief, which followed their consecration by the Chaplain General. This took place at Sennelager, on the ubiquitous 'Windmill' parade ground, scene of so many spectacular parades in the past. However, all who were there would affirm that this was probably the best parade of its kind put on by the Regiment. Don Featherstone wrote about it in *Tank* under the title of 'Military Theatre at its best':

Standards Parade, 12 July 1985. All four Regiments took part in a spectacular parade at Sennelager in July 1985, when our Colonel in Chief, HM The Queen, presented new Standards, which were then consecrated by the Chaplain General. TM

Chinese eyes at rest in a forest of antennae, as crews of 4 RTR dismount at the end of Ex Zodiac Zest, West Germany 1986. TM

The Standards Parade was a stage-play of many acts, a colourful, memorable kaleidoscope played out on a vast military stage where rapid scene-changing produced theatrical-style reprises. The overture and finals of long and hot coach rides and boring boats was anti-climatic, but the main event at Sennelager was too expensive for any producer in the world of stage, and the numerous other 'Sets' and backcloths were inimitable. There was The Barrack-Room set, depicting sparse but

adequate accommodation, noisy and echoing from about 5am as Old Soldiers resumed shouting and stamping about as though there had been no forty years' interval. In my room, new acquaintances, middle-aged executive types, once amateur soldiers in 48th Royal Tanks (TA), compared then-and-now photographs taken in the Gothic Line, and matter-of-factly told grim anecdotes that said much for man's resilience. Queueing for huge breakfasts far removed from one's usual Shredded Wheat, we revealed training was not wasted when taking dirty plates back to the counter. The Duty Free Shop; was it to be gin or whisky at about £3.25 a litre, or perhaps a cheap TV or Hi-Fi equipment?...

The Main Event was the Windmill Arena set at Sennelager - the highlight of the Show, greater even than the Royal Tournament, Massed Bands at Wembley or Andrew Lloyd Webber's Starlight Express. Graced by the foremost Leading Lady in the World, plus a galaxy of past and present Top Brass, supported by a chorus of hundreds of immaculately costumed soldiers, it featured mechanical vehicles worth a king's ransom, so many as to cause General Foote, VC, to murmur that only once had he seen so many tanks at one time - and they were all German and coming towards him! All hearts beat proudly when, under cloudless skies, the order was given 'The Royal Tank Regiment will advance in Review Order' and, to a backing of brown, red and green smoke, two hundred engines started up and put smoke clouds high into the air. Her Majesty in the Land-Rover, dwarfed by the comfortable figure of General Jerram, inspected the parade; old and new Standards were trooped, consecrated and presented before the Drive Past, surely among the most spectacular events devised by man. Several hundred Old Comrades had rehearsed getting from their seats and assembling behind Branch Colours in 6½mins whilst 4 RTR pipers played before the Queen; in the event, the 400 who eventually marched did so in style - after all, that was the moment we had really come for, wasn't it? A serving soldier's wife said she found the march-past a real tear-jerker - so did we! The musical accompaniment to all these events was both impressive and stirring, and marching and nostalgic tunes played full part in arousing emotion and fervour...

Of course, it is not possible to conclude without the inevitable comment that officers and soldiers look younger than ever, and we respect your generation as we hope you respect ours, we admire your bearing and professionalism, certain that if the unthinkable occurs then you will handle those mechanical marvels as well as we did their primitive predecessors. No doubt about it, those New Standards are in good hands!

Off to Lincoln. Cambrai veteran, Flirt II, being loaded at the Tank Museum, en route for the city of its birth, prior to being restored by the apprentices of Ruston Gas Turbines and presented to Lincoln. It is now on show at the Lincolnshire Life Museum. TM

A 4 RTR Scorpion in a position of observation. This excellent photo was used on the front cover of Tank *to illustrate an article by Lt-Col (later Brig) C.J. McBean on Reconnaissance in 2020.* TM

LINCOLN'S PRIDE

20 November 1985, saw the handover ceremony of *Flirt II*, a female heavy tank which had fought at the Battle of Cambrai 68 years earlier. Post-war it had returned to Bovington where it remained on a plinth outside the Tank Museum battle-scarred and at the mercy of the wind and rain. Now it was being presented back to Lincoln, the city of its 'birth' - after two years of careful restoration work by the apprentices of Ruston Gas Turbines. The historic old tank is now housed in the Lincolnshire Life Museum.

REGIMENTAL SUCCESS ON SNOW

In 1980, four members of 2 RTR (Potter, Brown, Pugh and Wallington) were chosen to race for Great Britain at Lake Placid USA, in the Winter Olympics. Then in 1984, 2 RTR achieved even greater success by fielding 'Great Britain One' - four-man Bobsleigh Team (Pugh, Wallington, Brown and Tout) for the 1984 Sarajevo Winter Olympics - a unique achievement!

PRISON GUARD FORCE

One of the oft-occuring tasks for regiments in Germany were unaccompanied tours, usually lasting for six months, in Northern Ireland and one of the jobs they often had to do was to provide the Prison Guard Force at the Maze. For example, 1 RTR provided a squadron in November 1986, whilst Huntsman of the 2nd did the same in 1989. Their tasks included providing General Defence Area Troops, Patrols Troops, and Guard Towers Troop. The first of these was the busiest, the last of the three, the most mind-numbing. Nevertheless all still found it an interesting experience and even had time for sport - Huntsman, for example, raising money for charity by running 50 times around the perimeter wall (once round was 2.2miles)!

LAYING UP OF STANDARDS, 15 SEPTEMBER 1985

Following on from the spectacular Standards Parade of 12 July, came a more solemn occasion, when the old Standards of the four Regiments, were laid up at the Regimental Church of St Peter upon Cornhill in the City of London. The service was conducted by the Regimental Chaplain, the Reverend Alan Cook and the sermon given by the Dean of Windsor. Standard Parties consisted of the RQMS of each Regiment carrying the Standard, together with a Staff Sergeant escort. They were commanded by RSM Hepburn of 3 RTR, the senior RSM. The Standards were hung next to the Standard of 5 RTR. Over 300 people attended the service, which was followed by luncheon at the Duke of Yorks HQ.

THE THIRD MOVE TO UK AND CYPRUS

After a number of years when all four Regiments were serving in Germany, the 'mould' was finally broken when 3 RTR left at the end of 1986: 'At last we

have made it!' they reported in *Tank*, 'The Third has finally left BAOR in toto with 'F' Sqn firmly established in Cyprus and the rest back in England with squadrons at Bovington and Lulworth. After seven long busy years in Germany we are now not only back in England, we are sitting in the middle of our recruiting area. Although our stay is not planned to be more than 15 months, we are already having to add new expressions to our vocabulary. People can be seen in small huddled groups all over the RAC Centre muttering such phrases as "sports afternoon" and "home for the weekend". ...It is indeed a revelation that the weekly programme does not have to read "Monday to Friday – Tank Park" and before long we will see those veterans of a season in

Left: *3 RTR at Bovington, Lulworth and Cyprus. Whilst most of the Regiment was in UK, lucky 'F' Sqn was soaking up the sun in Cyprus and carrying out regular patrolling in their Saladins and Ferrets, February 1987.* TM

Below: *Northern Ireland again. 4 RTR was in Northern Ireland in 1986, guarding amongst other things, the inmates of the Maze. This is 13 Troop of the 4th, looking suitably warlike with rifles instead of the usual SMGs.* TM

Germany pulling up a sandbag to tell the new boys what it was really like on Soltau in 1986.' Meanwhile, 'F' Sqn, a composite squadron formed in August 1986, was now the Sovereign Base Area Recce Sqn in Cyprus, having: 'handed in their Chieftains, taken over a multitude of Ferrets and Saracens, and drawn up the flip-flops and suntan oil' - clearly they were destined for sun, sea , sand and sangria - or that is what they fondly imagined! The 3rd's tour in Dorset and Cyprus would last until in early 1988.

THE PRAIRIE BLUES

The monotony of the BAOR training cycle was of course still broken from time to time by trips to Canada such as *Medicine Man* 7 when 4 RTR reported that: 'The wind whistled through the baskets and the tracks groaned and creaked as we came to a stop. The gun kit went off line and 'O' could be heard giving another bollocking on the air. The commander stirred from his dream as the driver's hatch swung open and clicked. A blast of cold air swept into the turret. Over the intercom Cookie croaked: "I'm just getting out for a pee. I may be some time…" The commander and loader looked at each other and sighed. We were in Canada on *Medicine Man 7*.'

Fortunately, by the second paragraph of this report, the downbeat mood had changed and the writer talks estatically about: '…glorious weather, clear blue skies and a crisp wind' , whilst the days flew by as they: 'attacked, counter-attacked and moved across the prairie from box leaguers to hides to circular leaguers…then the heavens dropped snow, the temperatures fell to minus 20 and commanders had grins frozen on their faces.'

The temperature finally dropped to minus 38 degrees Fahrenheit!

Right: The armorial bearings of the Vintners' Company. The apposite motto reads: Wine gladdens the heart. Formal affiliation began with the RTR in 1987. TM

Not all visits to BATUS were of course made so late in the year and many of those who were hooked in to the *Medicine Man* cycle of exercises had to contend with the duststorms of boiling hot summer days, however, much of the Canadian weather was wonderful. Nevertheless, whatever the time of year, they afforded marvellous training periods, a complete change from BAOR and, in addition, a chance for everyone to take part in really 'adventurous' Adventure Training from the Rockies to California.

AFFILIATION WITH THE VINTNERS' COMPANY

1987 saw the beginning of the formal affiliation between the Vintners' Company and the Royal Tank Regiment. Eleventh in the precedence of City Companies,it began as a trading fraternity which undertook religious and charticable duties on behalf of its members. Its first Charter was drawn up on 15

The Armorial Bearings of
The WORSHIPFUL COMPANY of VINTNERS of London.

Her Majesty The Queen dining with officers of the Regiment and members of the Vintners' Company at the Vintners' Hall, 1987. TM

July 1364. The Company is ruled by a Master, three Wardens and a Court of Assistants. About one third of its members belong to the Wine Trade. Reciprocal visits were arranged and the 1987 Officers' Annual Dinner, was held at the Vintners' Hall, in company with HM The Queen.

A HIT CAN'T BE MISSED

One of the main problems with past exercises has been that you could not actually fire at a live enemy. All you could do was to let off a blank round (or shout 'bang') and wait for an umpire to assess the result. This all changed in 1986-87, with the introduction of SIMFICS which was designed to work through the tank's IFCS (Improved Fire Control System). With the system an 'enemy' tank that had been successfully engaged emitted a plume of orange smoke and displayed a flashing light. SIMFICS thus allowed the tank crew to operate as a crew, both in the loading and firing sequences whilst on dry training - a dramatic improvement in training value for the crew, so that all were now involved all the time.

ARRIVAL OF CHALLENGER 1 MARK 2

The most important happening of early 1987 for Badger 2 RTR, was the arrival of its brand new Challenger 1 Mark 2s. The 2nd had of course been the first RTR Regiment to be equipped with CR 1 Mark 1, now they received the Mark 2s, which were fitted with TOGS (Thermal Observation Gunnery System), a passive system which enabled the commander and gunner to detect, observe, track and engage targets no matter the light or weather conditions. To help them to assimilate the new MBT, parties from the squadron had been flying back to UK since before Christmas, to be instructed on the new ICSS sighting equipment at the RAC Gunnery School, Lulworth.

Also invaluable was the revolutionary Singer-Link-Miles simulator which the company loaned to 2 RTR for two months and installed 'in a shroud of mystery' in early February. Badger was working up for the Canadian Army Trophy (CAT) 1987, when they would be up against serious international opposition.

A cheerful looking group of crewmen and their Challengers from 'D' Sqn 3 RTR. The original caption said that it should be 'D' Coy as it was being commanded at the time (1987-88) by Maj John McCall of the Royal Anglians, who was attached 3 RTR and can be seen in the centre. (Tank)

Haus Panzer. The Regiment acquired Haus Panzer in Bavaria for winter training and relaxation in 1988 and kept it for the next five years. TM

HAUS PANZER

In 1988, the Regiment acquired a large farmhouse/pension at the foot of the Grunten in the Allgau district of Bavaria. The acquisition of Haus Panzer had three aims: firstly as an Exercise *Snow Queen* base for RTR Regiments serving in Germany (Snow Queen being ski training for beginners and other forms of winter training); secondly, as an Adventure Training and Challenge Pursuit Base for RTR personnel wherever they were serving; thirdly, to provide holiday accommodation in summer and winter for use by all RTR families. Four Flats were available for DM20 per night for two people, either married couples or soldiers on holiday. It would remain in RTR hands until early 1993.

4 RTR IN CYPRUS

In June 1989, the 4th took over as the Cyprus Emergency Roulement Regiment (CERR), leaving a Rear Party of over 100 men back in Osnabruck responsible for the maintenance of the vehicles and the welfare of the families. In Cyprus, the rest of the Regiment was split with RHQ (CO, Adjt and Ops Offr) and two squadrons as part of the UN Force in Nicosia, whilst the other two squadrons and a second RHQ (2IC, Asst Adjt and OC HQ Sqn) were in Dhekelia some 40 miles away. Their task as part of the UN peacekeeping force was to patrol and protect the Buffer Zone which divided the island in two. This was the Green Line that was set up 15 years previously following the uneasy peace after the Turkish invasion. The six-month unaccompanied tour proved

to a challenge for everyone, as one member of the Regiment wrote: 'In essence the Cyprus tour would seem to be hard work and challenging. It is giving junior commanders at all levels the opportunity to prove their worth and gain valuable experience. From a visitor's point of view the Regiment seems to be enjoying the new challenges and environment. The only black mark to the tour must be that it is unaccompanied and six months is a long time for the wives to remain in Osnabruck alone.'

A BUSY DECADE

The eighties thus closed with all but one of the four Regiments in Germany as they had been at the beginning of the decade. However, the locations of each Regiment had changed at least twice over the ten year period, viz:

1 RTR was in Herford, Germany, in 1980, went to Bovington from 1982 until 1984, then to Hildesheim from 1985 onwards, but had one squadron in Northern Ireland for six months in 1986.

2 RTR was in Omagh in 1980, went to Wolfenbuttel in 1981, then on to Fallingbostel in 1984 until the end of the decade, however they had a squadron in NI at the Maze for six months in 1989.

3 RTR was in Paderborn in 1980, moved to Sennelager in 1981, then on to Bovington and Cyprus (one sqn) in 1987 and finally, on to Deilinghofen in 1988.

4 RTR was in Munster in 1980, then went to Tidworth in 1982, on to Osnabruk in 1985 where it remained (apart from its six-month unaccompanied tour in Cyprus 1989-90).

THE ROYAL TANK REGIMENT

Goodbye to Germany. Challengers of 2 RTR on parade with their Standard, drive past the reviewing officer Lt-Gen Sir Charles Guthrie, Commander 1st British Corps, during their farewell parade in Germany. TM

Hitting the beach at Warbarrow Bay. During the summer of 1991, Scorpions of Badger 2 RTR, carried out some amphibious training with the LSL Sir Bedivere, *coming ashore near Lulworth.* TM

Chapter 17
ON TO THE MILLENNIUM

THIS SPORTING LIFE

Sport has always played an important part in Regimental activities throughout every decade. An interesting statistic for the early 1990s, was, that at a rough count, the RTR Regiments had been almost continually active in nearly 40 different types of sports, with varying degrees of success, gaining Army Championship status or higher in some, but playing an active part in a large range of others - for example, at the start of 1990 the list for just one regiment read: athletics, cross-country running, rugby football, football, basketball, swimming, hockey, cross-country, marathon running, triathlon, decathlon, bobsleigh, Nordic and alpine skiing, squash, sailing, board-sailing, tennis, golf, squash, archery, ten-pin bowling and orienteering - 23 different sports - when did they find time for soldiering I wonder! However, they all did, of course, the Ist being so busy in 1989 that they were unable to find time to celebrate Cambrai Day until December!

Later in the decade three of our athletes would reach the ultimate pinnacle of sporting success, namely representing Great Britain. Cpl (later Sgt) Mark Tout, who had been a member of the 2 RTR 'Great Britain One' four-man Bob at the 1984 Winter Olympics, won the 'Federation International Bobsleigh and Toboggan Best Junior Driver Award' in the World Championships at St Moritz, in the 1984-85 Season. This initial success as a driver led to him being selected to represent Great Britain in the next three

Winter Olympics. He would later be awarded the BEM and retire from the Army in 1994. Cpl Scott of 2 RTR would be selected for the British 1992 Olympic Team in Nordic Skiing and later for the World Cup, whilst L-Cpl Gee would represent Great Britain in the Biathlon at the Winter Olympics in 1993, then again in the World Cup the following year.

Cpl (later Sgt) Mark Tout, BEM, in action at the 1992 Winter Olympics. TM

THIS SPORTING LIFE

THIS SPORTING LIFE

2 RTR returned to UK in early 1990 and were split between Catterick, Bovington and Lulworth. The photograph shows crewmen of 'Huntsman' working on vehicles at Lulworth, where they supported the RAC Gunnery School. (Hattie Young)

INTO THE NINETIES

The 1990s would continue the turbulence that had become a recognised part of regimental life as we moved towards the Millennium. Infantry tours in Northern Ireland and unaccompanied service with the UN Forces in Cyprus were now interspersed with - and almost just as frequent as - more normal armoured battlegroup training in Germany, Canada and later, Poland. In August 1996, 2 RTR became the 1st Lead Armoured Battlegroup in the new Joint Rapid Deployment Force (JRDF), then the following September, 1 RTR took over the same task. However, as the highlights below will show, even more tumultuous happenings were soon to take place.

2 RTR RETURNS TO THE UK

The 2nd began 1990 with a move back to the UK, to become heavily involved in the RAC training machine. However, unlike 3 RTR which had been all together in Dorset as the RAC Centre Regiment 1986-88, the 2nd found itself split between Dorset and Yorkshire. The main portion of the Regiment was in Catterick, carrying out the role of the RAC Training Regiment, whilst two of its squadrons were down South - Badger was in Bovington with almost 200 'A' & 'B' vehicles to look after plus additional military personnel (eg: Artillery Troop, Engineer Troop and Warrior Section) and numerous civilian drivers. Their primary task was to supply all the vehicles (which they also maintained and repaired) for the

Garrison, their three main 'customers' being the Driving & Maintenance School, the Signals School and the Tactics School. 'A' Vehicles included the first of the new Driver Training Tanks, which used a Challenger MBT hull, engine, gearbox and transmission, but instead of a turret it had a a cabin to house the instructor and students. They would also find their 'summer seasons' really hotting up with the preparations for the RAC yearly extravaganza - Battle Day - which normally attracted over 20 000 visitors on one hectic day! The other detached squadron, Huntsman, was the Support Squadron for the RAC Gunnery School at Lulworth and included a special composite troop, known as: 'Guided Weapons/Warrior Troop'.

NORTHERN IRELAND AGAIN

July 1990 saw the majority of a specially organised 3 RTR moving en masse, from Germany to Northern Ireland, with 'X' Sqn in Bessbrook, County Armagh, acting as a fifth infantry company for 1 Cheshires; 'Y' Sqn in Middletown, with a troop in Keady and another with 2nd UDR in Armagh City; 'Z' Sqn was in Aughnacloy, only 700metres from the Irish border. Back in Deilinghofen was 'R' Sqn, with the key role of maintaining the Regiment's tanks and associated equipment. The Regiment's pretour training had ensured that they all now possessed a high standard of infantry skills, whilst 80 volunteers from other regiments helped to boost numbers.

Fighting on Home Ground. The troubles in Northern Ireland continued to impinge regularly on the lives of most soldiers, all RTR regiments taking their turn in the infantry role. TM

AND CYPRUS

Towards the end of 1990, a large part of 1 RTR, deployed to Cyprus as 'T' (Tank) Squadron in support of The Queen's Own Hussars, for a four-month tour. Simultaneously, the rest of the Regiment was getting ready for the next *Medicine Man* in Canada, together with not only the requirement to find a rear party but also having to find a 90-man Site Guard Force, so the elastic was stretched almost to breaking point. No wonder their *Tank* notes commented: 'the Quartermaster goes greyer by the day'!

OPERATION GRANBY

On 2 August 1990, Iraq had invaded the tiny, oil rich state of Kuwait, thus precipitating the Gulf War. The United Nations first undertook *Desert Shield* - the air war, to be followed in January 1991 by ground operations. However, before these could be launched the men and vehicles had to be made ready and shipped out to Saudi Arabia. In Operation *Granby*, as this preparatory phase was codenamed, the 2nd played a major role preparing vehicles for shipment to the Gulf, the RAC Centre being the hub of armoured activity in the UK. War Maintenance Reserve Main Battle tanks, Scorpions, Scimitars and many other vehicles appeared and had to be prepared, including an overall desert camouflage with sand-coloured paint. Personnel had also to be found as maintenance crews on board the ships bound for the Gulf and to man the Armoured Delivery Squadron in

Operation Granby. Preparing for the Gulf War was a massive operation for everyone, especially at the RAC Centre, where 2 RTR had to prepare vehicles for shipment. Note on the Challenger 1, the additional external fuel tanks on the rear and additional armour on the sides. TM

Arabia. Preparations to send two armoured brigades meant long hours of shift working with Badger at one time, holding more than a complete regiment's worth of Challengers.

Although no RTR Regiment served in the Gulf War, there were many RTR soldiers of all ranks - the most senior being Brig Christopher Hammerbeck, CB, who commanded 4th Armoured Brigade - both as reinforcements to major and minor units. Here for example, is Maj Bryan Broadhurst and three other 2 RTR soldiers, who were part of the HQ Delivery Squadron. TM

OPERATION DESERT STORM

Op *Granby* had had a profound effect on life throughout the Army and, although none of the four RTR Regiments was actually part of the two armoured brigades that were deployed operationally in the 1st (UK) Armoured Division, many RTR personnel were there, helping to bring the RAC regiments up to their war establishment, or filling some of the many operational and administrative staff appointments that were so necessary to keep everything running smoothly - even the 2 RTR Band was deployed as part of the casualty evacuation chain! And of course many of the AFVs in Germany had equipment and parts removed to provide vehicle spares, as they were in such short supply. The most senior RTR officer to serve during Operation *Desert Storm*, as the ground operations against Saddam Hussein's invading Army were called, was Brigadier Christopher Hammerbeck, who commanded the 4th Armoured Brigade. Challenger 1 and its American equivalent the Abrams M1A1, swiftly made short work of the enemy armour, the ground war lasting for just two weeks, by which time the cream of the

Iraqi Army - the Republican Guard - had been destroyed. The Regiment had certainly played its part in ensuring victory, and in total, the medals presented to members of the RTR were: one CB, one CBE, one OBE and four MBEs.

BESSBROOK RETROSPECTIVE

3 RTR was now back in Deilinghofen, now re-formed into four sabre squadrons and with post-tour leave over, one of their young officers had this to say in retrospect of their Northern Ireland tour:

During our training we had learned a lot about Northern Ireland and the terrorists with whom we might come face to face during our tour. We had learned the lessons drawn from past experience and practised how we would react in almost every situation that we might encounter. Of course after 20 years in the province the British Army has become more and more skilled and the terrorists have become more and more devious. So in the short time available to us, we had a lot of knowledge to absorb. This intense training left

3 RTR in Northern Ireland. Training for the street battles in Northern Ireland, was often almost too realistic! (Tank)

us with a sensibly wary, but keyed up, image of the area into which we were to be deployed.

I can vividly remember the day I arrived with ther Advance Party at Bessbrook Mill, the Security Force Base. The weather was beautifully clear and hot. As the Chinook landed and we stepped off to see the familiar perimeter fencing, sangars and barbed wire, it finally came to me what Northern Ireland was all about. Bessbrook Mill, a huge drab, grey building, surrounded by defences like a medieval fortress, seemed in itself indicative of the hostile environment of South Armagh.

After the first weeks of the tour, we all became more street-wise, or in our case, field- wise, and I began to see South Armagh in its true colours; a beautiful rural county with majestic lakes and mountains and lakes, inhabited by normal people of each religion who wanted nothing more than to be able to go about their normal business, unhindered by terrorism and everything that goes with it.

I found the people of Northern Ireland quite remarkable almost unique. Where I had expected to encounter mass hatred, I found placid patient people who, in many cases, amazed me by their friendliness. Of course there were those who didn't like us, but I wonder how the average Englishman would react to constantly being stopped and sometimes searched as he tried each day to commute from comfortable suburbia to his office.

What I find most sad about Ireland is that the people fully accept our presence on the streets and seem unperturbed by their police force patrolling fully armed and surrounded by soldiers. They clearly have resigned themselves to the fact that they are doomed to live amongst a violent minority for the foreseeable future.

It is hard to measure success in military terms with a problem such as that of Northern Ireland. However, the fact that all of 'X' Squadron returned unscathed can be considered a resounding success. It is a tribute to the professionalism of all the soldiers who served there and maintained such a high standard of alterness, despite the monotony and the deprivation that they suffered.

NEXT IN LINE

The 1st would be the next RTR regiment to deploy troops to Northern Ireland, with almost two squadrons being deployed there as the Prison Guard Force at the Maze, where they took over from 4/7 DG. Prior to their departure, Tofrek Barracks became their training ground much to the dismay of others in Hildesheim Station! At the time speculation was rife about the prospect of reintroducing internment, so it was no unsurprising that the job was taken very seriously, as one PGF commander commented:

Although historically a quiet area, the potential for a large-scale breakout, probably combined with a diversionary attack on the guard force, can never be ruled out. This is enough to make it an important challenge and one to which everyone rises and enjoys. Fortunately during our tour no one escaped and I still have a job!

THE 4TH IN CYPRUS

'Once again the 4th finds itself basking in the sun of a Cyprus summer,' they chortled in the November 1991 issue of *Tank*, going on to say that very little seemed to have changed since their last visit in 1989. This time they were to be the first regiment to carry out the 'Roulement Regiment' tour of six months' unbroken duty on the Peace Line. 339 officers and men, organised into *Arras* and *Cambrai* Squadrons provided the Line coverage, whilst *Rhine* Squadron provided the HQ and support element. As it turned out, their workload was considerable as it was a time of great change in the island's political situation, plus an enhanced profile for the UN itself. Back in Osnabruck, the rear party was getting to grips with the mountainous task of sorting out the ravages of Op *Granby*.

REGIMENTAL RESTRUCTURING

In late 1991, it was announced that, under the 'Options for Change' it had been decided that the RTR would be reduced from four to two regiments, whilst retaining Regimental Headquarters at Bovington. In July 1992, 2 RTR and 3 RTR would come together at Fallingbostel to form the new 2nd Royal Tank Regiment; a year later at Tidworth, 1 RTR and 4 RTR would merge to become the new 1st Royal Tank Regiment. 'No organisation can possibly welcome a massive reduction in its strength and capacity,' wrote the Representative Colonel Commandant, Gen Sir Antony Walker, KCB, to the Commanding Officers: 'however, I know that under your leadership your Regiment will face the future with confidence and optimism. Unlike some others the Royal Tank Regiment capbadge will remain in the Army's Order of Battle. We will take care to design for the future in such a way that we safeguard that which is best from the past and relevant to the present.'

CHANGES IN DRESS

The restructuring would also lead to certain changes in regimental dress, viz:

All officers and WO1s will wear black guernseys. All other ranks will wear black wool patched pullovers
Red lanyards will be worn by all ranks at regimental duty with 1 RTR; saffron lanyards will be worn by all ranks at RD with 2 RTR; when posted outside their regiments all ranks will wear black lanyards.
There will be no shoulder flashes, just plain black slides, with white embroidered badges of rank (where applicable)
Black denims and all other normal forms of dress would continue to be worn unchanged.

FORWARD TO THE FUTURE

'Goodbye to the Green on Black'
(by WO2 Dai Marsh, 3 RTR)

The axes fall, chop here, chop there
No one is safe, all must beware.
For there is peace in Europe's East
No mighty Russian bear,
But lots of little angry cubs to fight
amongst themselves

But peace is peace and armies cost,
And so traditional names are lost,
With few traditions and short of years
It had to be our biggest fear;
The day would come when They would say
No more the Green on Black

The Green will go, the Black will stay,
The politicians have had their way.
Half will go but half survive
To carry on their tankie lives.
With heavy hearts and no look back,
We all salute the Green on Black.

The life I had was full of fun
Was full of mates both old and young.
But now my feelings just aren't the same,
It's no one's fault, no one's to blame,
An era's gone, it's got the sack!
Farewell my friend, the Green on Black.'

Prior to the formal, final amalgamation parade, which did not take place until the autumn, both the 2nd and 3rd held their own parades

Beknighted Colonels Commandant. In 1993, for the very first time in the Regiment's history, all three Colonels Commandant were Knights. Left to Right: Maj-Gen Sir Laurence New, CB, CBE; Lt-Gen Sir Jeremy Blacker KCB, CBE and Gen Sir Antony Walker, KCB. (Tank)

An impressive parade took place at Fallingbostel on 9 October 1992, when 2 and 3 RTR were amalgamated to form the new 2 RTR. The parade was taken by the Representative Colonel Commandant, Lt Gen Sir Jeremy Blacker, KCB, CBE. (Hattie Young)

and other farewells, which included laying up the 3rd's Standard in the Regimental Church on 13 September 1992. These events, inevitably tinged with sadness, were followed by an upbeat, impressive parade and other celebrations, which marked the formation of the new 2 RTR at Fallingbostel on 9 October 1992. The parade was taken by the Representative Colonel Commandant, Lt-Gen Sir Jeremy Blacker, KCB, CBE.

BEKNIGHTED COLONEL COMMANDANTS

For the first time in the Regiment's history, in 1993, all three Colonels Commandants were Knights as the photograph on the previous page shows.

1 ELVERTON STREET

1993 saw the demolition of 1 Elverton Street, London, which had been RHQ RTR from 1959 until 1988, when RHQ moved down to Bovington.

1 RTR AND 4 RTR AMALGAMATION PARADE

As with the other two regiments, there were sad farewells to the old 1st and 4th, including the laying up of the 4th's Standard at the Regimental Church on 12 September 1993. The 4th also ended its final range firing with the CO symbolically firing the last round

1 Elverton Street, London. This was the 'home' of RHQ RTR from 1959-88. It was pulled down in 1993, just after this photograph was taken. (The Journal of the Westminster Dragoons)

of 4 RTR – a memorable moment. Both Regiments also had to move to Tidworth, 1 RTR bidding farewell to Hildesheim, where they had been since 1985, with 4 RTR doing the same in Osnabruck where they had also been since 1985. 1 RTR began its new tour in Tidworth with an internal amalgamation parade in Aliwal Barracks with the sabre squadrons renamed as A, D, G and H representing the old 1, 4, 7 and 8 RTR, with HQ Squadron retaining its original title. The formation of the new Regiment was represented symbolically by the lowering of the old 1st and 4th flags for the last time, followed by the raising of the new flag by RSM Roberts. This was followed by a short service to re-dedicate the Regimental Standard to the new Regiment.

The amalgamation parade took place at Tidworth of 1 October 1993, with the Representative Colonel Commandant, Lt-Gen Sir Jeremy Blacker, KCB, CBE, once again taking the parade. The day consisted of a mounted parade followed by lunch in the respective messes, a series of displays in the afternoon and an All Ranks Dance in the evening. 'What a Day! What a Spectacle!' wrote one junior officer: 'After weeks of painful preparation we were finally ready for the "Big Day", the parade was on. On receiving the command to advance, the Regiment began its move to the parade site which included a manic charge through smoke, a game of moving chess to get into position and then a regimental advance from dead ground, stopping some 100m in front of the spectators... Despite all the hard work and effort that went in at all levels of the Regiment it was an enjoyable parade for everyone - not just for those watching. I am sure that many of us will remember it in times to come.'

2 RTR were OPFOR (Opposing Force) at BATUS 1995-96. Here the CO, Lt-Col (later Brig) Stephen White greets Gen Sir Jeremy Blacker, at the entrance to the OPFOR hangar. TM

2 RTR GO BACK TO CYPRUS

The new 2nd became the United Nations Roulement Regiment (UNRR) towards the end of 1993, going to Cyprus for another six-months unaccompanied tour. 'Compared with Fallingbostel, for the single man/woman Cyprus is heaven. The weather is obviously better, but generally there is more to do. The Adventure Training opportunities are excellent and Cyprus is ideally located within the Mediterranean for travel enthusiasts. Eating and drinking out is incredibly cheap and most of the locals speak English and are very friendly.'

THE RUSSIANS ARE COMING!

One of the unique developments which came with the end of the Cold War, was the arrival of military teams from the other side of the now defunct 'Iron Curtain', both to check what vehicles regiments were holding - they were known as: 'Joint Arms Control Implementation Groups' (codename: *Rebecca*), and also other teams to evaluate a formation as a whole and assess its fighting capability (codename: *Apollo*). How times have changed!

RESTRUCTURING THE COLONELS COMMANDANT

At the Regimental Council meeting in November 1993, it was decided to have in future a single Colonel Commandant at the head of the Regiment, supported by two Deputy Colonels Commandant who would each adopt certain executive duties. The Council considered that the new organisation better reflected the needs of our smaller Regiment.

OPFOR

1995 saw 2 RTR providing the OPFOR (Opposing Forces) element at BATUS, so they acted as a live enemy for the visiting battlegroups such as QDG, RDG, KRH and Coldm Gds. Inevitably there was also the 'Clash of Titans', when 1 RTR visited Canada on Ex *Medicine Man 5* in the September. 2 RTR had to maintain a sizeable rear party, so only half the Regiment was in Canada at any one time. They completed their highly successful tour at Suffield in March 1996. 1 RTR moved from Tidworth to Paderborn in August/September 1996, re-equipping with Challenger 1, having been the last Regiment in the British Army with the Chieftain MBT.

SIXTY YEARS WITH THE REGIMENT

1995 was an important year for our most famous living soldier, Field Marshal Lord Carver, GCB, CBE, DSO and Bar, MC. Not only did he celebrate his

2 RTR OPFOR at BATUS. Maj Spicer and the tanks of Tank Coy 2, with the snow-clad prairies stretching away behind them. TM

80th Birthday on 24th April, but he had also then served sixty years with the Regiment. He entered the RMC, Sandhurst in 1933, passing out the following year top of the order of merit, gaining the King's Gold Medal and the Anson Memorial Sword, plus prizes for Economics, Military History and Military Law. Commissioned in the RTC on 31 January 1935, he was posted to 2 RTC, then in 1938 went with 1 RTC to Egypt. When 7th Armoured Division was formed there in 1940 he joined its staff, on which he held appointments as Captain, Major and, finally as Lieutenant Colonel, being chief of its General Staff until the closing stage of the North African campaign. He then assumed command of 1 RTR, holding it in Italy and then in North-West Europe, being promoted to command 4th Armoured Brigade soon after landing in Normandy - at 29 he was the youngest brigade commander in the British Army. Post-war he continued up the ladder, and held all the highest posts in the Army and Services, including Chief of the Defence Staff, returning to the Regiment in 1968 as one of our Colonels Commandant, a post he held until 1973.

On the evening of 16 March 1995, the Colonels Commandant and Officers held a dinner at the Vintners Hall to celebrate Field Marshal Lord Carver's 80th birthday. The photograph shows Gen Sir Jeremy Blacker with the Field Marshal after presenting him with a silver salver. TM

RESTRUCTURING RHQ RTR

In 1995 the last serving officers left RHQ and were replaced by Retired Officers, the first incumbents being: Regimental Colonel - Col (Retd) J.L. Longman; Regimental Secretary - Maj (Retd) A. Henzie, MBE; Regimental Adjutant - Maj (Retd) C.A. Parr. RHQ was now located in Stanley Barracks, Bovington and was scheduled to move into Bovington Farmhouse in 2002.

LOCOMOTIVE 45041 'ROYAL TANK REGIMENT'

Dedicated at Crewe on 14 July 1996, was Diesel Locomotive 45041, now renamed ROYAL TANK REGIMENT. It was built in Crewe in 1962 and originally known just as number D53, it is a 2500-horsepower, 133-ton giant, which originally operated in the Midlands and Yorkshire. Bought by the Midland Railway Centre and lovingly restored externally, it was due to return there after the ceremony for full internal restoration.

2 RTR NORTHERN IRELAND 1997

Yet again, the RTR were on duty in Northern Ireland. And on this occasion, whilst two of their patrols were on duty with the RUC in the Ardoyne area of Belfast, they were attacked by the Provisional IRA, one of the vehicles being hit on the side with a shoulder-launched anti-armour missile. Fortunately only one of the team sustained a minor injury and in the

ensuing follow-up , the alleged prepetrators were captured - that was the Regiment's closest encounter with PIRA during their tour

THE RTR REUNION, BOVINGTON, 1997

On Friday, 30th May, the sun shone all day long, as members of the Regiment, young and old, celebrated at their spiritual 'home' of Bovington, Dorset. They were joined there by our Commander in Chief, Her Majesty The Queen, who looked radiant throughout her visit and clearly enjoyed herself. Luncheon was taken in the George Forty Hall of the Tank Museum which Her Majesty later toured, showing great interest in the wonderful collection of armoured fighting vehicles, these included opening the very latest state-of-the-art 'Iron Fist' exhibit. Many of the Regiment's past and present AFVs were also on parade outside, together with contingents from both the First and Second, with their Regimental Standards; the Band and Pipes & Drums; and of course the Old Comrades, their Branch Standards waving proudly in the breeze, as they marched past their Sovereign.

It was a day to remember and we were joined in our celebrations by representatives of the renowned tank builders Vickers Defence Systems, whose AFVs we have manned for so many years and who were celebrating their 150th anniversary in 1997. The 'icing on the cake' was still to come, with the commemoration of the 80th anniversary of the Battle of Cambrai 'on site' in France

2 RTR Northern Ireland, January to July 1997. This trooper was a member of the back-up force to the Black's - the Operational Support Unit for 'D' Division, RUC. TM

Her Majesty arriving at Bovington for the RTR Reunion on 30 May 1997. She was accompanied by Maj Gen R.W.M. McAfee and drove in on the Tank Museum's immaculate 1920 pattern Rolls Royce armoured car. (Crown Copyright)

Above: *The Regiment awaits the inspection by Her Majesty, Bovington, 30 May 1997.* (Crown Copyright)

Members of all branches of the RTRA marching past Her Majesty at Bovington, 30 May 1997. (Crown Copyright)

Cambrai 1997 - The Officers' Dinner was held in the Salle de la Manutention of the Hotel de Ville at Cambrai. (Crown Copyright)

Wreath laying at the Cambrai War Memorial. Maj-Gen Rob McAfee was accompanied by Sir Michael Jay, HMA Paris and Dr John Reid, Minister for the Armed Forces. (Crown Copyright)

The Drumhead Service at the cemetery at Louverval, taken by the Regimental Padre, the Very Reverend Graham Roblin, OBE. (Crown Copyright)

THE 80TH ANNIVERSARY OF THE BATTLE OF CAMBRAI

Formal activities during the Cambrai visit included a comprehensive battlefield tour, the mist and rain adding to the drama; the final of the Cambrai Cup football; stirring parades and wreath laying in Cambrai town, at which we were joined by Dr John Reid, Minister for the Armed Forces and Sir Michael Jay, HMA Paris; a candlelit officers' dinner in the Salle de la Manutention of the Hotel de Ville and numerous All Ranks social gatherings. However, the highspot was undoubtedly the simple, yet incredibly moving Drumhead Service, held the Louverval Cemetery, one of the most atmospheric cemeteries out on the battlefield.

MEMORIAL GARDEN

On Sunday 8 March 1998, Padre Robert Green consecrated the RTR Memorial Garden adjacent to St George's Church in Allenby Barracks, Bovington. The garden, which incorporates a Portland stone carving of the RTC crest, together with a selection of roses and heathers, will became a focal point for all serving and ex-members of the Regiment wishing to pay their respects to members of the Regiment who have gone the the Green Fields Beyond.

1 RTR AND THE JOINT NBC REGIMENT

In early July 1998 the Secretary of State for Defence announced the outcome of the Strategic Defence Review (SDR). One of the enhancements to defence capability was to be the formation of the Joint NBC Unit from 1 April 1999; an organisation that would be manned by both the Army and the RAF in the ratio 75 per cent-25 per cent. The 1st Royal Tank Regiment was nominated to be the main Army element. Implementation of this decision was to begin on 1 April 1999, with 1 RTR manpower starting NBC training from 1 September. The Jt NBC Regiment was to be operational by 31 December 1999. Thus for the second time in its relatively short history, the RTR was to be in the forefront of the latest developments in military technology. Along with preparing to re-role the bulk of its soldiers, the 1st also was tasked to provide the armoured squadron as part of the Combined Arms Training Centre Battlegroup (CATC BG) at Warminster, equipped with Challenger 2 - the first time CR2 was deployed in the UK. The principle will be that all soldiers joining the RTR will first serve on tanks in order to gain a level of proficiency before they move on to the NBC role.

The re-roling went according to plan and all ranks of 1 RTR have won high praise for their professionalism and high morale. 'It is not a job that

1 RTR becomes Jt NBC Regt. Under the SDR of July 1998, 1 RTR was re-roled from 1999 as the Army element of the Joint NBC Regiment and later returned to UK. They are now based at RAF Honington. The photograph shows one of their Fuchs Radiological and Chemical Survey vehicles, being decontaminated after carrying out a survey of a contaminated area. (RAF Official)

2 RTR received the latest Challenger 2, at Fallingbostel in November 1998. (Foto Boesel)

'A' Sqn, 1 RTR, the armoured squadron at the Combined Arms Training Centre, Warminster prepares to deploy. (1 RTR)

Get your knees brown! Men of the Jt NBC Regt in the Gulf during exercises in 1999. (Crown Copyright)

any of us had anticipated or volunteered for but we have learnt to respect it,' wrote one of the 1st's senior officers: '...we are proud of what we do and proud of being Bio Warriors. At the end of the day any one of my vehicles is far more important than an entire squadron of Challenger 2s and will have an operational and strategic impact far in excess of any other vehicle on today's battlefield!' The Regiment is now regularly manning, for example, the Biological Detection component of the force protection package at Ali Al Salem (AAS) Airbase in Kuwait. For the future, the Army Chiefs of Staff have endorsed a plan that will significantly improve the Regiment's ability to deliver its Full Operating Capability in 2004. The first step in this plan has seen the Jt NBC Regt transfer to operate directly under RAF Strike Command.

UNVEILING THE RTR STATUE

'The day of the unveiling finally arrived and we were told that taxis had been booked to take us to the parade site'. So wrote Cpl Hanns of 2 RTR, who had been chosen with his wife, Chelle, to be one of the lucky few to be introduced to Her Majesty The Queen during the Reception at the Banqueting Hall that would follow the unveiling. 'Unfortunately we must have had the only taxi driver in London who didn't know where the junction of Horse Guards Parade and

Whitehall was - not a good start to the day!' Fortunately they did eventually arrive safely and were shown to their seats. 'The parade started with the Pipes & Drums playing 'Highland Cathedral' which instantly brought the hairs on the back of your neck to attention. Next the Old Comrades marched on parade followed by the Guards of Honour from 1 and 2 RTR and the Standards Party. ...Once Her Majesty The Queen arrived she was shown to her seat on the dais and at that point we listened to the dedication to the Memorial Statue by Maj Gen Ridgway. Then The Queen was invited to unveil the statue and meet some of the Old Comrades. I felt extremely proud to be part of this auspicious occasion. After the parade finished the reception party was ushered round to the Banqueting Hall to meet Her Majesty, rounded up into a semi-circle, palms sweating, waiting with mounting anticipation for The Queen to arrive. The moment finally arrived and we were each introduced to Her Majesty... Afterwards I turned to my wife and said: "Well Chelle, it's not every day you get to meet The Queen, shake her hand and stand in a Banqueting Hall drinking champagne and eating raw tuna wrapped in spinach." Don't get me wrong. I could get used to it, well, all but the raw tuna in spinach and that's got to be an acquired taste!

To sum up the whole trip was a most memorable occasion and by far the best thing I have ever been asked to do in the Army so far.'

The RTR Memorial Statue. The Colonel Commandant, Maj Gen Andrew Ridgway, CBE, beginning his address to Her Majesty The Queen before the unveiling, 13 June 2000. (Crown Copyright)

Her Majesty having just unveiled the Statue. It is located at the corner of Whitehall Court, just beside the corner of the Old War Office Building. (Crown Copyright)

C SQN 2 RTR IN BOSNIA

As the Millennium closed part of the Regiment was once again on operations - this time it was Cyclops, 2 RTR, which went off to Bosnia on Operation *Agricola 5*. They would be followed to the Balkans in February 2001 by the rest of the Regiment who departed on a six months unaccompanied tour to Kosovo, leaving Cyclops to follow on as part of the Scots DG Battlegroup on Op *Agricola 6*. Thus between April 2000 and November 2001 some 450 members of the Regiment will have completed three operational tours in the Balkans spanning some 14 months. They have conducted a number of troop, squadron and Task Force operations outside the brigade area in support of other multi-national brigades, the most notable being on the Macedonian border to interdict extremist activities in that region.

2 RTR in Kosovo. The crew of a Scimitar recce vehicle keeping a sharp lookout from high ground some 800m from the Macedonian-Kosovo border. Using thermal imaging sights they can keep a 24-hr watch for illegal incursions or arms smugglers.
(Crown Copyright)

Other tasks have included foot patrolling and insertions by helicopters.

2 RTR also introduced towards the end of 2000, with the blessing of the RTR Council, two new names for E and F Squadrons, to go with the existing Badger, Cyclops and Nero. So there are now: Egypt and Falcon, the names being derived from tank names used in the First World War.

'DOUBLY IS OURS A GREAT ADVENTURE'

In our short history the Regiment has undergone enormous changes, greater than those which even the most radical of the first tank pioneers could have ever imagined. And the speed of these changes shows no signs of slowing down. We have seen the

Operation Agricola 5. *Keeping the Peace. CO 2 RTR's CR2, complete with 7th Armd Bde 'Desert Rat' is seen here on the edge of Podujevo.* (Sgt Maddams, 2 RTR)

The shape of things to come? 2000 saw the unveiling of the DERA ACAVP (Advanced Composite Armoured Vehicle Platform) demonstrator developed in partnership with Vickers Defence Systems. It has a plastic/glass fibre composite hull – the most revolutionary change of AFV materials since the aluminium hull of the early 1960s. (DERA)

effective compromise between firepower, protection and mobility which first produced the tank change many times over the years, until it has now led to Challenger 2, a modern, costly, 70-ton main battle tank, with its automated fire control system, powerful engine, transmission and suspension, and its composite armour, all making it a vastly different machine to *Mother* and her original brood, but capable of dealing easily with most other weapons on the modern battlefield. Now some pundits say that the age of the heavy main battle tank is over and that a radically lightened, air-portable, cheaper version will have to be the backbone of any future armoured force. Others go even further, saying that the age of the tank itself is over and that it will shortly be replaced by the attack helicopter. Whatever the outcome, the chances of our Regiment staying in its present form for long is unlikely. However, I believe that our future is sustainable, especially as some of our soldiers are already 'Bio Warriors', embracing new technologies for a second time and thus giving our Regiment a double chance to survive. No doubt, such radical thought would have been understood by men of vision like our great founder, Major General Sir Ernest Swinton, who said of those who were going into action for the first time at Flers, on 15 September 1916: 'They were setting out on a crusade and were pioneers in a new form of warfare. Doubly was theirs a great adventure.' At the end of the Millennium I can do no better than to paraphrase his words: 'We are setting out on a crusade and are pioneers in a new form of warfare. Doubly is ours a great adventure.' FEAR NAUGHT!

OPFOR 2000. Most of 2 RTR were back again in Canada acting as OPFOR for the QRH Battlegroup in April 2000, whilst 'C' Squadron deployed to Bosnia on an operational tour with KFORBR Battlegroup - and they say there's no over-stretch these days! TM

SERVICE OVERSEAS
Since the end of the Second World War

KOREA

1 RTR	1952-53
5 RTR	1953-54
7 RTR ('C' Sqn)	1950-51

CYRENAICA

2 RTR	1959-62
5 RTR	1955-57
6 RTR	1957-59

EGYPT

1 RTR	1954-55
4 RTR	1947-53
6 RTR	1947, 1956 (Suez operation)
8 RTR	1946-47

HONG KONG

1 RTR	1957-60, 1965-66 (sqn only)
3 RTR	1949-52
7 RTR	1952-54

MALTA

1 RTR	1956
6 RTR	1956

ADEN & PERSIAN GULF

1 RTR	1965-66
4 RTR	1963-64

MALAYSIA

3 RTR (sqn only)	1950-52
4 RTR	1964-66
5 RTR (sqn only)	1966

INDIA

7 RTR 1947

ULSTER (ALL or part of regiment)

1 RTR	1972, 1973-74, 1977, 1981, 1984, 1991-92
2 RTR	1962-64, 1973-74, 1975, 1979-80, 1983, 1989, 1997
3 RTR	1973, 1974-75, 1990-91
4 RTR	1971, 1976, 1978, 1986

CYPRUS (ALL or part of regiment)

1 RTR	1975-75, 1982-84, 1990, 1998
2 RTR	1964-65, 1993-94
3 RTR	1976-78, 1986-87
4 RTR	1983, 1989, 1991
6 RTR	1957-58

PALESTINE

4 RTR	1948
8 RTR	1946

ITALY / AUSTRIA

2 RTR	1945-46
4 RTR	1946-47
6 RTR	1945-47
8 RTR	1945-46
12 RTR	1945 then disbanded

GERMANY (ALL or part of regiment)

1 RTR	1945-52, 1960-63, 1976-77, 1978-82, 1985-92, 1996-98
2 RTR	1947-48, 1952-59, 1966-70, 1972-79, 1980-84, 1985-89, 1992 to date
3 RTR	1945-47, 1953-62, 1964-67, 1970-75, 1979-86, 1987-92, then amalgamated with 2 RTR
4 RTR	1945, 1954-63, 1966-73, 1975-82, 1984-93, then amalgamated with 1 RTR
5 RTR	1945-53, 1960-65, 1968-69, then disbanded
6 RTR	1952-56, 1959-60, then amalgamated with 3 RTR
7 RTR	1945-46, 1958-60, then amalgamated with 4 RTR
8 RTR	1951-60, then amalgamated with 5 RTR
9 RTR	1945, then disbanded
11 RTR	1945, then disbanded

UK (ALL or part of regiment)

1 RTR	1952, 1955-57, 1967-68, 1974-75, 1983-84, 1993-96, 1999 to date
2 RTR	1948-52, 1965, 1970-72, 1990-91
3 RTR	1948-49, 1962-63, 1968-69, 1976-78, 1986-87
4 RTR	1953-54, 1963, 1973-75, 1982-83
5 RTR	1957-59, 1965-67
6 RTR	1948-51
7 RTR	1948-52, 1955-57
8 RTR	1947-51

BALKANS

2 RTR	2000-01

CANADA

2 RTR	1995-96, 2000

SPECIAL FEATURES

REGIMENTAL STANDARDS

The custom of carrying Colours and Standards goes back to the days of early man, who fixed his family badge to a pole and held it aloft in battle for the dual purpose of indicating his position and acting as a rallying point should the need arise. Standards evolved from the banners of the Knights of the Middle Ages and are now carried by both of the regiments of the Royal Tank Regiment.

Standards were first presented to the RTR by HM The Queen at Buckingham Palace in October 1960. These were laid up in the Regimental Church of St Peter's upon Cornhill in September 1985, after Her Majesty had presented new Standards to the four remaining Regiments in July 1985. The Standards of

Standard Bearers of the RTR Association Branches waiting to greet their Colonel in Chief when she visited Bovington in June 1997. (Crown Copyright)

The Regimental Standards of the 1st and 2nd Royal Tank Regiments outside the Town Hall, Cambrai, November 1997. (Crown Copyright)

3 RTR and 4 RTR were laid up in the Regimental Church in September 1992 and September 1993 respectively. The two remaining Regiments carry similar Standards, the only difference being that individual Regimental numbers are embroidered above the letters 'RTR'in the top right and bottom eft hand corners. The Battle Honours shown below in italic type are emblazoned on each Standard.

BATTLE HONOURS

The First World War. *Somme 1916-18, Arras 1917-18, Messines 1917, Ypres 1917, Cambrai 1917*, St Quentin 1918, *Villers Bretonneux, Amiens, Bapaume 1918, Hindenburg Line*, Epehy, Selle, *France and Flanders 1916-18*, Gaza.

The Second World War. Arras counter-attack, Calais 1940, St Omer-La Bassee, Somme 1940, Odon, Caen, Bourguebus Ridge, Mont Pincon, Falaise, Nederrijn, Scheldt, Venlo Pocket, Rhineland, *Rhine*, Bremen, *North-West Europe 1940, 1944-45, Abyssinia 1940*, Sidi Barrani, Beda Fomm, Sidi Suleiman, *Tobruk 1941*, Sidi Rezegh 1941, Belhamed, Gazala, Cauldron,

Knightsbridge, Defence of Alamein Line, Alam el Halfa, *El Alamein*, Mareth, Akarit, Fondouk, El Kourzia, Medjez Plain, Tunis, *North Africa 1940-43*, Primosole Bridge, Gerbini, Adrano, *Sicily 1943*, Sangro, Salerno, Volturno Crossing, Gargliano Crossing, Anzio, Advance to Florence, Gothic Line, Coriano, Lamone Crossing, Rimini Line, Argenta Gap, *Italy 1943-45, Greece 1941, Burma 1942*.
Korea. *Korea 1951-53*.

ALLIED REGIMENTS AND OTHER AFFILIATIONS

Australia – 1st Armoured Regiment, Royal Australian Armoured Corps
Canada – 12e Regiment Blindé du Canada, Royal Canadian Armoured Corps
India – 2nd Lancers (Gardner's Horse), Indian Armoured Corps
New Zealand – Royal New Zealand Armoured Corps
Pakistan – 13th Lancers, Pakistan Armoured Corps
France – 501e/503e Regiment de Chars de Combat
Royal Navy – HMS *Kent*

Our two Second World War VCs Maj Gen Bob Foote and Maj Pip Gardner try out a Chieftain tank at Bovington Camp. (Lt Col S W Crawford)

HONOURS AND AWARDS

This summary of British Honours and Awards (no foreign decorations are shown) is divided into four periods in line with the division of the main text. The large number of decorations awarded during the First World War were won in only two years, showing clearly how committed the Corps was from the very outset.

(a) First World War (1916-18)

Officers		Other Ranks	
VC	4	MC	1
CB	1	DCM	144
CMG	6	Bar to DCM	1
CBE	2	MM	604
OBE	23	Bar to MM	23
MBE	1	MSM	106
DSO	73		
Bar to DSO	9		
MC	447		
Bar to MC	42		

(b) Inter-War (1919-39)

Officers		Other Ranks	
KCB	1	GC	2
CB	5	DCM	4
CBE	3	MM	14
OBE	10	MSM	2
MBE	9		
DSO	4		
MC	14	Bar to MC	2

(c) Second World War (1939-45)

Officers		Other Ranks	
VC	2	MBE	18
GC	1	DCM	45
GCB	1	MM	343
KCB	2	Bar to MM	10
KBE	3	2 Bars to MM	1 *
CB	10	GM	1
CBE	20	BEM	23
DSO	88		
Bar to DSO	13	*Sgt F W Kite was the only soldier in the British Army to be awarded three Military Medals during WW2	
2 Bars to DSO	1		
OBE	36		
MBE	79		
MC	282		
Bar to MC	33		

(d) Post-War (1945-2000)

Officers		Other Ranks	
Life Peerage	1	MBE	12
GCB	2	MM	7
KCB	8	BEM	36
CB	20	RVM	1
KCMG	2	MSM	24
KBE	2		
CBE	20		
DSO	1		
OBE	54		
MBE	85		
MC	3		
DFC	1		
AFC	1		
QGM	2		
QCVC	1		
QCVS	1		

COLONELS COMMANDANT
(1923 –2000) (Ranks and decorations shown are as on appointment)

		Representative
Maj-Gen Sir John E. Capper KCB, KCVO	1923-34	
Maj-Gen Sir Ernest Swinton KBE, CB, DSO	1934-38	1934-38
FM Sir Archibald A. Montgomery Massingberd GCB, KCMG, LLD, ADC	1934-39	
Gen Sir Hugh J. Elles KCB, KCMG, KCVO, DSO	1934-45	1939
Maj-Gen G.M. Lindsay CB, CMG, DSO	1938-47	1940-43
Lt-Gen Sir Charles E. Broad KCB, DSO	1939-48	1944-47
FM The Viscount Montgomery KG, GCB, DSO, DL	1945-57	
Maj-Gen Sir Percy C.S. Hobart KBE, CB, DSO, MC	1947-51	1948-51
Gen Sir John T. Crocker GCB, KBE, DSO, MC	1949-61	
Maj-Gen N.W. Duncan CB, CBE, DSO	1952-59	1952-57
Maj-Gen H.R.B. Foote VC, CB, DSO	1957-64	1958-61
Lt-Gen Sir Harold E. Pyman KCB, CBE, DSO	1959-65	
Maj-Gen H.M. Liardet CB, CBE, DSO, DL	1961-67	1962-67
Maj-Gen A. Jolly CB, CBE, DSO	1964-69	1968-69
Maj-Gen J.R. Holden CB, CBE, DSO	1965-68	
Gen Sir Michael Carver KCB, CBE, DSO, MC, ADC	1968-73	1970-71
Maj-Gen P.R.C. Hobart DSO, OBE, MC	1968-78	1971-74
Maj-Gen R.E. Ward CB, DSO, MC	1970-75	1974-75
Lt-Gen Sir Allan Taylor KBE, MC	1973-80	1976-77

Maj-Gen J.G.R. Allen
   CB   1976-81   1977-80
Maj-Gen R.L.C. Dixon
   CB MC   1978-83   1982-83
Lt-Gen Sir Richard Lawson
   KCB, DSO, OBE   1980-82   1980-82
Maj-Gen I.H. Baker
CBE   1981-86
Maj-Gen R.M. Jerram
   CB, MBE   1982-88   1983-85
Maj-Gen A.K.F. Walker 1983-87   1985-91
Maj-Gen L.A.W. New
CB, CBE   1986-92

	Colonel Commandant	*RCC*
Maj-Gen A.S.J.Blacker		
CBE, BA	1988-95	1992-94
Brig R.W.M. McAfee	1993-94	

	DCC	*Col Comdt*
Maj-Gen R.W.M. McAfee		
CB	1994-95	1995-99
Brig A.C.I. Gadsby ADC	1994-2000	
Brig A.P. Ridgway CBE	1995-1999	1999-
Brig A.D. Leakey CBE	1999-	
Maj-Gen P. Gilchrist	2000-	

REGIMENTAL DISTINCTIONS AND DRESS

The ash plant. Officers of the Tank Corps during the First World War took to carrying long ash sticks with them, so that they could test the firmness of the ground before their tanks moved forwards on the thick mud of the Somme battlefields. To commemorate this practice all RTR officers now carry Ash Plant Sticks both on and off parade.

The arm badge tank. Designed by Swinton, this arm badge was originally intended as a unifying symbol for all ranks of the Tank Corps, because they wore their old regimental badges and insignia. It is still worn by all ranks of the right arm, four fingers width below the shoulder.

The black beret. Originally tank crews were supplied with primitive brown leather 'crash helmets', together with chainmail visors to protect their faces. However, both were hot and uncomfortable, so instead they wore their service caps, peak to the rear, and hung blankets around the inside of the tank to help stop the flakes of metal which chipped off inside whenever the outside was struck by a bullet or shell splinter. In the summer of 1918, Gen Elles began looking seriously for a suitable form of headgear and was certainly influenced in his choice by visiting the French Chasseurs Alpins, who wore a type of floppy beret. Black was selected as the best colour, as it would not show the oil stains which were impossible to avoid when working inside a tank. The beret was officially approved by HM The King on 5 March 1924.

The badge and motto. The present regimental badge dates from the formation of the RTC in 1923, but the crown above the tank changes depending upon whether a King or a Queen is on the throne, so the present badge came into use in 1953, when HM Queen Elizabeth II became Colonel in Chief. The motto: 'Fear Naught' appears on a scroll below the tank which is surrounded by a laurel wreath.

Coloured shoulder straps and lanyards. In January 1917, coloured shoulder straps were introduced for each battalion. They are now no longer worn, however the two remaining regular regiments have always had the following colours: 1st - Red; 2nd - Saffron. Traditionally a black lanyard was worn by all ranks of the RTC who had served in India and Egypt between the wars, whilst during the First World War every man awarded a gallantry decoration was allowed to wear a lanyard in the Corps colours. Appropriately coloured lanyards are now worn by all ranks at Regimental Duty (RD), but when posted outside their regiments black lanyards are worn. Neckscarves of the appropriate colour are worn with black denims.

Above: A staff sergeant (SQMS) of 1 RTR in Mess Dress (No 10 Dress) circa 1996-97. (NEXUS)

A good selection of officers' uniforms circa 1996, featuring five subalterns of 1 RTR at Aliwal Barracks, Tidworth (NEXUS))

Lt A.V. Golding of 5th RTC, models the full dress uniform of the Royal Tank Corps circa 1928-29. TM

F/4. The Regimental Sergeant Major of 1RTR, WO1 N.H. Kellett, at Aliwal Barracks, Tidworth, 1996 (NEXUS)

259

Flags and colours. The Regimental Colours are Brown, Red and Green (see Chapt 3 for the story of their choice). A Regimental Flag is always flown with the green uppermost. It was Fuller who coined the apt interpretation of the colours: 'From the mud, through the blood to the green fields beyond'. The three original flags, made by Mrs Elles from the material bought by her husband, are now on show in the Regimental Museum and were flown as follows: one by Elles on his tank at Cambrai; one across the Rhine (in both wars); one entering Berlin in 1945.

Regimental Day. The anniversary of the Battle of Cambrai, 20 November 1917, is always celebrated as the Regimental Day throughout the Regiment.

Dress peculiarities. Officers and WO1s wear black shoes, black socks and black Sam Browne belt, sword sheath, knot and frog; all ranks wear black gloves and black webbing. Between the wars all ranks wore black overalls when working on tanks and on mounted ceremonial parades. This custom was reintroduced after the Second World War and the RTR is now the only regiment allowed to wear black overalls instead of the normal green denims. Black guernseys are worn by Officers and WO1s and black wool patched pullovers by all other ranks in barrack-dress or shirt-sleeve order as necessary. A stable belt in the Regimental colours is worn with barrack dress or shirt sleeve order.

THE BANDS OF THE ROYAL TANK REGIMENT

The first official Staff Band was formed in February 1922, although before that date an unofficial band had been funded from Tank Corps funds, so most of the official bandsmen came from it. During the Second World War the RTR Staff Band played in the UK and Mediterranean theatre. In 1947 two Regimental Bands 'A' and 'B' were formed out of the Staff Band, then in 1949 both were regranted Minor Staff Band status. They were later joined by a third Minor Staff Band ('C'). Soon afterwards they took the names of Cambrai, Alamein and Rhine. In the early eighties they lost their Staff Band status to become the Regimental Bands of the 1st, 2nd and 3rd, while the 4th retained its Pipes and Drums which had been formed in 1971 and officially recognised in 1979. They wear the Hunting Rose tartan. August 1992 brought more changes, the 3rd RTR Band was dissolved and the musicians moved to the other two bands. Two years later in the next Army review, the two bands were combined to create the Royal Tank Regiment Cambrai Band, a Staff Band, headed by a Director of Music, with a Bandmaster and 35 musicians. A busy programme is maintained and the Band plays throughout Europe. They also have a wartime role as regimental medical assistants (see Chapt 17).

Below: *Two members of the crew of a Scimitar CVR(T) in Combat Dress (No 8 Dress) circa 1997.* (NEXUS)

The first Staff Band, as formed in 1922, many of whose members came from the unofficial band which had existed before that date. (TM)

The Royal Tank Regiment Cambrai Staff Band and the Pipes & Drums of 1 RTR make an impressive sight on Horseguards Parade, prior to leading the Cenotaph Parade on Sunday, 19 November 1995. (Crown Copyright)

REGIMENTAL MARCHES

My Boy Willie. The Regimental March 'My Boy Willie' was based on the old Worcestershire song Billy Boy and was arranged and used as the Regimental Quick March during the twenties. Its association with *Big* and *Little Willie*, the original tanks is obvious. Soon after the Second World War it was felt that the tune was too short and repetitive and so a second tune was added, called Cadet Roussel, a folksong from the area of Cambrai in France, scene of the Tank Corps' first great victory. The revised version was approved by HM King George VI on 12 November 1946 and Bandmaster N.L.Wallace's march is now famous throughout the Army. It is played both in slow and quick time.

Other marches. Over the years other marches have been associated with various RTR regiments including: 'Lippe Detmold', 'Saffron', 'On the Quarterdeck' and 'Blue Flash' which at one time or another were adopted by 1, 2, 3 and 4 RTR.

THE REGIMENTAL MUSEUM

With the end of the First World War, Tank Corps units in Europe and overseas, as well as their training establishments at Bovington, Lulworth, Wareham and Swanage, began to reduce in strength upon demobilisation. Large numbers of tanks accumulated on the heath north of Bovington Camp, where many remained until they were broken up and sold for scrap. Twenty six specimens from the Tank Park – examples of each Mark of current or experimental vehicle - were collected and moved to about half an acre of ground, fenced off with chestnut paling. These were the beginnings of the present museum. In 1923, Rudyard Kipling, during a visit to Bovington, expressed disappointment that so little was being done to preserve these machines and in 1924 a start was made by housing a selection of them, including *Little Willie* and *Mother* in an open-sided shed in the Driving and Maintenance Wing of what was then the Royal Tank Corps Central Schools. In 1923 an equipment store was taken over to house souvenirs and relics, and the embryo museum was considerably enlarged in 1928. It was not open to the general public but was kept up for the instruction of all members of the RTC and selected parties and individuals from all the Services. Various experimental machines of the inter-war years were added to the collection whenever they had outlived their usefulness. A visitor at this time wrote:

Down below I could see some large buildings, obviously workshops. But almost rubbing shoulders with them were a few - three or four - low tin-roofed shelters behind a red fencing, looking for all the world like a farm. And this likeness to a homestead was the more faithful by token of a flock, or small herd or whatever you call it, of a dozen or so beasts on the heath this side of the fence. Strong humpbacked cattle, they looked rather on the big side. Bellies to grass and sterns to the wind they looked impervious to a monsoon. Calling the dog to heel, I legged it pretty briskly for the big gate and shelter. Here I found 'Ted'. Ted looks like a jovial farmer in overalls, he said he was NCO i/c Museum. He isn't. He's the curator of the Wonder House. I know. I spent two topping hours in his company 'doing' the museum, which my farm proved to be: The Royal Tank Corps Museum. The old building at Lahore fascinated Kim, this one just absorbed me. In a few minutes the rain was forgotten in my interest and I found an afternoon well spent. No charge either. A chap doesn't even have to leave his brolly at the door. The exhibits of things historical and heroical are there to be seen and Teds's there to show 'em.

1939 saw the formation of the Royal Armoured Corps, comprising the Cavalry of the Line, the Royal Tank Corps (thereafter called the Royal Tank Regiment) and certain Yeomanry and Territorial Army units. It was decided to enlarge the scope of the existing RTC Museum to cover the interests of all the regiments then making up the RAC, but the project had to be abandoned on the outbreak of war, when the museum closed for the duration. During the invasion scare of 1940 *Little Willie* guarded an airfield in Gloucestershire and a number of other museum exhibits were used in local defence schemes. The Mark V was stationed on the Wareham road , while the Vickers Medium, with the Independent, covered the road from Bovington to Wool. Other machines were positioned on the coast near Lulworth Cove. These and a number of other tanks were thus saved from the drive for scrap steel which destroyed many irreplaceable relics, such as *Mother*, the experimental electrically-driven tank, Gen Martel's own home-made light tank, the Medium 'C' and many other unique machines.

In 1945, space for about 50 vehicles was again found at the Driving & Maintenance School, but the buildings were not very suitable, so between 1947 and 1952 the present central hangar, currently the World War 2 Hall, was taken into use. The Museum was opened to the general public in 1947 when some 2500 people visited. A collection of Allied and Foreign AFVs, which had accumulated during the Second World War, came to the Museum in 1951. In 1984 a License Agreement was signed with the Secretary of State for Defence, which gave the Museum security of tenure for 50 years and the ability to charge visitors so as to generate addi-

The Tank Museum's Trench Exhibition, depicting the Mark I bringing manoeuvre back to the battlefield, breaking into a German trench and crushing the barbed wire. TM

Tanks in action! A Chieftain taking part in one of the mock battles during a mobility display at the Tank Museum. TM

263

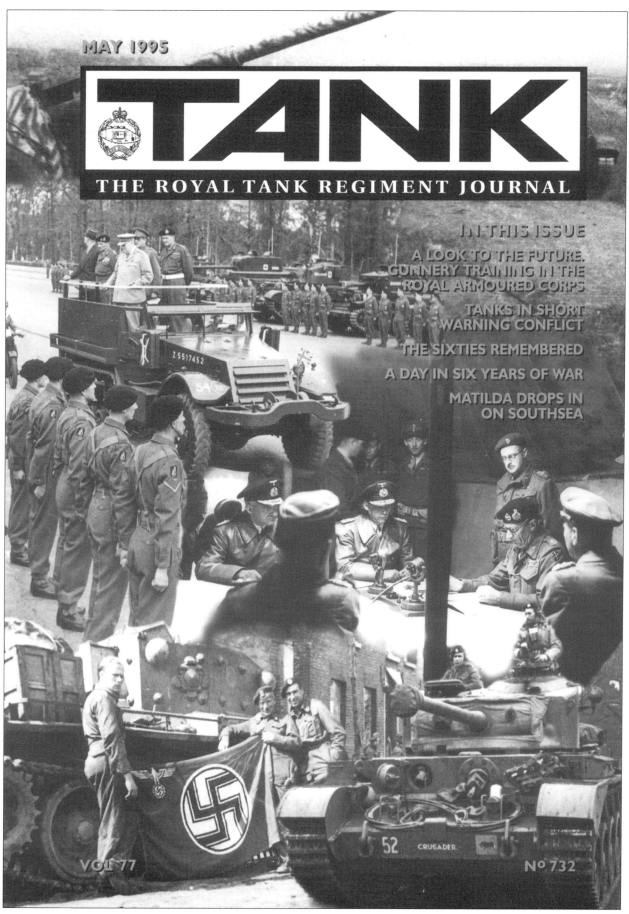

Front cover of the May 1995 edition of the quarterly Tank Journal, *commemorating the 50th Anniversary of the end of the Second World War.* (Tank)

tional income to care for the collection by redeveloping the Museum. Under the leadership of the then Curator, Lt-Col (Retd) George Forty, some £3m was raised to provide additional halls and displays that would relate to the needs of the general public. This change in approach has ensured the survival of the Museum which now averages some 140 000 visitors a year making it one of the largest attractions in southern England and certainly the most successful Regimental Museum.

The Museum aims to tell the story and concept of armoured warfare by placing the tanks in context by bringing the combined effect of the soldiers who fought in tanks with that of their techological development. A typical example is the 'Trench Exhibition', opened in 1998, which explains why the tank was invented. The role and part played by the RTR soldiers in the development of of the tank and the concept of armoured warfare is explained by having exhibitions throughout the Museum to explain the Regiment's involvement. In the summer season the Museum is brought to life with mock battles that explain and demonstrate the roles of the different AFVs to the public, who have little understanding of the subject but love to experience tanks in action.

Planning is in hand for further development of the Museum so it can continue to record the Regiment's history for the benefit of all.

THE REGIMENTAL ASSOCIATION AND BENEVOLENT FUND

The RTR Association has the aim of promoting by any means considered necessary, including financial aid, the efficiency andésprit de corps of the Royal Tank Regiment. The Regimental Secretary, RTR at RHQ RTR, looks after the day to day business of the Association. At present there are 38 branchs of the RTRA throughout the UK. The Benevolent Fund's is to assist less fortunate members of the Tank Corps, RTC and RTR and their families, who are in difficulties through no fault of their own. The Colonel Commandant is President and the Regimental Secretary, administrator.

THE TANK JOURNAL

Tank came into existence as the *Tank Corps Journal* on 9th April 1919 and has been published without a break ever since, although the issues during the Second World War were very sparse. It is now published every quarter and contains a mix of information about regimental matters, covering both serving and Old Comrades, together with a mix of historical and technical articles about armoured matters. It thus provides an invaluable historical record as it covers all the important regimental events in words and pictures. Many of the first-hand battle accounts quoted from in this book are taken from the pages of *Tank*.

REGULAR REGIMENTAL EVENTS

RTR Remembrance Sunday and March to Cenotaph. The Royal Tank Regiment is unique in that it holds its annual Remembrance Sunday and March to the Cenotaph on the Sunday after Remembrance Sunday, because this is the nearer of the two to Cambrai Day. In 1998, the Old Comrades were joined by detachments from both Regiments and the Cambrai Band , together with the Pipes & Drums. It is the intention to always have a detachment of serving soldiers marching with the Old Comrades and, whenever possible, the Cambrai Band.

Officers' Dinner. This yearly event is held at the Officers' Mess, The Armour Centre, Bovington, on the Friday evening of the week in which the RTR Council holds its meetings (invariably the week in which Cambrai Day falls)

Annual Reunions. Every year the RTR Association holds a Regimental Reunion Weekend, hosted by one of the regular regiments, although the 80th was held centrally at Bovington (see Chapt 17) in 1997. In addition, the 1st/4th/7th RTRA and the 2nd/3rd/6th RTRA hold yearly reunions, as do 5 RTR, 8 RTR and some of the other disbanded regiments, whilst all other RTRA branches hold regular Cambrai dinners ever year.

The Memorial Statue miniature maquette (6.5 x 5 x 2in), which was presented to HM The Queen. A limited number of copies were then made of cold cast bronze resin and sold to members of the Regiment.
(Crown Copyright)

RHQ RTR EMAIL ADDRESS

RHQ now has a website and an email address: rhqrtr@cwcom.net

CADETS

The Regiment has had a long association with the Army Cadet Force with affiliations in various areas, such as Merseyside, where in 1942 at the Park Street Barracks of 40th RTR(TA) a cadet unit known as 40th (Cadet) RTR was formed and a number of cadets from there joined the Regiment during the war. Post-war, the TA reorganisation led to the ACF detachment moving to Hightown, Merseyside. A second detachment was later formed at Prescot. Over the years many cadets from both detachments have joined the RTR, whilst others have joined other regiments or become local TA volunteers. In the 2001 New Year's Honours List, their executive officer Maj Gordon Corbett was appointed MBE after thirty years' dedicated work. The other main affiliated area has been Kent, where the ACF has maintained a number of RTR badged cadets within their sub-units. Other cadet units are King's College CCF and I31 Detachment RTR of the SW London ACF.

Commemorative enamelled box, made to commemorate the 80th Anniversary of the Battle of Cambrai and the 50th Wedding Anniversary of our Colonel in Chief. A similar limited edition was produced in 2000 for the unveiling of the Memorial Statue (Crown Copyright)

Thumbs up to the Regiment! The Army Cadets of Merseyside ACF are very proud of the RTR capbadge that they wear. (Maj R Bevan)

(A Dedication)

The Regiment is a precious thing.
A many sided diamond in a ring.
Each man may a shining facet be,
But its brilliance lies in unity.
Yours is the Regiment, heart and mind.
Multiplied by thousands of your kind.
They have made it, to you they gave it,
You are the heir, and you inherit,
A heritage of selfless merit.
Invisible, it lives in the lives of men,
And in their death relives again.
It is spirit, form and flesh and blood,
A potent power for all that's good.
A blend of youth and age and history,
A conundrum and a mystery.
It is more than men and guns,
'Legends' have passed the torch to sons.
It is a flag, a motto and a creed,
A tune, a badge, a valiant deed,
A 'battle honours day' when we recall
The sacrifice and glory of it all.
It is a code of conduct and a guide
Based on loyalty and pride.
It is a unifying element to bind
All the best that's in mankind.
Even the ultimate in sacrifice,
A 'greater love' beyond all price.
A trail of footsteps to be followed,
Customs old, revered and hallowed.
It is even drill and church parade,
Squads on the square and friends you made.
And it is a positive identity,
That makes a man of a nonentity.
Adds a rank and number to his name,
No target then outside his aim.
It is names evocative of faces,
Comrades' graves in foreign places.
Those with whom you shared a 'fag'
Who saved your sanity 'in the bag'.
Graves: in serried rows they stand
Or, unmarked like in an alien land.
So, wherever in life you may later be,
You have met the 'cream of society'.
It is autonomous; on its own,
But gives allegiance to a crown.
Your Regiment is all these things and more.
What else could add up such a score?

Edward Body

BIBLIOGRAPHY

Browne, Capt D.G.: *The Tank in Action*
  (William Blackwood & Sons, 1920)
Duncan, Maj-Gen Nigel: *79th Armoured Division Hobo's Funnies*
  (Profile Publications, 1972)
Foot, Stephen: *Three Lives and Now*
  (William Heinemann Ltd, 1937)
Forty, George: *Desert Rats at War, North Africa*
  (Ian Allan Ltd, 1975)
– *Tanks Across the Desert* (William Kimber, 1981)
Fuller, Col J.F.C: *Tanks in the Great War 1914–1918*
  (John Murray, 1920)
Liddell Hart, Capt Sir Basil: *The Tanks*, Volumes One & Two
  (Cassell, 1959)
Macksey, Major K.J.: *The Tanks 1945–1975*
  (Arms & Armour Press, 1979)
– *A History of the Royal Armoured Corps* 1914–1975
  (Newtown Publications, 1983)
– *To the Green Fields Beyond* (privately by RHQ RTR, 1965)
Maurice, Major R.F.G. (Ed): *The Tank Corps Book of Honour*
  (Spottiswoode Ballantyne & Co Ltd, 1919)
Swinton, Maj-Gen Sir Ernest: *Eyewitness*
  (Hodder & Stoughton Ltd, 1932)

Various Authors: *A Short History of the Royal Tank Corps*
  (Gale & Polden, at various dates up to 1938)
Privately published works or unpublished papers
Chadwick, Kenneth: *Seconds Out*
Lawson, General Sir Richard: *A Soldier's Story*
Jolly, General Sir Alan: *Blue Flash*
Fearnley, Major A.J.: *On the Road to Mandalay*
  (unpublished ms held at Tank Museum)
War Diary of Heavy Section
1 RTR Korean Journal
Short History of 4 RTR
7th RTR Diary
Short History of 42nd RTR
History of 44th RTR
History of 50th RTR
'A' Sqn 46th RTR, accounts of operations at Anzio
'B' Sqn 48th RTR, *'B' Line Magazine*
Various reports and papers, as contained in the RTR Regimental
  boxes at the Tank Museum Library
The Tank Journal, the *RTC Journal*, the *Tank Magazine*, *Tank*, etc,
  including special issues such as the *50th Anniversary
  Souvenir*, published in November 1967

SUBSCRIBERS

R. M. Allen MBE, Oulton Broad, Lowestoft, Suffolk
Captain L. P. Ashbridge MBE, Sauchie, Alloa
C. F. Ashmore, Redfield, Bristol
A. G. Atkinson, (Capt. 50th RTR) Condover,
  Shropshire
Edward and Joy Atkinson, Oldham, Lancashire
Trooper Harold Baker
Major General I. H. Baker C.B.E., Hook, Hampshire
Tomasz Basarabowicz, Krakow, Poland
Ian Baston, Brieselang, Germany
Major General Simon Beardsworth, Minety,
  Wiltshire
Richard Bellamy-Brown
Ken Bennell (Ben), Bushey, Herts.
Dick Bennett, Maidstone, Kent
WOII George V. Benns, Dundee, Scotland
(Sgt) Paul Betteridge, Richmond, North Yorkshire
L-Cpl Charles H. Bigg, Woolmer Green, Herts.
  44th RTR
Major James K. W. Bingham
Tom Bishop, Tudeley, Kent
Colonel John Blackwell, Cobham, Surrey
Sgt Albert S. Blatchford, Exeter, Devon
Geoffrey J. Bourne, Plymouth, Devon
Anthony Bowden, London
MCPL Alain P. E. Brogniez, The Redcoats Society,
  Belgium
Ivan E. A. Brogniez, The Redcoats Society, Belgium
Oliver Brookshaw, Thorpe Underwood Farm,
  Northants

Peter Brown, Wimborne, Dorset
John F. J. Brown, Hordley, Shropshire
Edward W. Budgen, (2 RTR) Winchester
Revd George Butler, Wool, Dorset
TPL Ron C. Calcutt, Wallingford, Oxon
Sergeant John Campton, 2 RTR Yeovil, Somerset
Philip J. Carey
Carts, NLBA, London
Sgt Bert Charman, Arundel, West Sussex
Major Ian Clooney, 1st Royal Tank Regiment
Major D. H. Conran T. D., Oxford
Lieutenant Colonel T. B. J. Coombe
Trooper Joseph Cottrell, 23709134
Captain A. D. Cowley M.B.E. and Mrs Felicity
  Cowley, Uffculme, Devon
Major Brian C. Crowder, Barton Mills, Suffolk
Major Trevor A. Dady, Halling, Rochester, Kent
Corporal Allan Dale (4 RTR), Bilton, East Riding
Mr Roy Davis, Bovington, Dorset
SQMS Ron De'Ath, 7th-4th Gosport, Hants.
Mr Rodney Dew, York
Major General Roy Dixon, Salisbury, Wilts.
Major Stephen Doble, Oriental Club, London
Bill Dodd, (Ex 11th/49th) Portchester, Hants.
P. H. Dunford, Wareham, Dorset
WO2 Kevin Edwards, Nuneaton, Warwickshire
Cpl R. Elson, 2 RTR, BFPO 38
SSGT Jeff Elson, Recce TP 2 RTR
Lt-Col Richard (Dick) M. Everard MBE,
  Bradford-on-Avon

SUBSCRIBERS

Mr Edward C. Fagg, Westgate-on-Sea, Kent
Major A. F. Flatow, T. D., RTR. Surbiton, Surrey
Bob Fullerton, Inverness
Major Howard Gater-Smith
Graham A. Gibson
Capt Stainslaw Grabowski, London
Major (Ret'd) John F. Green, Telford, Shropshire
Cliff Greensitt, Gonubie, South Africa
H. V. (Bert) Greenwood, Groby, Leicester
Sgt Harry Guest, Southend-on-Sea, Essex
Lance Corporal Darren A. Halligan, Warrington,
   Cheshire
Major Stuart Hamilton MC., Shaftesbury, Dorset.
   (ex 8th RTR)
Mr Charles M. Hayter
Major Colin E. Hepburn, East Burton, Dorset
Sgt Terence R. Heslop, B Squadron 3 RTR
Corporal Marcus R. Heslop, Badger. 2 RTR
Cpl Marcus R. Heslop, Lulworth, Dorset
Steve 'Izzy' Hiscock, Milborne St Andrew, Dorset
Captain Nick Hoareau, Marlborough, Wiltshire
Richard Hodson, Celbridge, Co. Kildare, Ireland
Adrian Hunt, S. Yorks. Former WOII (RQMS(T)
   2 RTR
S. L. Hunter-Cox, 4 RTR
James A. Hynson, Rochester, Kent
Lieutenant-Colonel R. F. Jammes RTR
Sgt Ron Jarrett, Coulsdon, Surrey
Major P. N. Jarvis, Kensington
Colonel W. M. S. Jeffery, Waddington, Lancs.
Chris Johnson, Newcastle, Ontario, Canada
L-Cpl John Johnstone, 24359146. 4RTR Pipes and Drums
WOII (Ret'd) E. C. Jones, Kent (7896381)
Mr William P. Kavanagh, Dublin, Repb of Ireland
P. Kay, Stanwell, Middlesex
Peter M. Kerr, East Calder, West Lothian
Keith Kerwood, Midsomer Norton, Bath
Geoff Key, Kenilworth, Warwickshire
Mr Geoff M. Knights, Windsor, Berkshire
J. Knowles, Weybridge, Surrey
Mr A. de Leeuw, Ede, Netherlands
L-Cpl C. P. Lewis 706, Manchester
Brian Llewellyn, Teddington, Middlesex
Norman J. Long, Sheerness, Kent
Dave Marsh, 3 RTR, Wareham, Dorset
Sgt Karl Robert Martin, Dunfield, Glos.
Sergeant Charles Martyn, 4th Royal Tank Regiment,
   1949-52
Major Neil B. Mason, Bovington Camp, Dorset
Ray (Jess) Matthews, Highworth, Wilts.
Major (Ret'd) Eyre R. Maunsell, Hastoe,
   Herefordshire
Major (Ret'd) Robert E. Maunsell MC, Milford-on-
   Sea, Hampshire
Captain A. J. M. McAfee, RTR
Major General R. W. M. McAfee CB, London
Keith McIntosh, Ex- 4RTR
Mr Bryan McVitty, Doncaster, S. Yorks
Sgt D. A. Mears, Atherstone, Warwicks

Lieut Colonel D. N. Moir, Tavistock, Devon
Mr Philip J. Morrish, Wool, Dorset
Dr Charles Mould
Mr J. G. Naish, Wool, Dorset
Tpr. Alan R. Normanton, Merthyr Tydfil, Wales
P.J. Fellow I.M.A., NLBA, London
Ernest Pang, Newcastle-upon-Tyne
Brigadier Roger Plowden, Westley, Suffolk
Lieut. Anthony H. Pyatt, Waldringfield, Suffolk
Guernsey R. G. Paul, (5 RTR)
Major R. B. Ramsay (Ex Sgt 3rd RTR), Edinburgh
Brigadier J. D. Rash, Westcott, Surrey
Roger T. Rathmell
Captain Maurice G. Reaney, Wallington, Surrey
Tpr K. Reid, Plymouth, Devon
Captain Michael E. Roberts, Mark Beech, Nr
Edenbridge, Kent
Merlin Robinson, Aurora, Ontario, Canada
Colonel Michael H. Rogers, Chichester, West Sussex
Captain M. P. N. Rowe
Leiutenant Colonel Wade H. Russell,
Lt-Col (Ret'd) Brian D. Rutterford, Dumfries,
   Scotland
Sergeant Reginald F. Scammell, Dinton, Salisbury,
   Wiltshire
Captain John H. Sibson, Church Aston, Shropshire
Alan RN Simcock, Verwood, Dorset
Major A. E. Simmons M.C.
Eric W. Smallwood FRGS, Blakedown,
   Worcestershire
G. T. Smith, Gillingham, Kent
Mr Ken Smith, Poole, Dorset
Ex-Trooper Maurice F. Spencer, Stubbington, Hants.
Col (Retd) D. S. Squirrell OBE
Captain Douglas H. Stokes, Bath, Somerset
Captain Dick Taylor, Poole, Dorset
George A. Thornalley, Worlington, Suffolk
S/Sgt J. E. Towle, 3RTR, Weymouth, Dorset.
   1974-1996
Lt-Col D. B. Vale, West Sussex
Brigadier Peter Vaux, Hampshire
Mr Don Verity, Leeds, West Yorkshire
Peter J. Vine, Talbot Village, Poole, Dorset
Mr P. Waddington (Waddy), Poole, Dorset
Sgt Craig Wann, Fife, Scotland
Lance-Corporal Albert Edward Warren M.M.,
   (7th Armoured) East Ham, Lon
Lt-Col, Hon. Ret'd, A. Michael Warrington,
James (Jimmy) Watchus, 2 RTR
Bryan Watkins
Mr R. P. Wheeler (Joe), Weymouth, Dorset
Mr Graham Whitehead, Oldham, Lancashire
Capt Pip Willcox MBE., Rutland
Edward Wilson, 5RTR, 1944/46
Mr Martin S. Witmond
Ian F. Wolstenholme B.A.(Hons),
Sergeant Chippy Wood MBE, Tyldesley, Manchester
L-Cpl Steve Woods, Redruth, Cornwall
Mr George H. Woolley, Runcorn, Cheshire

INDEX

INDEX